MW01393649

Prophets, Sages, & Poets

To Nita on the occasion of
our golden anniversary,
June 10, 2006.

Prophets, Sages, & Poets

JAMES L. CRENSHAW

CHALICE
PRESS
ST. LOUIS, MISSOURI

Translations in this book are by the author except where otherwise noted.

Cover art: © The Crosiers
Cover design: Elizabeth Wright
Interior design: Hui-Chu Wang

Visit Chalice Press on the World Wide Web
at www.chalicepress.com

10 9 8 7 6 5 4 3 2 1 06 07 08 09 10 11

Library of Congress Cataloging-in-Publication Data

Crenshaw, James L.
Prophets, sages, and poets / James L. Crenshaw.
p. cm.
ISBN-13: 978-0-8272-2988-4
ISBN-10: 0-8272-2988-7
1. Bible. O.T.–Criticism, interpretation, etc. I. Title.

BS1192.C74 2006
221.6–dc22

2006021513

Printed in the United States of America

Contents

Acknowledgments vii

Introduction 1

I. Wisdom

1. "Flirting with the Language of Prayer (Job 14.13–17)" 6
2. "Wisdom and the Sage: On Knowing and Not Knowing" 14
3. "The Primacy of Listening in Ben Sira's Pedagogy" 20
4. "Qoheleth's Understanding of Intellectual Inquiry" 29
5. "A Good Man's Code of Ethics (Job 31)" 42
6. "Unresolved Issues in Wisdom Literature" 46
7. "A Proverb in the Mouth of a Fool" 53
8. "From the Mundane to the Sublime (Reflections on Qoh 11:1–8)" 61
9. "Deceitful Minds and Theological Dogma: Jer 17:5–1" 73
10. "Qoheleth's Quantitative Language" 83
11. "Beginnings, Endings, and Life's Necessities in Biblical Wisdom" 95

II. Psalms, Prophecy, and Torah

12. "The Book of Psalms and Its Interpreters" 106
13. "The Deuteronomist and the Writings" 125
14. "Reflections on Three Decades of Research" 132
15. "A Living Tradition: The Book of Jeremiah in Current Research" 137
16. "Who Knows What YHWH Will Do? The Character of God in the Book of Joel" 147
17. "Freeing the Imagination: The Conclusion to the Book of Joel" 153
18. "Joel's Silence and Interpreters' Readiness to Indict the Innocent" 163

19. "Transmitting Prophecy across Generations" 167
20. "Theodicy in the Book of the Twelve" 173
21. "Theodicy and Prophetic Literature" 183
22. "The Sojourner Has Come to Play the Judge: Theodicy on Trial" 195

Notes 201
Hebrew/Greek Index 265
Scripture Index 267
Author Index 275
Subject Index 283

Acknowledgments

I wish to thank three people for helping me with the publication of this book. First, Gail Chappell guided the manuscript through its several stages, always with efficiency and grace. Second, Anne Weston handled the task of securing permissions from the publishers to reprint these essays. Third, Carol Shoun rendered valuable service in scanning several articles and providing clean copies for the press. An expression of gratitude is also extended to Trent Butler for generating this project, Sarah Tasic for her enthusiastic support, the editorial staff of Chalice Press for expert shepherding of this book, and Chad Eggleston for preparing the Index.

The original place of publication of the articles is as follows:

"Flirting with the Language of Prayer (Job 14:13–17)," *Worship and the Hebrew Bible: Essays in Honor of John T. Willis.* Ed. Patrick Graham, Rick Marrs, and Steven McKenzie. JSOTSup 284. Sheffield: JSOT Press, 1999), 110–23.

"The Sages: On Knowing and Not Knowing." *Proceedings of the Eleventh World Congress of Jewish Studies.* Jerusalem: World Union of Jewish Studies, 1994), 137–44.

"The Primacy of Listening in Ben Sira's Pedagogy," *Wisdom, You Are My Sister. Studies in Honor of Roland E. Murphy, O. Carm., on the Occasion of His Eightieth Birthday.* Ed. Michael L. Barré. CBQMS 29. Washington, D.C.: The Catholic Biblical Association of America, 1997, 172–87.

"Qoheleth's Understanding of Intellectual Inquiry," *Qoheleth in the Context of Wisdom.* Ed. A. Schoors. BETL CXXXVI. Leuven: University Press, 1998, 205–224.

"A Good Man's Code of Ethics (Job 31)," *The Family Handbook.* Ed. H. Anderson, M. S. Van Leeuwen, I. Evison, and D. Browning. Louisville: Westminster John Knox, 1998, 221–23.

"Unresolved Issues in Wisdom Literature," *An Introduction to Wisdom Literature and The Psalms: Festschrift Marvin Tate.* Ed. H. Wayne Ballard, Jr. and W. Dennis Tucker, Jr. Macon: Mercer University Press, 2000, 215–27.

"A Proverb in the Mouth of Fools," *Seeking Out the Wisdom of the Ancients. Essays Offered to Honor Michael V. Fox on the Occasion of His Sixty-fifth Birthday.* Ed. Ronald L. Troxel, Kelvin G. Friebel, and Dennis R. Magary. Winona Lake, IN: Eisenbrauns, 2005, 103–16.

"From the Mundane to the Sublime: Qoh 11:1–8," *From Babel to Babylon: Essays on the Primary History in Honour of Brian Peckham*.Ed. Joyce Rillett Wood and John E. Harvey. Sheffield: Sheffield Academic Press, forthcoming. Reprinted by permission of the Continuum International Publishing Group.

"Deceitful Minds and Theological Dogma: Jer 17:5–11," *Utopia and Dystopia in Prophetic Texts*. Ed. Ehud Ben Zvi. Helsinki and Goettingen: Finnish Exegetical Society, Vandenhoeckard Ruprecht, 2006, 105–21.

"Qoheleth's Quantitative Language," *The Langauge of Ooheleth in Context: Symposium in Honor of Antoon Schoors*. Leuven: Peeters, forthcoming.

"Beginnings, Endings, and Life's Necessities in Biblical Wisdom," *Wisdom Literature of Mesopotamia and Israel*. Eds. Richard Clifford and Peter Machinist. Atlanta: SBL, forthcoming.

"The Book of Psalms and Its Interpreters," preface to Sigmund Mowinckel, *The Psalms in Israel's Worship*. Grand Rapids: Eerdmans, 2004, xix–xlv.

"The Deuteronomist and the Writings," *Those Elusive Deuteronomists: The Phenomenon of Pan-Deuteronomism*. Eds. Steven McKenzie and Linda Schearing. JSOTSup 268. Sheffield: Sheffield Academic Press, 1999, 145–68. Reprinted by permission of the Continuum International Publishing Group.

"Reflections on Three Decades of Research," *Religious Studies Review* 20 (1994), 111–12, in conjunction with "James L. Crenshaw: Faith Lingering at the Edges," *RSR* 29 (1994), 103–10 by Walter Brueggemann.

"A Living Tradition: The book of Jeremiah in Current Research," *Interpretation* 87 (1983), 117–29.

"Who Knows What YHWH Will Do? The Character of God in the Book of Joel," *Fortunate the Eyes that See: Essays in Honor of David Noel Freedman in Celebration of His Seventieth Birthday*. Eds. A. B. Beck et al. Grand Rapids: Eerdmans, 1995, 185–96.

"Freeing the Imagination: The Conclusion to the Book of Joel," *Prophecy and Prophets*. Ed. Yehoshua Gitay. *Semeia Studies*. Atlanta: Scholars Press, 1997, 129–47.

"Joel's Silence and Interpreters' Readiness to Indict the Innocent," "*Lasset uns Brücken bauen...*" Eds. Klaus-Dietrich Schunck und Matthias Augustin. BEATAJ 42; Berlin: Peter Lang, 1998, 255–59.

"Transmitting Prophecy Across Generations," *Writings and Speech in Israelite and Ancient Near Eastern Prophecy*. Eds. Ehud ben Zvi and Michael H. Floyd. SBLSymS 10. Atlanta: SBL, 2000, 31–44.

"Theodicy in the Book of the Twelve," *Thematic Threads in the Book of the Twelve*. Eds. P. L. Redditt and A. Schart. BZAW 325. Berlin: de Gruyter, 2003, 175–91.

"Theodicy and Prophetic Literature," *Theodicy in the World of the Bible.* Eds. A. Laato and J. C. de Moor. Leiden: Brill, 2003, 236–55.

"The Sojourner Has Come to Play the Judge: Theodicy on Trial," *God in the Fray: A Tribute to Walter Brueggemann.* Eds. Tod Linafelt and Timothy K. Beal. Minneapolis: Fortress Press, 1998), 83–92.

I am grateful to the publishers for granting permission to print these articles in a single volume.

Introduction

The unstated title of this book, "Attentive Listening to" *Prophets, Sages, and Poets,* implies both an extraordinary description and an urgent plea. The description makes a claim, audacious to some, that the author has occasionally succeeded in bridging the chasm that separates modern readers from ancient texts. The plea invites others to join the author in crossing that bridge in the hope of discovering ways of viewing reality other than those often taken as natural and therefore correct.

The differences between Israelites of the biblical period and citizens of the early twenty-first century who cherish their written legacy are enormous: e.g., a pre-Copernican understanding of the universe, a pre-Darwinian concept of nature, a pre-Freudian notion of the psyche, a pre-Marxist idea of economics, a pre-Nietzchean belief in providence. Having been formed intellectually and spiritually by postbiblical ideologies, in the same way that men and women in biblical times were shaped by entirely different ways of looking at the world, contemporary readers find themselves standing at the door of a sacred text without a key.

It is not that they have failed to search diligently for that elusive key, for eager readers have expended considerable time and energy looking for the right way to read ancient texts. The rich history of hermeneutics reaches back into the early stages of the composition of the biblical canon and extends to the present day. This endeavor attests the polyvalency of a text, its inherent multiple meanings even when the grammar and syntax are unambiguous. That capacity for a richness of interpretation is often enhanced by purposely ambiguous language.

For example, the disclosure to Moses of the divine name in Exodus 3:14 ("I AM WHO I AM"), simultaneously revelatory and concealing, is open to several theological readings. A causative reading emphasizes the creative or generative power as the essence of deity; viewing the form as a simple Qal imperfect of the root *hyh* (to be) places the emphasis on philosophical issues of constancy and reliability in both the present and the future; and seeing the verb as a form of *hwh* (to blow) points to historical dynamism that is at home in the ancient world of a text.

The earliest interpreters recognized the openness of the text and sought to capture the different senses by distinguishing between the literal or historical meaning on the one hand, and other levels of interpretation such as the allegorical, the spiritual, and the tropological on the other hand. Many of the readings attributed to Paul, early Church Fathers, and the rabbis strike modern interpreters as bizarre, but at the very least such wrestling with the text bears witness to its potential for multiple meanings. Practitioners of modern historical critical approaches to the text sometimes lost sight of this richness and came close to a rigid one-dimensional reading, being saved by its inherent critical principle. Perhaps that hermeneutic of suspicion explains the shifts that have characterized this endeavor for the last two centuries. From these emerging changes in perspective an entire cottage industry has evolved consisting of such disciplines as source criticism, textual criticism, literary analysis, form criticism, tradition history, sociological analysis, structuralism, canon criticism, archaeology, theology, feminist and womanist theories, and post-modernist criticism.

The articles reprinted in this book reflect the changes in interpretive analysis over the past quarter of a century. My fundamental concerns have been (1) to discern how the composers of biblical literature thought they arrived at truths concerning the world and (2) to understand these insights insofar as humanly possible. That lofty goal has required a suspension of disbelief, not always easy for me, and a willingness to embrace an alien worldview.

The broad scope of these essays is offset by their narrow focus on prophets and sages. At first glance these two groups have little in common, for the former claim a divine origin for their oracles while the latter take full credit for their teachings. On closer inspection it is clear that the matter is much more complex than first meets the eye. To be sure, intermediaries throughout the ancient world claim to act as spokespersons of various deities, sometimes receiving the divine word without seeking it and at other times employing various techniques to uncover the hidden will of the gods. The same individuals who utter what they understand to be the deity's exact words give their own interpretations of these messages and their ethical implications.

Conversely, the sages of the ancient Near East present their very own understandings of the world around them, primarily to the young as a means of shaping character. Still, these guardians of culture do not hesitate to make bold claims concerning a mediator of heavenly origin whom they call *Ḥokmâ*, Wisdom, from whom they have learned much about divine activity and essence. Moreover, specialists in the second century B.C.E. practice a type of wisdom that remotely resembles divination, and the earlier author of the book of Job does not shrink from attributing speeches to the deity that reprimand a defiant servant. The presence, therefore, of sapiential insights within the present book attributed to Jeremiah is not surprising. I explore this extraordinary literary unit in "Deceitful Minds and Theological Dogma: Jer 17:5–11." The essay on "A Proverb in the Mouth of a Fool" also deals with traditional wisdom that has been placed in literary settings that belong to entirely different genres than those usually characterized as wisdom literature. The goal is to assess claims about sapiential editing of the Psalter.

Several essays probe the subject of knowledge and its transmission, along with the perplexing issue of limits imposed on the intellect. The programmatic treatise that has the title, "The Sages: On Knowing and Not Knowing," raises this epistemological question, one that is pursued further in "Qoheleth's Understanding of Intellectual Inquiry," which examines the special vocabulary for cognitive investigation. The nature of the instructional task is treated in "The Primacy of Listening in Ben Sira's Pedagogy." "Qoheleth's Quantitative Language" is an attempt to use vocabulary as a means of discovering the daily tasks of scribes during the third century and to determine the extent of the influence of Hellenistic philosophy on Qoheleth.

The sages were not always stuck in the banal, for they frequently discussed issues approaching the sublime. This feature of their thought can be seen in four essays. "Flirting with the Language of Prayer: Job 14:13–17" asks whether or not the author of the book of Job viewed death as final, while "Beginnings, Endings, and Life's Necessities in Biblical Wisdom" inquires about the sages' values and their sense of the existential limits imposed on human beings. An ascending movement in thought from life's ordinary events to the miraculous origin of life occurs in "From the Mundane to the Sublime: (Reflections on Qoh 11:1–8)," and the brief study of "A Good Man's Code of Ethics: Job 31" examines this remarkable confession of innocence as an ethical treatise.

The ongoing nature of research is signaled by "Unresolved Issues in Wisdom Literature." "Foreword: The Book of Psalms and Its Interpreters" discusses the nature of that book and its interpretation over the millennia, with special attention to the contribution of Sigmund Mowinckel.

"The Deuteronomist and the Writings" functions as a transition from the singular attention to the sages and the other major literary work that is written from below, that is as human prayer and praise rather than a divine word from above. The brief assessment of my professional career, "Reflections on Three Decades of Research," covers the two subjects, wisdom and prophecy.

The essays dealing with Israelite prophecy in the context of the ancient Near East are best understood in the light of my discussion of the way oracular traditions were preserved for posterity ("Transmitting Prophecy across Generations"). The essay entitled "A Living Tradition: The Book of Jeremiah in Current Research" attends to the same basic issue, albeit with a narrower concentration.

My long-standing interest in the so-called Minor Prophets has resulted in three articles that arose during the writing of a commentary on Joel in the *Anchor Bible.* One treats a liturgical formula that occurs in a number of places and ultimately derives from the confessional statement in Exodus 34:6–7 ("Who Knows What YHWH Will Do? The Character of God in the Book of Joel"). The second examines Joel's utopian dream of a restored community ("Freeing the Imagination: The Conclusion to the Book of Joel"). The final Joel article explores the way an assumption of guilt has been imposed on the Judean community in Joel's day ("Joel's Silence and Interpreters' Readiness to Indict the Innocent").

Two essays cover the problem of divine justice as seen in the prophetic corpus. "Theodicy in the Book of the Twelve" and "Theodicy and Prophetic Literature" were written in conjunction with my recent book, *Defending God: Biblical Responses to the Problem of Evil* (New York: Oxford University Press,

2005). These explorations represent the heart of my research over the years, as evidenced by the final essay, "The Sojourner Has Come to Play the Judge: Theodicy on Trial," the sole entry pertaining to the Torah. Its presence serves as a reminder that the present collection of essays is the contribution of a mere sojourner with no bargaining chip in his pocket. I am fully aware that, as Plato observed, written words, forever mute even when confronted by desperate readers eager to discern their meaning, cannot choose their readers. My hope is that those who study these investigations of biblical texts will use the occasion as a stimulus to discoveries of their own.

I.

Wisdom

CHAPTER 1

Flirting with the Language of Prayer

Job 14.13–17

In her stimulating commentary on Job 14.13–17, Carol A. Newsom writes that "Job starts to be drawn into the language of prayer," only to turn away in 14.18–22 because this mode of discourse "is still too powerful and too seductive for Job to trust himself to speak in its accents."[1] Job's momentary shift from attack to imagined refuge, from angry talking about the deity to plaintive addressing of that sovereign one,[2] reveals the lingering power of an intimate relationship with the divine, despite the total collapse of Job's belief-system. His hasty abandonment of a renewed effort to sustain direct discourse with God indicates the extraordinary force at work aimed at driving a permanent wedge between him and the deity. The next few centuries witnessed several such stabs in the dark brought on by horrific personal circumstances and energized by an undying love for the sacred.[3] The persistence of an undying hope, now generalized to embrace everyone born of woman, invites closer scrutiny of Job's bold ruminations.

14.13 Oh that you would hide me in Sheol,
you would conceal me until your anger abates,
you would fix a statute of limitations, and remember me.
14.14 If mortals[4] die, will they live again?
All the days of my service I would wait
until my release arrived.
14.15 You would call and I would answer[5] you;
you would long for[6] the work of your hands.
14.16 For now you number my steps,
you do not watch over my sins.

14.17 My transgressions are sealed in a bag;
and you cover over my iniquity.

The translation requires comment at two points: *ḥoq* in 14.13 and *kî 'attâ* in 14.16. The former may signify nothing more than temporality, hence a set date on which the deity will remember Job, hidden in the underworld, just as the avenging YHWH remembered Noah and the animals shut up in the ark, according to ancient legend (Gen 8.1). The forensic language permeating Job's complaints, however, invites another interpretation, one facilitated by the legal concept of a statute of limitations, a precise date at which criminal culpability becomes null and void.[7] This translation permits one to retain the usual sense of *ḥoq* as statute.

The temporal force of *kî 'attâ* poses difficulty. Ordinarily, it connotes the present which presents a contrast with what has preceded. The translation adopted above implies a change in point of view; Job imagines that the deity conceals him[8] in Sheol until the divine fury passes, which brings about a decisive change toward a wronged Job. Then he places himself in that sheltered situation, at least in his imagination, and encounters a different sovereign, one who solicitously counts every step Job takes and no longer spies on him to catch every misstep. In such an altered context, Job need not worry, for the deity has sealed the evidence against him, whitewashing his offenses the way the Chronicler covered up David's villainy.

The absence of a negative particle in 14.16a may favor an alternative rendering, "Whereas now you count my steps." The final two verses of this imaginary meditation would then harbor an ominous thought, one that has already abandoned the optimism of the initial three verses. This interpretation accords with the usual meaning of language about the deity's numbering of an individual's steps; however, the unique concept envisioned by Job may also imply a rare understanding of divine surveillance as well.[9]

Even when the translation lacks problematics, its meaning remains obscure at some points. What imagery is conjured up by the words *ṣeba'î* and *ḥelîpatî* in v 14 and *ḥatum biṣrôr* in v 17? Does Job refer to arduous labor as a slave and to the relief at day's end,[10] or to conscription in the military and release from service when a replacement arrives?[11] Use of *geber,* which frequently has the sense of a warrior, may tilt the evidence in the direction of military language. The conscious effort to include the whole human race in the larger context, where three other words designating mortals occur (*'ādām* in v 1, *geber* and *'ādām* in v 10, *'îš* in v 12, *'enōš* in v 19; *'iššâ* in v 1) encourages caution, as does the apparent synonymous use of *geber* and *'ādām.*

The allusion to sealing transgressions in a bundle likewise evokes two possible practices. According to an obscure reference in 1 Sam 25.29, it was thought that YHWH kept certain favored persons secure by placing their life in a bundle of the living.[12] Scholars have explained this image as a reflection of a practice in accounting whereby shepherds entrusted with animals would keep pebbles in a bag to indicate the precise number under their care.[13] The problem with this interpretation of Job's imagery is the word *ḥatum,* for such bundles would have been closed by means of a drawstring. Therefore, some interpreters view the expression in terms of official written documents, papyri containing important data and sealed in a bundle by means of hot wax.[14] These documents provided decisive evidence in judicial proceedings once the seal was broken and the contents were examined. The two images convey opposite dispositions when applied to the deity. The former suggests providential care, whereas the latter points to an exact, but fair, judgment, an idea that seems at odds with what follows immediately: a divine pardon for all offenses.

The belief that a transgressor could hide from YHWH in Sheol was dealt a death blow by the prophet Amos, who denied that anyone could escape divine punishment.

> If they hide in Sheol,
> from there my hand will take them;
> if they ascend to heaven,
> from there I will bring them down;
> if they conceal themselves on top of Carmel,
> from there I will search and capture them;
> if they hide from my sight in the bottom of the sea,
> from there I will command the Serpent[15] and it will
> bite them,
> if they go into captivity before their enemies,
> from there I will command the Sword[16] and it will slay them.
> I will fix my eyes on them for evil and not for good (Amos 9.2–4).

Similarly, the psalmist who composed the following meditation believed that YHWH's dominion extended to Sheol.

> Where can I go from your spirit,
> where can I flee from your presence?
> If I ascend to heaven, you are there;
> if I make my bed in sheol, you are there.
> If I take the wings of dawn
> and dwell at the outermost region of the sea,
> Even there your hand guides me,
> your right hand holds me.
> If I say, "Surely darkness will conceal me
> and light around me will become dark,"
> Even darkness is not dark to you
> and night is bright as day,
> for darkness is like light to you (Ps 139.7–12).

Such boundless confidence about the extent of the deity's domain does not translate into a perfect society, for the psalmist complains mightily about evildoers.[17]

Job's incisive question, "If mortals die, will they live again?" evoked different answers in the ancient world. In the absence of firsthand knowledge about what happens after death,[18] one was left to speculation. The gradual decomposition of the body could be observed, as Gilgamesh discovered following the demise of his companion Enkidu. In mythic lore, the gods possessed the capacity to rise from the dead, waxing and waning like the processes of nature itself in its seasonal unfolding. Do mortals have the same power?

According to the myth in Gen 2–3, the tree of life became permanently inaccessible to mortals, who joined the hapless serpent in transgressing divine limits and provoked the deity to declare the tree off limits. In the Gilgamesh Epic the snake snatches a branch from the tree of life, sheds its skin, and rejuvenates itself, leaving the hero to face his mortality. In ancient Egypt this pessimistic view did not prevail, for these people believed that their soul (*ba*) survived death. Not surprisingly, the Hellenistic author of Wisdom of Solomon assumes that people possess souls that make them immortal.[19]

The larger context of Job's question comprises three distinct units.[20] The first, 14.1–6, reflects on life's brevity and unwelcome limitations. The finality of death is the subject of the second unit, the eternal sleep into which mortals fall (14.7–12). The third unit, 14.18–22, graphically describes the deity's destruction of human hope. All three units contrast certain aspects of nature with the experience of mortals. The motivating thought seems to rise from the kinship between humankind and the natural world, proclaimed in the YHWHistic creation story, where the *'ādām* is fashioned from the dust of the earth, *'ādāmâ,* and receives the divine animating breath. Have the mythic discussions of nature's periodic resuscitation spilled over into reflections on the destiny of humankind? The commingling of earthly body and divine breath corresponds to the two prevailing concepts regarding human destiny: the largely Mesopotamian and Canaanite notion of dying and rising gods representing nature's transformation and the Egyptian belief in an immortal soul (*ba*).

Job 14.1–6

The fragility of flowers in the searing heat of the Near East must have been obvious to any observer. How much more true if the author thinks of cut flowers before the days of air-conditioned houses. The poet who composed Deutero-Isaiah used a similar analogy to describe the fleeting nature of all flesh. Here grass stands alongside flower as a metaphor for the human condition; in contrast to both of these elements of nature, the divine word endures. The repetitive language gives the impression that the poet has hit upon an apt analogy and does not want to give it up before exhausting its emotive range.

> A voice says, "Proclaim."
> And I said, "What shall I proclaim?"
> All flesh is grass
> and all its loyalty is like the flower of the field.
> Grass withers, flowers fade
> when YHWH's breath blows on them.
> Surely the people is grass.
> Grass withers, flowers fade;
> but the word of our God stands forever (Isa 40.6–8).

Something more is at play here than the composition of humankind from elements of nature. Deutero-Isaiah characterizes the bonds uniting mortals with one another and with the sacred as short-lived and therefore unreliable. In his view, all that humans constitute, together with whatever they produce in the affective realm, resemble the most transitory of things, grass and flowers. Both that which exposes human fragility and whatever affirms divine permanency come from God's mouth, a scorching wind in one instance, an utterance in the other case. The specification, "flower of the field," goes beyond Job's simple "flower," indicating, like grass, something that grew without human cultivation. Springing up hither and yon, such grass and flowers were entirely subject to the whims of nature.

In characterizing humankind, the unknown author of Psalm 144.4 combines the notions of breath and passing shadow, an astonishing shift from what takes place in Psalm 8, which 144.3 echoes. Instead of remarking on human grandeur and expressing amazement over divine attentiveness, this text likens mortals to a breath and a fleeting shadow.

> Humanity (*'ādām*) resembles breath (*hebel*;)
> its duration is like a moving shadow (*kĕṣēl 'ōbēr*).

The resemblances between this assessment of mortal existence and Qoheleth leap to mind, for not only does he frequently characterize human existence as *hebel,* by which he means transitory, futile, and absurd,[21] but he also uses the comparison between life under the sun and a shadow, a natural accompaniment of sunshine (Qoh 6.12). Here, too, Qoheleth associates this simile with that penetrating question attributed to Job concerning the future, now formulated in different language: "For who can inform a mortal as to what will take place afterwards under the sun?" In this teacher's view, death brings about the original state of things: Dust returns to earth and the divine breath goes back to its source. Neither departure brings a modicum of comfort to Qoheleth.

Job's assessment of the human condition in 14.1 comes close to Qoheleth's dismal picture.

> A mortal (*'ādām*), born of woman,
> short in duration and sated with trouble,
> emerges like a flower and withers,
> flees like a shadow and does not tarry (14.1).

The expression, *yĕlûd 'iššâ* functions comprehensively; it includes everyone and in no way suggests a flawed nature[22] resulting from association with a woman, who was thought to be impure at certain times. The description of human existence as brief and painful gathers force from its variation on a traditional formula for a good life (old and full of days; cf. Gen 35.29, 1 Chr 29.28, and Job 42.17).

Having established the incontrovertible nature of human existence as transitory and onerous possibly by generalizing from his own case, Job proceeds to argue against anything that would increase life's burden. It seems that the deity has fixed a gaze on miserable Job, and by extension on everyone, for the purpose of catching them in a misstep. Such extraordinary surveillance strikes Job as excessive, given the severe restrictions on mortals and divine foreknowledge. Job has no quarrel with the deity's placing restrictions on the mythological chaos monster, for those limits are essential to cosmic order.[23] Neither Job nor his fellows pose a threat to society. Why, therefore, does the deity hedge them in and limit their days?

This line of thinking leads Job to utter a plea on behalf of beleaguered mortals.

> Look away and desist
> so that, like laborers, they may take pleasure in their sojourn (14.6).

In asking for some relief, Job stops short of petitioning for radical measures, for example, the immediate removal of the causes for trouble unrelated to the deity's steady gaze. He continues to assume that life will resemble hard labor, which the darkness of night alone brings to an end.

Job 14.7–12

It occurs to Job that nature also offers an analogy for permanence, a longevity occasioned by dormancy and resuscitation. In contrast with ephemeral flowers and grass, a tree has the capacity to renew itself under certain conditions. For emphasis, Job personifies a tree, ascribing to it hope when circumstances seem to imply otherwise. Not without cause does mythic lore point to a tree of life and do genealogies depict family trees.[24] In Job's imagination, the mere scent of water activates the process of rejuvenation for a felled tree. Pressing beyond the conviction expressed in Isa 11.1 that the Davidic monarchy will rise from its stump to former glory, Job broadens the thought to universal dimensions. The idea of vibrant growth utilizes the same verb (*ḥdl* with negative particle) that conveyed the notion of ceasing when applied to the deity's close scrutiny.

In v 8 Job concedes that trees resemble humans in the aging process; their roots grow old in the ground and their stumps decay. That process of rotting comes to an abrupt halt with the arrival of water. Perhaps in the case of *mût* the difference indicates degree, for according to ancient mentality a person became enmeshed in death to a greater or lesser extent.[25]

Water, the rejuvenating agent in v 9, cannot boast a similar staying power, according to v 11. Large bodies of water disappear, either from shifts in terrain or from absorption and seepage. This vanishing agent of renewed life ironically mirrors the permanent disappearance of women and men.[26]

> Mortals die and are weakened,
> human beings expire and where are they?...
> So people lie down and do not rise;
> until heavens cease they will not awake
> or rouse from slumber (14.10, 12).[27]

The unexpected use of the verb *ḥlš* in v 10 may have arisen as a compelling contrast to the noun *geber*. Whatever intimations of strength individuals may entertain are quickly negated. The process of death drains away every pretence of might, leaving individuals unable to lift themselves from earthly graves. Now Job asks a variant of the deity's first address to Adam and Eve: "Where are you?" has become "Where are they?" (cf. Gen 3.9). Unlike the eternal heavens, mortals are no more.

Job 14.18–22

The images chosen to symbolize human existence have gone from a fragile flower and a fleeting shadow in the first unit to a stately tree and substantial streams and beds of water in the second one. In this final unit they become even more durable: a mountain, a rocky crag, a stone, and dirt. Now, however, the same quality that has demonstrated its evanescence shows yet another face. The enormous velocity of cascading water wears away mountains, dislodges rocky crags, smoothes out small stones, erodes soil. Nature's caprice thus comes to expression in the opposing descriptions of water, first as a disappearing entity and later as a force at work altering the most durable surface as the years go by.

The logic of the argument from first to last demands one conclusion: so mortals succumb to the erosive power of time. Just as water alters mountains, the succession of days and nights wears down the body. That anticipated conclusion does not appear; instead, Job accuses the deity of destroying human hope. Whereas a tree possessed that positive attribute, hope, mortals were denied its fruition. For them, hope constituted a delusion. No one saw this fact with more clarity than Qoheleth, who ironically identifies the advantage of the living over the dead as a hope defined by certainty of death (Qoh 9.4–5).

The depiction of the deity as an inexorable flow of energy gradually demolishing human hope demonstrates the short-lived nature of Job's fanciful thinking in vv 13–17, for he relentlessly pursues the attack against the destroyer of hope.

> You always triumph over them and they die;
> you change their appearance and dispatch them (14.20).

Job harbors no illusion that mortals could prevail in combat with the deity; the natural outcome of such futile endeavor is death. The verb *hălak* in this verse is elliptical for the traditional formula announcing one's journey to dwell in Sheol with ancestors (cf. Qoh 3.20; Ps 39.14 [Eng, 13]). The irrepressible force distorts human visage, leaving the tell-tale signs of age, until at last sending mortals on their way. In this new state, they do not participate in reality as we know it, either the swelling of pride and joy over positive social feedback or the shrinking in dismay resulting from negative sentiment. A deep abyss separates residents of Sheol from family members left behind, and no one has access to knowledge about things on the other side of the divide. The bane of sickness, its utter isolation,[28] has replaced the social being; the threat to existence has focused thoughts inward. All that remains is physical pain and psychic grief.[29] Every vestige of hope has vanished forever.

Conclusion

To expose Job's personal struggle in the face of utter vulnerability, the poet grounds his fantasy on an intimacy that refuses to surrender before perceived breach of trust. For him, survival beyond death, if it happens, springs from profound love rather than from belief in either divine justice or power.[30] Ultimately, however, Job abandons this hope as unrealistic; the enemy has triumphed, as Job's name implies.[31] Nature's extraordinary capacity to renew itself may have generated myths about dying and rising deities,[32] but the flimsy analogy that Job entertains, that of a tree's trunk sprouting at the scent of water, cannot offset the crushing weight of widespread decay. In the end, he sees his own destiny symbolized by the wilting of grass and flowers, the sinking of ponds and wadis into the voracious earth, and the wearing away of mountains, crags, stones, and soil.

CHAPTER 2

Wisdom and the Sage

On Knowing and Not Knowing

Contemporary researchers have cast considerable light on the limits of ancient knowledge imposed from outside the human intellect.[1] The axiom that human beings propose but the gods dispose was undoubtedly borne out in daily experience, for even best-laid plans sometimes go awry. An incalculable factor permeates existence, casting a shadow over all pretense to knowledge and its accompanying power. Controls of various kinds encumber daily activity,[2] both intellectual and physical: deliberate controls such as laws and norms established by society, latent controls that influence decisions unconsciously and when least expected, cognitive controls intended to hold things in check, coercive or seductive controls that others enforce and thus limit free expression. Our language shapes discourse and determines thoughts; the myths we fashion become the script in which we read the drama of our lives and the truth to which we ultimately submit; the groups to which we belong, and those to which we do not, impose hidden pressure on us in subtle and not so subtle ways; our anticipation of rejection and isolation issues in a particular code of conduct and a system of beliefs; the level of access or availability of a given choice enters heavily into our decisions; and expected compensation for an action determines to some degree whether or not the reward or punishment justifies it in our eyes.

As for obstacles to learning from within, modern interpreters have yet to give an adequate analysis of students' resistance, despite translations of Sumerian and Egyptian scribal texts[3] and corresponding comments in Sirach. A constant complaint runs through these school texts that some students resisted all effort to educate them. Assuming that a selective process weeded out the intellectually challenged, why did students incur their teachers' anger by spurning what they had to offer?

The Sumerian text, "A Scribe and his Son," addresses the problem of vocational choice, evidently a difference of opinion between father and son over the desirability of the scribal profession. "The Disputation between Enkimansi and Girnishag" exposes inevitable competition when more than one student must vie for a teacher's approval, as well as the discomfiture felt by timid persons in an unruly situation. "A Colloquy between an *ugala* and a Scribe" highlights the arrogance of supposed intellectual superiority and the potential boorishness of erudition. "Schooldays" acknowledges the harshness of physical punishment in the classroom and the plain reality of economic redress.

Egyptian scribal texts further illuminate ancient student mentality. "P. Lansing: A Schoolbook" introduces a host of difficulties associated with teaching, not the least of which is an attraction to sensual pleasure with a woman. This text resorts to traditional defenses of the scribal profession by extensive contrast with less enviable occupations, emphasizing miseries associated with each. In addition, it takes special note of hardships facing soldiers, presumably because the attraction of fast-earned booty made the military option particularly desirable. In this extensive text one finds reference to undeveloped potential, learning stimulated by the motive of fear of punishment, a teacher's inability to discover a means of arousing students' interest, and mischievous youngsters. The reluctant student, Wenemdiamun, seems to have overcome his objection to the intellectual life through frequent beatings. In his own words to the teacher, "You beat my back; your teaching entered my ear."

Other texts imply that some students did not like to be confined in a building. In P. Sallier I,6,9–7,9 Pentawere is scolded for carousing and for choosing farm labor, with its attendant supervisors, to the scribal profession where one has no boss. P. Anastasi I,8,1–9,1 warns against idle pleasures, noting that by the application of sufficient force one can teach dumb animals. In P. Anastasi IV,9,4–10,1 the scribe Inena is told that the beatings received by soldiers resemble those applied to papyrus stalks in making writing material.

The teacher's argument in Prov 1:8–19 was provoked by a compelling counter-argument, specifically that the most effective scheme for acquiring wealth was to join hands with others in using force to extract wealth from targeted victims. The lure of comraderie, pecuniary equality, and ready cash must have appealed to many students faced with prospects of endless competition, meager earnings, and delayed gratification. Moreover, generational conflict naturally increased students' tales of woe, for by the nature of things sons are always subject to a higher authority.[4] Elsewhere in the initial collection of Proverbs a father imagines that his son may have to bemoan a poor choice, that of a loose woman,[5] rather than heeding the advice of his teachers (5:7–14).

In light of Sumerian and Egyptian school texts, canonical wisdom is astonishingly silent about anything connected with classrooms. Israelite sages never rebuke students for refusing to learn, although Prov 4:1–9 comes close with its intimate recollection of learning from both father and mother. In their extensive warnings against the notorious *'iššâ zārâ* or *nokrîyyâ*, never do sages specifically relate her threat to pedagogy the way Egyptian scribes do. Even the supposed similarities between teachers' examination questions in Egyptian onomastica and the deity's lively questions in Job 38:1–41:6 hardly change the situation. Despite similar themes, Israelite wisdom literature simply ignores the kinds of problems that occupied the authors' thinking in Sumerian and Egyptian scribal texts. That silence speaks more eloquently than a host of abecediaries, transposed letters, and primitive drawings.[6] Given the later rabbinic observations about types of students, this omission in canonical wisdom is puzzling. Nothing prepares us for various metaphors in Pirke Aboth indicating different aptitudes. Nor does biblical wisdom discuss the matter of access to education, whether, that is, special qualifications such as birth, native intelligence, and affluence affect admission to a school. In this respect as in the actual periodization of life into educational units rabbinic literature resembles Egyptian scribal texts, not biblical wisdom.

The earliest surviving reflection on resistance to learning consists of a dialogue between the scribe Ani and his son Khonshotep. Father and son have distinct views about the embodiment of knowledge; Ani knows from experience that wisdom can be expressed in one's lifestyle, but Khonshotep thinks of the task as too demanding. The essential virtues–controlling one's passions such as anger, envy, lust, and appetite, mastering the tongue by avoiding gossip and slander, learning timing and eloquence–transformed an informed person into a wise one. Khonshotep recognizes the bitter reality that mere desire to do good does not suffice, any more than simply reciting classics. The centrality of speech and hearing in this dialogue derives from the oral feature in Egyptian education, the emphasis on reciting ancient texts from memory. In Sumer this practice led to strange imagery of *apkallus* with four ears. A person learned primarily from hearing, although the Sumerian riddle about a school, "What does one enter with closed eyes and depart with open eyes?" indicates that observation also featured prominently in learning. Blindness due to ignorance, prejudice, and erroneous information vanishes with the arrival of knowledge, the altering of preconceived notions, and the substitution of fact for fiction.

An interesting feature of this debate between father and son concerns human nature. Khonshotep insists that nature determines one's actions, suggesting that he follow the path of least resistance, but Ani refutes the claim by pointing to Nubians and Syrians who have learned to speak Egyptian and to various wild animals that have been domesticated. Khonshotep wishes to convince his father to lower the requirements for admission into the scholarly guild, and he notes that the masses follow their base inclinations, making an individualist rare. P. Insinger comments on this phenomenon as follows: "Whoever raves with the crowd is not regarded as a fool." In this debate between father and son, the two reach a stand-off, as if shouting "Does!" "Does not." Appealing to physical development, Khonshotep pleads for food digestible by an immature child, whereas Ani insists that adult nutrition is now appropriate. The argument concludes on a surprising note. Ani states that resistance is futile, for just as carpenters shape a piece of wood to a desired form, so the iron will of teachers succeeds in the end, unless corruption has occurred. Perhaps that possibility justifies the allusion to prayer for divine assistance in the educational endeavor and the acknowledgment that even Ani's wisdom was bestowed on him by the god. Sages realized that a single generation could destroy everything they believed, for the teachings depended on a chain of tradition.

True to form, the much later P. Insinger doubts that teachers' determination can actually overcome students' reluctance to learn. An entire chapter, the tenth, is devoted to the task of instructing one's son. Here the teacher concedes that dislike cancels every possibility for learning. The text may refer to a teacher's contempt for students or for the pedagogical task and its subject matter; alternatively, it may allude to a student's dislike for a teacher or for the topic under consideration and the process of learning itself. In this text two major factors encouraged students' malaise: the sacrifices essential to success in intellectual pursuits and severe physical lashings administered by supervisors. Control of the belly and phallus was obviously difficult for young students, if the frequent observations about these temptations provide a valid sense of their threat to students' well-being. The text states that the god Thoth created the stick to be used on lazy students and observes that a son does not die from its effects; the implied contrast is that failure to punish the child does result in death. The Aramaic Ahiqar compares beatings to manure for gardens and restraints for animals. As in biblical wisdom, P. Insinger recognizes different forms of punishment for various types of learners. Some students function better by contemplating the power of shame; a refined conscience and remorse distinguished the instructed from the uninstructed. In this context the text makes an astonishing concession that a willingness to learn is superior to biological descent.

P. Insinger generally ends each chapter with a set of paradoxes and two concluding thoughts. The first paradox in chapter ten introduces the idea of intuitive intelligence, a sort of recognition without benefit of instruction. The earlier Ptahhotep mentions natural eloquence among untutored maidens, indicating that native intelligence will find a way of coming to expression regardless of personal circumstances. The second paradox concerns a sinister side of knowledge, the possibility that learned scoundrels exist. The text refers to the fact that not all informed persons actually embody the teachings. Moreover, it avoids the facile explanation that such persons have acquired faulty knowledge. Here P. Insinger contrasts with Ani, who links knowledge and virtue much more closely. The two concluding observations apply a heuristic standard to sonship in place of the usual biological one and introduce religion into the educational task at every point, including the disposition to learn, the resulting virtue, and life itself. This divine gift is Insinger's way of explaining recalcitrance among some boys; in the last resort, the teacher's effort cannot overcome dislike if the god put it in a student's mind.

A section in Sirach dealing with difficulties confronting teachers and students demonstrates the extent of affinities between Egyptian and Israelite wisdom literature. In 6:18–37 Ben Sira ponders the educational dilemma, noting that one never ceases to learn and thus dissolving to some extent the sharp chasm between students and teachers. Ben Sira concentrates on irksome aspects of learning, using images from agricultural labor and recalling the desirable season of harvest. In trying to understand why so many obstacles stand between learner and a desired goal, Ben Sira suggests that knowledge plays a game of hide and seek, testing students to determine whether or not they deserve any reward. Here he uses a popular etymology for *mûsār*, either a play on the noun "discipline" and a participle *môsēr*, "bond" or *mûsār* in the two senses of "discipline" and "withdrawn."[7] A hint of esotericism attaches itself to this argument, conflicting with Ben Sira's express desire to attract students to his house of instruction. He elevates all learners to royal status, something also achieved in Wisdom of Solomon by the well-known rhetorical device, *sorites*, in 6:17–20.

Like his Egyptian predecessors Ben Sira explores the paradoxical relationship between freedom and determinism, combining students' choice with divine activity. The importance of conversation with learned persons first comes to prominence in Ben Sira's remarks about listening to companions' reflections and studying their metaphors. A later rabbinic saying captures this idea nicely; "Much have I learned from my masters [teachers], more from my colleagues, but from my disciples most of all." Again like Ani and P. Insinger, Ben Sira concludes by encouraging religious meditation because God gives all knowledge. In other sections Ben Sira mentions an additive factor in learning, indicating that students did more than merely preserve ancestral teachings. Every generation assessed the *traditum* in light of changed circumstances (21:15). He knew that maxims possess multiple meanings, every answer opening up a new question. Ben Sira also differentiates between constitutive and ornamental features of thought (22:16–17) in the same way Amenemope identifies the teachings as mooring posts for the tongue. Because Ben Sira believed that speech revealed the quality of a mind, he emphasized a positive correlation between clarity of expression and mental capacity (27:6).

Another feature of Ben Sira's teaching about education has extraordinary evocative power because it appeals to a fundamental drive, *eros.* Like the author of Prov 1,8 & 9, he emphasizes the erotic dimension of knowledge (Sir 15:2, 51:13–30). The harnessing of sexual energy for intellectual ends has generated powerful poetry in which lover and beloved play out love's drama, one that includes a *femme fatale*. Insofar as I can tell, Egyptian and Mesopotamian sages ignore this fascinating interplay between the one who pursues knowledge and the object of that search. Egyptian P. Chester Beatty IV (British Museum 10684) calls the scribe's books heirs, his instructions a tomb, the reed pen his children, and the stone writing-surface his wife; but this symbolism lacks the compelling force of love's reciprocity issuing in conjugal bliss as in Wisdom of Solomon, where Solomon is the ideal representative of the scholar. In this respect, Greek philosophers who stressed the erotic relationship of intellectual pursuits, specifically through the term *sophia*, an equivalent of *ḥokmâ*, stand close to biblical wisdom. Nevertheless, Egyptian scribes had access to the figure *ma'at*, which could easily have evoked similar speculation. When faced with the prospects of a passionate lover, who can remain a reluctant learner?

To the question I have addressed in this paper, "Did biblical scholars think of knowledge as an achievement or a gift?" I offer the following tentative answer. Having emphasized human achievement so much that a kind of meritocracy developed, they increasingly perceived the inadequacy of such a rigid system and stressed the activity of the deity in intellectual pursuits. The marvel is that such an easy answer to overcoming ignorance did not squelch all resistance to learning, for "Ask and you will receive" provides a means of wresting knowledge from its source through religious devotion. That affirmation concludes the three discussions of resistance in Ani, Insinger, and Sirach. Do these ancient sages refer to the shock of recognition when informed intuition arrives at insight about something entirely unfamiliar? How can anyone recognize the unheard of and radically new unless through a gift of intuitive insight? I am positing two distinct types of knowledge, the familiar and the affective surprise. The first type yields to disciplined research; the second catches us wholly unawares, coming like a gift from a generous but mysterious teacher. This phenomenon, rare in a society that venerated the *traditum* far more than any *novum*, must surely help explain the restraint of reason and humility of prayer[8] in ancient observations about knowledge and its acquisition. Our post-Enlightenment celebration of reason has brought commendable results, but often at the price of humility, the admission that all knowledge has an ultimate source beyond the human intellect and that insights occasionally come as a gift. This *testimonia* is the legacy transmitted over the centuries by Ani, P. Insinger, and Ben Sira.

CHAPTER 3

The Primacy of Listening in Ben Sira's Pedagogy

The last three decades have brought remarkable progress in clarifying the text of Sirach, the historical background for the author, his central concerns and means of presenting them, and the place of the book in the development of Israelite wisdom.[1] Scholars have also addressed special issues with considerable vigor: was Ben Sira a priest?[2] why did he omit Ezra in his catalogue of national heroes?[3] what canon of scripture did he use?[4] how did he view women?[5] Nevertheless, a notable gap in the discussion exists, particularly with regard to Ben Sira's pedagogy.[6] Did he understand education primarily as a matter of listening to intelligent people talk or did he assume that students read literary texts? That is the subject of this investigation, one that explores the extent of literacy in second century Yehud.[7]

Recent Research on Sirach

Establishing the text of Sirach is notoriously difficult, but that task has become less daunting as a result of discoveries of more than two thirds of the Hebrew text (four manuscripts from the Geniza in Cairo, a manuscript from Masada, and a portion of one from Qumran),[8] as well as the publication of the Greek text in the Göttingen Septuagint project.[9] Two concordances,[10] text critical studies on specific chapters[11] and on the Syriac text,[12] and the text in various languages, set out in parallel columns,[13] have greatly assisted those students who wish to learn more about Sirach.

Examinations of the context of Ben Sira have oscillated between wholesale endorsement of Hellenism as the prevailing spirit in his teachings[14] and insistence that Jewish thought adequately explains his vocabulary and interests.[15] The older claim that he declared war against Hellenism[16] has been nuanced further by awareness of the extent of Greek influence on Judaism as a whole.[17] Ben Sira's affinities with Demotic wisdom, especially Papyrus Insinger, and his apparent acquaintance with the older Egyptian Instruction for Duauf, commonly known as The Satire of the Trades, indicate that he truly was cosmopolitan in spirit.[18] That recognition has not carried over into a conviction that he subscribed to Stoic philosophy,[19] despite some linguistic similarities with this system of thought.

The structure of the book has eluded detection, although several attempts to solve this enigma have been made. These vary from an effort to view Sirach in terms of a textbook of increasing difficulty[20] to a more plausible understanding of it in the light of separate units introduced by hokmatic or doxological reflections.[21] The concluding praise of men of worth has evoked a theory about the epic as a charter ideology for the temple[22] and has prompted the suggestion that two encomia conclude the book, the first in praise of wisdom, the second lauding the creator and honoring heroes of the past, as an appropriate way of paying homage to Simeon, the high priest in Ben Sira's time.[23] The correctness of the Greek genre, encomium, has elicited criticism,[24] and the mixture of genres within the entire book contributes in large measure to the difficulty of breaking it down into convenient sections that cohere from the modern standpoint. In this respect, Sirach resembles earlier biblical wisdom,[25] but in significant ways it marks a decisive transition to a new kind of piety.[26] That has been labeled priestly instruction in written form, although precious little in the book pertains to exclusive concerns of the priestly profession.

Perhaps the most extensive discussions have focused on themes within the book. Does Ben Sira think first and foremost in terms of religious piety,[27] the fear of God, or does he draw more heavily from sapiential categories? Does he accept the concept of free will,[28] or does he subscribe to a theory of two inclinations, the good and the evil, as later developed in rabbinic literature? What function does theodicy play in his thinking,[29] particularly in light of his rhetorical flourishes that seem directed at persons who questioned divine goodness and justice? Was Ben Sira actually a misogynist, or does he cite prevalent views regarding women, from which he separates himself? What does Ben Sira think about the ancient commandment to honor one's parents?[30] What principle of selection operates in the praise of famous men? What role does prayer play in Ben Sira's piety?[31] How do suffering and death affect his pedagogy and theology?[32] Does he believe in a messiah[33] and in the resurrection of the dead?[34]

In the realm of commentaries, progress has been extremely slow, perhaps owing to Sirach's dubious canonical connection and textual uncertainty, but students need not despair. They will find reliable translations and notes,[35] exhaustive treatments of linguistic features, and literary/theological analyses[36] that should stimulate interest and encourage them to examine the wide range of secondary literature on the book.

Orality versus Literacy

The virtual silence of commentators on the subject of education in Ben Sira's environment matches that on ancient education generally, one that has resulted from the dirth of direct evidence in the Hebrew canon. Recent epigraphic finds have prompted a more venturesome approach to the problem,[37] particularly when parallels with ancient Near Eastern cultural centers are taken into account. Still, methodological difficulties abound,[38] and renewed interests in the oral register have raised the issue of the extent of literacy in ancient Israel.[39] Where does Ben Sira fit in this oral/literacy continuum? Is he closer to parental instruction implied by earlier proverbs or to the explosive literary activity indicated by the remarkable texts at Qumran?[40]

None would question the presence of a core elite group of scribes in the great city states of Mesopotamia from c. 3100 BCE and from Egypt a century or so later, but this specialized education was directed inwards and was characterized by manipulation of scarcity.[41] For the most part, education served the wishes of royal administrators, eventually filtering down to benefit wealthy entrepreneurs and commerce of all kinds. Much of the literary activity was highly technical. Religious texts of various types (omens, execration texts, myths and epics, hymns, prayers), royal propaganda, inventories and archives, mathematical texts, and grammatical aids (word lists, bilingual vocabularies, scribal exercises, school texts). Because of the difficult character of the cuneiform script and Egyptian hieroglyphs, literacy was restricted to a tiny percentage of the population, perhaps one to two per cent. Schools certainly existed, but admission into the ranks of scribes was severely limited.

The development of a phonetic alphabet in fourteenth century Syria-Palestine and its eventual adoption throughout the Ancient Near East–an interesting case of a vanquished culture exercising linguistic dominance over its victors–introduced a different situation into the entire Fertile Crescent.[42] Still, an Aramaic lingua franca did not usher in mass education and literacy, for no positive correlation between simplicity of an alphabet and literacy exists–witness the illiteracy in Medieval Europe and the exceptional literacy in China. An agrarian Israelite society lacked an incentive to introduce widespread literacy, although from the eighth century on certain features of society begin to elevate writing as something of value.

To what extent did the Israelite monarchy employ professional scribes? The answer to this important question is highly controversial, and even a maximalist response does not settle the matter of educational opportunity in the land. Even if, as is likely, the royal administrations in Israel and Judah employed trained scribes like their counterparts elsewhere, this does not necessarily suggest that such training proliferated among rank and file Israelites. Vested interests undoubtedly kept the number of professional scribes sufficiently low to guarantee employment. The customary guilds among artisans and craftsmen functioned as a protective measure for the family; and scribes, who experienced a comparable vulnerability, must have guarded their ranks both to enhance their prestige and to increase their earnings.

Any learning acquired by ordinary citizens would probably have been minimal–perhaps an ability to read and write their names, to recognize various items from inventories, and the like. An actual verse in the book of

Isaiah (29:11–12) posits a situation in which wholly different responses occur: one person lacks the ability to read whereas another possesses that skill. Ancient Hebrew texts were not "reader friendly," for they lacked the several aids to understanding contributed by later guardians of sacred literature, Sopherim and Massoretes. Small wonder a coterie of trained interpreters of the torah in Ezra's day engaged in the task of assisting the populace to become familiar with the written word imposed on the people who returned from exile in Babylon.

Composers and guardians of canonical wisdom fall into an exceptional category where education is concerned–at least, one would think. After all, these individuals valued learning and devoted their waking hours to transmitting their teachings to youth, or so it seems. Nevertheless, they rarely use the verb *kātab*, and, unlike Egyptian Instructions such as Merikare, Amenemopet, Anii and Anksheshanky, Israelite sages never instruct students to read a text or to write anything as an exercise in learning.[43] The text in Prov 22:17–24:22 that shows affinities with the Instruction of Amenemopet opens with a question about the author's having written thirty sayings; an epilogist to Qoheleth observes that the teacher wrote reliable words (12:9–10); and a distraught Job imagines a written testimonial to his integrity (19:23–24). In two instances the teacher in the initial collection of sayings within Proverbs urges the son to write his, or divine, teachings on the tablet of the heart (3:3 and 7:3), but the language is necessarily symbolic–unlike comparable instructions in Deuteronomy, which enjoin hearers to write the divine commandments on doorposts and to wear them on the body.

A similar situation exists in the Sayings of Ahiqar, where one finds a single instance of the verb *qārā'*, but with the sense of naming rather than reading, and not one occurrence of *kātab*.[44] Given the ostensible setting of this work in the royal court, although removed by circumstances to a place of incarceration, the absence of direct allusions to reading and writing stands out. Necessity forces Ahiqar to adopt a literary medium until his reinstatement as the king's counsellor takes place. Ben Sira's restricted use of the verb *kātab* to his own literary endeavor, with rare exceptions, accords with longstanding reluctance among Israelite sages to employ verbs of writing and reading. For him, the verb *kātab* applies to sacred texts (a prediction about Elijah's role in eschatological times, 48:10), musical compositions (44:5), engraving (45:11), and his own teachings (39:32).

Education in Canonical Wisdom

In the canonical book of Proverbs emphasis falls on hearing as the medium of learning. The ears play the decisive role in the acquisition of knowledge, and whenever the eyes come into play they observe human behavior rather than poring over written texts. According to Prov 18:15, the ear of the wise actively seeks knowledge, just as an intelligent mind (*lēb*) acquires it. Culpability comes from failing to listen to instruction, not from refusing to read assigned texts (5:13–14). This extraordinary concession on the part of a teacher, like that of the pharaoh Merikare who admitted to having committed an act of wrongdoing, removes the gulf between student and teacher that Anii's son, Khonshotep, felt so keenly.[45] The biblical sage confesses that he did not obey his teachers or incline his ears to his instructors, thereby jeopardizing his place among the assembled people. His offense concerned listening, not refusal to do what he had read.

The collection in Proverbs that incorporates several sayings that also appear in the Instruction of Amenemopet begins with explicit reference to inclining the ear (22:17) and proceeds to mention, in interrogative form, written sayings (22:20), but the emphasis within this section reverts to hearing as the means of acquiring knowledge. Thus one reads in 23:12, "Apply your mind to discipline and your ears to knowledgeable sayings." In 23:26 the teacher invites the student (*benî*, my son) to observe him and to delight in his conduct. Personal example, rather than written texts, however lofty, serves here as inspiration to the object of instruction.

Not all instruction derived from words. A particularly informative narrative in 24:30–34 describes the process of acquiring knowledge through keen observation of circumstances, in this instance a neglected vineyard coming to ruin. The combination of laziness and time's passage gradually brought devastation, leading the observer to conclude that even a little indolence will open the gate for poverty to enter like a robber.

Nevertheless, the parental warning in 19:27 best exemplifies the importance of hearing to biblical sages: "My son, stop hearing instruction only to depart from words of knowledge." This silence about written instruction persists in the two collections of foreign wisdom, the sayings of Agur in Prov 30:1–14 and the Instruction to Lemuel by his Mother in Prov 31:1–9. Furthermore, the late acrostic in Prov 31:10–31 has nothing to say about written instruction, all the more noteworthy if the word *sôpîyya* in 31:27 contains an aural pun on the Greek word for wisdom, *sophia*.[46] This remarkable wife opens her mouth with wisdom, and gracious teaching adorns her tongue (31:26).

The choice of the verb *we'izzēn* in Qoh 12:9 may owe something to an audial pun, connoting both listening and assessing.[47] In preparing to teach the people knowledge, he listened and weighed the significance of what he heard, probing deeply and arranging numerous aphorisms. Then he endeavored to discover pleasing expressions, which he subsequently recorded in writing. The following caveat against the intellectual enterprise, its endless preoccupation with producing more written texts, evokes a different environment from that reflected in the book of Proverbs, justifying the placing of the epilogues of Qoheleth toward the literacy end of the oral/literacy continuum.[48] Whether or not that judgment applies to the rest of the book is unclear, but the poem in 3:2–8 does not include the polarities "reading and writing." Evidently the author did not consider it necessary to isolate times for normal scribal activity. The epilogist did not hesitate to identify Qoheleth as a professional sage, a *ḥākām* (12:9), and to associate him with literary activity, but Qoheleth himself seems to have lived up to his name, the assembler, and to have addressed hearers with his oral teachings, which he later wrote for posterity.

A similar ambiguity prevails in the book of Job. On the one hand, the instruction within the book always belongs to the oral register. The three friends verbally harangue Job, as do Elihu and the deity. In return, Job tries to set the friends right by word of mouth; he says nothing to Elihu and only slightly more to the deity. On the other hand, this "slightly more" consists of a surprising rejection of what he had heard at some time in the past in favor of immediate sight (42:5). Still, the preference for sight over hearsay, or the potent combination of hearing divine speeches with the accompanying insight, has absolutely nothing to do with reading and writing. The unreliable and therefore dismissable hearing constituted second hand reports about divine mystery, now seen for what they were. This means little more than that all teaching has to be evaluated in the light of one's own experience.

To sum up, canonical wisdom literature presupposes a predominantly oral culture.[49] That is true not only of older proverbial sayings, most of which probably arose among the populace and were transmitted orally from parents to children, but also of later instructions, domestic and foreign.[50] Similarly, the books of Job and Qoheleth imply that teaching came primarily, if not exclusively, in the form of oral sayings. The occasional references to writing fall into the category of a testimonial for the benefit of deity and posterity, or they represent a sort of colophon inscribed by another hand than the speaker of the original work.

An Oral Culture?

The question arises, however, whether or not such concentration on hearing can exist in a literate sub-culture. In ancient Sumerian educational circles an emphasis fell on hearing, leading to a bizarre description of the learned Marduk as possessor of four ears. Similarly, Egyptian scribes identify a sage as "one who hears,"[51] and the Instruction of Ptahhotep has a long conclusion that makes this point most tellingly. The true scribe is the one who hears, which means that his actions embody the teachings. Such remarks about the importance of hearing may have originated in earlier times when instruction was oral, but they persisted in later times when scribes practiced the art of reading and writing. Writing certainly existed, as demonstrated by copious inscriptions and letters that have survived in Syria-Palestine,[52] but such evidence does not erase the overwhelming impression within canonical wisdom that instruction took the form of oral delivery.

Ben Sira as Scribe

Did that situation continue into the first three decades of the second century when Ben Sira took on the role of teacher? On the basis of his own advice to the youth of his day, the answer is "yes." Presumably, Ben Sira resided in Jerusalem, although most of Yehud was rural. He refers to a hierarchy in society, with the ruler at the top, followed by the High Priest, judges, physicians, sages, artisans and craftsmen, merchants, ordinary citizens.[53] The cult at the temple exercized a significant influence on Ben Sira, at least aesthetically, but he seems to have remained on the periphery insofar as strict dietary laws were concerned, and indeed, he ignores the ritual features of priestly legislation. For this reason, the claim that he belonged to the priesthood lacks cogency; moreover, his silence in this regard makes no sense if he actually could have made such a boast. Nevertheless, he was definitely moved by pomp and circumstance associated with special religious days, as his ebullient description of Simeon demonstrates.

Ben Sira really understood himself as a sage, a teacher who continued in the tradition of earlier *ḥakamîm*, with one decisive difference. He resisted the earlier isolation of Israelite sages, their self-conscious universalism. Instead, he joined together the national heritage in religion and the Jewish legacy of international wisdom. Viewing his own contribution to the latter as inspired and therefore worthy of inclusion in a treasury of sacred literature, he sought eagerly to instruct disciples who would transmit that legacy to the next generation. To that end he boldly issued an invitation to students, urging them to seek instruction in his *bēt hammidraš* or his *yešivâ*. Such language has nothing to do with institutional schools, whether one thinks in terms of Greek schools or later Jewish instruction in synagogues.[54] It rather implies private instruction in a teacher's home, a type of training akin in some ways to peripatetic instruction by Greek philosophers. The emphasis in Ben Sira's teaching fell on moral formation, an ethics firmly grounded in theology. This approach to learning was both elitist and practical. Ben Sira considered most people ineducable, a judgment based on their indifference to morals.

The goal of education, in his view, was to demonstrate the reality that righteous actions issue from religious allegiance. The fear of God, the ancient sages' term for religion, manifested itself in compassionate deeds. This conviction explains a curious feature of Ben Sira's teachings–the manner in which the concept "fear of God" rivals the notion of wisdom. Subscribing to the introductory motto in the initial collection within the book of Proverbs, 1:1–9:18, which asserts that wisdom begins in and achieves its highest expression in religious devotion, Ben Sira tries to spell out the implications of this insight. Nevertheless, he does not teach torah, for all his insistence that students meditate on it. The subject matter of his teaching always belongs to the category of wisdom, even when he enters the realm of doxology.

Despite the lofty enterprise to which he subscribed, Ben Sira remained very much a child of his times.[55] In at least two areas his views raise modern eyebrows: his attitude to women and slavery. In the latter area, the author of Deuteronomy moved from theological perceptions about the people of Yahweh in Egyptian bondage to humane treatment of slaves,[56] but Ben Sira's compassion for the poor did not extend to slaves. Nor did his frequently-expressed admiration for good wives prevent him from obscene remarks about daughters.

In retrospect, it appears that Ben Sira pitched his camp with representatives of the past rather than the future. His deep respect for the priestly class and temple cult, his refusal to endorse radically new views such as life beyond the grave, his elitism–these attitudes placed him nearer the later Sadducees than the Pharisees, whose openness to popular ideas and deep piety appealed to the masses.

A Test Case, Sirach 6:18–37

Returning to the question posed earlier, "Did an oral culture persist as late as the first quarter of the second century BCE?" The preliminary answer is "yes." To test that response, we turn to the discussion of educational training in 6:32–37. The larger context, 6:18–37, consists of twenty-two bicola, suggesting comprehensiveness like the complete alphabet. Its topic appeared obvious to the person who added a title in the Vulgate (*De Doctrina Sapientia*). An inclusio built on the Hebrew noun *ḥokmâ* links the first and last verses of the unit, 18 and 37, and a direct address, *benî*, sets the three sub-sections apart from the whole. The imagery of farming and hunting dominate the first two smaller units, whereas the third graduates to a picture of vigorous conversation and deep thought.

Although Ben Sira thinks of education as especially applicable to the young, he recognizes its lifelong appeal. His language concedes the harsh nature of ancient education, about which scribes in Mesopotamia and Egypt had much to say.[57] Ben Sira urges the youth to approach their education eagerly, like farmers who plow the ground and sow seed, anticipating a bountiful harvest. A short-sighted person stoops to pick up a heavy rock but quickly drops it, rather than relocating it to help control the rapid runoff of heavy rains. Like the discarded stone, wisdom conceals its real use. Here Ben Sira probably plays on the words *mûsār* (instruction) and *sûr* (to turn away, in its passive form), the latter root returning in v 33 (*tiwāssēr*). With its allusion to *hoi polloi*, the Greek rendering of this complex pun sounds elitist (*kai ou pollais estin phanera*).

The second sub-section continues the idea of wisdom's seeming harsh ways but quickly transforms the images. Students are likened to oxen and urged to submit willingly to the yoke. Then the image changes to hunting, with the hint that wisdom wishes to be found so as to grant rest to the weary hunter. Ben Sira's love of lavish apparel manifests itself in an extended description of conversion: fetters become protection, a collar turns into a splendid robe, the yoke changes to a golden ornament, and bonds are transformed into a purple cord. Work clothes have been cast off in favor of royal attire, a purple robe and a crown. With this bold description of transformation through education, Ben Sira gives his personal view about the social ramifications of an education. These words are not just anybody's opinion, but that of an authoritative teacher. Verse 23 stresses Ben Sira's authority through the threefold repetition of the possessive pronoun "my," at least in the Hebrew; the Greek translator drops one of them but makes up for the difference by an intensive form, *me apanainou*. The notion of receiving the torah like a yoke struck a responsive chord in later Christian and rabbinic literature (Matt 11:29; Pirqe Aboth 3:6; Erubin 54a).

Not every image in this section is transparent, giving rise to suggestions that the idea is that of nets, and to weights used by athletes in training, or blocks placed on slaves' ankles. Ben Sira employs three imperatives to describe the hunt. Besides the verbs *deraš* and *beqaš*, which refer to careful searching, the imperative *hāqar* implies that one traces out a route.

Combined, the three imperatives suggest thorough research leading naturally to discovery, *wetimṣā'*. An adverb of time (at last) and a personal pronoun (for you) express the decisive nature of this turnaround (*nehpak*), as does the word "joy."

The third sub-section stresses the importance of motivation, the firm resolve to acquire an education at any cost, indicates the diverse character of learning, and gives it a theological complexion. Ben Sira advises young people to keep their ears open in the assembly of elders, listening for intelligent speech. Then they are told to take advantage of every opportunity to learn from perceptive individuals–even to the point of making themselves a nuisance. Moreover, Ben Sira alerts his hearers to two different kinds of intelligence, one that expresses itself in witty sayings, another that takes the form of exposition. Here he characterizes wisdom as preserved in the canon: aphorisms and reflective, or theoretical, discourse. Finally, he insists that those who want to learn should meditate on torah, confident that God will reward them with wisdom. Here Ben Sira uses a rare word *śîḥâ* which occurs only three times in the Hebrew Bible (Job 15:4; Ps 119:97, 99). An educated mind achieves its loftiest expression in a divine gift of insight.

Conclusion

Nowhere in this unit does Ben Sira mention the reading of texts or exercises in writing. His students learn by listening to intelligent conversation; Ben Sira still lives in a predominantly oral culture. He himself reads torah and writes what he hopes will be viewed as inspired teaching, yet he transmits his instructions to students orally, and he expects them to learn by astute listening.[58]

CHAPTER 4

Qoheleth's Understanding of Intellectual Inquiry

Consider two scholars of equal ability and accomplishment. The first externalizes her presuppositions, lays bare her particular concerns, discusses her methodological procedure, identifies her intended audience, and furnishes personal assessments of the data being explored. She consciously leaves nothing to chance, taking her readers by the hand and guiding them safely through difficult terrain. The second interpreter does not state the perspective from which he comes to the data, says nothing about his own personal interests, shuns any mention of theoretical issues guiding the analysis, seems oblivious to any specific audience, and maintains scholarly detachment from beginning to end. He trusts readers to enter into a dialogue with the text and to detect what the first scholar freely provided. Nevertheless, the second scholar reflected self-consciously about the things he left unstated and chose to challenge his audience intellectually rather than risk underestimating their ability to recognize perspective, personal agenda, method, reader, and authorial involvement.

Which of the two interpreters is more subjective, the one who leaves little to the imagination? Not necessarily, for the scholar who withholds data that he considers self-evident in order to involve readers more actively in an intellectual journey has made a conscious pedagogical decision. He has also acknowledged the intelligence of his audience. The first scholar, on the other hand, may have recognized that her readers lacked the experience and expertise necessary to sift through sophisticated arguments and to discern what does not lie on the surface. She, too, has chosen the pedagogy that she deems most appropriate to her subject and audience. In short, the mere articulation of ideological bias (e.g., form critic, feminist, social scientist, archaeologist, theologian) does not indicate a higher degree of ego-consciousness or subjectivism than silence about ideology does.

Qoheleth resembles the first of these two scholars, for in him an intrusive ego intervenes between the topic under exploration and the audience's perception of his discoveries.[1] He observes reality and reflects introspectively on the experience. Indeed, he turns his own intellectual inquiry into the study of personal reflections. The impression he leaves approximates that of confession: then I saw, considered, knew, thought, pondered, said, and so forth. He was not the first, however, to interpose his subjective consciousness between experience and audience, nor was he the last. The unknown observer in Prov 7:6–27 who describes a fateful encounter between an adulteress and a young man opens the account with personal information concerning vantage point and then piles up verbs for observation: I looked out, saw, and perceived.[2] Similarly, the composer of the anecdote in Prov 24:30–34 consciously reflects on a personal journey of discovery: I passed by, saw, considered, looked, and learned.[3] The difference between these epistemologies and Qoheleth's may be measured in degrees; whether the latter thinker deserves the adjective "new" is doubtful. The same goes for "revolutionary." The later Ben Sira, the first Israelite sage to succumb to the temptation to claim authorship of a written text,[4] allows his healthy ego[5] to manifest itself on several occasions. Similarly, the unknown author of Wisdom of Solomon considers the state of his soul and the details of his love life worthy information to convey to readers.[6]

The extraordinary teaching attributed to Agur in Prov 30:1–14 throbs with personal introspection, all negative in character. He confesses his abysmal ignorance, both about wisdom and about deity. Whatever the meaning of his initial observation, it seems to conclude with an acknowledgment of weakness, a perceived incapacity to measure up to the demands of existence. The language of this extraordinary wise man stands as a powerful warning against hasty assessments of vocabulary, for theistic sentiment (a twofold reference to El, allusion to the Holy One) is negated by powerful skepticism in vv 1–4, which end on a mocking note familiar from the divine speech in Job 38:5.[7]

Other factors also affect one's determination of a text's subjectivity, especially the author's selection of a particular mode of narration.[8] Omniscient narration may take place in first person or in third, and the author may opt to maintain distance by means of a persona, or even multiple personae.[9] Do these choices indicate different degrees of egocentricity? On the surface, it appears that first person dialogue signals heightened subjectivity, but a sentient self hovers over narration in the third person and makes its powerful presence felt at every step of the way. In a sense, such reticence increases the mystery and calls attention to the godlike presence behind the speaking voice. A persona, too, permits an author to remain in the shadows while focusing attention on an imaginary figure. Insofar as a persona replaces the actual author, the level of subjectivity recedes because it is once-removed.

Both of these authorial decisions on Qoheleth's part further complicate matters. On the one hand, he selected a narrative style in the first person, giving the impression of total involvement in the learning process. The epilogues heighten the sense of immediacy by emphasizing the achievements of the individual who speaks under the name Qoheleth.[10] Readers follow him through one experiment after another, watch him agonize over injustice and life's utter futility, and sympathize with his effort to salvage something from the daily treadmill-existence. On the other hand, the author chose to speak through a fictional persona, King Solomon. For some reason, Qoheleth abandoned this royal mode of address after the initial attempt in 1:12–2:26. Was this decision the result of a desire for immediacy with his audience?

These ambiguities imply that, like most questions pertaining to Qoheleth, his understanding of intellectual inquiry is multifaceted and complex. In *The Gift of Asher Lev,* Chaim Potok has Picasso say to Lev: "Truth has to be given in riddles. People can't take truth if it comes charging at them like a bull. The bull is always killed, Lev. You have to give the truth in a riddle, hide it so they go looking for it and find it piece by piece; that way you can learn to live with it..."[11] With this warning in mind, we shall attempt to tease out some fundamental principles pertinent to a discussion of Qoheleth's epistemology, examine the sapiential language for acquiring wisdom, and explore the sages' acknowledgment of limits imposed on the intellect.

I. Asking Pertinent Questions

A. Prose, Poetry, and Philosophy. The scope of Qoheleth's own contribution to the book continues to baffle the experts. An older way of dealing with this problem, the positing of voices in dialogue,[12] has taken on a new wrinkle, the assumption that Qoheleth's voice coincides with the prose components of the book, which was subsequently challenged in various ways by additions in poetry. Whatever one thinks of the colometry lying behind Osswald Loretz's hypothesis,[13] the effort to detect early forms of Jewish philosophy is surely salutary.[14] Critics have often commented on the extent of abstractions within the book, together with Qoheleth's striving to formulate a philosophy of existence.

Merely breaking away from traditional constraints of poetry does not constitute philosophy, although it may be an initial step in this direction. Clearly, Qoheleth's tenuous venture into allegory fails to grasp its vast potential for philosophizing;[15] for that advance one looks to Philo, whose fertile mind perceived the easy transition from sacred story to speculation about stages of intellectual and spiritual development. Likewise, the author of Wisdom of Solomon seized the idea of personified wisdom and formulated a philosophy of history that included an active governing principle, Wisdom, who participated in the divine essence. Both authors enjoyed the intellectual stimulation of an immediate environment steeped in Hellenism;[16] Qoheleth was further removed from the Greek cultural center, even if his expressions for human destiny approximate the Greek concept of fate.[17] Like Ben Sira, Qoheleth adopted traditional Jewish modes of presenting his teachings, although at times deeply touched by Hellenism.[18]

This claim rests on a relatively late dating of the book of Ecclesiastes, now under attack from two directions. Daniel Fredericks' case rests on dubious grounds methodologically, for a demonstration that Qoheleth uses some early features of language does not offset the overwhelming evidence for late vocabulary and syntax.[19] Leong Seow's arguments, both linguistic and socio-economic, indicate the difficulty of establishing the date of any ancient text.[20] Tracing the detectable first appearance of a word or expression does not fix the time of its occurrence in another body of literature, even if one accepts Seow's view about the cessation of a given usage (e.g., *šalîṭ*, which I question).

Equally unreliable is the attempt to postulate the exact socio-economic reality reflected in the book.[21] Apart from the problem presented by any literary work (i.e., does the author furnish accurate information about the actual context giving rise to the thoughts, or does one encounter an imaginary world?), how many eras of the past are distinctive enough to be recognizable millennia later? How do we know that Qoheleth's society alone experienced an excessive compulsion to "strike it rich," to climb the social ladder by whatever means, and to risk ruin in the process?[22] While Persian rulers may have presented an ideal situation for such preoccupations,[23] so did the Ptolemaic ruling hierarchy.[24] Prophetic attacks on certain segments of eighth century Israel and Judah suggest that the drive to get rich, with its accompanying risks and privileges, did not originate with Persian hegemony, although the means of attaining wealth differed significantly.

B. Embedded Tradition from Stoic Teachings. A related issue concerns the nature of attitudes embedded within poetic sections of the book, specifically in the poem about times for everything in 3:2–8 and the reflection about cyclical events in 1:4–11. If Joe Blenkinsopp's reading of the facts can be sustained,[25] namely that 3:1–8 is a citation from a Stoicizing Jewish sage or a Stoic composition translated into Hebrew, and that 3:9–22 constitutes idiosyncratic commentary, it follows that Qoheleth entered into dialogue with philosophical ideas about timely action (*eukairia*). In his view, no amount of studying the events that fill human experience enabled one to detect the right action for the occasion. Far too much randomness rendered the future uncertain. The circle of destiny trapped one and all, as the poem in 1:4–11 demonstrates so effectively.

The extent of polemic within Qoheleth's teachings, as well as the exact target of this attack, raise additional questions about the degree of subjectivism underlying his rhetoric. Such expressions as "crisis" and "bankruptcy of wisdom" served an important function as long as they were not generalized and absolutized.[26] Qoheleth's disillusionment with many traditional views does amount to a crisis arising from the sharp disparity between inherited beliefs and experienced reality, but his awareness of this gulf does not entirely invalidate the sapiential enterprise. He understands his own intellectual quest as a continuation of what earlier sages engaged in, and he insists that he is guided rationally. Regardless of whether or not his bold denial in 8:10–17 refers to another *ḥākām* or to his own deliberations, the final word rules out any claim to absolute truth.

One may justifiably speak of a personal crisis, a painful recognition that old answers no longer sufficed, but the experience enervated the honest thinker rather than paralyzing him.[27] One could just as easily designate the personal event a creative moment leading to a revolutionary breakthrough,[28] an acknowledgment that one cannot control human destiny through acts of virtue or piety. Living in accord with nature was not possible, regardless of what Stoics taught, nor could anyone conduct life in a manner that would guarantee longevity, health, wealth, and social esteem. Qoheleth resists a particular kind of wisdom in the same way the author of the book of Job undermines certainty,[29] but neither author opposes wisdom as such.

C. An Empirical Thinker? Much has been written about the empirical grounding of sapiential thinking, its thorough basis in experience. That claim applies to the book of Proverbs, with minor exceptions. Obviously, the speculation about Wisdom's role as witness during the creation of the world (Prov 8:22–36) did not arise from ordinary experience. Certain features of the book of Job also transcend empirical investigation, particularly the material in the Prologue and Epilogue, as well as the divine speeches from the whirlwind.[30] One could quibble about the latter point, insisting that encounter with the Holy belongs to human experience. In any event, few interpreters would deny the overwhelming experiential basis of Qoheleth's teaching. Michael Fox, who refuses to grant that wisdom literature is empirical, bestows that honor on Qoheleth alone.[31]

That claim certainly applies to Qoheleth's method of study, but it obscures the extensive impact of non-experiential data on his thinking. Where, one asks, did he learn so much about the deity who, on Qoheleth's own admission, remains hidden, thus concealing the essential character of divine activity? What empirical facts conveyed the following insights: that God has appointed a time for judgment, dislikes fools, will punish rash vows, created the world good/appropriate, dwells in heaven, creates the embryo within its mother's womb, chases the past, tests people in order to make them fear, gives human beings unpleasant business, keeps them preoccupied with joy,[32] made men and women upright, has already approved one's actions, and rewards those who fear/worship the deity.

Such unsubstantiated assertions about God are not Qoheleth's only departure from an empirical base. How does he know what has been will recur, that people will not be remembered, that everything belongs within an ordered scheme, that the crooked cannot be straightened, that sadness makes the heart glad, that no righteous person exists? After all, he claims an active memory of all who preceded him on Jerusalem's throne. Did he, like Jeremiah, search high and low for a single righteous person? Has he not heard that in certain circumstances (educational, carpentry) the crooked can indeed be straightened, and vice versa, as Anii insisted to his son, Khonshotep?

The simple truth is that Qoheleth accepted an astonishing variety of transmitted teachings without submitting them to the test of experience. Occasionally, he uses emphatic language, e.g., "I know," when asserting something that none can confirm (3:14–15 and 8:12–13). One suspects that rhetoric aims at obscuring faulty logic in such moments. In light of overwhelming evidence of *a priori* knowledge in Qoheleth's teaching, it may be necessary to qualify the claim that a new era of empirical knowledge dawned when he appeared on the scene.

D. Orality and Genre. Susan Niditch has brought the matter of orality into the forefront again,[33] but without the assumptions accompanying previous discussion. In passing, she considers Qoheleth within the literacy end of a continuum, although her "trial runs" or "scenarios" necessarily belong to the realm of conjecture. My own independent study of Sirach emphasizes the primacy of orality in Ben Sira's pedagogy, his insistence that students attend to human discourse rather than written texts.[34]

If one goes far enough back to the moment when individuals first perceived the insights presently embedded in the proverbial sayings within the biblical collections attributed to Solomon (Prov 10:1–22:16; 25–29), at least two things stand out. One, the discovery has nothing to do with literacy,[35] and two, the mode of arriving at the new understanding is entirely empirical. At the later stage of transmission, Fox may be right that the saying reinforces ethos,[36] but that admission does not rule out a prior discovery based on experience. Sages, like Qoheleth, may well have generalized on the basis of limited experience; and they undoubtedly applied some insights to inappropriate categories. Nevertheless, they reached their conclusions by studying reality as they encountered it, and they tested these perceptions by observing patterns of behavior and repeatable events. In this respect, they functioned as pioneers in the search for knowledge; a later Qoheleth followed the same pathway.

Contemporary interpreters find it helpful to identify a text's genre, for this information provides a clue that assists in placing similar texts alongside one another and in this way to discover the unique features of each. Christian Klein's penetrating analysis of Ecclesiastes may say all that can rightfully be asserted, but calling a text *sui generis* amounts to an admission that every text is unique.[37] His useful observation that a *māšāl* has parabolic and paradigmatic force helps readers appreciate Qoheleth's elusive appeal. Over the centuries, skeptics and orthodox, philosophers and neophytes, have been drawn to this book, and their fascination is rooted in its enigmatic quality, an open invitation to its use as a mirror.

Like genre, structure assists critics in their analysis of the book's message. Here, too, modern principles of investigation have proved ineffectual.[38] Some probabilities exist: poetic sections (1:4–11; 11:7–12:7) enclose the main body of teachings; a thematic statement precedes and follows these poems (1:2–3; 12:8); a pivotal section appears at the beginning of the main body (1:12–2:26; 3:1–22); certain refrains and repeated statements give an impression of unity despite frequent contradictions; and editorial additions provide orientation for readers (1:1; 12:8–14). Such indications of intentional arrangement do not offset the baffling effect of random sayings with no discernible relationship to the progress of Qoheleth's argument. Ingenuity has not been lacking in a modern attempt to crack the code; but it, too, has been *hebel*, futile.

II. The Acquisition of Knowledge

Although the sages never quite drew up a compendium of terms relating to learning, they did occasionally reflect on the pursuit of knowledge in ways that draw attention to specific verbs and nouns having to do with the intellectual process. In a few instances these teachers actually gather together several verbs that cover the entire scope of learning, and at other times they seem to discourage certain types of speculation. An examination of this vocabulary for intellectual achievement throws additional light on Qoheleth's epistemology.[39]

Vocabulary for Teacher

Two expressions in Gen 12:6 and Judg 7:1 seem to reflect a period when Israel endeavored, through the assistance of trained technicians, to ascertain the divine plan for the future by means of divination. The teachers' terebinth near Shechem (*'ēlôn mōreh*) and hill of instruction (*gib'at hammôreh*) respectively allude to the places of access to divine secrets. Belief in God as teacher occurs in several texts, but Job 35:11, Isa 28:26, and 30:20 stand out as particularly significant manifestations of this notion. Elihu describes Eloah as "one who gives songs during the night, who teaches us (*mallepēnû* with missing *aleph* ; the root is *'lp* and one expects *me'allepenû*) more than the beasts of the earth and bestows more wisdom than the birds of the sky." The comparison appears to be between experiential observation, the basis of conclusions about reality in the sayings within the book of Proverbs, and revelation.

The two approaches to learning, the one horizontal, the other vertical, come together in Isa 28:23–29, for the farmer observes a certain rhythm in planting and sowing; but Isaiah insists that God also instructs him rightly, indeed that YHWH of hosts, the one who works wonders in counsel (*hiplî' 'ēṣā*) and excels in perspicacity, oversees this natural rhythm. The other text from the book of Isaiah, probably postexilic, concedes that YHWH will afflict Judah sorely, bestowing "bread of affliction and water of adversity," but promises that its teacher (*môreykâ*) will no longer hide, enabling eyes to behold the divine Instructor (*môreykâ*) and ears to discern a word from behind: "This is the way; walk in it," when the people veers either to the right or to the left. The divine enclosure of Judah, front and rear, is a noteworthy theological concept. In a text from the same general period, a personal name in 1 Chr 5:13, *yôray*, may be a short form of *yôreyyâ*, with the probable meaning "whom YHWH teaches." Elihu sums up this theological conviction in the following words: "Look, El is sovereign in power; who is a teacher (*môreh*) like him?" This religious conviction manifests its power in the Psalter (e.g., 94:12 with the Piel of *ysr* and *lmd*, 119:108 with *lammedēnî*) and in a hymnic text in Sirach (51:17, with *melammedēnî*; cf. also 11Q Psa). This religious ideology shows signs of encountering skepticism over the effectiveness of divine instruction, given recalcitrant human nature. Accordingly, a text in Jer 32:33 places blame squarely on human shoulders. Even persistent effort on God's part, expressed by an infinitive absolute of *lāmad*, failed to overcome resistance.

Abstract qualities were also thought to possess the potential for instruction, not always for good. In Job 15:5 Eliphaz contends that Job's wickedness dictates his speech (*ye'allēp 'awōnekā pîkā*) with the result that his tongue chooses crafty retorts. Ben Sira notes that a person's mind (Greek *psyche*) informs him (*yaggîd*) more reliably than seven watchmen (37:14), a viewpoint at odds with the observation in Prov 28:26 that a fool relies on his own insights (*lēb*) but the person who walks in wisdom will survive. Even the dead continue to function as teachers, according to Bildad, who in Job 8:8, 10 urges Job to inquire about the reasoned conclusions they have bequeathed to society (*ḥēqer*). This resorting to ancestral teaching is his way of compensating for life's ephemerality. Our remote ancestors teach us (*yrh*) across the centuries by reasoned utterances (*millibbām*).

A list of living teachers within Israelite society would include virtually everyone, inasmuch as instruction is both positive and negative, intentional and unintentional. Sages, priests, parents, prophets, specialists of all kinds taught others both in word and in deed. Not always successfully, as a student confesses in Prov 5:13 ("I did not obey my teacher [*môrāy*], did not incline my ear to my instructor [*limlammeday*]"). Teachers did not necessarily escape a certain amount of pride in their ability to communicate effectively. Thus Elihu promises to teach Job rationality ("Be quiet, and I shall teach you wisdom" [*haḥarēš wa''aallepkā*], Job 33:33b).

From these texts one can discern the broad semantic range in Hebrew for teaching. The more frequently used verbs include Piel forms of *'lp*, *lmd*, and *ysr*, Hiphil forms of *bin*, *škl*, and *yrh*, but various circumlocutions enrich this vocabulary (e.g., *yôsîp leqaḥ*). A measure of reproof often characterized ancient instruction, graphically indicated in the Egyptian symbol for a teacher as a strong arm poised to strike with a cane. This predilection to punish uncooperative and dull students was given a theological basis in Prov 3:11–12 ("YHWH's discipline, [*mûsār*]) my son, do not reject, nor loathe his teaching; for whom YHWH loves he instructs (*yôkîaḥ*) and afflicts (reading *weyak'ib* with LXX) the son in whom he delights"). This understanding of corrective discipline led to the use of the verb *ykḥ* in the sense of "to teach" and to circumlocutions such as "to receive *tôkāḥôt*."

Vocabulary for Students and Their Activity

The considerably richer vocabulary designating students and their activity indicates the focus of countless aphorisms and Instructions. The familiar form of address, "my son" (Hebrew *benî*), occurs throughout the ancient Near East in Instructions; with a single exception, Egyptian Instructions limit this direct address of father to son to the Prologue, whereas Mesopotamian and Israelite texts intersperse it throughout the Instruction. Initially, this language actually indicated blood relationship, although it eventually came to signify a student, at least in Mesopotamia. Similarly, father (Hebrew *'āb*) at first referred to the head of a household, subsequently it may have taken on the extended meaning of "teacher." The word *limmûdîm* ("those who are taught") connotes an acquired response that has become habitual–in animals as well as among human beings. One embarking on the task of acquiring such ingrained behavior bore the title *talmîd* ("pupil") in a late text, 1 Chr 25:8 ("Both small and large, teacher and pupil [*mebîn 'im-talmîd*, assuming chiasm in the parallelism]).

The primary responsibility of students was to observe and listen, eye and ear uniting to convey knowledge to the mind for storage in the belly until released through the mouth. Such corporal imagery underlined the belief that the act of cognition involved more than the mental faculty, the heart (*lēb*). Curiously, writing does not play a significant role in canonical wisdom literature. The verb *ktb* occurs only five times (Prov 3:3; 7:3; Job 13:26; 19:23; Qoh 12:10). The two occurrences in the book of Proverbs may echo Deuteronomic influence, the symbolic etching of divine teaching on the tablets of the heart (*kātebēn 'al lûaḥ libbekā*). The two occurrences in the book of Job mark emotional peaks in the struggle to maintain Job's integrity. In the first, he accuses God of writing bitter things about him, bringing to mind youthful indiscretions. The idea of God keeping a ledger is familiar from various texts in the Bible, as is the notion of YHWH writing on tablets of stone or on a wall. This idea, too, finds symbolic expression in Jer 31:33 ("...my teaching I will put within them, and I will write it on their hearts"). In the second text from the book of Job, the victim of God and friends expresses the wish that his words be written down, indeed inscribed in stone with an iron pen and lead as a perpetual testimony to his innocence, like the exploits of Darius recorded on the Behistun Rock.

The only use of *ktb* in Qoheleth occurs in the First Epilogue and presents a textual difficulty. The verb should be pointed as an infinitive absolute, *wekātôb*, in accord with Qoheleth's linguistic usage.[40] The words *wekātûb yōšer dibrê 'emet* conclude an enumeration of activities that Qoheleth is said to have performed: "he wrote the most reliable words." This reluctance to use the verb *ktb* continues in Sirach, despite the obvious engagement of Ben Sira in literary activity (39:32). Nevertheless, he urges students to associate with learned people and to listen to their discourse. Nowhere does he tell them to read and write texts, but he assumes that they will become thoroughly familiar with traditional literature, possibly viewed as sacred by his time (cf. 48:10; 44:5). He does urge the keeping of careful records of income and expenses (42:7), and he refers to engraved gem stones and jewelry (45:11).

The learning process began with observation. One looked carefully (*rā'â*, *ḥāzâ*, *śākal*), exploring thoroughly (*tûr*, *dāraš*, *bāqaš*, *ḥāqar*), assessing data by arranging them in an orderly way (*tāqan*). Listening supplemented ocular discovery, (*'āzan*, *šāma'*, *nātan lēb*). Reflecting on something and talking about it followed (*sît lēb* and *sāpar*). The actual discovery of an insight was expressed by verbs for finding and knowing, *māṣā'*, *yāda'*; attaining a full grasp of an idea, by *bîn*, *lāqaḥ mûsār*, *qānā*, and *kûn*. Once an individual had acquired knowledge, he was obligated to hold on to it (*ḥāzaq*), guard it (*šāmar*, *nāṣar*), love it (*'āhab*), not abandon it (*'āzab*), or neglect it *pāra'*), or despise it (*bāzâ*, *šāna'*), or let it drop (*rāpā*). The end product of this quest for learning went by many names, but one word, *ḥokmâ*, served as a supernym for all the rest (*da'at*, *mûsār*, *tôra*, *bînâ*, *tebûnâ*, *'ōrmâ*, *tušîyyâ*, *tôkaḥat*, *nābôn*, *'ārûm, kišrôn*). For Qoheleth that word *ḥokmâ* combined with the preposition *b* designated rational inquiry, and *ḥešbôn* stood for the process of thinking and its result.[41] The person who possessed such knowledge was *ḥākām*, a sage.

The verbs for investigating the nature of things sometimes appear in clusters, probably in additive fashion, although the exact relationship in poetic parallelism cannot easily be determined. In Eccles 7:25, a context explosive with reflection about the nature of rational calculation, one finds the following sequence: *tûr*, *bāqaš*, *yāda'*, and *māṣā'*, together with the result of this inquiry into things–*ḥokmâ* and *ḥešbôn* as the general conclusion, with specific manifestations involving the evil nature of folly and madness, and a certain type of woman, a femme fatale. Qoheleth refers to the process of drawing conclusions and associating them with one another to reach a total assessment of things ("one to one to find the sum [*ḥešbôn*], 7:27b), regrettably acknowledging that, despite all his effort, he has not found it (7:28a). He admits to having discovered one man among a thousand but not a woman, and also that God made humans morally upright but they have sought out numerous contrivances.[42] Perhaps this suggests that they have replaced the single absolute, the *ḥešbôn*, with multiple alternatives, *ḥiššebōnôt*.

Qoheleth's use of the infinitive *lātûr* with abstract qualities, wisdom and the sum of things, represents a shift from its usual application to tangible qualities like the land that spies explored. His modest findings are introduced by a concession in 7:23b that wisdom always retained its essence, which was so profound as to remain permanently hidden ("Far off...and deep, deep, who can find it?," 7:24). This admission that none can unravel life's mystery recurs in 8:1, often taken as a later gloss.[43] It reads: "Who is like the sage, and who knows the interpretation (*pešer*) of a thing?" Usage demands that the rhetorical question be taken as a denial: "nobody knows the meaning of a matter" (*dābār*).[44]

The epilogist who evaluated Qoheleth's contribution to society (*hā'ām*) as sage and teacher used a total of six verbs to characterize his intellectual approach (12:9–10). Qoheleth listened (*we'izzēn*), probed deeply (*weḥiqqēr*), and arranged (*tiqqēn*) numerous sayings; he sought (*biqqēš*) to discover (*limṣō'*) pleasing expressions, and he wrote (*wekātôb*) reliable things. The verb, "he listened," implies that people constituted the "texts" that he studied. The absence of a verb for reading at this late date, probably mid-third century, is noteworthy, although its effect is weakened by the further reference to writing. Presumably, Qoheleth expected someone to read his observations and to appreciate their form and substance.

An unusual verse in Sirach also juxtaposes six verbs to indicate the goal of students (6:27). Ben Sira urges them to seek (*drš*), probe deeply (*ḥqr*), hunt for (*bqš*), discover (*mṣ'*), and having found the answer, to grasp it firmly (*ḥzq*) and not to let it fall (*rph*). The second half of the verse echoes Prov 4:13, "Hold on to instruction; do not let it fall" (*haḥazēq bammûsār 'al terep*).

The thoroughness implied in the verb *ḥaqar* made it particularly appropriate as a description for divine exploration of human thoughts. In Ps 139:1–3 the Psalmist confesses that as a result of YHWH's penetrating search nothing lies hidden in a dark corner of the mind: "YHWH, you have searched me (*ḥaqartanî*) and known me (*wattēdā'*); you know my sitting and rising, you comprehend (*bantâ*) my musings from afar; you measure (*zērîtā*) my path and couch; you are familiar with (*hiskantâ*) all my ways." The same knowledge extends to speech prior to its utterance (v 4). The psalmist's invitation to further divine scrutiny may resemble Cleanthes' famous prayer, "Teach me to do your will, O Zeus, for whether I want to do so or not I will do it," but the excitement over YHWH's extraordinary knowledge seems boundless. "Search me (*ḥāqrēnî*), God, and know my mind (*weda' lebābî*), test me (*beḥānēnî*) and ascertain (*weda'*) my anxious thoughts. See (*ûre'ēh*) if any harmful way exists within me" (Ps 139:23–24).

An angry Job resented God's relentless searching for his sins despite the prior knowledge of his innocence ("that you seek [*tebaqq*ēš] my sins and search for [*tidrôš*] my transgressions," Job 10:6). Such inquiry on God's part placed the deity on the dubious level of humans, who by nature are of short duration. For modern readers there is something shocking about depicting God as having to search diligently to discover Job's wrongdoing, but the biblical YHWH cared about good and evil, and lacking omniscience, searched the human heart. This qualification explains why verbs for seeking were usually restricted to human subjects. Prov 18:15 is no real exception, for the human ear, the subject of the verb *tebaqqēš*, functions as *pars pro toto.* Seeking belongs to the essence of humankind, according to Eccles 3:6 (*'ēt lebaqqēš*), along with its opposite, losing (*we'ēt le'abbēd*), possibly through a lapse of memory, or perhaps as a consequence of negligence and inattention. In one notoriously difficult text, Qoheleth characterizes God's activity as chasing the past (*yebaqqēš 'et nirdāp*), as if God attends to events that are present to human beings but were previously present reality to the deity (cf. Sir 5:3).

III. Limits to Knowledge

In contrast to God's full knowledge as celebrated by the author of Ps 139, human discovery invariably came up against a teacher's tight fist, the restriction of knowledge. Qoheleth makes this point in opposition to anyone who insists that he has actually found knowledge, apparently of divine activity (8:17). The diligent toiling and seeking notwithstanding, one result follows–even a sage will be unable to discover that rare thing called knowledge. In 3:11 Qoheleth makes a similar point, at the same time granting that the deity created things beautiful and implanted something positive in the human mind. This unknown quality (*ha'ōlām* in the MT, but, it probably should be pointed *hā'elem*)[45] bestows a sense of the unknown and unknowable on all intellectual inquiry. Here, as well as in his notion of time, death, and rational inquiry, Qoheleth gives voice to his belief that all human endeavor comes up against absolute limits that affect the very nature of thought itself.

When negated, the Niph'al form of the root *ḥāqar* regularly connotes the unfathomable and immeasurable. Matitiahu Tsevat reads only one positive use in twelve Niph'al forms of *ḥāqar*.[46] Seven have a negative particle, either *'ēn* or *lō'* (Job 5:9; 9:10; 34:24; 36:26; Ps 145:3; Prov 25:3; Isa 40:28), two are objects of rhetorical questions and therefore negated (Job 11:7; 38:16), one appears in a corrupt text (Prov 25:27), and one is uncertain. The sole positive assertion occurs in Job 8:8 ("...and consider what their ancestors discovered"), unless Prov 25:27 also belongs to this usage ("nor the discovery of their honor, honorable"). The unfathomable usually refers to God's ways and deeds, although it can apply to extraordinary human beings such as kings (Prov 25:3, "the minds of kings are unsearchable").

The unfathomable nature of *ḥokmâ* comes to expression in the remarkable poem comprising the twenty-eighth chapter in the book of Job. Against the backdrop celebrating the extraordinary accomplishments of human beings in exploring the bowels of the earth in search of precious stones, the author remarks that even such ingenious effort cannot make a dent in the barrier separating humans from wisdom. The most anyone can do, even mythical Sheol and Abaddon, is eavesdrop on a rumor. Here these two locations for the realm of the dead are personified. Job will later discover how terribly unsatisfactory secondhand knowledge really is–when he comes face to face with the one who rebukes him from a whirlwind, prompting him to say: "By the hearing of an ear I heard about you, but now my eye sees you..." With regard to God's knowledge of Wisdom, the poet says: "God sees her way and knows her place, for he looks to the ends of the earth and sees under all the heavens" (28:23). The sovereign of wind and ocean, rain and lightning, saw wisdom, discussed it, established it, and probed it deeply (28:27).

This verse covers four distinct stages in the intellectual process. The first, observation, engages the eyes as they examine an observable phenomenon. It connotes immediate knowledge, firsthand experience, thus intimate knowledge. The second, discussion, involves the organ of speech as the agency through which an individual endeavors to articulate whatever conclusion he has reached in a way that communicates with others. This discussion also entails hearing with discernment. In this way private insights become public commodity, and the collective knowledge of a given community makes its contribution to private knowledge. The third stage, establishing hypotheses and reaching provisional conclusions, functions within the mind, for the discoverer ultimately bears sole responsibility for any new insight. The final stage, analytic assessment by exploring every facet of an idea, returns to the earlier image of probing the recesses of earth in search of precious gems, then examining them for possible flaws. The four verbs–*rā'â; sāpar*, *kûn*, and *ḥāqar*–nicely describe the cognitive analytic process as the poet understood it.

Ben Sira proceeds even farther than the author of Job 28 toward limiting intellectual inquiry. Whereas the poet responsible for the above description of indefatigable energy in the pursuit of the unknown grudgingly conceded that this effort ultimately aborted when wisdom was its object, Ben Sira considers some kinds of curiosity not only futile but also inappropriate. He writes:

> 3 [17]My son, when prosperous comport yourself humbly and you will
> be appreciated more than those who are generous with gifts. [18]Defer

> before the great ones of society and you will discover favor with God, [19]for God's compassion is vast, and he reveals his secret thoughts to the lowly. [21]Seek not unfathomable wonders, nor probe into things concealed from you. [22]Attend to what is entrusted to you; hidden things are not your business. [23]Do not talk about what exceeds your grasp, for more than you (understand) has been shown to you. [24]Indeed, human speculations are numerous, and evil conjectures lead one astray.[47]

One naturally thinks of Am 3:7, "Surely the Lord YHWH does not do anything without revealing his secret counsel to his servants the prophets," but Ben Sira extends this divine generosity to the humble. Having said that, he stresses the sufficiency of such revelation. Not willing to let readers draw their own conclusions on the basis of this principle of disclosure, he presses the point that some sorts of rational inquiry have perverse consequences, echoing a similar viewpoint in Deut 29:29 [MT 28], "The secret things belong to YHWH our God, but the revealed things belong to us and to our posterity…" This attack on the very essence of rational inquiry, the desire to penetrate the unknown and make it comprehensible, does not automatically follow from humble acknowledgment that the intellect can never explain the mystery of life. The necessities of polemic have forced Ben Sira into an untenable position: some things are not subject to cognitive analysis. Regardless of whether this restriction of knowledge refers to Greek astrological and cosmological speculations or to Jewish variations of such efforts to control one's fate, it clearly expresses the view that certain types of intellectual endeavors bode ill for those with a curious mind.

By reading *tō'mar* for the meaningless *tōmar* in v 23, one brings this discussion into line with a significant thrust in Ben Sira's apologetic. The formula of debate, introduced by *'al tō'mar*, normally appears in contexts dealing with theodicy.[48] He may reject certain kinds of speculation about divine justice within society, and in doing so he insists that Israel's wonder-worker, alluded to in v 21, has conveyed sufficient information to enable those buffeted by life's waves to trust confidently in divine goodness.

Conclusion

With respect to subjectivity, or the amount of involvement of the ego in the learning process, Qoheleth differs from other biblical sages only in degree, and this difference may reflect varying pedagogical strategies. As for the empirical base of his insights, Qoheleth resembles earlier sages at the time of initial discovery. His attempt to forge philosophical concepts, while innovative and bold, never quite got off ground, but the failure may have little to do with the matter of poetry versus prose. In his understanding of the intellectual enterprise, he was quite at home with sages who preceded him and who came after him, if his choice of language and recognition of the outer limits of knowledge have any bearing on this issue. Perhaps Qoheleth was epistemologically less revolutionary than some critics have imagined.

CHAPTER 5

A Good Man's Code of Ethics

Job 31

The book of Job is a literary masterpiece, and chapter 31 reveals the basis for the deity's extraordinary assessment of its hero as blameless and upright, a religious man who avoided evil. Forced by circumstances to defend his innocence, the hero unveils his heart for public scrutiny of inner motive and resultant deed. His oath of innocence is directed beyond the ears of the three friends with whom he has contended for two rounds of debate, plus a partial third one. Convinced that he will receive a more favorable hearing from the deity, Job first ventures into the land of nostalgia while recounting happier days, then contrasts those times with his present misery, before at last bombarding heaven's gates with a declaration of integrity aimed at undermining any indictment against him, human or divine.

Whether viewed as oath or ordeal, the confession is intended to force the silent deity to respond. Instead, the youthful Elihu berates the friends and Job for six chapters before the Lord answers from a whirlwind, entirely ignoring Job's claims and focusing attention on the wonders of nature beyond the human domain. Unencumbered by the urgency of a human social order, the Creator views the world from the standpoint of eternity, which removes humankind from the central position. The speeches silence the hero, without giving enough information to enable readers to discern the real nature of his submission. The framing narrative in prose recreates the idyllic past, oblivious to the intervening skepticism that has undermined such a worldview.

Job's declaration takes the form of an oath: "I swear by El that if I have done X then let Y happen to me." Presumably, one who emerges unscathed after such a bold outcry cannot be guilty. Parallels for these imprecations exist in the Egyptian Book of the Dead (chap. 125) and the Code of Hammurabi. Normally, the result clause is omitted, possibly to increase the psychological dread by leaving the punishment unspecified. Job dares to defy tradition, stating four times the actual punishment envisioned (vv. 8, 10, 22, 40). The total number of offenses is unclear; the complete number fourteen (twice seven) may be intended. The entire confession, an ordered cacophony, teems with verbal links and rhetorical features, the most powerful of which is Job's defiant appeal for a divine weighing of his heart (against the feather representing justice) and the upheld defense, personally signed by a proud prince who is prepared to display an indictment on his shoulders. On two occasions Job's words carry barbs directed against the deity, who in contrast to Job has abused a loyal servant and has neglected to set a guard over divine eyes.

Job's code of ethics is grounded in a primal bond akin to that of an infant for its mother. It is relational, not an abstraction of principles. An "I" has acknowledged a kinship with another, a "Thou." This bond extends to all others regardless of social status, and it reaches within the mind where motives and thoughts reside long before they issue in deeds. When a valued relationship fails, this code moves an individual to risk death in an effort to restore the lost ardor. The bond links all humankind in a single family, assuring protection for marginalized citizens–the widow, the orphan, and the resident alien in the Bible–and even producing goodwill for enemies. Nevertheless, even Job's code of ethics suffers from the controls exercised by all worldviews in at least two respects. It presents a proud man whose view of women needs refinement ("If I have committed adultery, let my wife become someone else's sex object," v. 10, author's translation). It also indicts the deity when virtue is not rewarded.

However much this chapter rises above others of its day, both in literary power and religious sentiment, it still belongs to an ancient era. How can modern readers appropriate its insights and apply its teachings within the narrow confines of family life? The only legitimate means of doing so is by analogy, and the restraints of space in this volume prevent elaborate discussion. They do allow some suggestions that readers may carry to their logical conclusions.

A beginning point is the distinction between secret sins and those apparent to society at large. Naturally, sexual offenses span both areas, for even a secret rendezvous affects at least two persons. Job's insistence that he has not lusted implies that he has refused to view another person as an object of personal gratification. Similarly, his disavowal of adultery means that he recognizes the sacred bond of marriage and the sanctity of a family. The image of placing a guard over the eyes recalls that of securing the lips from unbecoming speech in Psalm 141:3. Both imply that the deity searches the mind and heart, so that nothing is hidden. The contemporary bombardment of the eyes with images chosen for maximal erotic appeal can be resisted by those who appreciate other persons' vulnerability and who value the family as the glue holding society together.

Other secret sins have social consequences as well. Deception, for example, in the form of fraudulent business practices, deprives others of good even though they do not know anything about the nefarious deeds. So, too, coveting. Greed leads to a consumerism characterized by slavery to "creature comforts" and the latest electronic gadget. This endless competition, already recognized by the observant author of Ecclesiastes, threatens the fabric of the community, resulting in disparity between the "haves" and the "have-nots." The natural capacity to deceive ourselves fuels this drive to obtain more. It can be overcome only by acknowledging the true owner of all things.

The social sins that Job disavows include a heartless abuse of power, an arrogance and unfeeling that denies the reality that all human beings constitute a single family, an inhospitable attitude that ignores suffering, and a vulnerability to peer pressure. Job views all people as creatures of one deity, and that includes the unfortunate of his day–slaves, widows, orphans. His compassion embraced them all, and he refused to bow to pressure from influential citizens. The modern reader can readily transfer God's concern for others to the contemporary scene with its vast array of citizens who have been marginalized on the basis of their race, religion, and income. One who takes seriously the link that unites us all in one big family will be compelled to feed the hungry, clothe the naked, and strive for a more just society. Like Job, this modern hero will become a parent to orphans, learn to extend goodwill to those who subscribe to dubious causes–the KKK, members of the free militias–while resisting their racism and paranoia to the end. Like Job, too, the modern individual who rises above the crowd will work to overcome the roots of poverty (and racism). Immigrant and migrant workers will be welcome in this person's society.

Two sins belonging to the secret category relate solely to the deity. Job denies having committed idolatry in either form, the worship of money or the adulation of nature. The issue is one of priority, the determining of ultimate concern. Job's inclusion of these two temptations stands as a constant reminder that the human creature, for whatever reason, tends to substitute perishable things for the eternal. The unknown author of the contest of Darius's Guards, recorded in 1 Esdras 3:1–4:41, relegates possessions and the sun to those things that eventually pass into oblivion, while the God of truth endures forever.

The declaration of innocence concludes on a surprising note, one that recalls the divine curse of the ground in Genesis 2–3. Job insists that he has honored the land, letting it lie fallow at appropriate seasons. The modern reader can certainly appreciate this ecological concern, and Job's counterpart will work at recycling, composting, preserving natural resources, saving endangered species, and the like. This will entail a lifestyle that attends to, among other things, the consumption of meat, use of water and other types of energy, the protection of the environment through every available means, planned parenthood, and the fair distribution of resources. The central role of the family in this concerted effort will move a step beyond Job 31, where the patriarch enjoys a position of honor above women and children. Happily, this concentration on the male hero, partly dictated by the plot, belongs to a bygone era. Not only has Job honored the land. He has not concealed his offense the way Adam (and Eve) did.

What does Job's confession of innocence contribute to contemporary ethical discussion as it pertains to family life? It goes beyond the external expression to inner motives; it pushes beyond legal requirements regarding slaves to the greater demands imposed by primal bonds; it defines ethical conduct comprehensively, embracing the whole body; it enlarges family ties to include the needy and even the hated; it acknowledges a single human family and only one creator. In short, Job answers Cain's question "Am I my brother's keeper?" with a resounding "yes." And my sister's keeper too.

CHAPTER 6

Unresolved Issues in Wisdom Literature

Eurocentric male dominance in the interpretation of wisdom literature during the first three quarters of the twentieth century has eased in the last twenty-five years. The rich variety of voices has introduced new questions and applied different presuppositions to the ancient corpus. By highlighting the male perspective of the texts and by searching for the significance of depicting wisdom as female, feminist readings[1] have been particularly suggestive, but Asian and liberationist interpretations have also widened the parameters of investigation and forced interpreters to question their own assumptions about the worldview hidden within the literature.[2]

The sharpest challenges to the reigning hypotheses fashioned by white males have, nevertheless, arisen largely in their own circle, harsh rhetoric from other interest groups notwithstanding. The most extreme view dismisses the entire literary corpus and professional sages as a figment of the imagination.[3] More moderate revisionists raise the issue of correctly identifying the extent of wisdom literature,[4] its unity,[5] and its consistency over time.[6]

1. Fact or Fiction

The designation "wisdom literature" has no Hebrew or Aramaic equivalent in the Old Testament. The modern construct derives from the prominence of the word *ḥokmåh* and various synonyms in the books of Proverbs, Job, Ecclesiastes, Sirach, and Wisdom of Solomon. The authors of these books clearly considered wisdom a worthy acquisition, the bestower of long life and its desirable assets, or they reflected on its hiddenness and special relationship with the deity. Such unbridled speculation came very close to philosophy, for its mythic ruminations eventually equated wisdom with the divine thought process.[7]

By analogy, interpreters of Egyptian and Mesopotamian literature dubbed certain texts "wisdom" because of their similarity with the above-mentioned biblical books.[8] The occasional caveat indicates early acknowledgment that non-biblical sources contained omen texts presupposing a magical base, as well as noun lists compiled for scribal instruction, and laments.[9]

Once the analogy was made, the move also occurred in the other direction. Biblical interpreters began to use ancient Near Eastern texts to fill in gaps of knowledge about the composition and function of Proverbs, Job, and Ecclesiastes. This move led to the supposition that Israelite sages served royal administrators, composing educational texts to instruct fellow courtiers.[10] The cultural gap between the courts of Egypt and Mesopotamia on the one hand, and Israel, on the other hand, was largely ignored.[11] Perhaps the decisive reason for overlooking Israel's differences in administrative development was this: linking them provided an explanation for the presence of foreign material in the book of Proverbs. If courtiers graced the courts of Solomon or even Hezekiah, the incorporation of portions of the Instruction of Amenemope in the book of Proverbs makes sense, as do the Sayings of Agur and Lemuel's mother.[12]

A major difficulty remained, however, for the overwhelming impression given by the book of Proverbs is that of instruction within the family in small villages,[13] whereas few indications of courtly interests have survived. Parents convey vital information to their children, preparing them to cope with whatever circumstances they encounter. Clues derived from Sumerian wisdom literature, where the references to fathers and sons function metaphorically for teachers and students,[14] suggested that the same may occur in Israel. Although the allusion to maternal instruction lacks a parallel outside the bible, it has not been considered sufficiently weighty to nullify the evidence of metaphorical language.

When the mode of composition entered the picture, matters were further complicated. The primacy of oral instruction within the family and the unsettled question of the extent of literacy in Israel left many unresolved issues.[15] The frequent appeal within Proverbs for a hearing, together with the total absence of any reference to reading a text and copying it so that teachers could make corrections, gave a different impression from that generated by similar texts in Egypt and Mesopotamia.[16] The resulting uneasiness was only minimally assuaged by the knowledge that literate people in the ancient world, few in number, read aloud.

The books of Job and Ecclesiastes, moreover, seemed ill-suited as parental instruction for young boys; like Sirach and Wisdom of Solomon, they raised theoretical questions more appropriate for a learned audience. Did such texts offer guidance to advanced students, or did they represent serious intellectual activity of ordinary adults who sought answers to existential questions?[17] The striking use of *ḥakāmîm* in Ecclesiastes as a technical term and Ben Sira's high regard for sages when compared with other professions imply that something more than parental advice has found expression.[18]

Whatever its origin and locus, this literature assisted in the formation of character and the socialization process.[19] It went a long way toward shaping a world view, making explicit the things to cultivate and those to avoid. In this precarious environment, a certain kind of woman seems to have posed the gravest danger to young men.[20] Alongside this peril from seductive words and limbs, other dangers lurked, especially drunkenness, lack of control of one's temper, and malicious talk. Very little in this socialization applies solely to prospective courtiers; the vast majority of the instructions and warnings were intended for society at large.

2. Identifying a Specific Type

The force of the argument against professional sages comes from things other than the absence of this class among the lists of officials in Solomon's bureaucracy.[21] If sages existed in Israel, why did they not compose unique literature? Their failure to do so has raised the issue of correctly identifying a type.[22] The argument, necessarily circular, goes like this. Certain books within the Bible share various features: non-revelatory address, concentration on humankind, emphasis on what promotes positive results in society, concern for unraveling life's mysteries, an absence of sacred traditions relating to Moses, David, or the patriarchs. One naturally assumes that these features indicate the presence of wisdom literature, and when they are absent, the texts belong to another category.

A degree of slippage can be detected even within the three classic texts, especially the book of Job. Both divine revelation through theophany and a profusion of laments suggest either that the type has been too rigidly defined or that other texts have a claim to inclusion in wisdom literature.[23] The widespread incorporation of Yahwistic tradition in Sirach and Wisdom of Solomon, together with the inclusion of sentence-like literature in texts such as Tobit, imply that the interests commonly attributed to the sages may have been broader than usually thought. Similarly, the posing of intellectual queries about life's meaning in the face of injustice and physical suffering is not limited to the books of Job and Ecclesiastes, but comes to expression in several psalms, notably 37, 49 and 73.[24] Should these psalms be included in wisdom literature? Most specialists have thought so, but what about other texts in the Psalter? Should learned psalmography be attributed to sages, and does the same judgment apply to so-called torah psalms like 119? Do indications of educational intent signify sapiential composition, particularly those psalms based on a reading of sacred history–the exodus and wanderings in the wilderness, for example? Are such "midrashic" readings a precursor to Sirach 44–50? Do meditative and self-reflective psalms such as 139 derive from groups who place a premium on cognitive achievements?

The sages did not hold a monopoly on intellectual queries demanding a high degree of sophisticated thinking. The wrestling with the issue of theodicy by the prophetic books of Habakkuk and Jonah[25] suggests that certain problems were universal. Similarly, some rhetorical features seem to have found utility in various settings, which explains their presence in wisdom and prophetic books. The sages were not the only ones interested in controlling their destiny or in the written word.[26]

The resulting dilemma has hampered the study of Israelite wisdom, for interpreters have not been able to agree on what constitutes the phenomenon. Some of them collapse the literature into a single corpus; when the wisdom texts themselves remain silent about traditional Yahwism, they simply take it for granted.[27] Others view the lack of national particularities and "special" revelation as proof that wisdom constitutes an alien body devoid of salvific content.[28]

These issues have thus far resisted resolution. A recent wrinkle concerns the affinities between wisdom and apocalyptic, especially in light of developments at Qumran and the post-biblical traditions associated with Enoch, a notable figure in both wisdom and apocalyptic.[29] Does the extraordinary character of God in the book of Job pave the way for introducing additional apocalyptic concepts into the wisdom tradition?[30]

The affinities between wisdom and torah seem distant because the texts do not confirm a postulated common origin in the clan, about which very little can be known.[31] Why do sages remain quiet about the law until the second century Ben Sira, who takes the unexpected step of equating the Mosaic legislation with a highly developed concept of personified wisdom. Despite this extraordinary move, a minimum of legal data occurs in Sirach. Either Ben Sira did not take the identification seriously, or he used the broadest possible language when referring to the law.

The meager evidence in Proverbs and Ecclesiastes does not lend support to the view that a group of scribal traditionists was responsible for composing Deuteronomy. The superficial similarities between this book and wisdom literature and the substantial differences suggest that the two derive from different circles. A test based on vocabulary hardly carries conviction, for any number of factors easily skew such compilations.[32]

Perhaps the search for a particular type should be guided by the knowledge that categories in biblical literature have considerable flexibility.[33] Prophecy, for instance, includes both narrative and oracle. The former prophets consist largely of a view of history in which prophetic proclamation exercises controlling power, and the latter prophets comprise oracles and visions, with occasional biographical narrative and meditation. This broad characterization of the prophetic literature still leaves out the book of Jonah, a story about a prophet, and Malachi, a series of discussions with an audience largely about matters of purity. If one takes into consideration prophecy at Mari and Neo-Assyrian texts, even more latitude is necessary, given the prominent place of divination here as opposed to its role in ancient Israel.[34] A similar situation exists in torah, which includes far more than legislation, whether casuistic or apodictic. A story of the beginnings of the cosmos and peoples of the earth, replete with genealogies, and an account of family conflict introduce the corpus in which legal matters later find expression.

3. Unity

In one sense the individual books in the wisdom corpus lack unity; so does the collection as a whole. This statement applies most directly to the book of Proverbs, which has at least eleven separate collections,[35] but also to the other books. Although modern interpreters have made valiant efforts at understanding the book of Job as a work of literary integrity,[36] it nevertheless has strong indications of developmental stages. Similarly, Ecclesiastes shows signs of later adjustments to soften its pessimism.[37] As a product of a different culture from that reflected in the books of Job and Ecclesiastes, one that prizes authorship, Sirach seems to derive from a single mind, except for the translator's prologue. Wisdom of Solomon, too, was crafted by a highly educated person, one steeped in Greek thought and fully at home in the niceties of the Greek language.[38]

The book of Ecclesiastes comes close to philosophical speculation in the Greek sense. Despite its sustained argument that everything is futile or absurd, the book still has occasional collections of unrelated sayings. The modern reader gets the impression that the author incorporated earlier material into the work, sometimes without comment and occasionally with corrections to bring it into line with the rest of the book.[39] The most glaring indications of editorial intention occur here, however, for the book concludes with two epilogues that most likely derive from a later hand than that of the author of what precedes. This judgment rests on style, tone, and content. The first epilogue, which refers to the author in the third person and makes an assessment of his role among the wise, reads almost like an epitaph. The second epilogue, more distant and cooler in tone, introduces entirely different views from those championed by Qoheleth. Torah piety, fearing God and keeping the commandments, now sums up the human requirement, and the prospect of divine judgment awaits everyone.

The affinities between the final epilogue in Ecclesiastes and torah piety as reflected in Sirach have been pointed out.[40] Has an editor attempted to align the two books theologically? It has even been conjectured that an editor has brought the book of Proverbs into the same theological ambiance by the addition of the prologue in the initial collection (Prov 1:2–7). The centrality of the fear of Yahweh as the avenue to acquiring wisdom, in other words the importance of religion for becoming wise, seems to function almost as a buzz word here. A similar theme finds expression in the poem (ch. 28) that comes after Job's dialogue with his three friends and before his great oath of innocence.[41]

4. Consistency over Time

If one assumes that wise men existed in ancient Israel as a professional class, it follows that the literature they produce ought to have a high degree of consistency. Certain themes should come to prominence, together with stylistic features and vocabulary. The search for characteristically wisdom themes has been only moderately productive. In the book of Proverbs, one can identify certain central features such as pithy sayings about human nature and animals, along with intentionally didactic instructions conveying strong moral suasion, but this type of teaching recedes to the background in the very different book of Job. Here the dialogical literary form, first with human partners in dispute and subsequently with the dominant voice being identified as the deity, give an entirely different impression. Moreover, the narrative that frames the dialogue links this text with a significant body of literature from elsewhere in the ancient Near East.[42]

With Ecclesiastes another literary form emerges, this time a quasi-philosophical exploration of the nature of reality. Moreover, the author formulates a thesis and endeavors to demonstrate its validity. Only here and there do moral maxims occur, and in some instances they are poorly integrated into the argument.[43] Sirach reverts to sayings and instructions, but these are joined in such a way as to create sustained treatments of various topics, a rare occurrence in the latest section of the book of Proverbs and entirely missing in earlier collections. Sirach goes beyond its predecessors in introducing hymnic texts. Like Proverbs, Ben Sira includes hymns about personified wisdom, and like the book of Job he praises the creator for the majesty of the universe. The unprecedented paean of famous men in the Bible has been seen as an attempt to create a national myth,[44] and its Hellenistic characteristics have caught interpreters' eyes. Although Wisdom of Solomon continues some of the earlier emphases such as celebrating wisdom's virtues, it does so in an entirely new manner. The linguistic difference alone cannot explain this shift, even if the author has become thoroughly Hellenized. The ambiguity of death issues in a sustained argument in which an immortal soul complicates matters, at least for anyone trained in traditional Jewish thought.[45] The author uses Greek categories and rhetoric with telling effect, both in praising wisdom and in midrash-like interpretation of the Exodus.

How can this development from moral maxims, often lacking religious significations, to fervent religious passion with apocalyptic inclinations be explained? All efforts to trace the various stages of wisdom literature have suffered from an absence of reliable historical data. The few attempts to specify a linear development have been criticized on several counts, largely because of the failure to recognize an oral stage alongside a literary one and the assumption that a secular tradition preceded a religious one.[46] The claim that wisdom moves resolutely within creation[47] runs the risk of trivializing the kind of thought underlying the majority of collections in the book of Proverbs. Perhaps one should qualify this dictum, thus leaving room for everyday maxims with specific moral functions, rather than submitting these to the cosmic ramifications of another kind of wisdom altogether. Both anthropocentric and cosmo-centric wisdom probably existed from the beginning.[48] The former may actually have consisted of two very different types of sayings, those with no religious intentions and others with theological purposes. Even the ones that appear secular from the modern standpoint must be understood against the background of a thoroughly religious society. This acknowledgment does not settle the debate over the extent to which modern interpreters may assume that Yahwistic monism has infused the sayings in Proverbs. On that issue, a minimalist position seems more appropriate than a maximalist one.

The long-held assumption that wisdom literature is a-historical has been effectively challenged,[49] but how far can one go in the other direction? With

Sirach and Wisdom of Solomon, the effects of adverse historical developments can certainly be detected, giving rise to fervent prayer and apocalyptic expectations of relief from persecution. A similar conclusion may apply to the book of Job but, like Proverbs, it conceals the social circumstances of its origins. The exilic and post-exilic environment provided the matrix within which much of the wisdom literature took shape, but almost nothing of this social context has found expression. Even Ecclesiastes has left few clues about its actual date of composition; the author's concerns transcend historical circumstances.[50]

Conclusion

The current controversy over the existence of professional sages in ancient Israel, and consequently a specific corpus of wisdom literature distinct from the rest of the Old Testament has arisen within the ranks of biblical criticism. Modern interpreters have resisted the tendency to view their conclusions as final, for they have understood their work as a process in need of constant refinement. The evidence has always been subject to multiple readings.

On the issue of a professional class of sages, the scant evidence seems to point to gifted intellectuals who combined the earlier product of instruction in the family with intellectual pursuits of a quite different kind. Eventually such individuals may have functioned as teachers in schools,[51] but this remains uncertain until Ben Sira.[52] Can one really imagine the first stages of philosophy that occur in Ecclesiastes, or even the intellectual dispute in the book of Job, apart from a circle of advanced thinkers?[53]

The peculiarities of language and style that characterize wisdom literature seem to confirm the existence of actual professional sages in Israel. Nevertheless, major problems remain, for the book of Job employs stylistic features more at home elsewhere than in sapiential enclaves that produced the book of Proverbs–or even Sirach and Wisdom of Solomon.

A professional group of sages may have had diverse interests. That would explain the lack of unity within the several bodies of literature attributed to them. If a few sages sought to shape the different books in a way that would suggest some grand scheme, one should not be surprised. A theological agenda need not alter the entire document, when introductory and concluding coda could orient the material in a given direction.

Still, the wisdom corpus was consistent only to a certain point. Orientation toward human beings existed in tension with cosmic focussing. Perhaps the same people held both views, but that seems less likely than positing separate circles for the two perspectives. In any event, describing a linear development of wisdom tradition, except in broad strokes, has proved enormously difficult. More progress has occurred in the literary realm than in the historical or social domain. The greatest challenge facing scholars at the beginning of the twenty-first century is to describe the social setting of wisdom over the years.

CHAPTER 7

A Proverb in the Mouth of a Fool

"When sight and hearing fail, the mute leads." This variant of "Among the blind the one-eyed is king" is embedded in the "historical romance in pseudo-prophetic form" attributed to Neferti, an Egyptian sage from the Middle Kingdom Twelfth Dynasty (1990–1785). As part of an apologetic discourse for Amenemhet I, the text describes a period of social chaos, real or imagined, and proleptically "predicts" the rise of a ruler who will establish order, inaugurating an era of peace.[1] Faintly resembling biblical prophecy and early apocalyptic, it has few affinities with the body of literature to which the adjective "wisdom" has been attached by modern scholars. Nevertheless, the author uses an aphorism to communicate a harsh reality: an absence of intellectual leadership leaves a vacuum that is rapidly filled by the inept. According to the proverbial saying, both organs of acuity, sight and hearing, are inoperative, while a speechless leader usurps their place. A single statement sums up such a situation: "Each man's heart is for himself." The result of numbness of observation and listening creates a situation of total lawlessness like that described in the scandalous stories at the end of the book of Judges that offer a persuasive defense of centralized rule (Judges 19–21; note the refrain in 19:1, "In those days, when there was no king in Israel," and 21:25, "In those days there was no king in Israel; everyone did what was right in his own eyes").

"Want is followed by deceit." This proverbial saying appears in "The Hymn to Hapy," a hymn to the personified Nile. Also from the Middle Kingdom, the literary composition praises the inundating river for nourishing life, and the section under consideration emphasizes the theme that bread sustains humankind.[2] The brief proverb suggests that hunger creates its own ethical norm,[3] a point also made in the prayer attributed to Agur in Prov 30:8–9,[4] and perhaps in Prov 6:30, "One does not despise a thief who steals to satisfy a hungry appetite."[5] "The Hymn to Hapy" seems to demean mercantile endeavors and religious rites in that the former secure no bread and the latter no meat.[6] Furthermore, it elevates bread and barley over gold, silver, and lapis lazuli in that the latter cannot be eaten or drunk. This early effort at prioritizing human possessions has a parallel in Ben Sira, who reduces life's necessities to water, bread, clothes, and a house (Sir 29:21), or, in a less Spartan mood, water, fire, iron, salt, flour, milk, honey, wine, oil, and clothes (Sir 39:26).

"Who would give water at dawn to a goose that will be slaughtered in the morning?" The final sentence in "The Tale of the Shipwrecked Sailor," this proverb captures the trepidation of an official who has been sent on a mission and failed.[7] The tale reckons with the arbitrariness of human destiny, against which excellence does not always succeed. Sometimes, it suggests, individuals put forth Herculean effort to achieve a desired goal only to be thwarted in the end by random events. The effect of following the proverb's implied counsel would be catastrophic, for no one would attempt anything worthwhile lest the effort be wasted. Another version of the saying has been widely formulated: "Humans propose, but the gods dispose." Whereas this version suggests that an unpredictable transcendent factor may alter the best-laid plans, the other contemplates a similar unknown: fate. In some religious systems, the two are equated.

"Mouth or muscles, men are what they're born." This obscure saying is from an epic poem that Benjamin Foster entitles "Tiglath-Pileser and the Beasts," a description of the Assyrian king's massacre of mountain peoples.[8] Depicted as a hunter stalking wild game, the king strikes terror in his prey, which they attempt to conceal beneath braggadocio. The meaning of the saying–a part of their response–is unclear, but it may intimate that education in both senses, intellect and skill (at hunting), is innate,[9] hence cannot be pressed beyond prescribed limits. A modern variant would then be "An apple does not fall far from the tree."

"Water flows under the straw." This proverbial saying is attributed to the god Dagan and is spoken by a prophet. The full oracle indicates the specific use to which the proverb was put. It reads: "The peace initiatives of the king of the city of Eshnunna are treachery, water flows under the straw. But I will capture him for the very net he meshes; I will destroy his city; and I will make plunder of his ancient possessions."[10] In short, the deity warns against pursuing a treaty with a sovereign who is covertly stalling and biding his time until a propitious moment, when he will launch an attack. Contemporary parallels easily come to mind, the most obvious being the argument by U.S. government officials that Saddam Hussein's political maneuvering was a calculated move to gain time to hide weapons of mass destruction.

"The bird takes refuge in its cage, and the cage saves its life." This Hittite proverbial saying from Muršili's "Second Plague Prayer" is the first of three analogies in support of the king's plea for relief from a devastating plague.[11] The metaphorical language, familiar from biblical psalms, envisions the deity as a refuge from danger.[12] Just as an endangered bird flees to its nest and then rests securely, the king seeks safety in the deity's presence. The other two analogies emphasize the servant relationship between the king and the god.

They note that a servant in distress flees to his master, who takes pity on him and gives protection from danger, and that a servant who has committed an offense, confessed the wrong, and made restitution has done enough to satisfy the master, who, if not in fact satisfied, can then tell the servant what else is required to set things right. The symbolism of a bird taking refuge under its mother's wings, which continues into New Testament times, is a domestication and democratization of the sentiment expressed by Hittite royalty.

"...he has put his one foot in the boat, may he not stay the other on dry land." This proverbial saying, which means that there is no turning back after a decisive step, occurs in a mythic text from ancient Sumer, "Enki and Ninhursaga."[13] In hot pursuit of the goddess Ninnisiga, Enki seeks encouragement from his page Isimu: "Is this nice youngster not to be kissed?" Obligingly, Isimu urges him on: "Is this nice youngster not to be kissed? With a (favorable) downstream wind blowing for my master, a downstream wind blowing, he has put his one foot in the boat, may he not stay the other on dry land!" Whereupon Enki makes love to Ninnisiga, and she conceives a daughter, Ninkurra. A similar scene later unfolds, and Enki impregnates Ninkurra, who gives birth to Nin-imma. The scene is perpetuated until Uttu, the daughter of Nin-imma, is forewarned about Enki's amorous ways. Uttu succumbs nonetheless, but the verbal chain is broken.

These seven proverbial sayings from Egypt and Mesopotamia[14] adorn a variety of literary types: historical romance, hymn, wondrous tale, epic, oracle, prayer, and myth. Who would ever think of classifying such texts as wisdom literature? Yet each of them uses a proverb to make an important point. In this regard, the proverbs resemble biblical sayings that are interspersed within narratives and oracles.[15]

"We must all die. We are like water spilled on the ground, which cannot be gathered up again" (2 Sam 14:14). Reflections on human mortality such as this one emphasize a return to the material from which we were created, "Dust you are, and to dust you will return" (Gen 3:19; cf. "Ashes to ashes, dust to dust," *The Book of Common Prayer*). The observation that all die is placed in the mouth of an astute woman from Tekoa, an accomplished actress who follows a script assigned to her by David's chief warrior, Joab. The Hebrew text leaves no doubt here; it states that Joab "put the words in her mouth" (2 Sam 14:3b), that is, he gave her specific instructions about what she was to say.[16] Indeed, he needed a woman for his subterfuge, a widow's appeal to the king for redress from grievous harm implicit in the law. Playing on royal ideology, particularly the belief that a king was the champion of widows, the speech evoked royal pity and opened the door for its extension to the king's own household.

"I shall go to him, but he will not return to me" (2 Sam 12:23). This statement of resignation is credited to David on learning of the death of the child conceived in a clandestine encounter with Bathsheba. The king is represented as truly practical, resorting at first to religious entreaty but wasting no time once that approach proves to be in vain. The statement's reasoning is based on the common belief, expressed in the Yahwist's story of creation, that humans are destined to return to their original source and then to exist in Sheol as pale replicas of their earthly form.[17] That journey was nothing to welcome with open arms, unlike the later Jewish and Christian hope of joining loved ones in another world.

"Let not the one putting on armor boast like the one taking it off" (1 Kgs 20:11). This aphorism contrasts proven valor with untested enthusiasm, noting that only an experienced warrior who has defeated the enemy and lived to tell it really knows the outcome of a contest of arms. The untried warrior may believe that he has superior strength and skill, and like many cocky athletes, he may talk a good game, but his inexperience may speak otherwise. In the last resort, the bragging comes to nothing, and death ensues. The verbal contest that precedes the armed conflict between the champion of the Philistines and David illustrates the role of rhetoric in ancient warfare, especially its psychological force.[18]

"The fathers have eaten sour grapes and the children's teeth are sensitive" (Ezek 18:2; Jer 31:29). Transgenerational punishment, a principle embedded in the old confessional formula in Exod 34:6–7–"visiting the iniquity of fathers upon the children and the grandchildren, to the third and fourth generation"–is harsh enough without the added freight of theological legitimation.[19] The decisions in Judah during the Babylonian threat had lasting consequences, according to the exiles who were paying the price for what their ancestors had done. With this proverb, the descendants of the guilty ones assert their innocence and protest the inequity of the situation, accusing the deity of treating them unfairly. Beneath this simple proverb glows a tiny coal that will soon threaten to consume faith itself. As is evidenced by the recent massive tome devoted to theodicy in the world of the Bible,[20] that smoldering ember erupted into a full-scale fire in Second Temple times with the loss of temple, land, Davidic dynasty, and religious autonomy.

Such proverbial sayings, biblical and extrabiblical, could easily be multiplied,[21] but these examples suffice to reveal the widely diverse contexts of their use. Not one of them comes from a sapiential text, nor does any of them constitute advice from a professional sage. The gathering evidence seems to support the conclusions based on paremiological studies in general that certain societies used proverbial sayings for argument in circumstances as diverse as entertainment and legal decision-making.[22] I firmly believe that we need to acknowledge as much for ancient Israel.

After all, even sages recognized that fools could cite proverbs. In Prov 26:9 we read:

> Like a thorn that penetrates the hand of a drunkard
> is a proverb in the mouth of fools.

An alternative translation may be preferable: "Like a thorn taken up by a drunkard..."[23] The first rendering suggests an individual whose oblivion to reality prevents him from recognizing the harm he inflicts on himself, while the second suggests one who grabs a thorn bush in his drunken stupor and wields it as a weapon or in fun. This proverbial saying resembles the one in verse 7, which has the same second colon but is introduced by the words "Like a lame person's legs which hang useless." The picture of a person suspended between two crutches may point to the external form of the biblical proverbs, their employment of two cola.[24] It would then mean that fools may use the correct structural device but the content of their proverb lacks effectiveness.

Whereas Prov 26:9 seems to refer to a comic or absurd figure, a drunk waving a thorn bush in the air, Prov 9:17 indicates real and present danger, the eloquence of the seductive woman of folly herself:

> Stolen water is sweet,
> and bread eaten in secret is pleasant.

This rival to personified wisdom[25] does her own wooing, making no use of servant maids to issue an invitation to her feast. Her use of furtive suggestion promises more than culinary delights, and by appealing to the illicit she taps into the human desire to throw off all restraint. That is why the warning that follows conjures up the dreaded Rephaim in the depths of Sheol:

> He does not know that the Rephaim are there,
> in the depths of Sheol, her guests. (v. 18)

Metaphors for adultery and erotic pleasure (cf. Prov 5:15–20) are thus matched by a literal reminder of death.

It naturally follows that biblical sages had no monopoly on such proverbial sayings, which would have found their way into common discourse from the very beginning. Moreover, it is probable that many, perhaps most proverbial sayings in the Bible arose from common experience rather than the study of professional sages.[26] The same can be said for related speech forms such as pedagogic incentives in parental, prophetic, and priestly instruction (e.g., "listen; pay attention"), macarisms about receptive hearing, and terminology pertaining to the intellect (e.g., smart, astute, clever, stupid). By analogy, the rhetorical devices in common use (e.g., cases of polygenesis, especially opposites and graded numerical sayings) and existential responses to nature's harshness and grandeur (e.g., expressions of awe and wonder, as well as musings about life's brevity and frailty) are better attributed to society in general. These features are universal, hardly limited to an elite professional group that made up a tiny percentage of the population in Israel. Like specialists in ancient Egyptian and Mesopotamian literature, biblical scholars should make a distinction between the general use of *ḥokmâ* 'wisdom' (and similar words for intelligence) and the technical use of such words among sages.[27] Anything short of that only brings confusion into an already complex situation.

If the assessment of the extrabiblical evidence of proverbial sayings as creations of the populace in general is correct, and if the conclusions based on that evidence are sound, it follows that biblical interpreters may have overlooked a natural source of many expressions that they have attributed to professional sages. The issue is complicated by the probability that many sayings in the book of Proverbs arose in the larger society before being assimilated into a text that eventually became the exclusive domain of sages.

For this reason, modern biblical scholars are divided over the scope of wisdom influence on prophetic, historiographic, and psalmic texts. That argument continues unabated, despite caveats about hidden assumptions and unwanted consequences from one side[28] and claims of canonical shaping from the other.[29]

In some ways, the most innovative insights into redactional structuring of a text relate to the Psalter, and the persons responsible for this activity are said to have had sapiential interests. One of the latest to make this claim is Samuel Terrien, no novice in the long-standing debate over wisdom influence. In his massive commentary on Psalms, Terrien frequently mentions sapiential influence, sometimes qualifying the observation with a "possibly" or posing the issue as a question.[30] This enormously erudite scholar has capped an impressive literary contribution with a testament to faithful reading. Its publication poses an old question anew: Did the sages influence the Psalter? What response can one make?

First, what indicators point to sapiential shaping of the book of Psalms? Terrien suggests that two "sapiential meditations," Psalms 73 and 90, form two poles on which the rest of the book is articulated, a variant of others' claim that the first of these two psalms is the book's "theological center." Moreover, he appears to trace to the sages the dogma of reward and retribution, in which he sees the risk of latent biblicism. Similarly, he views acrostic psalms–"artificial" poetry devoid of artistic spontaneity–as a product of sapiential teachers, and the "prolix and redundant" recitation of history in Psalm 78 as akin to sapiential instruction.

From my perspective, Terrien's association of dogma and acrostics with wisdom fails to do justice to their wide association with laments and prophecy, and his reflections about the pedagogy of Psalm 78 do not take into account the vast differences between this material and the use of Israelite history in Sirach 40–50 and Wisdom of Solomon 10–19. The argument about the two poles of the Psalter, while suggestive, is highly subjective. Still, some critics find the context of Psalm 73 too similar to the book of Job to ignore the possibility of sapiential origin, even if such thoughts appear in prophetic texts, especially Jeremiah and Habakkuk.

Second, Terrien thinks that the depiction of human grandeur in Psalm 8 and the comparable portrayal of divine majesty and human frailty in Psalm 90 derive from the sages, whose views were similar to those articulated in Hebraic myths of creation. He does not identify the particular myths he has in mind, but he does note that the myths of creation are more sapiential than cultic. Given the prominent place of cultic worship in his interpretation of Psalms and the book of Job, this acknowledgment of non-cultic myths of creation within wisdom literature is significant. Scholars have often described wisdom theology as creation theology,[31] by which they mean that it embraces the human as opposed to a particular nation and that it is open to the world.

Nevertheless, the myth of the ordering of society through cosmic conflict with chaos is very much at home in prophecy and sacred narrative in the Torah. Terrien does not demonstrate that specific features of sapiential reflection on creation that may correspond to those in Psalms 8 and 90 do not occur in other treatments of the theme.

Third, Terrien's sense of the radiant divine presence in the theology of Psalms leaves little space for religious doubt, despite its prominence in a few psalms (94:7–9; 14 and 53). He labels the speakers who deny divine justice rebels or empirical atheists from the sapiential circles.[32] The problem of theodicy, to which these and similar texts attest, lays no legitimate claim on Terrien. In this view he has modern allies, especially in the Barthian camp,[33] but ancient thinkers did not hesitate to raise the question of divine justice. Like the authors of the psalms of lament (with the exception of Psalm 88), Terrien suppresses the feelings of absence and anxiety while basking in the hoped-for deliverance.[34]

Fourth, Terrien tends to erase distinctions between wisdom and prophecy, especially in the case of Jeremiah and the Jeremianic tradition.[35] Again and again he links a psalm with this prophet and the sages; that association is made in Psalms 73, 88, and 119, while both Psalms 52 and 62 are said to show affinities with prophetic and sapiential discourse. Jeremiah's deep probing of the psyche is similar to that of certain psalms, particularly 39, but it also reminds Terrien of Qoheleth's inner questioning.[36] The differences, however, between the psalmist and Qoheleth are major, for the latter does not examine his life to make himself more acceptable in God's sight[37] but rather uses autobiographical fiction on the one hand and internal dialogue on the other to muse about life's absurdity.

Fifth, Terrien builds evidence of sapiential influence on assumptions about ancient Israelite society that need revision in light of current research, tentative as it is. At one point he suggests that nomadic terminology in Psalm 25 has been normalized among prophets, priests, and poetic musicians. Does he imply a nomadic past for the ancestors of these psalmists, as was typical of scholars in the first half of the twentieth century? That is not clear. He does, however, state that wisdom schools were fashionable in several cities of the Diaspora,[38] a claim that rests on analogy with neighboring cultures, which has been sharply criticized.[39] Terrien also writes that sapiential ethics addressed itself chiefly to the socially elite, ignoring decisive indications that many of the persons described in the book of Proverbs were peasants struggling to eke out an existence from the land.[40] True, Qoheleth advises the people to seize the day, but he appears to be teaching ordinary people, *ha'am*. It has been argued, on slight grounds, that the book of Job envisions two types of privileged people, the generous and the selfish,[41] but such an argument is difficult to sustain. Sirach, however, does fit Terrien's description of sapiential ethics, for he seems to have belonged to a privileged class.[42]

Sixth, Terrien relies on style and vocabulary to link psalms and the sages, despite the overwhelmingly negative conclusions that specialists in this endeavor have reached.[43] All such attempts founder on the incontestable fact that the limited vocabulary of ancient Hebrew is insufficient to yield such conclusions about exclusive use in certain sectors. It is highly probable that cognitive expressions belonged to every segment of the population.

Seventh, although Qoh 11:5 acknowledges human ignorance about the miracle of life within a fetus, it does not follow that, as Terrien suggests, Psalm 139 derives its interest in embryology from sages. In Israelite society, midwives and pregnant women seem like the logical sources of reflection about the mystery of embryology.[44] In any event, the harsh remark in Ps 139:19–22 distances this psalm from the sages, with a single exception (Sir 50:25–26).

Conclusion

The widespread use of proverbs in literary genres distinct from wisdom literature, both within the Bible and in ancient Near Eastern texts, can be explained in one of two ways. Either the sayings are the product of sages, or they derive from popular culture. The second of these options would render less likely the widespread claim of sapiential influence, for example, in the book of Psalms. The evidence is sufficiently ambiguous to point scholars in opposite directions. Those who, like Terrien, discern the influence of sages in prophetic books and in the Psalter may be right. In my view, however, their labeling of words and expressions as sapiential serves no useful purpose. After all, labels ought to clarify or to issue vital information. Perhaps it is time to move beyond such speculation to a different task, that of specifying *functional* similarities and differences among genres. After all, fools had access to proverbs. It was the *use* of proverbs that distinguished the fools from the wise.[45]

CHAPTER 8

From the Mundane to the Sublime

Reflections on Qoh 11:1–8

11:1 Send your bread on the waters,
for in many days you may find it.
11:2 Give a portion to seven–or even to eight–,
for you do not know what misfortune will occur on earth.
11:3 If the clouds are full of rain, they empty on the earth;
and if a tree falls in the south or in the north,
where the tree falls there it is.[a]
11:4 Whoever continually watches the wind does not sow,
and whoever keeps on observing the clouds does not harvest.
11:5 As[b] you do not know the way of the wind–like a fetus[c] in the womb of a pregnant woman–
so you do not know the work[d] of the deity who brings everything into being.
11:6 In the morning sow your seed, and toward evening withhold not your hand,[e]
for you do not know[f] whether this or that will succeed,[g]
or if both of them alike will be favorable.
11:7 Now sweet is the light;
seeing the sun, pleasant to the eyes.
11:8 Even if people[h] live many years let them rejoice in them all,
and remember the days of darkness,[i] for they will be many. Everything that comes is futile.

a. Whether one reads *hû'* with a few manuscripts or a postulated *yehweh* makes no appreciable difference.
b. The *ba'ašer* of a few manuscripts is not an improvement over MT.
c. There is no compelling reason to follow the Targum's *bā'aṣāmîm*.
d. LXX, Syraic, and Vulgate have the plural here; the meaning is the same.
e. Many manuscripts attest the plural.
f. The usual form *yôdēa'* is attested in numerous manuscripts, but Leningrad has *yôdē'*.
g. The *kî* in this clause is best understood as emphatic (true...).
h. Many manuscripts have *yikšar*, unlike Leningrad. *hā'ādām* is generic, hence the inclusive plural rendering.
i. "Days of darkness" anticipates the subject of the object clause, "for they will be many" (Schoors, 1992: 209).

The language of this brief unit can hardly be more down to earth, ranging from bread and water, the staples of life[1] to the simple pleasure of basking in sunlight.[2] Still, the images point to the complex tasks of eking out a living from the inhospitable ground, to unfathomable mysteries like wind and gestation, to the contingency of human existence, and to the incomprehensible activity of the deity.[3] A decidedly negative sentiment prevails from first to last,[4] the haunting reminder of the limits of human perception and anticipated darkness, signaling futility.[5] Nevertheless, the plain discourse is far from dull, for it conceals much from listeners or readers who fail to recognize the coded language.[6] With nearly embarrassing simplicity, Qoheleth ventures into the realm of the sublime where life begins.[7] He closes, however, where life does, in darkness that stretches into the unknown.[8]

Beginnings and Endings

A leading interpreter of Qoheleth has observed that "the beginning of a section is a rather relative notion when applied to the book of Qoheleth" (Antoon Schoors 1992a: 206). That being true, the task of determining the precise scope of a literary unit is notoriously difficult when it lacks stylistic markers that delimit a text.[9] That task is compounded by Qoheleth, whose thought processes seem to weave together common themes and to return to them at the slightest provocation.[10] A glance at some modern commentaries will confirm this observation, for they present a panoply of suggestions about the structure of Qoheleth. Apart from almost universal consensus on the framework enclosing the main corpus, consisting of a title (1:1), a motto (1:2), the corpus (1:3–12:7), another motto (12:8), and two epilogues (12:9–14), little agreement exists.

Various alternatives for the structure of the main corpus are presented by Thomas Krüger (2004: 5–8). They include his own proposal (1:3–4:12; 4:13–5:8; 5:9–6:9; 6:10–8:17; 9:1–12:7) for which he makes no claim that it is "correct or the only appropriate division of Qoheleth." Krüger mentions older views by Kurt Galling (36 sentences, later revised to 26), Addison D. G. Wright (1:2–11; 1:12–6:9; 6:10–11:6; 11:7–12:8)[11] and Norbert Lohfink

(1:2–3; 1:4–11; 1:12–3:15; 3:16–4:16; 4:17–5:6; 5:7–6:10; 6:11–9:6l; 9:7–12:7; 12:8), along with more recent suggestions by Choon-Leong Seow (1:2–4:16; 5:1–6:9; 6:10–12:8), Franz Josef Backhaus (1:2–3:15; 3:16–6:9; 6:11–8:17; 9:1–12:8), and Ludger Schwienhorst-Schönberger (1:3–3:22; 4:1–6:9; 6:1–8:17; 9:1–12:7).

Wright's proposal was influenced by new literary criticism,[12] whereas the Greek cultural environment provided the impetus for Lohfink and Schwienhorst-Schönberger.[13] Lohfink argued for a palindrome with critique of religion at its center, while Schwienhorst-Schönberger used the four features of classical rhetoric–proposition, development, defense, and application–as paradigm (cf. Backhaus: 1993). Earlier suggestions about Qoheleth's structure can be found in Crenshaw (1987: 34–49) and Schwienhorst-Schönberger (1997: 7–14).

My delineation of the literary unit to be studied flies in the face of almost universal consensus that verse 6 concludes this particular section. Why the departure? The reason: I understand *kol šebbā' hābel* in 11:8 to be a more appropriate conclusion of the unit than the expansive 11:6,[14] and I take the unique direct address to a specific group in 11:9 (śe*maḥ baḥûr*) as a marker of a new section. The frequent use of a comparable vocative, *benî*, to introduce a unit in Prov 1–9, Sirach, and the epilogue of Ecclesiastes (12:12) supports this interpretation, the few exceptions probably being emphatic.[15] Occasionally, other interpreters have preceded me by refusing to accept a break in logic at 11:8 (Franz Delitzsch: 1877; Walther Zimmerli: 1962, Diethelm Michel: 1988; Hans Wilhelm Hertzberg: 1963; Lohfink: 2003, although he begins the unit at 11:4). For the purposes of this paper, however, this division of the text is inconsequential.

The Immediate Context

Regardless of how one resolves this particular issue, the links between 11:1–6(or 8) and what immediately precedes and follows are noteworthy. The inability of humans to understand life's many anomalies or to anticipate future events (*lō' yēda' ha'ādām mâ šeyyihyeh*, 10:14B) returns in 11:1–2, 5–6. Likewise, *leḥem* in 10:19 is taken up again in 11:1, just as the verb *yeśammaḥ* recurs in 11:8 (*yiśmāḥ*) and the reference to inactive hands in 10:18 reappears as an element of sage advice in 11:6 (*'al tannaḥ yādekā*). Links between the unit under consideration and 11:9–12:7 include the verb *zākar* (12:1) and the noun *ḥōšek* (11:8) and the verbs *teḥšak* and *weḥāšekû* in 12:2 and 3. Moreover, *he'ābîm* and *še* (11:3) recur in the expression *wešābû he'ābîm 'aḥar haggāšem* (12:2), and šō*mēr* (11:4) is echoed in šō*merê habbayit* (12:3) in the same way *rā'â* (11:2) returns in 11:10. So, too, do *hābel* (11:8 and 10) and *hā'ôr* (11:7 and 12:2).

Although some linguistic overlap between the respective units may be purely accidental,[16] even then it indicates remarkable consistency in a thinker who is notorious for self-contradiction,[17] giving rise to a theory of *zwar/aber* (yes/but) to explain such apparently opposite views.[18] Others prefer to think that Qoheleth takes up traditional views only to relativise them in his own formulations.[19] A gradual shift from the realm of Ptolemaic officials in

10:16–18, 19 to farmers in 11:4 and 6 is much clearer than the intervening stage represented by parallel imperatives with substantiating *kî* clauses in 11:1–2. Simple human pleasures, represented by bread and wine, as well as the means of acquiring them *(kesep)*, are set against a huge backdrop: nature itself. The age-old use of analogy from the natural world (and the animal kingdom), prominent in the books of Proverbs and Job,[20] reinforces Qoheleth's ethical counsel. However unpredictable Mother Nature may show herself, she can also be depended on to perform in a reliable manner under given circumstances.[21] Of that fact, Qoheleth is certain (1:4–11), but he underscores the mystery of natural processes while simultaneously alluding to the most profound secret of all, the gift of life. Its sweetness, all too brief, turns bitter and then is no more.

Metaphorical Language?

How does the larger context influence one's reading of 11:1–8? That question is necessitated by the use of the noun *leḥem* in 10:19 and 11:1. The truism that bread effects laughter, wine gladdens the living, and money answers everything (10:19) contrasts with the problematic exhortation, "Send your bread on the surface of the waters, for in many days you may find it" (11:1). Aside from the rhyming conclusion of the first word and the beginning of the second (*šallaḥ laḥmekā*) and the metathesis in *hammāyîm* and *hayyāmîm*, which may have brought pleasure to astute listeners,[22] what is the point of this proverb?

Presumably, *leḥem* in 10:19 refers to actual sustenance, whether in a strict usage (a product of grain) or in an extended sense of food generally. A literal sense in 11:1 renders the advice satirical, and when combined with 11:2, "Give a portion to seven or even to eight, for you cannot know what misfortune will eventuate on the land," it indicates different ways of squandering resources. The outcome of the first act, releasing round flatbread on the surface of water, is soggy bread, that of the second, empty hands, assuming that the rare numerical gradation, at home especially in Ugaritic literature,[23] means a lot of people. Its only other occurrence in the Hebrew Bible seems to mean "a sufficient number" of defenders of YHWH's people to trample Assyrian invaders (Mic 5:4, "seven shepherds and eight human princes"). The use of this numerical sequence in Phoenician and Aramaic incantations[24] opens the door to a magical interpretation of Qoh 11:2. On this reading, Qoheleth advises the taking of extraordinary measures to secure divine assistance while distributing a little here and a little there as a hedge against calamity.

What if *leḥem* has a figurative sense here? Such a meaning is well attested, ranging from an erotic connotation to the spiritual, from contexts of war to romantic interludes. For example, Joseph is said to have been denied nothing by Potiphar except the *leḥem* his master ate, which Gen 39:9 identifies as his wife.[25] Similarly, the aphorism attributed to Folly in Prov 9:17 owes its poignancy to an erotic double entendre, bread and water ("Stolen water is sweet, clandestine bread, pleasant"; cf. Sir 23:17). In Num 14:9

Israel's enemies are identified as food; Ps 42:4 (cf. 80:6) uses the image of tears as food by day and night; and Jer 11:19 calls the fruit of a tree its *leḥem*.

Investment of Capital or Deeds of Kindness?

The Targum of Qoheleth[26] attributed a figurative sense to other words in 11:1–8, specifically the imperative *zera'* and its cognate accusative *zar'ekā*, the temporal expressions *babbōqer* and *lā'ereb*, even *yādekā*. Those critics who understand *leḥem* in 11:2 as figurative, far more numerous than those who view it literally, fall into two camps: (1) those who think Qoheleth advises charitable contributions arising from self-centered interest in preparing for sudden turns in fortune by multiplying the number of persons in one's debt, and (2) others who think of investments in commercial ventures. The extraordinary similarity between 11:1 and a saying in the Egyptian Instruction of Anksheshonky ("Do a good deed and throw it in the water; when it dries you will find it")[27] suggests a meaning other than social satire, yet without supplying any clue about how it was understood, or for that matter how a good deed can dry while floating in water. Risky mercantile enterprises during the Hellenistic era presented the possibility of a high rate of return on investments,[28] but this understanding of the verse assumes an unusual use of *hammāyîm*, where *hayyām* would be more appropriate and an understanding of *leḥem* as grain to be loaded on ships (Seow: 1997, 344–5). Above all, the aphorism says nothing about profit, the sole purpose of investment.

Diversification does appear to be the subject of 11:2, which in context seems to clarify the previous verse as advice about financial investments.[29] Even if one ultimately favors the interpretation of these verses as spontaneous generosity, viewing them against the Greek emphasis on friendship and the practice of philanthropy with vested interest, the advice to give away one's portion (why not *kesep*?) seems strange in light of the substantiation clause. Has not Qoheleth already cited the sad case of one who lost his wealth in a risky venture and was left with no means of caring for a son (5:12–16)?[30]

Nature's Inevitability and Mystery

Whereas Qoheleth's admonitions in 11:1–2 concern the interaction of humans and nature, the next verse restricts itself entirely to natural events. Both the outpouring of rain from saturated clouds and the falling of a tree, presumably during the accompanying windstorm, can have consequences for people. Does Qoheleth mean that human ignorance about the future is just as inevitable as the laws of nature?[31] Or does *'ēṣ* indicate a divining rod, as in Hos 4:12? In this case the final clause should be translated thus: "The place that the rod falls–there will be [water]." This ironical interpretation has more merit than rendering *'ēṣ* as lightning, even if the context is that of heavy rain, or construing *'ēṣ* as an ellipsis of *zera' 'ēṣ*.[32] If 11:2 ventures into the realm of magic, the accompanying verse may follow suit. The indicator of directions, south and north, must be specific, rather than serving as a merism to express ubiquity. None of these three (trees, divining rods, and lightning) falls everywhere.

In 11:4 Qoheleth returns to the interplay of humans and nature, but with a twist. Mere observation replaces action. The farmer who persists in watching[33] for a favorable wind will never sow, and whoever observes the clouds looking for perfect conditions will never reap. Only the dumbest of farmers[34] would be ignorant of Qoheleth's truism. Is something else at work here? Who else watches over the wind and observes clouds? Their maker, the *šōmēr* of humankind. Perhaps Qoheleth suggests that the deity will not attend to palpably human tasks, however much people resort to foolish behavior, magical incantation, and divining rods.[35] Such a reading of a deeper meaning for *šōmēr* is comparable to viewing *'āb* and *'im* in the Decalog as a transition to the heavenly father, but Qoheleth's thought is a long way from such ethical advice as found in the Decalog.

Divine Hiddenness

The actual role of the deity comes into play in magnificent fashion in 11:5. Although the meaning of the comparison is less than obvious, it can be understood in the following manner. Just as one cannot know the behavior of wind any more than one can understand the movement of a fetus within the womb of a pregnant woman, so no one can know the deity's work, except in the general sense that God brings everything into existence,[36] or more specifically both the wind and the fetus. This interpretation depends on reading *ka'aṣāmim* as synecdoche, bones standing for the entire fetus; at the same time, this analysis retains the *kaph* as the *lexio difficilior*. Qoheleth's point grows out of the reality that we can only see the results of the wind's movement, not the wind itself. Likewise, the kicking and rolling of a fetus within the womb can be readily detected, but the actual living being cannot be seen.

Qoheleth's remarkable movement to theology[37] from an anthropological reference to foolish conduct has taken place in the most intimate of places, precisely where human ignorance is greatest: the emergence of life.[38] Appropriately, he employs a rare term for a pregnant woman, *hammelē'ah*[39] and doubles up on the negation of human knowledge, *'ênekā yôdēa' / lo' tēda'*.[40] Alternatively, the double sense of *rûaḥ*,[41] together with an emended preposition–*ba'aṣāmîm* for *ka'aṣāmîm* –yields the following possibility: just as no one can know how the breath of life enters a fetus, so nobody has any knowledge of divine activity (cf. John 3:8).

The Imperative to Act

In verse 6 Qoheleth returns to the mode of exhortation,[42] urging decisive and persistent action in the face of abysmal ignorance about the future. Temporal adverbs, *babbōqer* and *la'ereb*, precede imperatives, *zera'* and *'al tannaḥ*. Because you cannot know what effort will succeed, Qoheleth observes, sow your seed in early morning and do not withhold your hand toward evening. The indirect questions, whether this or that, and disjunctive (cf. 2:19) *we'im* plus *šenêhem* indicate two actions rather than sustained sowing all day long. Or does the *ke'eḥad* refer to divine activity and human effort, the *hazeh -'ô-zeh* reaching back to the previous verse and allowing the *lamed* on *'ereb* to be construed naturally as indicating ceaseless labor?

An even bolder reading takes its cue from the allusion to the mystery of gestation in 11:5 and adopts a figurative meaning for the temporal adverbs, the imperative and its cognate accusative, and the object of the negated imperative. According to this interpretation, Qoheleth urges youth to be sexually active and dissuades old men from abandoning the begetting of children. The use of *yikšar* and *ṭôbîm* as equivalent expressions stands under the negated participle, *'êneka yôde'*, the theme word[43] of the unit to this point, along with the comparable *lō' tēda'* (11:2, 5, 6). If *ṭôbîm* contrasts with *rā'â* in 11:2, Qoheleth has prepared a smooth path to a general conclusion that will enable his auditors to avoid the mistakes adumbrated in 11:1–6, namely foolish waste, profligate squandering of resources, inaction, and ceaseless toil. Such human endeavor, he argues, is subject to a *miqreh*[44] that cannot be calculated, whether by resorting to magic or to gargantuan enterprise. What then should one do?

Accept the limits imposed on the intellect and bask in the sweetness of sunshine! It is little, and much. Qoheleth's return to an adjective that he employed figuratively in 5:11 ("*Pleasant* is the sleep of a laborer [or slave] whether he eats little or much...") may be dictated by the necessity for a parallel expression for *ṭôb*. The emphatic *waw* contrasts a sure thing with all the uncertainties that generated the futile activities Qoheleth has just ridiculed. The aural pun between the negative particle *'êneka* (11:6) and *la'ênayîm* only partially restores the balance in a decidedly ocular context.[45]

Qoheleth's basis for discovering a bit of nectar while suspended over the abyss[46] is a sober reminder that even a long life is no compensation for the extended sojourn in Sheol.[47] Still, he urges the individual possessing such favorable fortune to enjoy those years but at the same time to ponder the dark days ahead, for they will be numerous. The closing statement minces no words: "Everything that comes is futile."[48] The ironic contrast between *šānîm harbēh* and *yemê haḥōšek* matches the tension underlying the two jussives: "let him rejoice but remember..." but pales before the pathos expressed in a similar assessment in 6:3, where *yemê* is joined to *šānayw*[49] and a particular instance of longevity is said to be less enviable than the status of a stillborn. The entire unit has reached a resounding conclusion in a call to seize the moment but to reflect on the specter of death: *carpe diem* and *memento mori*.[50] These two themes will be highlighted in the final unit of Qoheleth's teaching, 11:9–12:7.[51]

How does the unit we have explored fit within Qoheleth's general argument? It does not treat four of Qoheleth's top ten vocabulary items, as tabulated by Oswald Loretz (1964: 167–81; the forty-nine instances of *'ādām* are not considered in this count for some reason. Those four are *ḥākām*, *'ēt*, *'āmāl*, and *kesil)*. Qoheleth's failure to insert his heightened ego (*'anî*) into the unit,[52] although striking, may be a function of the rhetoric chosen in this instance. More consistent is his preference for *'ādām* over *'îš* and *'enôš*, forms that rarely appear in the book (1:8; 4:4; and 9:15[2x] for *'îš*, 9:14 and 12:3 for *'anāšîm* and *'anšē heḥayil*). Qoheleth's inconsistent use of the *nota accusativa* may point to traditional aphorisms in 11:1–2, 4, whereas 11:5–8 may be his own formulation. Similarly, *'îš miskēn* in 9:15 (2x) may derive from traditional lore. Distinguishing between citations and material attributable to Qoheleth is still in its infancy, despite frequent attempts to discover adequate criteria to accomplish this task.[53]

Conclusion

Looking back over 11:1–8 as understood here, two themes stand out, human inability to know and the inevitability of random events. Against this depressing background, and the even more troubling dark days ahead, Qoheleth urges the young to seize every available pleasure. This is not his final word, however. That belongs to Qoheleth's formulaic assertion: "everything that comes is futile." One can add: just like everything that has been, and is now.

Bibliography for Qoheleth

Backhaus, Franz Josef
1993 '*Denn Zeit und Zufall trifft sie alle': Studien zur Komposition und zum Gottesbild im Buch Qohelet* (BBB 83; Frankfurt am Main: Anton Hain).
Barton, John
1984 *Reading the Old Testament. Method in Biblical Study* (London: Darton Longman and Todd).
Bickerman, Elias
1967 *Four Strange Books of the Bible: Jonah, Daniel, Koheleth, Esther* (New York: Schocken).
Bohlen, Reinhold
1997 'Kohelet im Kontext Hellenistischer Kultur," *Das Buch Kohelet: Studien zur Struktur, Geschichte, Rezeption, und Theologie*, ed. L. Schwienhorst-Schönberger (BZAW 254; Berlin: de Gruyter): 249–73.
Braun, Rainer
1973 *Kohelet und die frühhellenistische Popularphilosophie* (BZAW 130; Berlin/New York: de Gruyter).
Brown, William P.
2002 *Seeing the Psalms: A Theology of Metaphor* (Louisville/London: Westminster John Knox).
Brunner, Hellmut
1988 *Altägyptische Weisheit: Lehren für das Leben* (BAW.AO; Zurich: Artemis).
Burkes, Shannon
1999 *Death in Qoheleth and Egyptian Biographies of the Late Period* (SBLDS 170; Atlanta: Society of Biblical Literature).
Carr, David M.
2003 *The Erotic Word: Sexuality, Spirituality, and the Bible* (Oxford/New York: Oxford University Press).
Cathcart, Kevin J.
1968 'Notes on Micah 5, 4–5,' *Bib* 49:511–14.

Crenshaw, James L.

1978a *Samson: A Secret Betrayed, a Vow Ignored* (Atlanta/London: John Knox/SPCK).

1978b 'The Shadow of Death in Qoheleth,' in *Israelite Wisdom* (Fs. Samuel Terrien). (Philadelphia: Fortress), 205–16. (*Urgent Advice and Probing Questions*, 573–85).

1987 *Ecclesiastes* (Philadelphia: Westminster).

1995 *Urgent Advice and Probing Questions: Collected Writings on Old Testament Wisdom* (Macon: Mercer University).

1998a *Education in Ancient Israel: Across the Deadening Silence* (New York: Doubleday).

1998b 'Qoheleth's Understanding of Intellectual Inquiry,' in *Qohelet in the Context of Wisdom*, ed. A. Schoors (BETL 136; Leuven: University Press), 205–24.

2006 'Qoheleth's Quantitative Language,' *The Language of Qohelet in Context. Antoon Schoors' Festschrift* (Leuwen: Peeters).

Crüsemann, Frank

1984 [1979] 'The Unchangeable World: The "Crisis of Wisdom" in Koheleth,' *The God of the Lowly*, ed. W. Schottroff and W. Stegemann (Maryknoll, N.Y.: Orbis), 57–77.

Delitzsch, Franz

1877 [1875] *Commentary on the Song of Songs and Ecclesiastes* (Edinburgh: T. & T. Clark).

Dor-Shav, Ethan

2004 'Ecclesiastes, Fleeting and Timeless,' *Azure* 18:67–87.

Ehlich, Konrad

1996 'הבל–Metaphern der Nichtigkeit,' in *'Jedes Ding hat seine Zeit': Studien zur israelitischen und altorientalischen Weisheit*, ed. A. A. Diesel et. al. (BZAW 241; Berlin/New York: de Gruyter), 49–64.

Fox, Michael V.

1986 'The Meaning of *Hebel* for Qohelet,' *JBL* (105): 409–27.

1987 'Qohelet's Epistemology,' *HUCA* 58: 137–55.

1989 *Qohelet and His Contradictions* (BLS 18; Sheffield: Almond).

1998 'The Inner Structure of Qohelet's Thought,' in *Qohelet in the Context of Wisdom*, 225–38.

1999 *A Time to Tear Down & a Time to Build Up. A Rereading of Ecclesiastes.* (Grand Rapids: Eerdmans).

Galling, Kurt

1969 [1940] *Der Prediger* (HAT 1, 18; Tübingen: Mohr).

Gammie, John

1984 'Stoicism and Anti-Stoicism in Qoheleth,' *HAR* 9: 169–87.

Gordis, Robert

1939/40 'Quotations in Wisdom Literature,' *JQR* 30: 123–47.

1949 'Quotations as a Literary Usage in Biblical, Oriental, and Rabbinic Literature,' *HUCA* 22: 157–219.

Gorssen, L.

1969 'Le cohérence de la conception de Dieu dans l'Ecclésiaste,' *ETL* (46): 282–324.

Harrison, C. Robert
1991 *Qoheleth in Social-historical Perspective*, unpublished Ph.D. Dissertation, Duke University.
1994 'Hellenization in Syria-Palestine: The Case of Judea in the Third Century BCE,' *BA* 57: 98–108.
1997 'Qoheleth among the Sociologists,' *Bib Int* 5:160–80.
Hengel, Martin
1974 *Judaism and Hellenism* (Philadelphia: Fortress).
Hertzberg, Hans Wilhelm
1963 *Der Prediger* (KAT, n.s. 17, 4; Gütersloh: Gütersloher).
Jong, Stefan de
1997 'God in the Book of Qohelet. A Reappraisal of Qohelet's Place in Old Testament Theology,' *VT* 47: 154–67.
Kaiser, Otto
1985 *Der Mensch unter dem Schicksal* (BZAW 161; Berlin/New York: de Gruyter), 135–53.
1998 *Gottes und der Menschen Weisheit. Gesammelte Aufsätze* (BZAW 261; Berlin/New York: de Gruyter).
Keel, Othmar
1997 *The Symbolism of the Biblical World: Ancient Near Eastern Iconography and the Book of Psalms* (Winona Lake: Eisenbrauns).
Krüger, Thomas
1992 '"Frau Weisheit" in Koh 7, 26,' *Bib* 73: 394–403
2004 *Qoheleth* (Minneapolis: Fortress).
Kugel, James L.
1989 'Qohelet and Money,' *CBQ* 51 (1989): 32–49.
Lauha, Aarre
1978 *Kohelet* (BKAT 19; Neukirchen-Vluyn: Neukirchener).
1983 'Omnia Vanitas: Die Bedeutung von *hbl* bei *Kolelet*,' in *Glaube und Gerechtigkeit (Fs. R. Gyllenberg*). (SFEG 38; ed. J. Külunen et. al. Helsinki: Soumen Eksegeettesen Seura), 19–25.
Lichtheim, Miriam
1976 *Ancient Egyptian Literature*, vol. 1 (Berkeley: University of California).
1980 *Ancient Egyptian Literature*, vol. 3 (Berkeley: University of California).
Lohfink, Norbert
1979 'War Kohelet ein Frauenfeind? Ein Versuch, die Logik und den Gegenstand von Koh 7, 23–8, 1a herauszufinden, in *La Sagesse de l'ancien Testament*, ed. Maurice Gilbert (BETL 51; Leuven, University Press 259–87).
1990 'Qoheleth 5:17–19–Revelation by Joy,' *CBQ* 52: 625–35.
1998 *Studien zu Kohelet* (SBA 26; Stuttgart: Katholisches Bibelwerk).
2003 *Qoheleth. A Continental Commentary* (Minneapolis: Fortress).
Loretz, Oswald
1964 *Qohelet und der alte Orient: Untersuchungen zu Stil und theologischer Thematik des Buches Qohelet (*Freiburg: Herder*)*.
1980 'Altorientalische und kanaanäische Topoi im Buche Kohelet,' *UF* 12:67–78.

Machinist, Peter
1995 'Fate, *miqreh*, and Reason: Some Reflections on Qohelet and Biblical Thought,' in *Solving Riddles and Untying Knots (Fs. J. C. Greenfield)* ed. Z. Zevit et. al. (Winona Lake: Eisenbrauns), 159–75.
McKenna, John E.
1991 'The Concept of *hebel* in the Book of Ecclesiastes,' *SJT* 45: 19–28.
Michel, Diethelm
1973/74 'Vom Gott, der im Himmel ist (Reden von Gott bei Qohelet),' *ThVia* 12:87–100.
1989 *Untersuchungen zur Eigenart des Buches Qohelet* (BZAW 183; Berlin/New York: de Gruyter).
1990 'Gott bei Kohelet. Anmerkungen zu Kohelets Reden von Gott,' *BK* 45:32-36.
Müller, Hans Peter
1968 'Wie sprach Qohälät von Gott?' *VT* 18:507–21.
1986 'Theonome Skepsis und Lebensfreude zu Koh 1, 12–3, 15,' *BZ* 30:1–19.
Ogden, Graham S.
1985 '"Vanity" It Certainly Is Not,' *BT* 38:301–7.
Polk, Timothy
1976 'Wisdom of Irony: A Study of *Hebel* and Its Relation to Joy and the Fear of God in Ecclesiastes,' *St Bib et Theol* 6:3–17.
Schellenberg, Annette
2002 *Erkenntnis als Problem. Qohelet und die alttestamentliche Diskussion um das menschliche Erkennen* (OBO 188; Göttingen: Vandenhoeck & Ruprecht).
Schoors, Antoon
1992a *The Preacher Sought to Find Pleasing Words: A Study of the Language of Qoheleth* (OLA 41; Leuven: Peeters).
1992b "Bitterder dan de Dood is de Vrouw (Koh 7, 26)," *Biydr* 54; 121–40.
1999 'Words Typical of Qohelet,' in *Qohelet in the Context of Wisdom*, 17–40.
2002 'God in Qoheleth,' in *Schöpfungsplan und Heilsgeschichte. Fs. für Ernst Haag* (Rome: Paulinus), 251–70.
2003 'Theodicy in Qohelet,' in *Theodicy in the World of the Bible*, ed. A. Laato and J. C. de Moor (Leiden/Boston: Brill), 375–409.
Schwienhorst-Schönberger, Ludger
1994 *'Nicht im Menschen gründet das Gluck' (Koh 2, 24): Kohelet im Spannungsfeld jüdischer Weisheit und hellenistischer Philosophie* (HBS 2; Freiburg: Herder).
1996 *Das Buch Kohelet. Studien zur Struktur, Geschichte, Rezeption und Theologie* (BZAW 254; Berlin/New York: de Gruyter).
Seow, Choon-Leong
1997 *Ecclesiastes* (AB 18C; New York: Doubleday).
Sharp, Carolyn
2004 'Ironic Representation, Authorial Voice, and Meaning in Qohelet,' *Bib Int* 12:37–68.
Trible, Phylis
1994 *Rhetorical Criticism: Context, Method, and the Book of Jonah* (Minneapolis: Fortress).

Uehlinger, Christoph
1998 'Qohelet im Horizont mesopotamischer, levantinischer und ägyptischer Weisheitsliteratur der persischen und hellenistischen Zeit,' in *Das Buch Kohelet*, 155–247.

Whitley, Charles F.
1979 *Koheleth* (BZAW 148; Berlin/New York: de Gruyter).

Whybray, R. N.
1980 'The Identification and Use of Quotations in Ecclesiastes,' in *Congress Volume Vienna 1980* (VTS 32; Leiden: Brill), 435–51.
1981 Qoheleth, Preacher of Joy,' VTSup 23: 87–98.

Willmes, Bernd
1999 *Menschliches Schicksal und ironische Weisheitskritik im Koheletbuch: Kohelet's Ironie und die Grenzen der Exegese* (BTS 39; Neukirchen/Vluyn: Neukirchener).

Wright, Addison D. G.
1968 'The Riddle of the Sphinx: The Structure of the Book of Qoheleth,' *CBQ* 30: 313–34.
1981 'The Riddle of the Sphinx Revisited: Numerical Patterns in the Book of Qoheleth,' *CBQ* 42: 35–51.
1982 'Additional Numerical Patterns in Qoheleth,' *CBQ* 45:32–43.

Wright, J. Edward
2000 *The Early History of Heaven* (Oxford: Oxford University).

Zimmerli, Walther
1962 *Das Buch des Predigers Salomo* (ATD 16, 1; Göttingen: Vandenhoeck & Ruprecht).
1974 1974 'Das Buch Kohelet–Traktat oder Sentenzensammlung?' *VT* 24: 221–30.

CHAPTER 9

Deceitful Minds and Theological Dogma

Jer 17:5–11

The ordering of society into two distinct camps made up respectively of sinners and righteous is perhaps the greatest break with reality in the Bible. Truly utopian, this fictional society is constructed to bestow comfort on those whose religious values have lost their appeal for a significant number of people. The irony of such a worldview appears to have escaped detection: this construction of reality co-exists with a view of radical, indeed innate, perversity of will.[1] The anomaly: how can anyone whose mind is thoroughly perverse aspire to and acquire virtue, or for that matter, speak truthfully? The text to be studied here illustrates this commingling of self-negating understandings of the world. It reads as follows.

Jer 17:5 YHWH said this.[a]

Accursed–one who trusts in humans,
making flesh his strength,
and whose mind turns from YHWH.
6 He is like a shrub in the desert
oblivious when good arrives.
It dwells in the desert, destitute,
in a salty flat, uninhabited.
7 Blessed–one who trusts in YHWH
and YHWH is his security.
8 He is like a tree planted beside water,
its roots extending by a stream,
undaunted[b] when drought comes.
Its foliage is lush;

unperturbed in a year of dearth,
it does not cease bearing fruit.
9 Most perverse[c]–the mind,
and twisted[d] is it, who can grasp it?
10 I YHWH probe the mind,
test the conscience,
to bestow on a person according to his actions,
according to the fruit of his deeds.[e]
11 A partridge hatches what she did not lay:
one who accumulates wealth unjustly.
In the midst of his days they leave him;
ultimately, he is a fool.

a The Greek lacks the oracular formula, attributing the views expressed in what follows to humans (but cf. v. 10).

b Parallelism with v 6 suggests a form of the verb *r'h* as in Qere, fragments from the geniza at Cairo, and Targum. Against this reading is Ketiv, Septuagint, and Syriac.

c The Greek βαθεια may point to a Hebrew *'mq* (deep, profound).

d Symmachus has και ἄνθρωπος as if he read *we'anôš*.

e The Qere is amply supported, pointing to the plural form in Jer 32:19, where the same phrase occurs.

Locative and Utopian Constructions of Reality

Jonathan Z. Smith has argued in *Map is Not Territory: Studies in the History of Religions*[2] that there are two distinct worldviews, locative and utopian. In the first of these, society identifies its redemptive moments in specific locations within observable reality. People look to these special places and particular moments for spiritual health, viewing episodic events as divine disclosure. Worship takes place at sacred sites, chosen by a given deity, and by adhering to prescribed ritual devotees can tap into the power deriving from divine presence. Exact places and transformative episodes vary with religious groups and among ethnicities.

As a heuristic device, this reading of religious literature can be applied to ancient Israel and its environment. Accordingly, the event that took place at Sinai and its later connection to Zion became normative, along with the ideology of Davidic rule and the Aaronide priesthood. Elsewhere, the Canaanites elevated Mt. Saphon, the Babylonians looked to Esagila, the later Greeks cast their eyes toward Olympus (and Delphi), and Christians longingly beheld Golgotha.

This locative understanding of regenerative power permeates Israelite literature that eventually became normative, with wisdom literature the notable exception until Sirach and Wisdom of Solomon. Divine mandate was identified with the events unfolding at Sinai, while prophetic proclamation was grounded in the Exodus and in messianism associated with David. The extraordinary attraction of Zion and its earthly ruler is attested in the Psalter, which is replete with eloquent prayers linking the two. Beyond that, however, this same book illustrates the fate of every locative worldview. Things temporal and spatial are subject to decay (cf. 1 Esdras 4:37–38). Kingdoms fall, and with them their holy places. Fire ravaged Zion, and with its collapse came an abrupt termination of the sacred cult of YHWH. Sinai's ritualistic laws were rendered obsolete, at least for the moment because of a shortage of priests and a non-functioning altar. The fountain of life dried up, and new springs were sought.

The answer: an alternative worldview that does not rest on phenomena and therefore is not subject to disconfirmation. Such an understanding of the world is utopian, fantasy not yoked to time and place. Transcending temporality and spatiality, the competing worldview posits a redemptive status achieved solely through an act of choice involving both will and intellect. In this artificial realm of fantasy, wild animals feed peacefully alongside domestic ones, harming neither beasts nor people, and nature serves human needs beyond the wildest imagination. Deserts are transformed into paradise, ethnic hostilities overcome, often but not always for Israel's advantage, and that of its deity. Above all, the existential realities plaguing humanity–pain, sorrow, and death–are vanquished, with YHWH coming to dwell in the midst of this joyous throng. Tears, precious to YHWH, are dried and singing echoes far and wide in this paradise that corresponds to the perfect world that, from a certain perspective, a benevolent creator should have brought into being in the beginning.[3]

This fantastic world has at least two serious flaws: it makes the deity obsolete,[4] and it lacks the challenge and the joy associated with growth in moral character.[5] Such religious fantasy, moreover, has lost all touch with reality. That is why it gives prominence to bizarre creatures, heavenly mediators transporting select humans through storied heavens and conveying the secrets of the universe to them. Symbolic language, secret codes, periodization, and epic conflict in the heavens and on earth invite partisanship, creating a mentality characterized by "us versus them." Those who consider themselves chosen become militants in the service of the Great King and await a summons to participate in a final battle which will precipitate a judgment that will be good for "us" but dreadful for "them."[6]

It is tempting to view these competing worldviews as early and late, thus completely unrelated except as two elements in sequence. Unfortunately, such a reading of the facts overlooks the important exception mentioned above. Israel's sages prior to Ben Sira and the anonymous author of Wisdom of Solomon saw no need to locate sacred experience anywhere except in the human intellect. Their teachings had no borders and no priestly, prophetic, or royal mediators. Experience, open to everyone regardless of nation or religion, was the sole avenue to the divine. Truth therefore was universal, transcending both time and place.[7] While this view had the appearance of utopianism, it is actually embedded in daily experience. Nevertheless, in their zeal sages pressed their claims too far, and in doing so they succumbed to the powerful seduction of utopia. A rigid dogmatism came to expression;

it insisted that goodness almost always leads to well-being, villainy to downfall.[8] Where this view prevailed, a sharp break with reality also took place.

This evidence of life's untidiness suggests that utopian views can be cherished by the very people who paradoxically emphasize the experiences of this world, very much grounded in space and time. One might even say they have universalized the locative. The same tendency is observable in Jer 17:5–11, where absolute claims are made that seem to cancel one another: (1) trust in human beings leads to destruction but relying on YHWH produced fruit; and (2) the human intellect is wholly perverse. If the mind is corrupt, how can anyone trust any of its formulations, especially the assertion about an underlying principle governing the universe?

Trust and Its Consequences

The section under consideration consists of an oracle (vv 5–8), a gnomic saying (v 9), divine speech (v 10), and a gnomic saying ending in a critique (v 11). The initial oracle is comprised of contrasting parallel statements in virtual symmetry. Two gnomic sayings follow, interrupted by divine declarative speech. The first aphorism ends in a rhetorical question, the second in a dismissive assertion. The section begins with the name YHWH; its closing adjective is fool. This alternation between YHWH and human subject characterizes the entire unit.

The contested issue in vv 5–8 is trust, whether it is rightly placed or not. Together with *lēb*,[9] the intellectual and affective aspects of human existence, *bāṭaḥ*[10] determines destiny, or so it is claimed. Accursed, the opening word in the oracle itself, is worlds removed from the exalted beginning set by the divine name. To whom does this loathsome condition apply? To the person who trusts the creature rather than creator, who relies on human defenses (*bāśar* instead of *rûaḥ*, the spirit, to adopt the language of Isaiah which seems to lurk in the shadows). In context, this turning of the mind away from YHWH signals an act of idolatry (cf. vv 1–4). The opposite of this condemned individual relies wholly on YHWH for protection and therefore is heir to the promise contained in the performative act associated with *bāruk*, blessed (v 7).

As if the language of curse and blessing were not sufficiently explicit to describe the opposing status of the different types, the author employs a familiar image, that of plantings in vastly different locations, the one arid, the other well-watered. Lacking water, the shrub (*'ar'ar*)[11] occupies undesirable terrain and comes to nothing. The tree (*'ēṣ*) planted by a stream grows and retains its lush foliage in harsh times, always producing fruit. The comparison is so obvious that its presence in ancient Egyptian literature as well as in the Bible should not surprize anyone. Its double use in the Bible, here and in Psalm 1, raises the question of priority and dependence, although the two thinkers may have used a figure of speech from a common store of knowledge.

We may compare the biblical imagery with Amenemope 6, 1–2, which Miriam Lichtheim[12] translates as follows:

As for the heated man in the temple,
He is like a tree growing [indoors].
A moment lasts its growth of [shoots].
Its end comes about in the [woodshed].
It is floated far from its place,
The flame is its burial shroud.
The truly silent, who keeps apart,
He is like a tree grown in the meadow.
It grows, it doubles its yield.
It stands in front of its lord.
Its fruit is sweet, its shade delightful,
Its end comes in the garden.

This contrast between the fool and the wise begins with the undesirable person, like Jer 17:5, and proceeds to the desirable one, again like Jer 17:7. The descriptions of the two kinds of people use six lines each, with the fourth line of the first description prematurely referring to the end of the heated person, whereas the end of the silent person is reserved for the sixth line.[13] Appropriately, fire consumes the wood that symbolizes the person who cannot govern his passions,[14] but the one in control of emotions resembles a productive tree in a garden.

In some ways, this Egyptian text is closer to Jer 17:5–8 than Psalm 1 is, for the latter contrasts a tree with ample water and chaff that is vulnerable to the slightest breeze. Moreover, Psalm 1 lacks the symmetry of expression in *'ašer yibṭaḥ baYHWH*, as well as *welô' yir'eh kî-yābô' ṭôb* and *welô' yirā' kî-yābô' ḥōm*. The psalm uses the adjective *'a*šrē to modify *hā'îš* and lacks an equivalent of *'ārrûr* while reversing the sequence by opening with the favorable type. Rather than focusing on the interior source of actions, Psalm 1 stresses the modes of conduct while one is walking, standing, and sitting. It further emphasizes the centrality of torah in the life of the favored person, who incidentally is like a tree planted by streams of water. This tree's leaves are green, like the one in Jer 17:8, but its fruit is only seasonal in contrast to Jer 17:8 where ceaseless productivity is implied (cf. Amos 9:13 and Ezek 47:12).[15] Psalm 1:4 introduces the wicked abruptly with "Not so" (*lô'-kēn*), reserving the equivalent of "accursed" to the closing verb, *tō'bēd*.[16]

The similarities between Jer 17:5–8 and Amenemope 6:1–12 become even more striking when one takes into consideration the immediate contexts of both. The unexpected aphorism in Jer 17:11 about unlawfully acquired wealth that leaves him in the midst of days resembles an observation in Amenemope 9:16 and 10:4–5.

If riches come to you by theft,
They will not stay the night with you...
They made themselves wings like geese
And flew away to the sky.

An Israelite sage's acquaintance with at least some sayings in the Instruction of Amenemope is undeniable,[17] as is the adaptation[18] of fowl to the new locale in Prov 23:5, "You look on it [wealth] and it is no more; it grows wings and flies heavenward, like an eagle."

The agrarian character of Israelite life makes the contrast between two types of tree like the ones in Jer 17:5–8 and Amenemope 6:1–12 persuasive moral instruction.[19] The image of a well-watered tree was a staple in diverse literary contexts.

> As for me, I am like a thriving olive tree in God's house;
> I always trust God's deeds of compassion. (Ps 52:10)
> The righteous bloom like a date palm,
> thrive like a cedar in Lebanon;
> planted in YHWH's house,
> they bloom in the courts of our God.
> Green and full of sap,
> They still produce fruit when old (Ps 92:13–15).
> Even wisdom was called a tree of life.
> A tree of life is she to those who grasp her,
> and whoever holds her fast is happy. (Prov 3:18)[20]

Elsewhere the mind is said to be the source of life and must therefore be purified of perverse talk issuing from it (*'iqqešût peh*, Prov 4:24). With that association of the mind and perversity we come to the aphorism in Jer 17:9.

A Corrupt Mind

We have seen that there was some difference of opinion over the attribution of the contrast between two types of people in Jer 17:5–8 to the deity. That uncertainty also applies to v 9, which seems to be presented as a popular adage expressing a low opinion of human nature like the sentiment attributed to YHWH in Gen 6:5 and 8:21. Here, too, we are dealing with a view that was widely held in the ancient Near East. Two texts are remarkably similar in that they assert universal perversity and add a rhetorical question about anyone's intellectual grasp of the unknown.

> Men are slow-witted and know nothing,
> No matter how many names they go by,
> what do they know?
> They do not know at all if they are doing good or evil.
>
> "To Any God" in B. Foster, *From Distant Days*, 270–71.[21]

> His word,
> a very brewing vat,
> is covered,
> who is to know
> the inside of it?
>
> "The Verdict of Enlil" in T. Jacobsen, *The Harps That Once*, 481.[22]

To these may be added the well-known saying in the Babylonian Theodicy.

> Enlil, king of the gods, who created teeming mankind,
> Majestic Ea, who pinched off their clay,

The queen who fashioned them, Mistress Mami,
Gave twisted words to the human race,
They endowed them in perpetuity with lies and falsehood.

B. Foster, *From Distant Days,* 323.

If one adopts the Septuagintal reading βαθεια (deep) for the Masoretic *'āqōb* (insidious),[23] a parallel exists in *Enuma elish* vii, 117–18.

GIBIL, who maintained the...
Profound of wisdom, ingenious in perception,
Whose heart is so deep that none of the gods
can comprehend it.

B. Foster, *From Distant Days,* 49.

Naturally, Qoh 7:24 comes to mind as a poignant biblical expression of intellectual impotency when confronted with ultimate mystery.

Far away and deep–whatever is;
deep, who can find it?[24]

The judgment expressed in Jer 17:9 is equally sweeping: the human mind, it claims, is the most devious thing of all, thoroughly sick as well. The result is that no one can fathom it.[25] The adjective *'ānuš* [26] connotes illness of an incurable nature, thoroughly devoid of comfort as in Ps 69:21. Those texts linking *'ānuš* with grievous blows and other afflictions indicate the brokenness of the mind (Isa 17:11; Jer 15:18; 17:9, 16; 30:12, 15; Mic 1:9; Job 34:6).

Like Deutero-Isaiah and Qoheleth, the author of Jer 17:9 prefers *lēb* to the longer form *lēbāb*, the favored word in Isaiah, Deuteronomy, and the Deuteronomistic history. Jeremiah does not seem troubled by anthropopathisms, for he mentions YHWH's heart eight times. The heart was widely thought to have controlled physical, psychological, and intellectual functions. As the seat of the will and deliberation, this bodily organ was believed to have been responsible for perception, recognition, and remembrance. It also enabled one to achieve insight, evaluate, and make critical judgments.[27] The author of Jer 17:9 openly dissents from this exalted view of the human intellect, pronouncing it utterly corrupt. The concluding rhetorical question, equivalent to *mî yôdēa'* elsewhere,[28] sharply denies that anyone can fathom its depths.

Does this negative judgment about the probative power of the intellect apply also to deities? The Nanshe Hymn suggests otherwise.

Nanshe sees into the nation's hearts
as were it into a split reed,
sees its designs and its rulers' secrets.

T. Jacobsen, *The Harps that Once,* 138.

The Divine Assayer

Although Jer 6:27 has YHWH appoint the prophet to act as assessor of the people, instructing him to examine and test their ways, in Jer 17:10 the deity takes on this task. Unlike the earlier charge, which states the depressing results of Jeremiah's probe, characterizing the people as "stubbornly defiant and debased, they all act corruptly," YHWH's assessment seems to serve a single purpose: to assure that everyone is treated according to the full measure of merit.

As the parallelism between *lēb* and *kelāyôt* suggests, this divine probe extends beyond the mind to the conscience, the inner core of affection and ego that gives expression to ideas which are then reflected on and given verbal expression. The kidneys, *kelāyôt*, indicate the most private, hidden being of a person, accessible only to YHWH. By contrast, a person of understanding was said to have been able to draw out the deep waters in the *lēb*, laying bare the very hidden ruminations (Prov 20:5).

The two participles governed by the divine subject and reinforced by the personal pronoun, *ḥōqēr* and *bōḥēn*, derive from the realm of metallurgy. The root *ḥqr* designates the digging into unknown terrain in search of valuable ore, while the root *bḥn* refers to the subsequent process of evaluating the ore by which impurities were separated out and removed.[29] The verb was ideally suited to express YHWH's critical assessment of humankind, hence its use with reference to the deity is more numerous than its application to tests carried out by people. Its use is primarily for determining personal qualities, but exceptions do occur, as in Zech 13:9 where the testing of gold is involved and where the parallel root *ṣrp* occurs (cf. Ps 17:3).

The formulaic use of confessional language involving the participle *bōḥēn* is widespread,[30] several times with *lēb* and *kelāyôt* as objects. In Jer 11:20 the beleagured prophet appeals to the "just judge who tests the conscience and mind" and asks to see divine retribution on his enemies. The language of Jer 20:12 differs initially but concludes in much the same way: "O YHWH of hosts, who tests the righteous, who sees the conscience and mind, let me see your retribution on them, for I have laid bare my case before you." Similarly, Ps 7:10 voices a desire to see right prevail because YHWH, a just God, tests mind and conscience. The Chronicler even has a humble David acknowledge that "you, Elohim, test the *lēbāb* and desire uprightness" (1 Chron 29:17). Like a confident David, a much maligned Job also believes in his own innocence even when placed under the divine microscope (Job 23:10; cf. 7:18). The author of Ps 139:23 openly invites heavenly scrutiny: "Search me (*ḥaqrēnî*), O God, and discern my mind, test me (*beḥānēnî*), O God, and discern my thoughts (*śarʿappāi*)."

Ill-gotten Riches

The sweeping claim that rewards are dispensed in strict proportion to one's behavior may be subject to challenge in one important area: economic prosperity. That seems to be the reasoning behind the popular saying and its moral in Jer 17:11. The person who accumulates wealth by fraudulent means is like a partridge in popular imagination, a bird that appropriates eggs belonging to another bird and hatches them as her own brood. In the words of the moralist, the young will soon abandon their false mother, and in the same way wealth unjustly acquired will eventually find a new home.[31]

The emphasis of this aphorism falls on stupidity rather than wickedness, as the final word "fool" makes unmistakable. The erroneous ideas about partridges open the door to the possibility that the moralist was also wrong about riches, at least by overlooking the fact that their possessor enjoyed them for an unspecified time. And do not all birds eventually leave the nest? Perhaps the temporal *be'aḥarîtô* actually alludes to the death of the wealthy individual, for one could not really pronounce another person blessed until the hour of death, according to Ben Sira (Sir 11:28). In this case, *bahaṣî yāmāw* may be distant in time from "the end" awaiting the fool.

Conclusion: Utopian or Not?

Thus far we have ignored the linguistic connections between Jer 17:5–11 and its immediate literary context. It is now time to consider these links to see whether or not they provide a valuable clue for interpretation. Verse 1 mentions an inscription on the tablet of the heart of the nation Judah, and v 13 returns to the notion of an inscription that signifies apostasy,[32] a forsaking of YHWH, the fountain of living water. This national abandoning of YHWH, signified by the verbs *'āzab* and *sûr* in v 13, involved worship at sacred groves (by verdant trees, *'al-'ēṣ ra'anān*). The dual sense of *miqweh* (hope and fountain)[33] in this verse may mean that the author has not lost sight of the importance of water in the broader setting, although the image of YHWH as a fountain is by no means restricted to this section of the book attributed to Jeremiah.

Let us assume, then, that Jer 17:5–8 may have something to do with idolatry in its widest sense. If we understand inauthentic worship as that adoration directed at any source other than YHWH, it follows that placing one's trust in creatures of flesh and blood constitutes apostasy. Thus when Judah's officials relied on human ingenuity and Egyptian military power they engaged in an act of idolatry, from the perspective of the biblical author. The destructive consequences of willful apostasy had long been spelled out for them: isolation, abandonment, and barrenness. How different was the destiny of those who put their hope in the fountain of life instead of resorting to feeble alliances, or so the text asserts. They bear fruit.

Precisely how one reads the contrast between the shrub's and the tree's response to opposing conditions, good and dearth,[34] makes a great deal of difference. If one reads the same verb *rā'â* in both instances it suggests that the shrub is unable to benefit from good while the tree cannot suffer from drought. The alternative reading in the second instance, *yirā'*, makes a less grandiose claim that the tree does not fear adversity. In other words, the tree is not completely shielded from hardship but has sufficient strength to withstand even a harsh climate.[35]

How does the aphorism about the incurable intellect fit into this line of thinking? From a biblical perspective, is not the pretense to possess knowledge of divine mystery another form of idolatry? If this is true, the saying may seek to squelch all claims relating to the capacity of the intellect as the ultimate arbiter of truth.[36] The aphorism recognizes the profundity of the mind while at the same time exposing its sickness, but even more importantly, it accentuates the hidden realm that can never be penetrated.[37]

Or can it? We come now to what is potentially the supreme idolatry, human speech that claims to derive from the deity. The views presented here as YHWH's embrace twin claims: (1) that YHWH is the judge of every action and (2) that the proper reward or punishment is handed out without fail. The first claim is not subject to validation, and the second is arguably the most dangerous lie every advanced in the cause of religion. Its inadequacy eventually forced a revision, the pushing of the moment of reward or punishment beyond history.[38]

Finally, for many people the ultimate object of attachment is money. That worship of mammon is so strong that they will do anything to possess wealth. This chasing after riches by hook or crook is the subject of the popular saying about a partridge's appropriation of eggs laid by another bird. Because the worship of YHWH demanded allegiance of the whole being, a choice between God and money was required. In the opinion of the author of the closing critique that is attached to the adage, whoever prefers riches to YHWH is a fool, a term that is applied to practical atheists in Pss 14:1 and 53:2.[39]

The entire unit, Jer 17:5–11, is therefore understandable as a many-faceted, albeit brief, treatise on idolatry, but it can also be viewed as whistling in the dark. The utopian picture of a well-ordered universe in which people who use their ingenuity to secure existence are doomed to atrophy and those who place their trust in a transcendent power only prosper is not borne out in real life. Precisely because the human intellect is perverse, claims like these cannot be trusted. That also goes for human assertions cloaked in the garment of deity, especially when their purpose is to strengthen a non-existent principle of justice by defending YHWH's all-seeing eye. Just as the popular knowledge of the habits of partridges was erroneous, the observation that wealth unjustly acquired does not long benefit its new owner is seldom accurate. The discrete units therefore present utopian understandings of reality in ancient Judah. The irony is that they also highlight the incurable intellect that constructs such fantasy.

CHAPTER 10

Qoheleth's Quantitative Language

It is a special privilege and pleasure to participate in this symposium that honors one who has contributed so much to the understanding of Qoheleth's language and thought. My acquaintance with Professor Schoors stretches back over a quarter of a century when he came to the States and to Vanderbilt University, where I was teaching at the time. On that occasion we talked at length about a mutual interest, Qoheleth. I am also glad to join others in this tribute who have shed light on many facets of Qoheleth's teachings, some of whom will have the burden of advancing research in the next generation. My modest contribution today looks at Qoheleth's quantitative language, beginning with the universalizing *hakkōl* and particles of existence [and non-existence], then examining specific numerical terms, as well as generalizing vocabulary for quantity. I then suggest a socio-historical explanation for this rich vocabulary as well as a theological one. Finally, I raise some methodological issues related to an increasingly popular literary interpretation of Qoheleth.

Everything. Nothing. And everything between these opposites. Qoheleth's discourse is rich in quantitative language, but does it offer a clue about the author's social location?[1] Why such interest in numbers by one who questions the very idea of profit in human existence? Previous interpreters have used Qoheleth's vocabulary to illuminate his economic background, with limited success.[2] Perhaps an examination of his quantitative language will throw additional light on his immediate environment.[3] The critical realist, turned skeptic,[4] claims to be comprehensive in his observations about things under the sun (*'et-hakkōl ra'îtî bîmê heblî*, 7:15),[5] but is that claim absolute or is it always qualified just as we say today, "*Now* I've seen everything"? If the former, it is patently false, regardless of whether we translate *heblî* by "brief" or "futile."[6] Context alone favors the second option, an expression of dismay over a specific injustice, signaling the bankruptcy of traditional belief in a just universe.[7] Given the honoree of this colloquium's interest in that subject as reflected in his article, "Theodicy in Qohelet,"[8] this assertion by Qoheleth seems to be an appropriate place to begin an investigation.

Hakkōl

The significance of *hakkōl* for situating Qoheleth's realm of discourse has long been recognized and has been the subject of special studies by Y. Amir and N. Lohfink.[9] Their opposing views illustrate the subjective nature of hermeneutics and the polyvalency of the biblical text. Amir emphasizes the similarities between the motto in 1:2 and 12:8, *habēl habālîm 'āmar qoheleth habēl habālîm hakkōl hābel*,[10] and the Greek concept of *tà pánta* or *tò pân*, especially the claim by the philosopher Monimus that everything that is assumed as existing is mist![11] Lohfink views Qoheleth's language as anthropological, even the motto, which he thinks actually anticipates the next verse and thus refers to all human possessions. In Lohfink's view, the representation of the cosmos by the four elements (earth, air, fire, and water) in 1:4–11 instead of the merism, heaven and earth, falls short of the Greek philosophical idea of the "all." In his commentary, Lohfink concedes that a final decision about the Greek influence on Qoheleth's use of *hakkōl* cannot be made, but he shrinks from the thought that Qoheleth may have rung the orchestral clang of cosmic pessimism.[12]

It is difficult to sustain the claim that every use of *hakkōl* by Qoheleth has a limited reference.[13] Some statements are comprehensive, particularly 1:14; 2:11, 17; and 3:19. Whereas the first three of these texts subsume all human activity under the umbrella of futility, the fourth embraces existence itself, an equation of humans and animals who share a single *miqreh*.[14] The ambiguity of the references to *hakkōl* is attested by the primary interpretations over the centuries: (1) everything that humans do lacks meaning; (2) all assertions are either illusion or false;[15] and (3) everything is transitory.

The conclusion of 9:1, *hakkōl lipnêhem hābel*, lacks any referent and supports a comprehensive interpretation of *hakkōl*. Qoheleth determines to explore the anomaly that good people, specifically the righteous and the wise, together with their deeds, are in the deity's control, but no one can discern the emotional state, presumably of the deity,[16] whether favorable or unfavorable. This leads Qoheleth to a radical conclusion: everything before them, or in the future, is futile. My reading of the text depends on the assumption that a scribal mistake has occurred, the omission of a *serif* that graphically distinguishes a *kaph* from a *beth*, and this error has led to the premature placing of the *soph pasuk* after *lipnêhem*.[17]

To be sure, not every instance of *hakkōl* refers to every living thing (3:20 [3x]; 6:6), even to the summation of teaching (12:13). Were one able to determine the precise scope of the *hakkōl* assertions, whether the abstract "universe" or concrete things belonging to a series, the point of emphasis in the motto would still need to be settled. Does Qoheleth suggest that *everything* is futile, or that everything is *futile*. Where does the emphasis fall, on the subject or on the predicate?

We can trace the beginning of such universal claims about Israel's deity to Deutero-Isaiah and to late additions to the book of Jeremiah.[18] According to Isa 44:24 Yahweh made everything, stretched out the heavens alone, and spread out the earth without assistance or accompaniment. Was this remark a response to speculation in Prov 8:22–31 about a feminine presence at the moment of creation?[19] Similarly, Jer 10:16 (=51:19) uses the expression with reference to Yahweh, *yôṣēr hakkōl hû'*.[20] Other texts are less sweeping when asserting Yahweh's sovereignty over everything, one that is said to have been shared with humans. In Ps 8:7–8 *kōl* is defined closely as creatures subject to human control, and in Ps 103:19 *kōl* includes heavenly beings and the totality of divine activity. The complete offerings being dedicated to the deity for the construction of the temple in Jerusalem are designated as *hakkōl* in 1 Chron 29:14, a use to which the absolute *kōl* has been put in several texts about sacrificial offerings.[21] Job's initial response to the deity in 42:2 ("I know that you can do everything...") concedes ultimate sovereignty without affirming the pertinent issue of justice. In Isa 45:7 *kōl- 'ēlleh* is anaphoric, looking back to the created opposites of light and darkness, weal and woe. That may also be true of Ps 119:91, with *hakkōl* referring back to the divine word and integrity, which are identified as servants. An absolute use of *hakkōl* here is also possible, along with the translation "the universe."[22]

Ben Sira's use of *hakkōl*[23] may have been inspired by biblical precedent, but the observation in 43:26b-28 has the ring of Stoic philosophy[24]: "...and by his word he works pleasure. More things like these we shall not add; the last word–he is the all *hakkōl* [or with Otto Kaiser, "Alles ist nur ER"]...for we cannot search [him] out." For this important claim, the Greek has *to pan estin autos*. To guard against the hint of pantheism,[25] the Latin translator wrote *ipse est in omnibus*, even though the Hebrew of verse 28 states that the deity is *gādôl mēkôl ma'áśāw*. The laconic *weqēṣ dābār* that introduces *hu' hakkōl* recalls a similar remark in the epilog of Ecclesiastes (*sôp dābār*, 12:13a). The choice of *sôp* here may be due to the occurrence of a synonym (*qēṣ*) in the previous colon, unless the Aramaic *sôpā'* had already come to indicate the conclusion of a literary unit or entire book.[26]

A related text in Sir 11:10–14 has less affinities with the Stoic concept of *tá pàntá* than with Qoheleth's teaching.

> My son, if you do not run you will not attain,
> And if you do not seek you will not find.
> There is a worker. He toils, hurries, and is thus deprived.
> There is a sluggard. He moves miserably, lacks everything,
> Yet he has an advantage in that Yahweh's eyes look favorably on him;
> He shakes stinking dust from him, lifts his head,
> And exalts him so that many are amazed at him.
> Good and evil, life and death, poverty and wealth:
> They are from Yahweh.[27]

The Greek text of verse 10 is much closer to Qoheleth's observations about the uncertainties of running a race or searching for something (Eccl 9:11), for it does not promise success in either instance; indeed it asserts the opposite. Regardless of whether we follow the Hebrew or Greek here, Ben Sira recognizes the powerful role of chance in human lives, for all efforts can be overridden by the deity. At the same time, Ben Sira acknowledges that the reigning opposites encountered daily are somehow harmoniously bound up by the creator, a point he makes in the context of theodicy in another hymnic text (39:12–35).[28] The similarity between this argument for the ultimate justice of the cosmos based on opposites and Greek philosophical theodicy has occasioned considerable discussion.[29] I have explored the various biblical theodicies in *Defending God: Biblical Responses to the Problem of Evil.*[30]

In this regard we may also consider Ben Sira's epithets for the deity.[31] Most telling is "Yahweh, God of all" in 36:1, to which we may compare "Elyon, king of all" in 50:15, which in Greek is rendered "*hupsisto pambasilei*." The expression in 51:12, "the one who fashions all things," seems to echo Jer 10:16 (=51:19). Ben Sira's openness to Hellenistic ideas and practices has been widely documented, beginning with pride of authorship, and extending to the endorsement of the medical profession, participation in Greek-style banquets, use of a debate formula, "Do not say," acceptance of "friendship ideology," and more.[32] For someone so immersed in Hellenism even though committed to upholding traditional Hebraic values, the use of an expression like "He is the all" seems almost natural. Can one posit the same openness for Qoheleth?

On Lohfink's reading of Qoheleth, *hakkōl* is restricted to the product of human activity, a view formulated by Gregory Thaumaturgus. My own understanding of 3:11 and 11:8 leads to a different conclusion,[33] for the divine order of reality is said to be flawed at the very center, at least insofar as intellectual pursuits are concerned, and the consequent futility extends to Sheol and its inhabitants. Moreover, the obscure second colon of 3:15, *wehā'elōhîm yebaqqēš 'et nirdāp*, may mean that Qoheleth believed that the deity was also caught up in futile activity, a searching for what has already unfolded. It seems, therefore, that Qoheleth has made an epistemological claim[34] resembling that of the Cynic Monimus. If everything is *hebel*, as maintained in 1:2 and 12:8, that includes the seven so-called positive exhortations to enjoy life. Ironically, just as relativists belie their denial of absolutes by asserting one themselves, and Monimus becomes entangled in a web of illusion,[35] so Qoheleth's *hakkōl* sweeps everything into a common dustpan.

Qoheleth was not alone in discerning a flawed universe despite assertions in the priestly creation narrative that from the perspective of the creator, at least, everything was exceptionally good. A hidden flaw,[36] however, eventuated in a bold fantasy, the eradication of the existing universe as a way of emphasizing the eternality of Yahweh's redemptive acts (Isa 51:6). Trito-Isaiah's imagination stretches even further to include an imminent new heaven and earth that will erase the memory of former things (Isa 65:17). Qoheleth may have registered a decisive "no" to the latter utopianism while subscribing to the apocalyptic notion that the created order was enslaved to evil. The mere claim that something new exists has no validity, he insists (1:9b-10), precisely because human memories are of brief duration. Life's brevity (*hebel*) becomes almost a topos in the Psalter (39:6–7, 12b; 62:10; 144:4), and the association of *hebel* and *kāzāb* recalls Monimus' emphasis on illusion. Not only are human beings *hebel;* according to Ps 94:11, their thoughts are also, and possibly even the reasoning process itself (cf. Jer 17:9, *'āqōb hallēb mikkōl we'ānuš hu' mî yēdā'ennû*).[37]

How, then, does Qoheleth use *hakkōl*? Its ambiguity and openness serve beautifully to illustrate life's futility, for even human knowledge is cloaked in ambiguity. If Qoheleth does not declare the deity to be *hakkōl* in the way Ben Sira does, he certainly inches close to such a statement. In doing so, he appears to have succumbed to epistemological pessimism. Given the positioning of the motto[38] and the totalizing claims of 1:14; 2:11, 17:3:19; and 9:1, it is difficult to read Qoheleth in any other way. Furthermore, a deity who stacks the cards against the intellect in a well-ordered universe (3:11)[39] and who causes everything (11:5)[40] but conceals all feeling toward humankind (9:1) is surely caught up in the web of *hebel*, random gifts notwithstanding.[41] Whatever nectar Qoheleth sipped was that of a dying man desperately clinging to life's fragile vine while suspended over an abyss.

yēš (and 'en)

The particle of existence, *yēš*, appears sixteen times in Ecclesiastes, eleven and one-half per cent of its total uses in the Bible. That number compares with six in Proverbs and twelve in the book of Job. These thirty-four instances of the particle in wisdom literature comprise nearly one fourth of its biblical use, not surprising because *yēš* often expresses an existential paradox that is naturally at home in texts with a "philosophical" bent. It forces one to pause momentarily to reflect on an extraordinary reality, e.g. "There are friends who feign friendship, but there is an intimate who clings closer than a brother" (Prov 18:24) and "For there is hope for a tree; if cut down it will sprout again...but a man dies and is laid low, expires and where is he? (Job 14:7, 10).[42]

Qoheleth's use of *yēš* has been treated by Antoon Schoors[43] and needs little amplification from me. I shall therefore only venture a few remarks concerning the positioning of the particle. It occupies five different locations in sentences: (1) an introductory particle; (2) a particle preceded by emphatic *kî*; (3) mid-sentence; (4) following an introductory statement; and (5) with an attached prefix and following a verb with a pronominal subject.

Six times *yēš* initiates an observation and is pleonastic in English translation (1:10; 4:8; 5:12; 6:1; 8:14; and 10:5).

1. "Something of which it is said: See this; it's new" (1:10).
2. "One person and no second; he has neither son nor brother, yet his work never ends..." (4:8).
3. "A serious injustice I have seen under the sun: wealth kept for its owner unto misfortune..." (5:12).
4. "An evil I have seen under the sun and it is serious for one...[acquired wealth cannot be enjoyed by its owner] (6:1).
5. "An absurdity committed in the land: righteous treated as guilty and wicked treated as righteous..." (8:14).

6. "An evil I have seen under the sun as a mistake issuing from the ruler's presence: folly is often exalted but the rich are humbled…" (10:5).

Although *yēš* in itself is often emphatic, in three instances Qoheleth enhances its force with an emphatic *kî*.

1. "Truly, there is a person whose toil is intelligent, informed, and successful but he must give his portion to one who did not work at it; this, too, is absurd and a grievous wrong" (2:21).
2. "In truth, there are many words and much futility; what gain does one have?" (6:11).
3. "Surely, there is a time and custom for everything, although a person's evil is strong on him" (8:6).

Qoheleth seems to have reserved mid-sentence for a positive nuance of the particle.

1. "Two are better than one in that they have (*yēš*) a good reward from their work" (4:9).
2. "For the one linked with all the living *there is* hope; surely a living dog is better than a dead lion" (9:4).
3. "I have observed that *there is* an advantage to wisdom over folly like the advantage of light over darkness" (2:13).

The third example has the relative particle attached to *yēš*. The sole negative sentiment expressed by *yēš* in mid-sentence following an introductory statement is tantamount to the pleonastic use discussed above. It reads: "I have seen everything in my short life: an innocent perishing in innocence and a guilty person living long in guilt" (7:15). As for the intent of the gnomic saying about a live dog's superiority over a dead lion, I remain convinced that a sociological explanation[44] best explains its original use: a reply by a former widow who from necessity married a person of inferior social status to her previous husband.

The difference between Qoheleth's use of *yēš* and that of the author of the book of Job is striking. Five times there *yēš* is preceded by the interrogative (Job 5:1; 6:6, 30; 25:3; 38:28) and another three examples occur after a particle implying the unlikelihood of something, *lû* in one instance, (Job 16:4) *'im* in two others (Job 33:23, 32). On one occasion a negative *lô'* precedes *yēš*, although this form is textually uncertain, LXX and Syriac implying *lû* (Job 9:33).[45]

The negative particle *'en*, also treated magisterially by Schoors,[46] occurs 44 times in Ecclesiastes, approximately 5.3% of its uses in the Bible. The absolute use of *'ayin* in 3:9 is unique: "…and humans have no advantage over beasts." In four instances *'ēn* introduces a statement.

1:11 There is no remembrance…
2:24 There is nothing good in a person except that he eat…
4:16 There is no end to all the people…
8:8 There is no one who can control the spirit…

A *kî* precedes the particle nine times, *'ašer* twice.

2:16 For there is no remembrance...
3:12 I know that there is nothing good in them except...
3:22 I have seen that there is nothing good in them except...
4:17 ...For they do not know that they are doing wrong.
5:3 ...For there is no pleasure in fools...
7:20 Surely there is no righteous person on earth...
8:7 For you do not know what will be...
9:10 ...For there is no activity and reason, no knowledge and wisdom...
11:6 ...For you do not know...[47]
8:11 Because a sentence is not executed, evil deeds accelerate...
11:5 Just as you do not know...

Most often, the negative particle follows an initial observation.

1:7 ...but the sea is not full...
1:9 ...and there is nothing new under the sun.
2:11 ...and there is no profit under the sun.
3:14 ...unto it there is no adding, from it no subtracting...
4:1 ...and there was none to comfort them...and none to comfort them.
4:10 ...and there is no second (person) to raise him up.
5:11 ...the satiety of the rich will not let them sleep.
5:13 ...and there was nothing of anything that he desires...
6:2 ...and he lacks nothing of anything that he desires...
8:13 ...because he does not fear
8:16 ...they don't see sleep with their eyes.
9:1 ...whether love or hate, no one knows...
9:2 ...and to those who do not sacrifice...
9:5 ...and the dead know nothing nor is there a reward for them any longer.
8:15 ...that there is nothing good for a person under the sun but...
4:8 ...and no second, he has no son or brother, and there is no end...
9:6 ...and they no longer have a portion in all that is done under the sun.
9:16 ...and his words were not heard.
10:11 ...then there is no advantage to the charmer.
12:1 ...I have no pleasure in them.
12:12 ...of making many books there is no end...

As these examples show, Qoheleth frequently uses *'ēn* in cognitive contexts and in circumstances relating to feeling and experience, attaching pronominal suffixes to the particle when it is followed by a participle (1:7; 4:17; 5:11; 6:2; 8:7, 13, 16; 9:2, 5, 16; 11:5–6). The scope and substance of the negated objects give the book of Ecclesiastes a decidedly negative tone, one that lingers long after Qoheleth's summons to seize the moment has been heeded.

Specific Numbers

Qoheleth mentions the following numbers: one, two, three, seven, eight, a hundred, and a thousand. Of these, *'eḥād* occurs by far the most often (18 times). Its adjectival force, best translated by "a single," refers to *miqreh*, *rûaḥ*, *māqôm*, *'ādām*, *hôṭe'* and *rō'eh*. Used alone *'eḥād* means "one" as opposed to two or several. In 11:6 the meaning of *ke'eḥād* is best captured by the word "alike." The special case of a feminine form *'aḥat* in 7:27, used additively, probably derives from accounting. Peter Machinist understands *ḥešbôn* differently.[48] He thinks it represents second order thinking, that is, reflecting about the process of thinking itself. Besides *ḥešbôn*, he appeals to the way Qoheleth uses *miqreh*, *ma'aśeh*, and *'ōlām* as a more explicit conceptualization and abstraction than earlier notions of fate.

The seemingly redundant *'eḥād* that modifies *rō'eh* in 12:11 may betray the influence of Ezek 37:24.

> My servant David will be king over them, and a single shepherd (rō'eh *'eḥād*) will be
> for all of them. They will walk in my statutes and observe my ordinances.

This peculiar use of *ke 'eḥād* belongs to a late phase of biblical Hebrew.[49] According to the utopian description in Isa 65:25,

> A wolf and a lamb will feed as one, a lion will eat
> straw like an ox, and dust will be a serpent's food;
> they will do no evil nor destroy on the entirety of
> my sacred mountain. Yahweh has spoken.

Here the verb *rā'â*, the nominal form of which is shepherd (*rō'eh*), occurs alongside *ke 'eḥād*, and an aural pun with *yārē'û* follows. In 2 Chron 5:13 *ke 'eḥād* indicates musicians' playing in unison with singers, just as Ezr 2:64, 3:9, and 6:20 use this word for togetherness. Similarly, Neh 7:66 refers to a unified community, *kol-haqqāl ke'eḥād.*

The interplay of the numbers one, two, and three marks an intriguing section of Ecclesiastes in which Qoheleth makes a strong case for companionship. Introduced by one of his typical assessments of absurd realities, "Then turning I observed absurdity under the sun" (4:7), the unit contrasts the disadvantages of solitary existence with the benefits of having an associate (4:8–12). Qoheleth's own ego inserts itself into this anecdote, a phenomenon studied by P. Höffken.[50] By this means Qoheleth personalizes the narrative for added poignancy: "And for whom am I toiling and depriving myself of good?" (4:8b). A person who has no heirs and who possesses an insatiable appetite for wealth is engaged in a futile enterprise, a ceaseless Sisyphian rolling of the rock up a steep hill (4:8). This observation leads Qoheleth to defend basic collegiality, but his defense is purely self-oriented, far short of an altruistic ethic.[51] It pays to have an associate who can offer assistance in times of trouble, and from the warmth of whose body one can stave off the cold of night (4:9–12a). To clinch the point, Qoheleth cites a proverb that is also known from the Gilgamesh Epic: "A threefold cord is not quickly snapped" (4:12b).[52] The alternation of *'eḥād* and *šenî*, (2x) and *šenayîm* (3x), broken by a substitute for the latter, *ḥabērô*, his companion, in

4:10, ceases when the number three, *ḥamšullās*, raises the ante, albeit on the level of things (4:12).

The next number of Qoheleth's repertoire is joined in the numerical sequence, seven/eight (11:2) and has a distributive meaning indicating multiplicity, as in its only other biblical use (Mic 5:4). Like many biblical and extra-biblical numerical sequences, this one appears to function figuratively (cf. Amos 1:3, 6, 9, 11, 13; 2:1, 4, 6). This understanding of numerical gradations[53] was enhanced by those instances where the final number bore the weight of the observation (cf. Prov 30:18–20, 21–23, 29–31; Sir 50:25–26), the others existing mostly as ballast.

Qoheleth uses the number ten in a similar manner to the sequence seven/eight, that is, with reference to an unspecified number of people. He observes that wisdom strengthens a wise person more than ten officials in a city (7:19). The reference is to the Ptolemaic governmental policy of appointing a host of underlings to share responsibility for maintaining order and assuring that a steady flow of revenue reaches the central office. Qoheleth's attitude toward this type of provincial supervision approaches laissez faire politics, a refusal to be surprised at incidents of injustice under such a multi-tiered surveillance (5:7).[54] In this context, it may be possible to interpret *melek leśādeh ne'ebād* in 5:8 figuratively, implying that the ruler's local officials work the populace successfully by extracting huge tax revenues while simultaneously keeping a semblance of order in society.

The numerals *mē'â* and *'elep* occur twice each in Ecclesiastes 6:3 and 8:1 [textually uncertain] for the former, 6:6 and 7:28 for the latter. Both references to a hundred are intended as exaggeration: fathering a hundred sons (6:3), committing as many sins but going unpunished for a long time (8:12). When reflecting on an extended life span, Qoheleth increases the count ten-fold to *'elep* and then doubles that number with a modifier, *pa'amayîm* (6:6). Without experiencing *ṭôbâ*, even a life that stretches two thousand years is *hebel*, given the fact that everyone goes to a single place. The other use of *'elep* belongs to a set phrase within the Bible and in ancient Egypt, although the exact sense of "one in a thousand" is not clear. Does it simply suggest one among many in the way *e pluribus unum* functions in coinage within the United States? Qoheleth claims to have found, or not to have found, a single man in a thousand but not a woman (7:28), but he fails to give the operative predicate adjective that women, in his view, do not possess.

Another way of reading this difficult text is to connect 7:28a with the previous verse, yielding the following: "Look, I have found this, says Qoheleth, one to one to find the sum, which I continued to seek but never found." The second colon in 7:28 then becomes a gnomic saying that barely elevates man over woman, a view that Qoheleth disavows in 7:29 ("Only see this [is what] I found that God made humans straight but they have sought many sums").[55]

The author of the book of Job knows the above idiom: "Truly I know that it is so. Who can be innocent–a man before God? If one wishes to contend with him, he could not answer one in a thousand (Job 9:2–3). Presumably, Job means that humans cannot answer any of the many legitimate charges the deity can lay on them. Ben Sira also uses this phrase when counseling others to be especially careful in selecting persons with whom to consult (Sir 6:6) and when challenging the traditional concept that numerous children, "a quiver full of arrows" in his terminology, are a sign of divine favor (Sir 16:3, uncertain text; cf. also 39:11, and 41:12 where the variant, "greater than a thousand" occurs).[56]

Non-Specific Quantitative Words

Two non-specific terms for quantity in Qoheleth's teachings are *me'aṭ* and *harbēh* (or the variant *rōb*), few and many. The two words are juxtaposed in 5:11 with reference to the amount of food an unnamed person customarily eats. In an anecdote about a small village with few inhabitants (*me'aṭ*) Qoheleth mentions the presence of a wise man capable of thwarting the intentions of a powerful invader (9:14–15).[57] A verbal form *mi'ēṭû*, indicates the scarcity of teeth in old age or the paucity of workers grinding grain (12:3), and the plural *me'aṭṭîm* occurs in connection with a warning against loquacity in a sacred precinct (5:1). Its opposite, *rōb*, refers to wisdom (1:18), anxiety and chatter (5:2), dreams (5:6), years (6:3, 2x, once in the plural), times (7:22), contrivancies (7:29), and days (11:1). The referents for *harbeh* are equally diverse: wisdom and knowledge (1:16), possessions (2:7), vexation (5:16), words (5:6, 6:11), righteousness (7:17), years (11:8), sayings (12:9), books (12:12), and study (12:12). This adjective also occurs with the verb *yizkōr* (5:19).

Qoheleth employs another word, *mispar*, when alluding to unknown life spans (2:3; 5:17; 6:12). In all three instances *mispar* appears in a set phrase, *mispar yemê ḥayye* (+ pronominal suffixes in 2:3 and 5:17). Portion, *ḥeleq*, designates for Qoheleth the individual's share of pleasure granted by the deity (2:10; 3:22; 5:17–18; 9:9) and the amount of one's possessions that can under certain circumstances be passed on to someone who has not earned them (2:21). It also indicates the part one plays in the game of life (9:6), as well as disposable property that can be shared with others (11:2). This word contrasts with *ḥešbôn* in 7:25 and 27 and *ḥiššebōnôt* in 7:29. The first two references are to something that can be explored, searched out, and found as well as to the evaluative process of the intellect itself. The third instance, a plural form of an unattested ḥišš*abôn*, has negative connotations, as if the product of devious thinking, thus machinations or devices. The move to implements of war follows this route (2 Chron 26:15). Ben Sira's use of *ḥešbôn* in 42:3 emphasizes accurate recording of expenses: ["Do not be ashamed]...of an account with a companion or traveling partner or of apportioning an inheritance." The juxtaposition of language about keeping an accurate ledger and dividing one's possessions[58] with pious advice shows just how important Ben Sira considered *ḥešbôn*. He writes: "Do not be ashamed of Elyon's torah or statute, or of clearing the innocent of evil" (42:2).[59]

In 3:14 Qoheleth uses verbal opposites, to add and to subtract, in an avowedly theological context. He writes: "I know that everything that the deity brings into being will be forever; no one can add to it or subtract from it, and the deity has acted so that they will be afraid in his presence."[60] Similarly, Qoheleth cites a proverbial saying in 1:15 that "The twisted cannot be straightened; the missing cannot be counted" as confirmation that every activity under the sun is *hebel* and *re'ut rûaḥ*.

Other quantitative terms are scattered throughout the book. These include the opposites full/satiety and empty/lacking/naked, the concept of collecting and gathering, the notion of reward, the dual "handfuls," the ordinals first to last, as well as beginning to end, and the comparative "more than." Several instances of *yitrôn*, *yôtēr*, and *môter* indicate a surplus or lack of one.[61]

Conclusion

What can modern interpreters make of Qoheleth's rich quantitative language? Perhaps it means no more than that he was fond of enumeration, but to a greater extent than the authors of Proverbs and Job. One may hazard the guess, however, that his vocabulary implies new directions in professional activity, the daily immersion in the recording of business transactions of entreprenurial clients. One thinks of the copious documentation of business expenditures by the Ptolemaic governmental official Zenon,[62] and lesser officials in Yehud may have been required to keep similar records. Ben Sira's inclusion of careful record-keeping as something important enough to be mentioned along with observance of torah is instructive. If scribes actually kept tallies of expenses and profits for their affluent clients, Qoheleth's use of *'aḥat le'aḥat limṣô' ḥešbôn* may reflect the sort of thinking required of the wise in the pursuit of their duties.[63]

Can we draw any theological conclusions from Qoheleth's fondness for quantitative language? Perhaps not, but it may reflect an abandonment of the qualitative in life resulting from resigned subjectivism characterized by a pessimistic theory of knowledge. If we are correct in assuming that the early sages by and large heeded the priestly admonition to master the good creation[64] and understood their task as coping with reality by means of the intellect, we may surmise that such instrumentalism was no longer in force for Qoheleth.[65] In his view, the flaw was divinely imposed, a guarded secret made unattainable by an arbitrary deity.[66] Nevertheless, Qoheleth refused to give up on wisdom, which he thought had relative advantage over folly. His quantitative language served the purpose of assessing relative worth. Interestingly, he did not venture in the direction of reflective myth-making of the kind recently examined by M. Fishbane,[67] or even of the sort that brought the creator into closer relationship with humankind by a personified feminine presence (Prov 8:22–31; Sir 24).[68] Nor did he choose the path of sages who viewed the limits of the intellect as an opportunity to burst forth in hymnic praise, the personal choice of Ben Sira. Instead, Qoheleth took the world as it was, tallying up its plusses and minuses.

Curiously, he did not recommend the restricting of intellectual pursuits the way the author of Psalm 131 eschewed questions that pushed the limits of the knowable, nor did he warn against investigating things beyond the power of the intellect the way Ben Sira did (Sir 3:21–24). Very much aware of divine mystery, Qoheleth probed the limits of knowledge even when conceding that much was *'ēn mispar*, beyond comprehending.[69] Qoheleth's theory of knowledge was akin to the view expressed by Ezra in Second Esdras,[70] namely that possession of an intellect demands that it be used to the limit by asking hard questions about life's inequities, even when angels discourage such probing and when no answers are forthcoming.[71]

Do the conclusions of this paper throw any light on the literary analysis of the book, a growing interest in recent publications?[72] As one who greatly appreciates literary approaches to texts, I would like to answer my question in the affirmative, but I am not sure such a response is justified. Instead, I wish to conclude by raising some questions that have become unsettling as a result of the application of literary theory to Qoheleth's teachings.

1. Can one sustain the assumption of many that Qoheleth becomes more positive as the book progresses, early comments being less significant than later?
2. Is it appropriate to normalize anomalies within a book that, after all, is unique in Hebrew literature?
3. Given Qoheleth's controversial teachings, plus the analogy with editorial practice in other books of the canon, isn't it likely that his radical views were subjected to corrective glossing?
4. Are Postmodernists correct that the author may no longer be assumed as a factor in interpretation?
5. Is internal consistency a modern concept and therefore anachronistic with respect to Qoheleth's teachings?
6. Do the religious views of interpreters have a legitimate place in exegesis?
7. To what literary camp does Qoheleth belong: poet? philosopher? theologian?

Because an interpreter's assumptions about these issues shape conclusions, my final response is by necessity modest.

What has this study of Qoheleth's quantitative language demonstrated? That his world remains obscure, despite the many monographs devoted to Ecclesiastes in recent decades. Perhaps the best we can do is add one to one to find the *ḥešbôn*, only in the end to concede the following: *'ašer 'ōd biqešâ napšî welō' māṣātî*, the crucial word being *'ōd*. Even if we accept Qoheleth's judgment that *hakkōl* is *hebel*, we cannot be neutral to the intellectual tease: *'et-hakkōl 'āśâ yāpeh be'ittô*.

CHAPTER 11

Beginnings, Endings, and Life's Necessities in Biblical Wisdom

Biblical sages devoted an inordinate amount of time observing the mundane activities taking place around them and trying to put their acquired knowledge to optimal use. Even ants were not too tiny to convey significant insights about human productivity, nor drunkards too ludicrous to offer negative examples of behavior. The cyclical events of the seasons and the changing patterns of the weather revealed valuable truths about the workings of a universe believed to be governed by its maker. The sages' task involved the mental processing of information about reality[1] and its analogical application to conduct.[2] They did not always limit their gaze to the ordinary, however, for they occasionally cast their eyes toward the mystery of human origins and final destiny, together with the necessities for life itself.

The Origin of Life

Your hands fashioned and made me
　　but now you devour me altogether.
Remember that you made me like clay,
　　and will return me to dust.
Did you not pour me out like milk,
　　congeal me like cheese?
You clothed me with skin and flesh,
　　wove me with bones and sinews.
With life and kindness you endowed me;
　　and your solicitude watched over my spirit (Job 10:8–12).[3]

This reflection about Job's birth is embedded in his third speech. In it he descends from hymnic praise (9:5–10) to outright accusation of calumny on the deity's part (9:22–24) and imagines that a neutral figure (*môkîaḥ*) would set things right (9:33). Then Job sinks into troubled thoughts about himself as "the work of God's hands" (10:3–22), now despised. The language of crafting underscores the tyranny in the deity's treatment of a lovingly-formed object, particularly in light of one of three explanations for idolatry put forth by the author of Wisdom of Solomon.[4] In his view, a craftsman took such pride in what he shaped with his hands that it was set aside for reverential awe (Wis Sol 14:18–20).

It seems to Job that the deity's intimate knowledge of him serves a malicious purpose, enabling the hunter to kill his prey. Having destroyed the moral order, the arbiter of justice orchestrates uncontrolled violence against an innocent victim who must plead for mercy, an intolerable perversion of justice. The language of parody predominates here, with Job mocking the traditional notion that divine intimacy implies providential care. Such thoughts do not stop short of imagining the reversal of the original creative act, a return to primordial chaos like that envisioned by Jeremiah (4:23–26). The language of paradox occurs as well, for Job ponders an eerie world in which darkness shines. Such a world would seem to encourage a longing for death, as in Job's initial lament in chapter 3, but the forensic metaphor that Job now embraces drives out such thoughts and equips him with an unprecedented boldness that demands a fair trial.

The extraordinary picture of personal origin in 10:8–12 returns to the theme enunciated in 10:3, humankind as the work of divine hands. The language suggests toil, thereby throwing in relief the contrast between fashioning and destroying in 10:8. The two verbs connoting Job's origin (*'ṣb* and *'śh*)[5] are matched by a single verb signifying destruction (*bl'*). With feigned deference, Job implores God to remember that his own beginning echoes the first fashioning of humankind, with the deity's subsequent pronouncement of destiny: "You are dust, and to dust you will return." The potter's exceptional contribution to daily existence and the relationship between potter and clay provided a natural image for the mystery of birth. It did not convey the sensual aspects related to conception, however; for this idea, Job alludes to the result of ejaculation, the pouring out of the substance of life like milk and its mixture with an "unknown" in the womb (10:10). For this coming together of life's ingredients, he uses the familiar concept of congealing cheese (cf. Wis Sol 7:2, the mixing of semen with the woman's bodily fluid).[6] Reaching into another realm of daily life, Job likens the development of the fetus within the mother's womb to the act of weaving. He is clothed with skin and flesh, while bones and sinews are woven together (*skk*) like an intricate garment (10:11).[7] This tender care was extended (Job does not say how long) in order to preserve breath by solicitous care (*ḥayyîm* and *ḥesed*). The irony could hardly be greater. The loving care expended on knitting together the skeletal structure has been replaced by uncontrolled aggression aimed at destroying Job.

The similarities between Job 10:8–12 and Ps 139:13–18 have long been recognized, in general content if not in tone.

> Indeed,[8] you created my conscience,[9]
> fashioned[10] me in my mother's womb.

I praise you, for I am awesomely and wondrously made.
Wonderful are your works,
    which I know well.
My body was not hidden from you,
    when I was fashioned secretly,
    woven together in earth's recesses.
Your eyes beheld my unformed substance;[11]
    all of its parts were recorded in your book.[12]
In time they were formed,
    and not one of them [had existed].
How precious to me are your thoughts, God,
    their number, how great.
I count them–more than the sand;
    I stop–I am still with you (Ps 139:13–18).

The poem that has this acknowledgement of the awesome product of divine creativity begins with praise (vv 1–6) and ends with supplication (vv 23–24). It also contains a puzzling query about escaping from such complete divine surveillance (vv 7–12) and a cry for the extirpation of personal enemies, whom the psalmist considers enemies of the deity too (vv 19–22). This combination of themes is difficult to categorize beyond meditative reflection in the guise of a legal plea for divine judgment.

The initial section, marked by the language of intimacy, an "I" addressing a divine "You," explores the extent of Yahweh's knowledge of the psalmist. Traditional language indicates intellectual probing that exposes the inner being of the poet, whose every act and thought are fully known. Even the words that express this marvel are known before their articulation, the psalmist insists. Does such divine searching of every thought and deed limit human freedom and become oppressive in the long run?[13] Verse 5 seems to suggest a certain feeling of unease when asserting that the deity hedges the psalmist in "front and back," laying a hand on him. Is the touch a consoling one, like that alluded to in Ps 73:23 ("But I am always with you; you hold my right hand"),[14] or an intrusive invasion of privacy? The next verse may support either interpretation: (1) the mystery is wonderful, like the deity to whom the epithet "worker of wonders" is applied *or* (2) such awesome knowledge is more than the psalmist can endure (*lō' 'ûkal lâ*).[15]

The question that introduces the next section appears to support the second interpretation, for why would a contented worshipper ponder the possibility of fleeing from divine presence? Neither height nor depth offers any respite. The same is true for east and west, except that on this journey with the wings of dawn to the western horizon Yahweh's guiding hand holds the psalmist securely. Here the language echoes the consolation celebrated in Ps 73:23. That comforting thought quickly vanishes, to be replaced by words about hiding under cover of darkness, a familiar idea that is usually associated with practical atheists in the Psalter.[16] Unfortunately for one who is inclined to use darkness as a shield from divine observation, day and night are alike to Yahweh, or so the psalmist thinks.

The psalmist's imagination falls short of the hypothetical comments that Amos attributes to Yahweh (Amos 9:2–4). In this prophetic text sinners hoping to escape divine punishment are said to be engaged in a futile exercise, despite their flight to Sheol or heavens, to the remote Carmel or further west into the sea, or to far away exile. Even were they able to hide in the depths of the sea, Yahweh exclaims, a serpent awaits the divine command. Similarly, a sword is prepared to do the deity's will in exile. The oracle of doom sounds the death knell: "My eye is fixed on them for harm, not good."[17]

The psalmist's thoughts about his origin oscillate between self-praise and exaltation of the deity, who is called El here in contrast to Yahweh in verses 1, 4, and 21. A hint of hubris has been detected in the language of ascent into heaven,[18] an honor previously reserved for exceptional people like Enoch[19] and Elijah and later extended more broadly to the faithful in Pss 49:16 and 73:24. In apocalyptic texts[20] certain chosen ones are taken on a journey into heaven but make the return trip carrying with them special knowledge about the mysteries of the world–(contrast, however, Prov 30:4).[21]

Verse 13 opens with an emphatic *kî* (indeed), although it is possible to understand the particle as a justification for the previous statement that Yahweh's vision penetrates darkness ("*For* you created my kidneys"). When *kilyōtāy* is combined with *lēb*, the two nouns indicate the emotions and intellect respectively.[22] The personal pronoun *'attâ* gives added specification to the verb *qānîtā*, in which one hears an echo of Deut 32:6b ("Is he not your father who created you [*qānekā*]; he formed [*'āśekā*] and established you?"). The psalmist's choice of the verb *tesukkēnî* to convey the interweaving of bodily parts in the mother's womb suggests loving attention and consummate skill. The proper response to such creative activity finds expression in a single word, *'ôdekā* ("I praise you"). The reason: "for I am wondrously made–awesome." The doubling up of words that are frequently reserved for the deity's *ṣidqôt* and their awe-inspiring effect reinforces the exalted assessment of a mere mortal and rivals the praise in Psalm 8. The psalmist dares to include himself in El's *ma'aśôt*, of which he claims intimate knowledge (*wenapšî yōda'at me'ōd*). Returning to the notion of concealment, he asserts that El was equally familiar with the fetus when fashioning it in secret, weaving together its separate parts in earth's depths.

This allusion to the myth of mother earth leads naturally to traditional lore about divine scribal activity, a fixing of the destiny of all creatures, which then evokes the revered story about the divine promise of progeny to Abraham in Genesis 15. It seems that by alluding to Abraham and Moses the poet wishes to situate his own extraordinary origin within Israel's sacred history. Such thoughts about divine priorities (*rā'šêhem*) are believed to be as precious as they are innumerable. The psalmist imagines that in the act of counting he runs out of numbers. One thing is constant, however; he does not believe that he has reached the end of divine immediacy.[23]

> "Just as you can not know the manner of the wind–like bones in the womb of a pregnant woman–so you can not know the deity's work who makes everything" (Eccl 11:5).

Although many interpreters emend the text to read "in the bones" and understand the reference to be the entering of the life breath into the fetus, there is no need to alter the preserved text. Qoheleth observes that our inability to understand how the wind causes movement in the branches of a tree is exactly like our ignorance about the power that enables a fetus to move about inside the womb. Equally obscure, he remarks, is the deity's activity, although everything is the direct result of a divine act.[24]

> I do not know how you came into being in my womb.It was not I who gave you life and breath, nor I who set in order the elements within each of you. Therefore the Creator of the world, who shaped the beginnings of man and devised the origin of all things, will in his mercy give life and breath back to you again, since you now forget yourselves for the sake of his laws (2 Macc 7:20–23, RSV).

The impassioned speech of this mother of seven martyrs is said to have fueled a woman's reason with a man's courage, but the contrast with sapiential precedent could hardly be greater. Here the mother draws on familiar concepts about the deity's role in the mystery of birth as the basis for confidence in the ultimate rectification of gross injustice. The same power that originated life can, in her view, give it back as reward for faithfully observing the torah. Belief in divine bestowal of life now functions as theodicy.[25] How different this is from 4 Macc 2:21–22, which stresses the enthronement of the intellect amid the senses as the essential gift bestowed at birth.[26]

The End

Speculation about life's termination occupied the thought of the sages primarily as a result of the collapse of belief in a moral order.[27] Their thoughts were by no means unified, ranging from the assertion that death was both natural and final to the conviction that humankind possesses an immortal soul. A mediating position–that no one knows whether the human spirit ascends in contrast to a descending animal spirit–characterized the view of Qoheleth, whose preoccupation with death was nearly obsessive.[28]

In Job's view, life fades and withers like a flower, vanishing like a shadow (Job 14:2), whereas a tree can sprout new growth after being cut down (14:7). Once a person succumbs to death, there is no rising until the heavens are no more (14:12). All the more perplexing, Job thinks, is the deity's relentless destruction of hope, which he compares to water wearing away rocks and eroding the landscape (14:18–19).[29] The erosion of hope has taken effect in Qoheleth, whose agnostic position is summed up in his final words: "Dust returns to earth as it was, and the life breath returns to God who gave it" (Eccl 12:7). The words that follow prevent a positive reading of the second colon: "Utter futility, said Qoheleth; everything is futile" (12:8). Indeed, the graphic depiction of the aging process, set over against the encouragement to make the most of youth, emphasizes death's finality by the choice of images that signal the end: the snapping of the silver cord, breaking of the golden bowl, and smashing of the jug at the cistern (12:6). These irreversible moments inaugurate the journey to an eternal abode.

Ben Sira minces no words when declaring that death, the decree for all, is final (Sir 34:7); he, too, uses the symbol of a tree to convey his thought that when old leaves are shed new ones take their place. So one person dies and another is born, continuing the cycle of life. More importantly, he insists, there is a good death just as there is an unwelcome one, the latter coming when one is prosperous and healthy (41:1–4). Curiously, Ben Sira preserves the tradition that Elijah resuscitated a corpse (48:5), but temporary restoration of life was entirely different from the concept of resurrection that emerged shortly after Ben Sira.[30]

The Hellenistic environment that may have influenced the views of death in Qoheleth and Ben Sira, even if negatively,[31] was the formative influence on the author of Wisdom of Solomon.[32] In his opinion, the righteous dead are at peace, possessing the hope of immortality (3:3–4).[33] Adopting the persona of Solomon, the author claims to have been endowed with a good soul and an undefiled body (8:19–20). In this author's view, death marks the transition to an everlasting existence with God. Whether one understands death as final or transitional, it inevitably looms before one as a reminder that choices must be made about priorities. In the face of death, what are life's essentials?

The Necessities of Life

'archē zoēs 'udōr, kai ărtos, kai 'imation, kai oîkos kaluptōn archēmosúnēn (Sir 29:21).

> The principle things of life are water, bread, clothing, and a house to cover one's nakedness.

[ṭwb lṭ]wb ḥlq mr'š / kn lr'ym ṭwb wr'
[r' k]l [ṣrk lḥym] 'dm mym / w'š wbrzl wmlḥ
[ḥlb ḥth ḥ]lb wdbš / dm 'nb yṣhr wbgd
kl [ṭwb lṭwb]ym yytybw / kn lr'ym lr'h nhpkw[34] *(Sir 39:25–27)*

> From the beginning he (God) has apportioned good things for the
> virtuous,
> similarly for the wicked, good and bad things.
> The essentials of every human need are water,
> fire, iron, salt,
> the marrow of wheat, milk, honey,
> blood of the grape, oil, and clothing.
> All these become good for the virtuous,
> just as they are turned into bad things for the wicked.

In these two texts Ben Sira offers rather different responses to the same unstated question: on what does human life depend? The interpreter gains little from dwelling on the author's inconsistency or even from detecting signs of sociological advancement on Ben Sira's part, as if he mirrors Israel's cultural development from village life to an urban setting.[35] Perhaps a better approach is to recognize the two distinct aims indicated by the larger contexts. The Spartan list of only four basic needs is set within a discussion of social responsibility to offer assistance to members of the community who fall on hard times, whereas the expansive cataloging of life's fundamental needs functions as theodicy.[36]

In the first instance, Ben Sira understands that in the face of widespread hunger, regardless of its particular expression, life can be sustained by bread and water for nurture and clothing and shelter for protection from the elements and from the shame of uncovering one's nakedness to one and all. Everything beyond these four things is disposable property and therefore constitutes a fund into which one can dip to provide charitable assistance. Because of his astute study of human nature, Ben Sira realizes that lending money has undesirable features; nevertheless, he advocates compassionate action regardless of these possible consequences. By such acts of kindness to the poor, he believes, one can deposit assets in a heavenly treasury on which to draw when the need arises. Although Ben Sira recognizes that entering into relationships in which one provides surety for another person can have disastrous consequences, he still recommends compassion, but with open eyes. Above all, he warns, a person should not become dependent on others for subsistence, for such parasitic existence robs one of dignity. The Roman satirist Juvenal goes beyond Ben Sira when mercilessly poking fun at uninvited guests of the rich who were subjected to menial chores and demeaning treatment by their hosts.

In the second instance, Ben Sira reflects on divine largesse, which he considers to be far from niggardly. Blessings abound, he thinks, even when one restricts thought to the essentials of life. Possibly influenced by Greek philosophical theodicies based on the functional duality of opposites in nature,[37] he argues that various things are neutral until directed at specific persons, when they become either beneficial to the good or detrimental to the health of the wicked. In this context Ben Sira draws on familiar tradition about a promised land of milk and honey, as well as lavish descriptions of Canaan as a place of abundant grain, oil, and wine.[38] In addition, he mentions fire, iron, and salt–the last to enhance flavor, the second to improve the quality of life through tools and weapons, and the first as essential to cooking and to forge implements of agriculture and of warfare. Naturally, Ben Sira includes water, bread, and clothing in this longer list but curiously omits shelter.

Nature's unruly forces (such as fire, hail, famine, and pestilence) as well as dangerous creatures (Ben Sira mentions wild beasts, scorpions, and vipers) function in this well ordered universe to punish the wicked, according to this theodicy. Ben Sira trusts his reasoning so much that he puts it in writing,[39] having thoroughly examined its logic. He concludes: *m'śh 'l klm ṭwbym lkl ṣwrk b'tw yspwq* ("God's works–all of them–are good; he supplies all your needs in their times" Sir 39:33). It follows that anyone who makes superficial distinctions between good and bad things per se does not reckon with the reality that everything is appropriate for its purpose. In this judgment, Ben Sira concurs with Qoheleth's sentiment in Eccl 3:11 (*'et-hakkōl 'āśâ yāpeh be'ittô*, "He made everything appropriate for its purpose"). Everything has its special time, that is, even if the two thinkers differed radically about whether or not humans can put such knowledge to good use.

In both versions of life's necessities water takes precedence, perhaps because bread, the other ingredient that is absolutely essential, depends on it. Fire assumes the second position in the longer account, probably because of its role in transforming grain into bread. In neither list does meat appear, a noteworthy departure from Deut 32:13–14.

> He made him [Israel] ride on the top of the earth
> so that he feasted on the produce of the field.
> He made him suck honey from a crag
> and oil from a flinty rock;
> Curds from cattle and goat's milk,
> with fat lambs;
> Rams from Bashan and he-goats,
> with the best wheat;
> you would drink wine, the blood of the grape.

In the judgment of the poet, however, Yahweh's lavish provision failed to generate gratitude, yielding instead an arrogance that found expression in idolatry. The danger inherent to riches was not foreign to the author of the only prayer in the book of Proverbs. Here one reads: "Two things I ask from you; do not withhold them from me before I die. Emptiness and lying words keep far from me; do not give me poverty or riches but break off for me a portion of bread, lest I be sated and deny, saying 'Who is Yahweh?' or lest being poor I steal and sully the name of my God" (Prov 30:7–9).[40]

Ben Sira's shorter version of life's essentials has been taken as endorsing simple values associated with working the soil, but it is hardly that, for in his hierarchy of sociological status sages rank just behind rulers, priests, and possibly merchants.[41] The later author of Pirke Abot 2:7 comes close to stating a preference for austere existence, however, when listing the dangers of economic prosperity as gluttony, worry over theft, serial polygamy leading to witchcraft, and anxiety brought on by a house full of servants. Over against these products of abundance, he names the benefits of torah, study, counsel, and deeds of charity. They are, respectively, life, wisdom, understanding, and peace.

> Go, eat your bread joyfully and drink your wine merrily, for the deity has already approved your action. Let your clothes be white at all times, and do not let your head lack oil. Enjoy life with the woman you love all the days of your brief existence that he has granted you under the sun–all your brief days, for that is your portion in life and in your toil at which you labor under the sun (Eccl 9:7–9).

Although lacking Ben Sira's language indicating the essentials of life, Qoheleth's exhortation, strikingly similar to Siduri's advice to Gilgamesh,[42] approximates the short version discussed above. Life's injustices, together with its brevity, lend urgency to conduct that will maximize enjoyment, Qoheleth concludes. His understanding of life's essentials includes bread, drink, and clothing, but also soothing ointment and companionship.[43] In this text we hear an echo of the invitation tendered by Wisdom in Prov 9:5. Having slaughtered her meat and having mixed drinks for her guests, she issues the following invitation: "Come, eat my food (literally "bread") and drink my mixed wine." Not to be undone, Folly alludes to bread and water in a masterfully crafted seduction (Prov 9:17, "Stolen water is sweet, and bread eaten clandestinely is tasty"). In yet another context Qoheleth adds money to the other two necessities, bread and wine ("For laughter they prepare bread, and wine makes life joyful, but money answers everything," Eccl 10:19).[44]

> "Lambs are for clothing, and he-goats for the price of a field;
> goats' milk is adequate for your food–for the food of your house
> and the subsistence of your maidens" (Prov 27:26–27).

This proverb appears in a context dealing with survival, which depends in this case on the condition of a small flock of sheep and goats. It urges one to take special care of these precious commodities, for on their well being the survival of the family depends. Of what does that consist? Just two things: food and clothing; or at most, three, in that a field is essential for the animal's existence and ultimately for their owners' as well.

If it is true that "man does not live by bread alone," the door swings open for additional necessities. The first to enter, according to Prov 1:7, is the fear of Yahweh, the *rē'šît* (first principle) of knowledge. Religious devotion, that is, lies at the heart of the intellectual enterprise. In that spirit, the epilogist concludes the book of Ecclesiastes by observing that everything has been heard, and by proclaiming the end of the matter[45] to be "Fear God and keep his commandments" (Eccl 12:13). With the dual sense of *rē'šît* above (first principle and beginning), we return to the idea with which this discussion began, but now in the context of endings.[46]

II.

Psalms, Prophecy, and Torah

CHAPTER 12

The Book of Psalms and Its Interpreters

The history of interpreting the book of Psalms is a powerful corrective to the illusion of objective scholarship that has long prevailed in scholarly circles. The interaction of readers with the biblical text over the millennia rivals the passion of those who originally composed these psalms of praise, petition, and instruction. Behind the grammar and syntax of the psalms, interpreters have looked for the plain sense of the ancient linguistic expression (what Jewish rabbis called the *pešat*) but they have also searched for a deeper meaning, the *deraš* (*sensus plenior* in Christian exegesis). Longing for religious insights concerning themselves and their creator, they have inquired about the social realities that underlie individual psalms. These three interests–literary, theological, and historical–have motivated interpreters of Psalms for more than two thousand years.[1]

I. Interpretation before the Enlightenment

The need for interpretation, together with the impetus for hermeneutics, arises only after the cessation of the age of inspiration[2] and intensifies with the adoption of a new language replacing that of sacred texts. With the virtual disappearance of inspired prophets, priests, and teachers, their traditional legacy requires competent interpreters. The earliest evidence of such interpretation in the book of Psalms is found in the superscriptions, editorial glosses ascribing authorship and fixing specific psalms in historical contexts, especially events involving King David. To some extent also, metrical terms such as *selâ* and indications of genre and tunes like *mizmôr*, *maskîl*, *miktām*, and *šiggāyôn* function as aids to understanding.

The earliest extrabiblical evidence of interpreting the Psalms comes from Qumran, where four fragmentary commentaries were discovered.[3] Only Isaiah, with five, surpasses Psalms in this regard. The number of copies of the Psalter, 31, exceeds all other biblical books (the book of Deuteronomy is a close second with 25, and Isaiah is third with 18). Fragments of 115 biblical psalms have survived, along with a book of *Hodayot* composed by a member of the sect and containing about 25 psalms. Quotations of biblical books in the sectarian literature from Qumran put the prophetic book of Isaiah at the top ahead of Deuteronomy and Psalms in that order. A *pešer* on Psalm 37 illustrates the sect's tendency to apply scripture to its own historical context, understood apocalyptically.[4]

Roughly 55 citations of Psalms in the New Testament exceed all other biblical books, with Isaiah's 48 a close second and Deuteronomy's 42 third. Clement of Rome quotes Psalms 49 times, the Didache cites Pss 4:2, 37:11, and 118:26, and Justin's "Dialogue with Trypho" has 47 references to 24 psalms.[5] Augustine's "Enarrationes in Psalmos" (c. 416) illustrates the significance of this biblical book to early Christian theologians, and the Jewish philosopher Philo quotes Psalms more frequently than any other biblical book save the Pentateuch.

The controversy over a literal interpretation and an allegorical one divided both Jewish and Christian exegesis, although both groups assumed that David was the author of Psalms. Alexandria was the center of allegorical interpretation, with Antioch that of literal readings. Origen (c. 185–254) quickly moves to allegorical senses, even of Psalm 137:2, the hanging of musical instruments on the willows, which he takes to mean a soul sitting in a shadow and ignorance without practical ability. Jerome (c. 342–420) represents a mediating position between allegory and literal interpretation. Theodore of Mopsuestia (c. 350–428) emphasizes the latter, even if that requires a certain boldness–denying that a psalm refers to Christ.

During the medieval period Christian scholars–e.g., Alcuin, Peter Lombard, Albertus Magnus, Nicolas de Lyra, and Thomas Aquinas–view Psalms as a vehicle for transmitting the early Christian legacy and develop expository techniques such as glosses and scholia. In time a tradition of interlinear and marginal glosses on the biblical text becomes standard practice in exegesis.

Jewish interpreters make enormous progress in this period,[6] particularly in philology. Saadia Gaon (c. 892–942) views Psalms as a second Pentateuch, following the lead of the earlier editor who divided Psalms into five books, (1–41, 42–72, 73–89, 90–106, 107–50), each with a concluding doxology (41:13, 72:19, 89:52; 106:48; 150). Reacting against the Karaites' reading of Psalms as a human product, a book of prayer, Saadia understands them as a manual of theological and moral guidance from God. For Saadia, the literary features of the book are rhetorical husk and thus of little value.

The Karaites move in the other direction, robbing the Psalms of their historical specificity. Salmon ben Yeruham (10th century) refutes Saadia's views on three counts: (1) the frequency of the language of prayer in Psalms; (2) twenty verses in Psalms where the same verbs in the imperative mood appear in first person; and (3) the use of Psalms in the regular liturgy. Yefet ben 'Ali Halevi (10th century) treats Psalms as perfect prophetic prayers. He devotes considerable energy to discovering the authors of the psalms with no attribution to David or anyone else. On the basis of style and theme he links

Psalms 9 and 10, 32 and 33, 42 and 43, 70 and 71, 103 and 104. In addition, he attributes Psalms 90–100 to Moses because they follow the statement, "A prayer of Moses, the man of God." Similarly, Psalms 146–50 are ascribed to David, since they follow *tehillâ dawid* in Psalm 145. In this way, Yefet rescues seventeen psalms from anonymity.

The eleventh century Solomon ben Isaac (Rashi, 1040–1105), understands Psalms as compositions of David and views their meaning in light of events pertaining to the Israelite king rather than a future messiah. Moses Ibn Giqatilah considers Psalms non-prophetic prayers and poems. Valuing intellectualism, he downplays the miraculous and stresses the historical meaning of texts, even interpreting messianic prophecies as applicable to the biblical author's own time. Giqatilah does not hesitate to adopt unpopular views, for his use of Christian commentaries and historical emphasis render his faith suspect to some critics,[7] as does the dating of many psalms to the Babylonian exile, a new departure. Giqatilah views the anonymity of some psalms as proof that David was not their author and thinks the Asaph psalms were composed in Babylon, hence not by the earlier Asaph in Judah.

Abraham Ibn Ezra (1092–1167) views Psalms as prophetic and sacred poetry. His hastily written commentary elevates the sense of smell over taste and sight, credits the word *ledāwîd* with five or six possible meanings, and distinguishes between the Holy Spirit and the prophetic spirit. Ibn Ezra believes that Sages edited Psalms and that their prophecies apply to the time of origins, the age of David. Moreover, Ibn Ezra insists, the individual psalms must stand alone.

David Kimḥi (c. 1160–1235), known by his acronym Radak, develops Giqatilah's historical method, adopting an intermediate position on *pešat* and *deraš*, with preference going to *pešat*. For him, the Masoretic Text is sacrosanct, although he occasionally reverts to *Athbash* and *Atbah*.[8] Greatly influenced by his father, Joseph Kimḥi, who balances competing schools of interpretation–French Talmudic tradition and Spanish philosophy and philology–David Kimḥi emphasizes grammar and philosophy.

Kimḥi's commentary on the psalms of ascent (120–34) illustrates his method. He writes that Psalm 127 was composed in connection with the building of the temple and may refer to (1) Solomon (2) the messiah (Ishmaelites and Christians who destroy and rebuild Zion), or (3) everyone. Pride in Psalm 131 is viewed with respect to David's secret and public demeanor, an absence of haughtiness when slaying Goliath and of pride when being anointed by Samuel as king over Israel. For Kimḥi, the allusion to marvelous things recalls the bringing of the ark to Jerusalem. The association of an oath with Jacob's God in Psalm 132 leads Kimḥi to speculate that the deity revealed the future location of the temple to Jacob, who vowed to keep it a secret. How did God do that? By a dream in which a ladder inclined from Zion to Bethel. Similarly, Kimḥi writes, God gave Abraham a hint about the site of the future temple in the words "the place that I will show you" (Gen 22:2), and the patriarch kept this information to himself. In the feminine suffix on the words *meṣā'nûhâ* and *šema'anûhâ* in verse 6 Kimḥi finds an allusion to the divine presence, Shekinah. The reference to the vanity of rising early reminds him of Adonijah's futile conspiracy to overthrow his father and assume the throne.

Not surprisingly, the Psalter is the first book to appear in print (1477), and Felix Pratensis' *Psalterium ex hebreo diligentissime ad verbum fere translatum* appears in 1522. The Protestant reformers, Martin Luther and John Calvin, compose commentaries on Psalms that incorporate the three main concerns of their predecessors–philology, history, and theology. Luther's lifelong preoccupation with this biblical book, totaling about 2,500 printed pages, culminates in the lectures on the gradual psalms (1532–3). John Calvin soon follows with an impressive commentary on Psalms (1557).

This brief sketch of Christian and Jewish exegesis of Psalms before the Enlightenment reveals a widespread assumption that they reward rigorous investigation into their religio-historical context but that their full meaning can not be grasped through this means alone. Philological analysis is therefore complemented by theological reflection, both of which encourage close attention to literary artistry.

II. The Enlightenment and Beyond

With the Enlightenment comes increased emphasis on rational inquiry, to some extent aided by earlier philology, especially the achievements of Saadia. The humanist Johannes Reuchlin perfects the philological method, and historical positivism begins to dominate the intellectual scene in general. Every text, the Bible included, is examined as the product of a human author, or authors, and can only be understood correctly by clarifying the historical context in which the work arose. To achieve that lofty goal, philology is essential. The study of Hebrew grammar and syntax soon flourishes, as do the disciplines of literary analysis and the history of religions.

To be sure, greater appreciation for the literary dimensions of texts coupled with a reaction to what is thought to be excessive rationalism leads to romanticism, with important consequences for biblical criticism. J. G. Herder's profound insights into religious lyrics bring about an emphasis on personal religious experience. Commentaries on Psalms from this perspective follow, for example E. J. K. Rosenmüller's *Scholia in Psalmos* (1798–1804), and in 1811 *Commentar über die Psalmen* by the founder of historical-critical interpretation of the Bible, W. M. L. De Wette.

Julius Wellhausen's impact on the understanding of Psalms is far reaching, as is his approach to the Pentateuch which solidifies earlier insights by Graf, Kuenen, Hupfeld, and De Wette. His treatment of the religion of ancient Israel depicts an evolution from primitive to prophetic to priestly concerns, while at the same time popularizing source critical hypotheses about four literary strata underlying the Pentateuch (JEDP). His belief that primitive animism is replaced by an ethical monotheism championed by the prophets, which succumbs to arid legalism of the priests in what comes to be known as "late Judaism," greatly influences subsequent interpreters of Psalms, which in his view originate among circles of the godly in post-exilic Judaism. In the first decades after Wellhausen, biblical interpreters tend to date most of the psalms in this late period. Indeed, some critics go so far as to locate virtually all the psalms in the Maccabean period.

The historical paradigm, stemming from the Enlightenment, comes to rule the day, with each psalm being studied for evidence of its historical setting and the individual author's personal views. This atomistic personal approach is carried to extremes by Jewish and Christian interpreters, most notably Moses Buttenwieser and Julien Morgenstern on the Jewish side and Robert H. Pfeiffer and Norman Snaith on the Christian. This approach depends on an imaginative reconstruction of Israel's religious history, with literary development of the individual books of the Bible being tied to this evolution, or vice versa.

Although strongly opposed to Wellhausen's late dating of Psalms, Buttenwieser's commentary on Psalms best illustrates the method and conclusions of the atomistic historical approach. He writes: "Of the sixty-six post-Exilic psalms in which is reflected either a distinct historical crisis or a joyous turn in the affairs of the nation, of which fifty-nine can be dated exactly, and seven approximately, none was composed later than the year 312 B.C., when Ptolemy besieged and conquered Jerusalem."[9] Buttenwieser opposes a late dating on linguistic grounds, the decomposition of Hebrew as a result of its disappearance as a spoken language, but also on the basis of content.

He believes that there are twenty-six pre-exilic psalms, all of which he dates more or less to precise times.[10] These ancient psalms range in date from the time of the conflict with Sisera to the seventh and early sixth centuries. Psalm 68 derives from the author of the Song of Deborah, and Psalm 81:6–17 comes from Joshua's era and promotes the same agenda as that in Joshua 24. At least three psalms are genuinely Davidic (60:3–7, 12a b, 13–14; 57:8–11, 6, 8–12a + 60:1–2; and 24:7–10) and depict the situation after the disastrous battle at Gilboa that gave the Philistines temporary supremacy, as well as the subsequent removal of the ark to Jerusalem from the house of Obed Edom.

Psalms 65:10ab, 68:11a (ba), 65:10c, 68:10b, 65:10d, 65:11–14 aims at producing rain, while royal transitions become the occasions for some psalms. Those of Ahab, Joash, and Jeroboam generate Psalms 20 and 21:2–9, 13, 10a, 11–14, both reflecting times of foreign dominance and written by the same poet. The wedding ode, Psalm 45, comes from Ahab's reign as well.

Buttenwieser considers five pre-exilic psalms liturgical compositions (100, 95, 114, 136, 105, [24:7–10]). Asa's reforms, in Buttenwieser's view, probably inspired a poet to compose Psalm 95. Jerusalem's dramatic escape from the Assyrian threat posed by Sennacherib in 701 BCE gives rise to Psalms 48 and 76, which celebrate this event, and Psalm 78, which echoes the people's reaction to the grave danger and its miraculous removal.

Prophetic influence on the psalmists can be detected in both pre-exilic and post-exilic compositions, according to Buttenwieser. At least eight psalms from before the exile reveal the high moral conscience of eighth and seventh century prophecy (29; 104; 19:2–7; 8; 51; 50; 15; and 24:1–6). Similarly, Psalm 89 shows signs of prophetic passion, but with less genuine understanding than the others.

Not until 300 BCE does this prophetic influence wane, despite Wellhausen's claim that arid legalism sets in much earlier. Interestingly, Buttenwieser recognizes a different kind of decadence, a literary one, beginning in the third century. Accordingly, he views Psalm 145 as a product of such decadence. Nevertheless, he thinks that seventy-seven of the one hundred and fifteen post-exilic psalms continue to show prophetic influence.

Are there any Maccabean psalms? Buttenwieser can detect no compelling reason to place a single psalm in that period. In that regard, at least, his interpretation of the psalms is in line with subsequent research. That judgment cannot apply to the way in which Buttenwieser tends to rearrange the sequence of the literary compositions. A single example will illustrate his method. He thinks the correct order of Psalm 68B is 8, 9abcBca, 16–18, 12–13, 14b-15, 19ab, 25–28. In this procedure, as in resorting to frequent emendations, Buttenwieser is truly a product of the times. The chance discovery of the Dead Sea Scrolls and their subsequent publication soon decelerates this trend. Greater appreciation for the reliability of the Masoretic Text, together with a growing sense of literary artistry, especially poetic language, lure interpreters away from the consuming passion that Buttenwieser and others of his day represent.

The first onslaught against the historical atomistic approach to Psalms comes from Hermann Gunkel, who introduces a method of classifying types of literature based on form, function, and social context.[11] This basic approach, resembling that of Linnaeus in the field of botany, moves away from the specific to the typical, thus undercutting all efforts to isolate the unique features of individual psalms. Moreover, Gunkel's appreciation for oral tradition, honed while doing research on Genesis, carries over into his analysis of Psalms, where he finds extensive evidence of stereotypical language and mythic tradition hardly applicable to the personal experience of a single individual.

Gunkel divides the book of Psalms into five major and five minor categories. The first group is made up of (1) hymns, (2) communal laments, (3) royal psalms, (4) individual laments, and (5) individual songs of thanksgiving. Comprising the second group are (1) songs of pilgrimage (84, 122), (2) communal songs of thanksgiving (67, 124), (3) wisdom poetry (127, 133, 1, 37, 49, 73, 112, 128), (4) liturgy (15, 24 [Torah]), 12, 75, 85, 126 ([prophetic]), and (5) mixed psalms (40, 89–90, 107–8, 144).

Hymns, in Gunkel's view, derive from worship, both solos and choral pieces composed for use in enthronement festivals (e.g., 8, 19, 29, 33, 65, 68, 96, 98, 100, 103). Communal laments arise in everyday life and are expressions of manifold calamity (e.g., 44, 74, 79–80, 83), while royal psalms originate during the period of the monarchy (e.g., 2, 18, 20–21, 45, 72, 101, 110, 132). The "backbone of the Psalter," and by far the largest number, belong to the category of individual laments (e.g., 3, 5, 6–7, 13, 17, 22, 25–26). The final major class, individual songs of thanksgiving (e.g., 18, 30, 32, 34, 41, 66, 92, 116, 118, 138) are believed to be closely associated with the cult, hence with worship in the temple. Indeed, most of the psalms begin in the cult, he thinks, but are later freed from it and become more spiritual.

Gunkel's influence on subsequent interpretation of Psalms is second to none, despite various flaws that gradually come to light, most notably his dependence on Wellhausen's description of religious development in Israel and his use of conflicting criteria of classification–form *and* content. The form critical assumption that genres originate as pure forms and eventually deteriorate into a mixture of types, and from simple to complex, grows ever more implausible with time's passage, and the centrality of the cult as vital spiritual worship captures the imagination of influential interpreters, especially in Scandinavia.

To be sure, subsequent interpreters do not embrace all of Gunkel's views wholeheartedly. Instead, they refine them in various ways. By far the most significant revision comes from Sigmund Mowinckel, whose comprehensive studies on Psalms are influenced by the Danish anthropologist V. Grønbech, a pioneer in comparative explorations into "primitive" societies. From him Mowinckel borrows the notion of creative drama, which leads to a deepening appreciation of symbolic ritual and its accompanying recitation.

Mowinckel accepts Gunkel's method of studying psalms according to types, preferring to label it type-critical or type-historical, but uses only four main types: (1) praises and thanksgiving of the congregation, (2) private thanksgiving, (3) congregational lamentations, and (4) congregational prayer psalms. The first of these types has two sub-types, common praise and special thanksgiving, as does the fourth, general and special prayers. He resolves the problem of individual and collective psalms ("I" and "We") in the figure of the king, who embodies the whole.

According to Mowinckel, the Hebrew expression *YHWH mālak* means YHWH has become king, but also includes the idea of continual rule. Holding both of these views simultaneously was no contradiction to the ancient mind. The royal enthronement festival serves as an occasion of divine epiphany, he argues, with a sacral procession and the proclamation of a covenant that carries conditions as well as promise. The word is creative, hence the drama of threat and victory over chaos is powerladen. The royal processional along a *via sacra*, reflected in such psalms as 15, 24, and 132, is filled with expectation that culminates in the festal shout, *YHWH mālak*.

This positive view of the cult enables Mowinckel to locate nearly all of the psalms in it from beginning to end, unlike Gunkel who thinks it necessary to "free them from the cult" in order to appreciate their spiritual content. What is more, Mowinckel sees in the piety of the psalms an expression of temple singers who write for liturgical worship. In other words, the praise and petition do not come from private experiences of the laity. It follows that interpreters cannot use them to discover facts about individuals' personal conflicts or joys. As vessels of liturgy, the psalms treat themes that have general application rather than topics with limited scope.

What, then, of the enemies that so many laments complain about, workers of evil who seem to bring so much misery to the pious? Mowinckel thinks of them primarily as sorcerers, professional practictioners of magic, rather than foreigners, the view of H. Birkeland, or personal enemies resulting from ordinary interpersonal relationships. Here the psalms become cultic instruments aimed at establishing an orderly society that ensures well-being.

Above all, then, Mowinckel posits a New Year's festival in Israel (similar to the *akitu* festival in Babylonia) and links approximately forty psalms with it. He believes that the Israelite king was enthroned annually on the occasion of the New Year's festival and that this act brought promise of *šālôm* to the nation itself. This drama has ancient roots, in his view, going all the way back to the worship of *'el 'elyôn* in pre-Davidic times, but its reality lingers in the memory of later rabbis who allude to this festival. Mowinckel's lofty understanding of liturgy does not prevent him from developing the view that prophetic eschatology grows out of disillusionment with the cult and the royal figure depicted in the enthronement ceremony.[12]

Preferring the category "learned psalmography" to Gunkel's "wisdom psalms," Mowinckel views didactic poems as products of scribes who have no connection with the cult. Indeed, he considers "didactic psalms" a contradiction in adjective, for by its very nature a psalm is cultic. The following psalms are identified as learned psalmography: 1, 19B, 34, 37, 49, 78, 105, 106, 111, 112, and 127.

Mowinckel thinks of the present book of Psalms as the product of the period from the monarchy to about 400 BCE and stresses an incremental formation of small, independent compositions, basically 3–41, 42–83, 84–89, 120–34, 93, 95–99 (100), 113–18, 146–50, and 105–107. This process was complete, he thinks, by c. 300 BCE.

To sum up, Mowinckel understands the individual psalms, not just their prototypes, and structural models, as products of actual cultic situations such as festivals and rituals. Even the technical terms in the superscriptions and occasionally in the body of a psalm (e.g., *selâ*) are, in his view, the product of temple personnel to assist singers. Nevertheless, he resembles Gunkel in valuing emotional and mythical dimensions of the psalms over literary and historical positivism.

Further refinement of Gunkel's approach to Psalms comes along several lines: (1) a basic simplification of the types; (2) a fuller exploration of the sociological dimensions behind the biblical texts; (3) a greater appreciation for the symbolic world of Psalms; (4) a keener interest in philology and literary structure; (5) a desire to trace the history of interpretation of various psalms, their reception history; and (6) an attempt to give modern poetic form to ancient Psalms.[13]

Claus Westermann reduces the Psalms to two types, praise and petition, corresponding to the two fundamental emotions, joy and suffering. In addition, he divides hymns (praise) into reportorial and descriptive, the former indicating historical events and the latter applying to nature. Franz Crüsemann looks to grammatical construction for categories, opting for imperative and participial hymns. James L. Crenshaw contests the existence of wisdom psalms, which Mowinckel attributes to a group of learned teachers.

Still, Gunkel's general classification captures the imagination of interpreters with widely differing interests. Erhard S. Gerstenberger prefers the following terms: dirges/laments, complaints, thanksgivings, songs of praise (hymns), royal psalms, and wisdom psalms. Samuel Terrien works with three major types (hymn or praise, supplication or elegy, and festival liturgy), but he divides the last of these into four sub-categories: royal psalm, psalm of entrance, prophetic psalms, and wisdom psalm. Here, as in the case with Gunkel, both form and content supply the criteria of selection.

Not all interpreters are persuaded that the New Year's festival of royal enthronement was the primary one in ancient Israel. Artur Weiser postulates an indigenous covenant renewal ceremony, largely because of the theological significance of a bond between YHWH and Israel. Nevertheless, Hans Joachim Kraus, who is arguably the most influential interpreter of Psalms since Mowinckel, thinks of the royal Zion festival originating in Canaanite culture as central to a number of psalms. For them and many other interpreters, the temple liturgy provides the clue to the use of psalms in ancient Israel; Gerstenberger, however, posits family worship in small villages and in synagogues as their primary function. This shifting of Psalms from the temple cult to ordinary religious practices within the outlying regions of Judah and Israel contrasts sharply with the cult functional approach in which professional priests and singers both compose and recite the psalms on behalf of the populace.

Borrowing the categories of orientation, disorientation, and reorientation from Norman Gottwald, Walter Brueggemann stresses existential issues while endeavoring to capture the theological profundity of the Psalter. He perceives their relevance to contemporary pain and searches for the pastoral dimensions in individual psalms. Similarly, Patrick D. Miller emphasizes the petitionary features of Psalms and compares these prayers with related ones from ancient Near Eastern texts outside the Bible. J. David Pleins probes these psalms for examples of social justice, finding in them something equivalent to the theme popularized by Gustavo Gutiérrez, "a preferential option for the poor."

Sociological interest is not limited to the insights it contributes for contemporary theology. Michael Goulder continues to explore the possibility that early northern traditions come to rest in the final collection of Psalms, especially in those attributed to Asaph and Korah. Some interpreters reach further back into the past, especially noting the Canaanite features of certain psalms (29, 68) and the affinities between Psalm 104 and the Egyptian Hymn to the Aten. Othmar Keel's pioneering study of iconography from the ancient world assists those interpreters in fine-tuning numerous aspects of daily life, both at home and in the royal court.

The symbolic world of the biblical text is becoming increasingly clearer as a result of several explorations of specific metaphors. The most comprehensive such study is that of William P. Brown, who treats metaphors concerning refuge, pathway, a transplanted tree, the sun of righteousness, the voice of many waters, the song of Leviathan, birthing and protection. The notion of refuge is the subject of a treatise by Jerome F. D. Creach, while the image of being caught in a net is examined by Peter Riede and that of kingship by Marc Brettler.

Literary analysis of Psalms rivals the sociological. Mitchell Dahood's efforts to establish Canaanite linguistic patterns throughout the biblical text and the philological analysis of archaic poetry by Frank Moore Cross, Jr. and David Noel Freedman[14] to establish an evolutionary line for poetry like the pottery chronology of W. F. Albright continue to inspire students of Psalms to produce studies of individual psalms. Considerably more influential, however, is the work of Luis Alonso-Schökel and to a lesser extent Meir Weiss.[15] The former introduces new criticism into biblical studies, and the latter emphasizes holistic interpretation. A third influence, possibly the most important, is James Muilenburg, who calls on interpreters to press beyond form criticism to rhetoric.[16] The literary approach to the Bible quickly catches on and is popularized by Robert Alter, Meier Sternberg, Adele Berlin[17] and a host of others, so much so that some critics believe that a shift in paradigms has occurred–from the historical to the literary.

Initially, the literary approach focuses on the microstructure, examining in intricate detail the artistry of individual psalms. The authors of these exegetical gems–Anthony Ceresko, P. Auffret, and many others–call attention to such literary features as inclusio, chiasm, refrain, theme word, repetition, rhetorical question, puns, inverted sentence order, topos, metaphor, unusual grammar and syntax, and more. Some interpreters count syllabi, while others search for clusters, allusions, and meta-textual indications. James Limburg enumerates the following rhetorical features of repetition: question and answer, statement and quotation, a better than expression, A varies and B repeats, abstract and concrete, whole and synecdoche, two terms as a merismus, and simile and reality.

The initiative for structuring the entire book of Psalms comes from Gerald H. Wilson, whose canonical interest leads to an inquiry into the editorial process by which the psalms came together. In his view, the Psalter depicts the bankruptcy of the Davidic monarchy and YHWH's replacement of the human leader as king. Wilson infers the failure of David as king from the position of psalms about a human king within the five books of Psalms.

He argues as follows. In Book I the endorsement of the earthly monarch follows the introductory psalm, but the next two books place such royal psalms at the end. Whereas Psalm 2 identifies the king as YHWH's son and promises dominion over the nations, this optimism gives way to supplication on the king's behalf in Psalm 72. Psalm 89 recalls YHWH's promise to David but concedes that the one who is incapable of lying has removed the scepter from David's house. This awkward situation leads to a biting question: "YHWH, where is your former steadfast love?" and to a puzzled comment, "You swore to David by your faithfulness" (v. 50). Bracketing this query is a twofold appeal for remembrance and a formulaic "How long, YHWH, will you conceal yourself forever; will your anger burn like fire?" (vv. 47, 48, 51). Books IV and V depict YHWH as Israel's true king, and Book V transfers the royal claims of the Davidic family to the people. While Book IV explores the ramifications of the collapse of the Davidic empire, Book V offers hope in the divine ruler.

J. Clinton McCann, Jr. varies Wilson's hypothesis, interpreting Psalm 2 in light of a biblical tradition that recognizes YHWH as true king even when a human ruler occupies the throne. The emphasis in Psalm 2 falls on YHWH, not the earthly king, a position that is reaffirmed in Psalms 71 and 89 and reinforced by Psalms 93, 95–99, where the shout "YHWH" has become king" or "YHWH reigns" prevails. For McCann, the real transition takes place in Psalm 73, a microcosm of Old Testament theology. Book IV, then, is the theological heart of Psalms, to which Terrien adds Psalm 90.

Another suggestion derives from James L. Mays, who understands the torah psalms as the key to the final form of the book. Westermann holds a similar view, insisting that Psalms 1 and 119 introduce and conclude an original book of Psalms, to which editors have added later material. Both Mays and Westermann think that Psalm 1 shapes the Psalter as devotional reading, or better still, as meditation. Similarly, G. T. Sheppard and Klaus Seybold view Psalms as a "didactic guide to righteousness" and a "reflective guide to prayer and right living" respectively.

Some interpreters find a clue to the structure of Psalms in liturgy. Carroll Stuhlmueller moves beyond the older suggestion that lament gives way to praise toward the end of Psalms. He discerns a movement from ordinary to liturgical language as one progresses toward the end of Psalms. In Book III he detects a new attention to liturgical guilds and events, concluding in Book V with the most liturgical psalms of all. Here one finds a collection focusing on the three major festivals in ancient Israel (Psalms 113–18) and a booklet for pilgrims (Psalms 120–34).

Stuhlmueller thinks that a shift occurs also from a more secular word for blessing (*'ašre*) in Psalm 1 to the sacred verb *bārak* (bless), which occurs three times in Psalm 134. The closing exhortation, "Praise YHWH," belongs to sacred discourse, and this final psalm has ten *hallelujahs* (or *hallelûhûs*), thirteen if one counts the conclusion in verse 6 and the opening and closing ones. Stuhlmueller relates these numbers to the Decalogue and the thirteen attributes of YHWH disclosed to Moses in Exod 34:6–7 and the thirteen times God spoke in Genesis 1.

A different suggestion comes from J. Reindl and R. Norman Whybray, who believe that editors from the circles of wisdom have inserted verses representing sapiential interests throughout the Psalter. Reindl locates the wisdom compilers in the second temple and envisions them as Ben Sira's predecessors. Thus Psalm 1 shows students how to conduct their lives in accordance with torah. These editors add snippets here and there, rearrange psalms, and provide links that reflect their particular views. Whybray develops this hypothesis about sapiential additions further, applying it to individual psalms as different as 19, 37, and 78. Finding sapiential glosses in numerous psalms, he extends the scope of wisdom psalms to twelve or thirteen.

The extraordinary influence of Psalms on the church and synagogue attracts the attention of a growing number of scholars. William Holladay traces the emergence of Psalm 23 as a kind of icon in North America, while Baltasar Fischer looks at the use of Psalms in the early church, and Hans C. Knuth examines the history of interpretation of Psalm 6. The growing emphasis on reception history may also bring greater appreciation for the formative role of Psalms on Christian hymnody (e.g., Herbert, Watts, Wesley, and others).

Rare indeed is the attempt by modern poets to render their own version of biblical psalms. Laurance Wieder risks putting "words to God's music," after testing the waters with an edited publication largely occupied with earlier attempts to compose modern renditions of biblical psalms.[18] Others study the book of Psalms for devotional inspiration; these interpreters range from C. S. Lewis and Stanley J. Jaki outside the ranks of biblical scholars to Walter Brueggemann, Bernhard Anderson, and Nahum Sarna within its inner circle. Moreover, Erich Zenger endeavors to take the sting out of psalms of vengeance, which contain views no longer compatible with modern sensibilities.

By necessity, this survey of the history of scholarly approaches to Psalms omits the names of many contributors to its rich history. Concentrating on the main lines of investigation over more than two millennia, it situates the work of Sigmund Mowinckel in the dynamic so as to enable readers to appreciate the magnitude of his contribution.[19]

A Select Bibliography on the Psalms

Aejmelaeus, A. *The Traditional Prayer in the Psalms.* BZAW. Berlin and New York: Walter de Gruyter, 1986.

Argues that traditional language of entreaty in ordinary daily life is embedded in the laments within the Psalter and that this setting, not the cult, is the original home of such prayer.

Allen, Leslie C. *Psalms 101–150.* WBC, 21. Waco, Texas: Word Books Publishers, 1983, 2002.

A valuable commentary with full exegetical discussion, ample philological and stylistic analysis, and attention to theological dimensions of the biblical text.

Alonso-Schökel, Luis. *The Literary Language of the Bible.* BIBAL Collected Essays 3. North Richland Hills, Texas: BIBAL Press, 2000.

Two essays, chapters 5 and 8, assess the imaginative language of the psalms and interpret Psalm 104 in the light of ecology.

Anderson, Bernhard W. *Out of the Depths.* Philadelphia: Westminster, 1983.

In revised form, this study guide now includes closer attention to stylistic features of the psalms without sacrificing the primary emphasis on existential concerns.

Baker, Joshua and Nicholson, Ernest W. *The Commentary of Rabbi David Kimhi on Psalms CXX-CL.* Cambridge: Cambridge University Press, 1973.

This thorough and methodical commentary from the end of the twelfth and first third of the thirteenth centuries balances philological and Talmudic approaches, frequently citing rabbinic sources.

Barth, Christoph. *Introduction to the Psalms.* New York: Charles Scribner's Sons, 1966.

A convenient guide for laity, heavily weighted toward theological meaning for the church.

Bellinger, W. H. Jr. *Psalms. Reading and Studying the Book of Praises.* Peabody, Mass.: Hendrickson Publishers, 1990.
A reader-friendly exposition of the various types of Psalms, with an excursus expressing appreciation for sociological analysis as used by Walter Brueggemann, especially the categories of orientation, disorientation, and reorientation.

Bland, Dave & Fleer, David, eds. Performing the Psalms (St. Louis: Chalice Press, 2005)
Featuring addresses by Walter Brueggemann, J. Clinton McCann Jr., Paul Scott Wilson, and others, the editors present a symposium on how to transform the Psalms into modern sermon and worship.

Bratcher, Robert G. and William D. Reyburn. *A Translator's Handbook on the Psalms.* New York: United Bible Societies, 1991.
Focusing on the RSV and Good News Bible, the authors provide aids for translating Psalms.

Braude, William G. *The Midrash on Psalms.* Yale Judaic Series, xiii. New Haven: Yale University Press, 1959.
A significant repository for studying ancient Jewish interpretation of Psalms.

Brettler, Mark Z. *God Is King: Understanding an Israelite Metaphor.* JSOTSup 76. Sheffield: Sheffield Academic Press, 1989.
Examines the dominant metaphor of kingship, noting the grammatical ambiguity of the brief expression, *YHWH mālak.*

Brown, William P. *Seeing the Psalms: A Theology of Metaphor.* Louisville & London: Westminster John Knox, 2002.
Thoroughly theological, this book examines in great detail the dominant metaphors in Psalms (refuge, pathway, transplanted tree, sun of righteousness, many waters, animals, birthing, light and fountain) and concludes with a look at Psalm 139.

Brueggemann, Walter. *Abiding Astonishment. Psalms, Modernity, and the Making of History.* Louisville: Westminster/John Knox Press, 1991.
Examines the way Psalms looks at history; the author discards the earlier salvation history for more culturally open views (intergenerational, covenantally shaped, morally serious, dialogically open, and politically demanding).

_____. *The Message of the Psalms.* Minneapolis: Augsburg, 1984.
Homiletic insights for Christians focusing on orientation, disorientation, and reorientation.

_____. *Israel's Praise. Doxology against Idolatry and Ideology.* Philadelphia: Fortress Press, 1988.
Seeks to recover the sociological dimension of Hermann Gunkel's approach to Psalms by stressing the deployment and legitimation of social power.

Brunert, G. *Psalm 102 im Kontext des vierten Psalmenbuches.* SbB 30. Stuttgart: Katholisches Bibelwerk, 1996.
Studies a single psalm in its macrostructure.

Clifford, Richard J. *Psalms 1–72.* AOTC. Nashville: Abingdon Press, 2002.
Adopting a threefold scheme (literary analysis, exegetical analysis, theological and ethical analysis), the author provides a clear and perceptive look at the first two books of the Psalter.

Craigie, Peter C. *Psalms 1–50.* WBC, 19. Waco, Texas: Word Book Publishers, 1983.
A valuable conservative commentary, especially astute on theological issues. Updated 2004 edition by Marvin Tate.

Crenshaw, James L. *The Psalms. An Introduction.* Grand Rapids and Cambridge: Eerdmans, 2001.
Part I examines the different ways of interpreting Psalms (as prayers, resources for historical reconstruction, genres, and structured design) and Part II gives readings of Psalms 73, 115, 71, and 24. An excursus questions the utility of the category, "wisdom psalms."

Dahood, Mitchell. *Psalms,* Vols I-III. AB, 16, 17, 17A. Garden City, N.Y.: Doubleday, 1965, 1968, 1970.
Interprets Psalms in the light of Ugaritic texts, making frequent emendations of the Masoretic Text. Innovative but highly controversial in many of its conclusions; minimally theological.

deClaissé-Walford, Nancy. Introduction to the Psalms (St. Louis: Chalice Press, 2004)
Emphasizes the story connection that gives shape to the five books of the Psalter.

Delekat, L. *Asylie und Schutzorakel am Zionheiligtum: Eine Untersuchung zu den privaten Feindpsalmen* (Leiden: Brill, 1967).
Examines the concept of protection implied in oracles pertaining to Zion as a place of asylum, with reference to psalms of the individual.

Erbele-Küster, Dorothea. *Lesen als Akt des Betens. Eine Rezeptionsästhetik der Psalmen.* WMANT 87; Neukirchen/Vluyn: Neukirchener, 2001.
Applies reader response criticism to Psalms, discovering empty space that makes them useful in modern prayer.

Flint, Peter W. *The Dead Sea Psalm Scrolls and the Book of Psalms.* Leiden: Brill, 1997.
Examines the relationship of the earliest external evidence about the book of Psalms.

Gerstenberger, E. S. *Psalms, Parts I-II,* The Forms of the Old Testament Literature (Grand Rapids: Eerdmans, 1988, 2001)
Provides form critical classification and discussion of each of the units in the Psalter.

Gierlich, Augustinus M. *Der Lichtgedanke in den Psalmen. Eine terminologisch-exegetische Studie.* Freiburg im Bresgau: Herder & Co., 1940.
Examines the language of light (and darkness), and discusses the literal as well as the symbolic senses of the Hebrew words involved.

Gillingham, S. E. *The Poems and Psalms of the Hebrew Bible.* OBS. Oxford: University Press, 1994.
Places the poetry of Psalms in the larger context of prophetic, wisdom,

and legal poetic texts. Studies the Book of Psalms as poems and its true nature, whether hymns, prayers, or anthology, and traces the history of its interpretation.

Grossberg, Daniel. *Centripetal and Centrifugal Structures in Biblical Poetry.* SBLMS 39; Atlanta: Scholars Press, 1989.
Studies the tension in poetic works with both a uniform structure and a loose composition, focusing on the Psalms of Ascents (120–34) and Lamentations. Contains many insights into linguistic artistry.

Gunkel, Hermann and Begrich, Joachim. *An Introduction to the Psalms: The Genres of the Religious Lyric of Israel.* Macon, Ga.: Mercer University Press, 1998 (original publication, 1933).
This classic application of form criticism to the book of Psalms divides them into major and minor types, examines their social context, and inquires about their use. Thorough and seminal, it has exerted unprecedented influence on subsequent interpretation.

Hakham, Amos. *The Bible Psalms with the Jerusalem Commentary,* 3 vols. Jerusalem: Mosad Harav Kook, 2003.
Traditional Jewish interpretation joined to modern linguistic insights, both in the hand of a master teacher, make this commentary indispensable reading for biblical scholars and laity. The introduction, pages vi-xlv, contains massive details about the name of Psalms, headings, composition, function, structure, parallelism, poetic devices, order, parallels in other biblical books, and use in Jewish liturgy.

Holladay, William L. *The Psalms through Three Thousand Years. Prayerbook of a Cloud of Witnesses.* Minneapolis: Fortress Press, 1993.
An informative survey of the Psalms from the moment of composition to the modern era of interpretation, with an essay on the emergence of Psalm 23 as a sort of icon in North America, plus remarks about current theological issues.

Hossfeld, F. L. and Zenger, E. *Die Psalmen I: Psalms 1–50.* Die Neue Echter Bibel-Würzburg/Stuttgart: Echter, 1993.
An important commentary displaying recent trends of interpretation.

Howard, David M. Jr. *The Structure of Psalms 93–100.* Biblical and Judaic Studies 5. Winona Lake, Ind.: Eisenbrauns, 1997.
Using word association, syllable and stress counting, and structural arguments, the author seeks to prove that the present order of Psalms 93–100 is intentional and that YHWH's kingship is central to all the psalms, but that recognition does not imply a failure of the covenant with David.

Irsigler, Hubert. *Psalm 73–Monolog eines Weisen.* Arbeiten zu Text und Sprache im Alten Testament, 20. St. Ottilien: Eos Verlag, 1984.
Views Psalm 73 as a special kind of monologue before God and the worshipping community, using literary theory developed by Wolfgang Richter in which attention is paid to microstructure and macrostructure.

Jaki, Stanley L. *Praying the Psalms: A Commentary.* Grand Rapids: Eerdmans, 2001.

Unlike commentaries by biblical interpreters, this one offers a modern meditation on all 150 psalms, with insights drawn from the general culture, and frequent absolutist statements.

Janowski, Bernd. *Konfliktgespräche mit Gott: Eine Anthropologie der Psalmen.* Neukirchen/Vluyn: Neukirchener, 2003.

Develops an anthropology on the basis of human movements from "life to death" and from "death to life," focusing on Psalms 13, 58, 7, 41, 88, 30, 16 and 22.

Keel, Othmar. *The Symbolism of the Biblical World: Ancient Near Eastern Iconography and the Book of Psalms.* Winona Lake, Ind.: Eisenbrauns, 1997.

The pioneering study of iconography in the ancient Near East, with special attention to the Psalms. Covers cosmology, destructive forces, the temple, the deity, the king, and religious practice. Richly illustrated. Indispensable.

Kraus, Hans-Joachim. *Theology of the Psalms.* Minneapolis: Fortress Press, 1992.

Magesterial in analysis, comprehensive in scope, this volume treats the following topics: God, people, sanctuary, king, enemies, the individual before God, and the psalms in the New Testament.

_____. *Psalms* 1–59 and *Psalms* 60–150. Minneapolis: Fortress Press, 1988 and 1989.

The standard commentary on the book of Psalms by its foremost contemporary interpreter, mainly form critical.

Levine, Herbert J. *Sing Unto God a New Song. A Contemporary Reading of the Psalms.* Bloomington: Indiana University Press, 1995.

Discusses the conflict between harsh reality and religious praises especially in light on the Holocaust.

Limburg, James. *Psalms.* Louisville: Westminster John Knox Press, 2000.

Intended as a guide to laity, this commentary is both clear and informative, often with profound theological insights.

Mays, James L. *Psalms.* Louisville: John Knox Press, 1994.

A volume in the Interpretation series intended for teaching and preaching, this commentary leans toward the practical aspects of scripture, viewed from a conservative perspective, while attending to the usual demands of exegesis.

McCann, J. Clinton, Jr. *A Theological Introduction to the Book of Psalms.* Nashville: Abingdon Press, 1993.

_____. "The Book of Psalms," *NIB*, vol. IV, 641–1280.

Reflects on the psalmists' insights about God and humans that have contemporary value.

_____, ed. *The Shape and Shaping of the Psalter.* JSOTSup 159, Sheffield: JSOT Press, 1993.

A collection of essays by various scholars devoted to ascertaining the present arrangement of the psalms and rationale for it.

Millard, M. *Die Komposition des Psalters: Ein formgeschichtlicher Ansatz.* FAT 9. Tübingen: Mohr Siebeck, 1994.

A compendium on type-historical analysis of Psalms.

Miller, Patrick D., Jr. *Interpreting the Psalms.* Philadelphia: Fortress, 1986.
Intended for pastors and students, this book falls into two parts: (1) modes of interpreting Psalms, with special consideration of laments and praises; and (2) brief exegetical analysis of ten psalms (1, 2, 14, 22, 23, 82, 90, 127, 130, 139).

_____. *They Cried to the Lord: The Form and Theology of Biblical Prayer.* Minneapolis: Fortress, 1994.
Compares biblical laments in Psalms to those in neighboring cultures, while giving a perceptive theological assessment of Israel's own profound doubts and courageous faith.

Mowinckel, Sigmund. *The Psalms in Israel's Worship* (Nashville:Abingdon, 1962).
Standard work representing the Scandinavian myth and ritual school's interpretation of the worship practices that produced the Psalter.

Pleins, J. David. *The Psalms: Songs of Tragedy, Hope, and Justice.* Maryknoll, N.Y.: Orbis Books, 1993.
Using a sociological approach, the author concentrates on issues of suffering, social justice, and worship. He first examines individual and communal laments to determine the nature of the psalmists' suffering, then looks at political structures, finally studying the religious dimension of the Psalter.

Prothero, R. E. *The Psalms in Human Life.* New York: E. P. Dutton, 1903.
Looks at the way individuals over the ages have personalized the experiences of the psalmists, both their moments of turmoil and their times of joy.

Raabe, P. R. *Psalms Structures: A Study of Psalms with Refrains.* JSOT Sup 104.Sheffield: JSOT Press, 1990.
Esthetic interest in the function of repetition in key locations.

Sarna, Nahum. *Songs of the Heart: An Introduction to the Book of Psalms.* New York: Schocken, 1993.
Essays on some psalms, viewed against the ancient Near Eastern context and in light of classical Jewish commentaries.

Seybold, Klaus. *Introducing the Psalms.* Edinburgh: T. & T. Clark, 1990.
A valuable examination of virtually everything students, especially seminarians, need to know about Psalms' origin, genre, purpose, content, affinities with ancient Near Eastern literature, and influence until modern times.

_____. *Die Wallfahrtpsalmen. Studien zur Entstehungsgeschichte von Psalmen 120–134.* Biblische-Theologische Studien 3. Neukirchen-Vluyn: Neukirchener Verlag, 1978.
Understands the Songs of Ascents as originally composed for rural pilgrimages but subsequently adapted, not very smoothly, for use in the temple at Zion.

Seybold, Klaus, and Zenger, Erich, ed. *Neue Wege der Psalmenforschung: Für Walter Beyerlin.* Herders biblische Studien 1. Freiburg: Herder, 1994.
Essays on contemporary approaches to the Psalter.

Sheppard, G. T. "Theology and the Book of the Psalms," *Interpretation* 46 (1992): 143–55.
Views Psalms as a didactic guide to righteousness.

Simon, Uriel. *Four Approaches to the Book of Psalms. From Saadiah Gaon to Abraham Ibn Ezra.* Albany, N.Y.: SUNY Press, 1991.
A valuable study of Jewish commentaries on Psalms, with extensive examination of the intellectual context in which they were composed. Discusses Saadiah Gaon (Psalms as a second Pentateuch); Salmon ben Yeruham and Yefet ben 'Ali (Psalms as prophetic prayers); Moses Ibn Giqatilah (Psalms as non-prophetic prayers and poems); and Abraham Ibn Ezra (Psalms as prophetic and sacred poetry).

Soll, Will. *Psalm 119. Matrix, Form, and Setting.* CBQMS 23. Washington, D.C.: The Catholic Biblical Association of America, 1991.
Examines the acrostic form in ancient Near Eastern literature, identifies Psalm 119 as a lament/prayer, contests the claim that its purpose is didactic, and places it in an exilic context.

Smith, Mark S. *Psalms. The Divine Journey.* New York: Paulist, 1987.
Emphasizes divine presence in the temple and solar imagery as a means of appreciating the Psalms.

Steussy, Marti. *Psalms.* St. Louis: Chalice, 2004.
Part of Chalice Commentaries for Today that seek to provide theological application as well as exposition of the text from a Process perspective.

Tate, Marvin E. *Psalms 51–100.* WBC. Dallas: Word Books, 1990.
An indispensable commentary, with careful attention to grammar and syntax, copiously documented.

Terrien, Samuel. *The Psalms. Strophic Structure and Theological Commentary.* Grand Rapids: Eerdmans, 2003.
This massive tome emphasizes poetic units and religious expression, while rooting many of the psalms in festivals and attributing numerous concepts to sages. It contains a rich bibliography, a fresh translation for every psalm, and exposition of form, commentary, date and theology.

Tsevat, Matitiahu. *A Study of the Language of the Biblical Psalms.* SBLMS 9; Philadelphia: Fortress Press, 1955.
A statistical account of formulaic words and phrases within Psalms that indicate a linguistic tradition from which the poets drew.

Vosberg, Lothar. *Studien zum Reden vom Schöpfer in den Psalmen.* Beiträge zur evangelische Theologie, Band 69. München: Chr. Kaiser Verlag, 1975.
Views three psalms as immediate responses to the destruction of Jerusalem in 587 BCE (Psalms 74, 89, and 102), while Psalms 33, 115, and 124 are seen as early post-exilic and Psalms 95, 135, 136, 147, and 148 as post-exilic liturgical confessions that YHWH is creator and has not forgotten his people.

Wieder, Laurance. *Words to God's Music. A New Book of Psalms.* Grand Rapids: Eerdmans, 2003.
Poetic renderings of all 150 Psalms into modern imagery and concepts, with sensitivity to both language and religious insights from the ancient world.

Westermann, Claus. *Praise and Lament in the Psalms.* Atlanta: John Knox Press, 1981.

Argues for a simplification of Gunkel's main types of psalms and makes wide use of data from the ancient Near East. Re-evaluates the presentation of history in Psalms.

Wilson, Gerald H. *The Editing of the Hebrew Psalter.* SBLDS 76. Chico, CA: Scholars Press, 1985.

Dissertation arguing for the coherent editorial structure behind the present form of the Psalter.

Zenger, Erich. *A God of Vengeance: Understanding the Psalms of Divine Wrath.* Louisville: Westminster John Knox, 1996.

Investigates the theological scandal generated by the vindictive psalms and tries to exonerate them from such a charge by stressing God's sense of justice, which believers should share, as long as they leave vengeance to God.

CHAPTER 13

The Deuteronomist and the Writings

While writing this paper I found it necessary to resist a strong sense of *deja vu.* Thirty years ago a pan-sapientialism infected much research relating to the Hebrew Bible, as if to make up for years of ignoring or worse, disdaining, wisdom literature because of the prevailing theological interest in "salvation history." The prophets Isaiah and Amos were said to have been educated in wisdom circles–the first within the royal court, the second in wisdom of the clan–and the same general background, the court, was posited for the story of human origins in Gen 1–11 and the narrative about Joseph in Gen 37–50. In 1968 I suggested to my class that the next logical step would be to view the so-called succession document as a product of the sages. Before the quarter ended, R. N. Whybray proposed precisely that, arguing that the episodes in 2 Sam 9–20, 1 Kgs 1–2 reinforce the moral lessons found in aphorisms within the book of Proverbs. This tendency to posit wisdom influence throughout canonical literature seemed out of control, so that even such an unlikely candidate as the book of Esther was co-opted for the sages. Within a decade few books of the Hebrew Bible had escaped the claim of sapiential influence–one thinks of Deuteronomy, Ruth, Jonah, Psalms, Micah, Habakkuk, Song of Songs, and various textual units elsewhere. I determined to resist this trend on methodological grounds, at the same time launching a career in wisdom literature.[1] If now, considerably older, I continue that resistance, although on a new playing field, you will not be surprised.

The similarities between the two trends, pan-sapientialism and pan-Deuteronomism, are astonishing. Lacking adequate controls or agreed-on criteria, scholars make their cases by appealing to (1) phraseological similarities, (2) thematic considerations, (3) social location, (4) creative adaptation, and (5) oppositional ideology.[2] The reasoning, overwhelmingly circular, convinces only those who have already subscribed to the theory. The strongest argument, linguistic parallels, loses force when one considers the paucity of written material from ancient Israel that remains. We simply do not know what literature was available to ancient authors, for we cannot assume that all of it survived as the biblical canon. Seldom does anyone examine the underlying assumptions, particularly with respect to the extent of literacy in ancient Israel and the availability of exemplars of canonical texts.[3]

Some observations about terminology seem appropriate at this juncture. The distinction between Deuteronomist and Deuteronomistic should be retained, the former pointing to an original source and the latter to subsequent works in the same vein. The terms "Deuteronomistic movement" and "Deuteronomistic school" are more problematic, as is also "Deuteronomism."[4] Movements and schools imply definite social locations and specific language, perhaps even their own literature.[5] Evidence is lacking for any of these. Josiah's early death must surely have crushed the brief national-cultic reform movement, and the next sustained movement in Yehud was inaugurated by the Maccabees. Neither the scribal activity of Hezekiah's men nor the reforms of Ezra-Nehemiah amount to a movement. Similarly, no real Deuteronomistic school, in the institutional sense, existed, and no Deuteronomistic "school of thought" can reasonably be postulated on the basis of the evidence.

The task of assessing the relationship between the Deuteronomist and the Writings would be quite different if Deuteronomy actually arose in wisdom circles, as Moshe Weinfeld has endeavored to demonstrate.[6] His argument rests on too many improbabilities to carry conviction–turning the dating of the proverbial collections upside down, with no justification;[7] assuming an exclusive ownership among sages for common concepts in the ancient world;[8] attributing all scribal activity to sages;[9] and ignoring significant differences between Deuteronomy and wisdom literature.[10] Nevertheless, his list of verbal links between Deuteronomy and wisdom literature provides a point of departure for this discussion.[11]

The Deuteronomist and Wisdom Literature

I turn first to suggested affinities between Deuteronomy and the book of Proverbs. In Deut 4:2 the following prohibition occurs: "Do not add to the word that I command you, nor take away from it" (cf. Deut 13:1 [Eng 12:32], "Do not add to it or take from it"). The sayings of Agur in Prov 30:1–14 contain this warning: "Do not add to his words lest he rebuke you and you be made a liar." The first text concerns divine commands, the other palpably human reflections; one gives no rationale, the other specifies the reason underlying the warning. One uses the negative particle *lô'*, the other has *'al*. One balances the warning, giving both a positive and a negative; the other does not mention taking away from something.[12] Moreover, the expression in its balanced form is at home in treaty curses and scribal colophons, which suggests that others besides the author of Deuteronomy used it.[13] Which is more likely? That a foreign sage knew and quoted Deuteronomy, or that he used language from ancient Near Eastern treaty formulation and scribal remarks about faithful renderings of a text?[14]

The injunction in Deut 19:14 against removing a neighbor's landmark finds a parallel in Prov 23:10, "Do not remove a widow's landmark or encroach on the fields of orphans."[15] The differences in the language stand out: *lô'* versus *'al*, *rē'akā* instead of *'ôlām* or *'almānâ*. The typical Deuteronomic rhetoric ("in your inheritance which you will hold in the land Yahweh your God gives you to possess") is lacking in Proverbs. The ancient curse in Deut 27:17 has a participle (*massîg*); here the oath particle functions as negation and the pronominal suffix is third person plural rather than second person singular. Between Prov 23:10 and these texts only two words agree: *tassēg gebûl*.[16] Can anyone imagine that only the author of Deuteronomy worried about this treachery in an agrarian economy? An Egyptian parallel to this injunction suggests otherwise.[17] Egyptian usage also readily explains the phrase, "abomination of Yahweh," in Proverbs (3:32; 11:1, 20; 12:22; 15:8, 9, 26; 16:5; 17:15; 20:10, 23), for this idea belongs to wisdom circles as well as to legal texts.[18] There is nothing exclusively Deuteronomistic about *tô'abat Yhwh*; the whole society understood certain acts as repulsive to the deity.

The author of Deuteronomy urged a visually stimulating practice to assure the preservation of divine statutes: binding them on parts of the body (the hand and the forehead) and on entry ways (doorposts and gates, 6:7–9; 11:18–20). At the same time, the people must keep the commandments on the heart always, teaching children on rising, during the day, and at bedtime. In Prov 6:20–22 the father tells the son to bind parental teaching on the heart and to tie the instruction around the neck so that it will protect him during all circumstances. The differences are important: divine commandments as opposed to parental teaching, literal verbs of binding and writing over against figurative language (cf. Prov 7:3, "tablet of your heart"). From time immemorial parents have encouraged their children to put their teachings into practice, and the prominence of this admonition in ancient wisdom outside the Bible suggests that the author of Prov 6:20–22 did not need to be instructed by the book of Deuteronomy.[19]

The other supposed borrowings from Deuteronomy within the book of Proverbs have even less claim to credence. These include the warning in Prov 30:10 against slandering one's slave in the presence of his master, which has absolutely nothing in common with Deut 23:15–16 (a legal injunction against returning an escaped slave to his master); the expression, "to show partiality in judgment" in Deut 1:17 and 16:19 and in Prov 24:23b (cf. 28:21); the words "pursue justice" in Deut 16:20 and Prov 21:21; and "inherit the land" in Prov 2:21–22 and 10:30, frequently in Deuteronomy.[20] One must explain the change from prohibitive to participial assertion in Prov 24:23, as well as the sequel, replacing the merism, small and great, with "*bal ṭôb*." The prophet Amos, among others, understood the intimate connection between the pursuit of justice and life. This was no secret lore known only to the author of Deuteronomy. As for the reference to dwelling on the land in Prov 2:21–22 and 10:30 (cf. Job 15:19; 22:8), the idea has nothing to do with the concept of divinely promised inheritance in Deuteronomy. The sages merely meant that decent people will have land to occupy (*škn*) as reward for virtue.[21]

To sum up, resemblances in phraseology between Deuteronomy and Proverbs do exist, but always amid notable differences. When using a text, an author can make alterations, but once this occurs, later readers cannot determine whether or not borrowing actually took place.

When one moves beyond linguistic similarities to broad concepts, does the situation change? Three ideas have been said to indicate wisdom influence on Deuteronomy or vice versa: the fear of the Lord, theodicy, and reward.[22] Not every instance of the concept, fear of Yahweh, in Deuteronomy comes under the category of a covenantal relationship, otherwise how could the author accuse Amalek, a foreigner, of lacking this quality (25:18)?[23] Nevertheless, that falls far short of asserting that the fear of Yahweh constitutes the first principle and impetus of all knowledge. The author of Deuteronomy makes a similar point quite differently: foreigners will recognize that keeping the divine statutes is the people's wisdom and understanding (4:6). Moreover, the notion of fearing God is not even unique to Deuteronomy within the Pentateuch, for it looms large in contexts normally attributed to an Elohistic writer.

If the concept of theodicy were unique to Deuteronomy and Proverbs, one could reasonably argue that the two books are somehow related. Unfortunately, theodicy pervades the thinking of the ancient world, leaving virtually nothing untouched.[24] Its centrality to thinkers everywhere makes it pointless to claim that a special relationship exists between Deuteronomy and Proverbs, or Job, for that matter. Belief that deserving persons had a secure future (*'aḥarît*) and that their hope would not be cut off (Prov 23:18, 24:14; cf. Ps 37:38; 73:17) characterized prophets, priests, sages, and apocalyptists in the ancient world. Reward and punishment belong to this nexus of thought. The idea was so widespread that none could escape its influence, even when reacting strongly against the concept (cf. the book of Job). What about specific applications of the theory such as the claim that Yahweh disciplines the one he loves just as a father reproves the son who pleases him (Prov 3:12)?[25] When Deuteronomy makes a similar point, the language differs significantly: a form of the verb *yāšar* instead of *yākaḥ*, *'îš* for *'āb*, and no indication that the son pleases the father (Deut 8:5). In Proverbs the analogy moves from the divine to the human, whereas Deuteronomy argues the other way around–Yahweh behaves in the same way humans do. Strikingly, the author of Prov 3:12 stresses divine love, missing in Deut 8:5.

Deuteronomy and Ecclesiastes

Two contexts in Qoheleth require comment: 5:1–5 and 12:13–14. The author of Deuteronomy observes three things about vows: (1) when you make one, be sure to carry it out; (2) abstaining from making a vow is acceptable conduct; and (3) Yahweh keeps track of promises and requires a full reckoning (Deut 23:22–24 [Eng, 21–23]). In the context of warning against hasty speech, presumably of a religious nature, Qoheleth points to the vast gulf separating Elohim from humankind, one that invites reticence in speech. Qoheleth then turns to the topic of vows, after deprecating loquacity. He urges prompt payment of religious vows, inasmuch as the deity has no particular fondness for fools. Repeating the advice to pay the vow, this time in those exact words, Qoheleth expresses the opinion that abstaining from such promises is preferable to making them and subsequently failing to carry them out. He goes on to warn against any conduct that places the body in jeopardy; as a precaution against danger, he urges fear of Elohim, which apparently means exactly that rather than a mild notion of religious devotion. The importance of vows in Israelite society can be seen from the fact that even Qoheleth comments on the practice, and this daily occurrence, not the book of Deuteronomy, shaped the advice in Qoh 5:15. Admittedly, both Qoheleth and Deuteronomy use virtually the same vocabulary at one juncture: "When you vow an oath...do not put it off" (*kî-tiddōr neder...lō' te'aḥēr lešallemô* in Deut 23:22, *ka'ašer tiddōr neder...'al-te'aḥēr lešallemô* in Qoh 5:3), but the idiom was a common one.[26]

The second epilogue to Qoheleth sums up matters quite simply–fear Elohim and keep his commandments–although completely at odds with the overwhelming sentiment of the book.[27] The moderating effort to negate the impact of Qoheleth's skepticism may come from traditional Yahwism, but that does not result in a personalizing of the deity, who retains the general name Elohim here. Furthermore, this author envisions a final judgment when every secret thing will be exposed. The author of Deuteronomy also reflects on secret things, but they belong to the special knowledge of Yahweh as opposed to the revealed things in the Mosaic legislation (29:29).

Deuteronomy and Late Liturgical Prayers

Liturgical prayers in the ninth chapter of three books–Ezra, Nehemiah, and Daniel–use occasional language reminiscent of the book of Deuteronomy. Two reasonable explanations for this phenomenon come to mind. The several books reflect a special religious discourse[28] or they indicate conscious imitation of an original religious document, probably Deuteronomy.[29] The balance of probability goes to the first explanation for this phenomenon, although editorial activity cannot be ruled out. The conservative nature of piety encourages the use of traditional language, but the reservoir from which the worshipper draws is fed by more than one stream.[30] Similarities with Deutero-Isaiah and prose passages in the book of Jeremiah quickly come to mind.[31]

The relevant expressions in Ezra 9 include "thy servants the prophets" and "as at this day," together with the idea that Israelites must not inter-marry with their neighbors (Deut 7:3). The prayer in Nehemiah 9 adds the concept of Yahweh's uniqueness and mentions the importance of divine reputation ("thou alone" and "acquired a name"). To these expressions Daniel 9 adds an allusion to the curse recorded in Deut 28:15–45, while reiterating such language as "his servants the prophets" and "acquired a name." These prayers remind God, and indirectly the reader, of a host of experiences in the wilderness, but the episodes are not unique to Deuteronomy. The closest resemblance comes in the rhetoric, often wordy, but even here one finds more restraint than in Deuteronomy (cf. Dan 9:15, where "with a mighty hand" stands alone without the balancing "and a strong arm").

The matter becomes enormously complicated when one considers the relationship between Deuteronomy and the Psalter. To be sure, the same words appear here and there in both books, but one expects such overlap in similar discourse. Didacticism punctuates certain psalms, for example, 34, in the same way it shapes discourse in aphorisms and instructions, on the one hand, and Deuteronomy, on the other hand. For this reason, Weinfeld's assembling of common words in Psalms and Deuteronomy carries little weight–even the emphasis on Yahweh's uniqueness (Ps 83:19 [Eng 18]; 86:10), the necessity of acting "with all one's heart" (Ps 119:10, 34, 69), and the indication of allegiance, cleaving to Yahweh (Ps 63:9 [Eng 8]) or to his testimonies (Ps 119:31).[32] Such resemblances between Deuteronomy and a torah Psalm occasion little surprise.

The remaining books in the Writings operate in different realms of discourse from Deuteronomy–Song of Songs with its erotic lyrics, Lamentations with its heavy emotional distress, Ruth's idyllic story, Esther's realistic politics, and the Chronicler's revisionist history.[33] If Deuteronomistic editors really existed as late as the period from Nehemiah to the Maccabean revolt,[34] why did they overlook Esther, a book that invites a different understanding of divine activity than that proffered, one that identifies human actions as the determinant of the nation's fate?[35] The absence of distinct Deuteronomistic ideas in these books raises the issue of selectivity.[36] Why would redactors ignore a book that cried out for alternative interpretations of reality?[37] Did the editors not know Esther?

Some Methodological Observations

Having examined the linguistic connections between Deuteronomy and the Writings, I want to close with some comments about the assumptions underlying the current pan-Deuteronomism. First, several types of argument lack cogency: those based on a common social location (e.g., that both Deuteronomy and X derive from the Northern kingdom) and those that set two books over against each other (e.g., that the author of Job was reacting to the teachings of Deuteronomy).[38] Similarly, the approach that explains differences in phraseology between Deuteronomy and other books as developments in the linguistic expression of Deuteronomistic redactors seems inadequate. The same goes for attempts to attribute different themes to changing socio-economic situations. Such arbitrary claims make it impossible to establish controls over one's logic, which changes to suit the occasion. Languages do change, but this fact makes it impossible to establish literary dependence when the two expressions differ noticeably.

Second, most people in Israel and Judah were illiterate, even as late as the second century.[39] One wonders how Deuteronomistic redactors could have gotten access to exemplars of the individual scrolls of the Writings.[40] Only the wealthy could afford scrolls, and individual libraries probably did not exist.[41] Even if exiled Judeans were introduced to literature, they lacked the means of becoming literate.[42] The few scribal guilds probably guarded their craft,[43] and writing was incidental to learning, even for Ben Sira.[44] Those scholars who think Deuteronomistic redactors persisted from the sixth century onwards seem to think of a literate society with accessible libraries and copious manuscripts. The exceptional situation at Qumran[45] should not be read back into earlier centuries in Yehud. Apocalyptic understandings of reality produced entirely new ways of thinking about written texts;[46] so did *pešer* readings, which elevate a sacred text almost to the numinous.[47] Finally, if Deuteronomistic redactors were so active in late canonical texts, why did they ignore Sirach with its numerous possibilities?[48]

CHAPTER 14

Reflections on Three Decades of Research

In the early sixties when I completed my Ph.D. studies in Old Testament at Vanderbilt University, two fundamentally different approaches to the biblical text vied for acceptance. On the one hand, the archaeological school of W. F. Albright and his students emphasized the historical features of the Bible and insisted on confirming the biblical account through artifactual evidence. On the other hand, form critics were inclined to stress the general aspects of discourse throughout the ancient world. Biblical distinctiveness came up against shared features in various geographical areas, specifically Egypt, Canaan, and Mesopotamia. Conservatives tended to opt for an historical approach to the Bible, whereas more liberal interpreters gravitated toward an analysis of speech forms. One of the most significant critics of the previous decade and a half, Gerhard von Rad, championed a mediating position, the tradition-history approach, that permitted him to pay lip service to history while actually focusing on creedal formulations.

My own inclination, inspired by a degree in literature at Furman University and fueled by the unfortunate dismissal of many of my teachers at Southern Baptist Theological Seminary, leaned heavily toward form criticism. The language of Neo-Orthodoxy, especially the talk about "mighty acts of God," rang hollow, partly because of challenges by one of my theology teachers at Vanderbilt, Langdon Gilkey, but also because I tended to disbelieve all claims about the Bible's sacred character. I did, nevertheless, find its literary features fascinating; besides that, I always wished to acknowledge the impact of the Bible on my religious experience. From the very beginning, then, I understood myself as a dissident, and the products of my literary activity over the years indicate little change in this respect. Three foci of my work stand out: 1) an interest in the speech forms within the Bible; 2) a desire to anchor those patterns of discourse in specific social contexts; and 3) a fascination with religious conflict within the biblical record, whether overt or covert.

I. Speech Forms

My dissertation on the doxologies of Amos brings together all three foci, for it concentrates on ancient hymnic affirmations, endeavors to situate the poetic fragments in a specific religious setting, and posits a conflict within the later Jewish community as generative influence. In doing so, the dissertation addresses the issues of divine justice as understood in the ancient world. My primary interest, however, was literary, and that focus has remained constant, giving rise to numerous "aesthetic" studies in Hebrew and Greek texts. Sensing a need for purely literary analysis, I examined the Samson saga and proposed an approach that I called "aesthetic criticism," principally because the term "literary criticism" had come to mean source analysis. Literary interpretation was "in the air," for that book, *Samson*, appeared the same year two other volumes of this genre did, those by David Gunn on *The Story of King David* and Phyllis Trible on *God and the Rhetoric of Sexuality*, three years before Robert Alter's heavily touted book, *The Art of Biblical Narrative.* My interest in the exquisite use of language resulted in various essays on refrains, rhetorical suasion, riddles, and the phenomenon I have identified as clanging symbols, the dynamic tension between form and content within a given literary unit. Although the emphasis is new, the groundwork for such studies exists in form criticism itself, for Hermann Gunkel certainly appreciated stylistic niceties in the literature he studied. The same must be said of tradition historians such as von Rad, for example, who commented on the poignant beauty in the story about Abraham's sacrifice of Isaac (*Das Opfer des Abraham*) and described the exalted rhetoric of the counselors Ahithophel and Hushai.

II. Social Context

My interest in discourse analysis has not been divorced from my concern to discover specific circumstances that shaped the language of distinct groups. It seemed to me that this search for social context was particularly difficult. At what point did individualism emerge to break up conventional modes of expression, and what forces led to an awareness of the ego? Form criticism by its very nature stresses similarities in modes of expression, although speech forms are then thought to have been given specific loci. Sociological interests naturally follow, and I have occasionally found such investigations irresistible. My work on the Samson saga led me to propose an apologetic purpose for the three episodes about the hero's entanglement with foreign women. Similarly, my analysis of hymnic fragments suggested that guilt-ridden Israelites pronounced doxologies of judgment on themselves and that they struggled to maintain the integrity of Yahwism in a syncretistic religious environment.

That sociological interest has dominated my investigations of wisdom literature, partly because of von Rad's dubious hypothesis about a Solomonic Enlightenment and partly because of widespread theories about temple and scribal schools in early Israel. Caution has always seemed wise, especially when the evidence is non-existent, meager, or capable of different interpretations. I have tried to imagine the distinct settings in which learning transpired, and the family has loomed large in my findings. Claus Westermann's recent history of research in wisdom literature, *Forschungsgeschichte zur Weisheitsliteratur 1950–1990*, underlines the complexity of the problem, for scholars remain divided over two essential issues: 1) were the proverbial sayings originally oral or written, and 2) did education occur at home or in professional schools? Naturally, other problems of lesser import concern the nature of sapiential discourse, that is, its sacred as opposed to secular character, and the matter of royal patronage. Perhaps most vexing of all, the problem of dating the several proverbial collections and consequently of writing a history of sapiential thought have occupied much of my interest. Even the goal of determining a date for the composition of the books of Job and Qoheleth has by no means been achieved, despite reasonably plausible guesses.

From the outset, my study of wisdom literature arose as an effort to counter a tendency to minimize its distinctiveness. I have resisted that trend on methodological grounds, a position that seems right in view of ever-widening claims of wisdom influence. H. W. Wolff's initial foray in this regard struck me as wrong, and his further claims about clan wisdom in Micah and Joel hardly strengthened the case. Sages naturally used language that overlapped with that of prophets and hagiographers, for they spoke the Hebrew of their day. That is why the mere use of a few expressions by sages and others does not indicate wisdom influence; the sages did not have a monopoly on certain words dealing with knowledge and ethics. (Consider, for example, the fact that less than 18% of the forms of *ya 'aṣ* [to advise, plan] occur in wisdom literature.). That acknowledgment lies at the heart of my resistance to so many claims about the ubiquitous presence of wisdom influence throughout the Bible.

III. Religious Conflict

Perhaps as a result of endless denominational disputes in our day, I have constantly looked at biblical texts from the standpoint of an historian of religion. That interest led me to study popular expressions of religion within quotations attributed to opponents of biblical prophets on the assumption that authentic views, although satirized, often came to light. My own doubt about religious authority compelled me to ask whether or not the canonical prophets were actually received as authentic spokespersons for the deity. This question led to an analysis of false prophecy, which only served to highlight the thin line between true and false prophets. The apologetic features of religious claims could hardly be denied, and the confirmation that ancient religious communities struggled to articulate their faith in the same way modern ones do lent urgency to the task.

Perhaps the dominant theme of my research has related to divine justice. Ancient responses to the problem of theodicy intrigue me, and I have examined this literary tradition extensively. Of course, that research has concentrated on Job and its parallels, along with Psalm 73 and Jeremiah's "Confessions," as well as Qoheleth and Ben Sira. I have argued that skepticism is absolutely essential to viable faith and that expressions of doubt reveal the vitality of religion, not its decadence. Perhaps my emphasis has been too individualistic, as Walter Brueggemann has asserted, but I have tried to isolate the agonizing cry of bold thinkers who refused to allow revered traditions to silence their experience of reality, knowing that the voice survived only because it coincided with the cries of numerous others. From first to last I have resisted the impulse to exonerate deity at human expense.

After all, liberal existentialism nurtured me during the formative years of my theological training. Accordingly, I have searched for authentic expressions of self-understanding, for I think at the deeper levels of Angst, modern individuals differ little from their ancient counterparts. Believing this, I have explored the rich language describing suffering in the Bible, and I have tried to understand lonely persons of faith in a silent universe. Naturally, my concern has extended beyond what the text meant, although the latter investigation has certainly governed most of my research. Furthermore, it has prevented me from imposing Christian readings on the Hebrew Bible, for I have always asked what ancient Israelites would have heard in a given text.

Appreciation for later Jewish communities, which my teacher Lou H. Silberman taught me, guided my literary activity from the beginning. Nevertheless, profound religious understandings within the bible have tempered my skepticism now and again. Having chosen to attend a Christian church and to express my faith in this particular religious community as opposed to other viable options, I have tried to test my own religious sensibilities by the written testimony of my ancestors. More often than not, that endeavor has resulted in an emphatic "no" to the tradition. But not always. For me wisdom literature has offered a universal voice of reason, one untainted by particularistic claims. I am reminded, however, that an ancient sage, Ben Sira, finally felt it necessary to introduce divine mediation into his own reflection about the relationship between Israel and its deity. For many contemporary scholars, this intersection of the universal and the particular has become highly problematic.

My literary career has included considerable editing, first as editor of the Society of Biblical Literature Monograph Series, subsequently as a member of various editorial boards, presently also as editor of a series on Personalities of the Old Testament. I have understood that task as a labor of love, just as I have undertaken the editing of three Festschriften and a volume on wisdom for the Library of Biblical Studies. In all of my work–and especially as director of Ph.D. dissertations–I have tried to encourage others to express themselves freely, whether I agreed with them or not. Never have I assumed that I have sole access to the truth; often I have been humbled by how little I know. I am not an archaeologist, a specialist in text criticism, a master of various ancient Near Eastern languages. In all these areas, I have had to rely on the scholarship of others. Basically, I employ an eclectic approach to the Bible, remembering what my mentor, J. Philip Hyatt said ("Your second Bible is *ANET*"), and entering into dialogue with a text just as passionately as my teacher, Walter Harrelson, does to this day.

To conclude, for three decades I have studied the Bible and similar ancient Near Eastern texts from a literary and theological perspective in an attempt to understand the development of Israelite religion. My approach has been one among many, but it has enabled me to come to terms with my religious tradition and to appreciate ancient Israel's attempt to describe its experience with perceived holiness. My ongoing research, commentaries on Joel and Sirach, as well as a book on education in ancient Israel, will no doubt continue earlier interests and approaches, for the task never ends. Fortunately, neither does its lure.

CHAPTER 15

A Living Tradition

The Book of Jeremiah in Current Research

Careful study of the Book of Jeremiah helps us remain faithful to the prophet's legacy by learning from him to weigh the traditions of the past and to use them in the struggle to forge a better world.

The thirty-first meeting of the Biblical Colloquium at Louvain, Belgium on August 18–20, 1980, was entirely devoted to the Book of Jeremiah. The twenty papers of this session covered a broad range of topics; seventeen of them subsequently appeared in volume 54 of *Bibliotheca Ephemeridum Theologicarum Lovaniensium.*[1] In addition, two surveys of research on the Book of Jeremiah have recently appeared[2] and another was published in 1983.[3] Naturally, these assessments of the status of research on the biblical book were prompted by a spate of articles and monographs, and the future promises more of the same, including four commentaries currently under way.[4] Since others have provided comprehensive surveys of research, I shall restrict the present discussion to the issues that seem most problematic at the moment.

The fundamental issue can be stated forthrightly: How can we recognize authentic materials of Jeremiah when the book contains distinctive literary styles? The differences in style are so pronounced that they have given rise to a theory of four sources in chapters 1–45 (the remaining chapters 46–52 are usually considered secondary): (A) poetic oracles in 1–25; (B) biographical narrative in 26–45; (C) prose sermons in 1–45; and (D) a book of consolation in 30–31. The issue is further complicated by similarities in style and language between Deuteronomy and the "prose sermons." Five significant questions therefore require attention: (1) What texts really derive from Jeremiah? (2) Did the prophet borrow the language and style of a book toward which he must surely have felt ambiguous? (3) Who speaks in the book, Jeremiah or the later community? (4) Do the so-called confessions reveal anything about the prophet Jeremiah? (5) Did Jeremiah stand alone over against the other prophets of his day? In this essay we shall address these five issues and endeavor to clarify the basic problems that have surfaced thus far.

I. The Inspired Poet

Bernhard Duhm's legacy has come to dominate Jeremianic studies in one important respect. This is the assumption that prophets were inspired poets. To be sure, other scholars such as Hermann Gunkel and Hugo Gressmann took for granted the originality of the poetic word. This position has recently been reasserted with reference to Jeremiah by Robert Carroll. He writes: "The difficulties encountered by biblical scholars in determining which elements are primary and which secondary may be modified by attending to the poetic sections as primary, with some poetic additions, and the rest as secondary."[5] The qualifying phrase, "with some poetic additions," suggests that Carroll, like others before him, is unwilling to reckon every poetic saying as an authentic word from Jeremiah. In practice a further distinction has often been made: Inferior poetry is considered secondary. One could point to numerous instances of such reasoning, but it would serve no real purpose.

Now if, first and foremost, prophets were poets, it follows that we should look only to the poetic texts for authentic words from Jeremiah. Such is the conclusion that many critics have reached. But the situation becomes considerably more complex when the problem of the original scroll enters the picture, for our information about that early document comes entirely from the narrative accounts within the book. Both the fact of the scroll and the description of its contents derive from the prose itself.[6] What if the story about King Jehoiakim's destruction of the scroll is tendentious? This possibility has not prevented a search for the original scroll and the expanded version that Jeremiah is said to have dictated to Baruch.

Seizing a clue from the narrative description, scholars look for poetic oracles which pronounce judgment. For example, William Holladay believes that he has succeeded in isolating the contents of the original scroll and the expanded one. To the first scroll belong the call (1:4–14), the harlotry cycle (2:2–3, 5–37; 3:1–5, 12*b*–14*a*, 19–25), and the foe cycle (4:1–6:30; 8:4–10*a*, 13). The second scroll includes these poetic units plus a supplementary foe cycle (8:14–10:25).[7]

The title of Holladay's book calls attention to the architecture of the book. By this he means the rhetorical features that comprise the structure itself. Jack Lundbom's study of the rhetoric in the Book of Jeremiah[8] argued that chapters 1 through 20 comprise a distinct unit, one that is held together by the inclusio in 1:5 and 20:18 ("you came forth from the womb"/"from the womb did I come forth"). Whereas Lundbom restricted his analysis to inclusio and chiasmus, Holladay takes into account a wide range of rhetorical features. While I appreciate the emphasis on stylistic expression, especially by a scholar with the linguistic gifts of Holladay, I have reservations about his basic argument for two reasons. First, I fail to see why one inclusio (that observed by Lundbom) is preferred over several others, the most notable being the verbs about building and planting, tearing down and uprooting in chapters 1 and 24. The second reason is even more weighty. Given the extensive redactional activity that shaped the final form of the book, how do we know that a particular stylistic device indicates the original structure of the book? For instance, if chapter 24 is the result of redaction in Deuteronomistic circles, as most critics assume, then inclusios may derive from a later hand than the original compiler. How does one determine the stage at which such poetic niceties entered the text?[9] In the final analysis the issue is the *extent* of editorial work.

As a matter of fact, the argument from rhetoric cuts two ways. Helga Weippert has launched a concerted effort to demonstrate that a formal prose was widespread in the ancient Near East during Jeremiah's day.[10] Her most recent essay examines the Aramaic texts from Tell Deir 'Alla and neo-Assyrian salvation oracles, concluding that a formal prose similar to Deuteronomy was in existence throughout the area. If her thesis can be sustained, it calls into question the assumption about poetic oracles as the original nucleus and the claim that the Book of Jeremiah has been edited by persons who were influenced by Deuteronomy. In Weippert's view the formal prose within the book actually goes back to the prophet.[11] Here she moves one step further than John Bright, according to whom the rhetorical prose arose in the decade following Jerusalem's downfall,[12] and Artur Weiser, who believed that a liturgical prose was widespread in Judah, a type of preaching that occurs both in Jeremiah and in Deuteronomy.[13]

One significant feature of Weippert's argument is that the prose sermons are actually the paraenetic part of Jeremiah's attempt to move the people to repentance.[14] This demetrification of poetry had as its goal the turning of the people to God. The Deuteronomists are therefore dependent upon Jeremiah for the form of their sermons, Weippert contends. Naturally, her thesis collapses if one adopts the view that Jeremiah did not begin his ministry until after Josiah's death. Holladay, for example, believes Jeremiah modeled his prose sermons after Moses' speeches in Deuteronomy just as he used the form of Deuteronomy 32 as a model for his poetic oracles.[15]

II. Redactional Activity

The striking affinities between the prose "sermons" in the Book of Jeremiah and Deuteronomy have been explained in yet another way, specifically through the hypothesis of redactional activity by persons under Deuteronomic influence. One of the earliest efforts to clarify the nature of such editing was an article by J. Philip Hyatt[16] in which he significantly altered the predominant source theory proposed by Sigmund Mowinckel and essentially endorsed by Wilhelm Rudolph in his contribution to the *Kommentar zum Alten Testament* series. Mowinckel himself shifted from literary analysis to tradition history in 1946, and Hyatt later worked out his views in the *Interpreter's Bible.*

Two scholars have pursued this line of thinking with important results. Ernest W. Nicholson explained the prose tradition as preaching to the exilic community.[17] This means that the sermons addressed specific concerns of the Jews who resided in Babylon rather than those of Jeremiah's immediate environment. Nicholson thinks the likely place for such preaching and teaching activity was the synagogue.[18] Nevertheless, he regards some of the material in these prose sermons as Jeremianic and insists that the Deuteronomists have altered this authentic nucleus to meet their own needs at a later time. Other materials were, in his opinion, created *ad hoc* by the exilic teachers. In the first of these techniques, the adapting of earlier material to later situations, Jeremiah himself paved the way, according to Nicholson.

A similar emphasis underlies Winfried Thiel's exhaustive studies of the redactional activity behind chapters 1–45.[19] Authentic words of the prophet have been subjected to a thorough Deuteronomistic editing so as to present the people with a choice to accept or reject the divine word. This redactional activity led to the juxtaposing of a word of judgment and a promise of deliverance. The people's response to the two words in the exilic situation determined which one became operative in their own lives. If Thiel is right, the Book of Jeremiah illuminates the exilic community as well as the Judahite, and a mere surface reading of historical narrative in the Book of Jeremiah obscures the richness of the text.

Even this interpretation of the evidence may be less complex than the actual situation warrants, for Gunther Wanke's investigation of the so-called Baruch narrative has arrived at the conclusion that three different tradition complexes lie behind the biographical material in the book.[20] These are (1) 19:1–20:6; 26–29; 36; (2) 37–44; and (3) 45; 51:59–64. If Wanke is correct, we must reject earlier claims that the biographical sections were written by a single scribe[21] who wished to depict Jeremiah as a suffering prophet. Although first articulated by Heinrik Kremers,[22] the popular presentation of the *via dolorosa* by Gerhard von Rad has influenced countless students of the Book of Jeremiah.[23]

The overwhelming evidence for Deuteronomistic editing obviates the need for justifying Jeremiah's use of language and style from a book that promulgates a theology which the prophet seems clearly to have rejected. Whereas Deuteronomy establishes a single holy place, Jeremiah denounces that temple as destined for destruction. The old covenant was a failure, so Jeremiah proposes another one. The resulting picture of the prophet is somewhat disjointed. Although he insists that all genuine prophets proclaimed a message of judgment, hopeful words are attributed to him. How can we explain this apparent inconsistency?

III. The Book of Consolation

One explanation proceeds from similarities between Hosea and Jeremiah, which lead scholars to argue that chapters 30–31 contain a nucleus of an early message to the survivors of the Northern Kingdom. Even such a skeptic as Carroll concedes that 31:2–6, 15–20 represent Jeremiah's early preaching of hope to Israel.[24] This tiny ray of hope was subsequently transformed into the bright beam that shines forth from chapters 30–31. In a recent treatment of the themes of "gathering and return" in Jeremiah and Ezekiel, J. Lust acknowledges that an authentic nucleus may underlie chapters 30–31, but in his view the materials have been thoroughly edited by an exilic redactor.[25] In particular, the theme of "return" does not appear in the earliest strata of the Book of Jeremiah, but derives from an exilic redactor. Lust thinks this theme was later adapted to the Diaspora and probably compared with the exodus event. He makes the interesting observation that in several instances the theme is muted in the Septuagint. It is noteworthy that a strong case has been made for preferring the Septuagintal text over the Massoretic, which is expansionistic and represents later redactional activity.[26]

Another response to the question about the inconsistency of attributing positive words to Jeremiah focuses on the changed situation after the fall of Jerusalem in 587 B.C. This argument runs as follows: The collapse of the Judean state confirmed the authenticity of Jeremiah's message, demonstrating to one and all that he was indeed a true prophet. The Deuteronomists therefore chose to use him as a means of addressing their own people with an alternative to opt for or against the divine word. The irony is that they chose a prophet who failed miserably and attempted to bring about a different response to his message in their own day. Carroll perceived this irony quite clearly: "All the time the prophet Jeremiah strides through the tradition as the true prophet, the central focus of the community's life. This is not only hindsight; it is ideology."[27]

IV. The Quest for the Historical Jeremiah

The search for the real Jeremiah has recently been likened to the quest for the historical Jesus,[28] and the difficulty is said to be greater in dealing with the prophet from Anathoth. If the teachers in the exilic community shaped Jeremiah's words so as to address their own people, how can we be sure that the stories themselves are not literary creations without any solid basis in fact? What is to prevent critics from concluding, as Carroll has done, that Baruch was a "construct" invented by the Deuteronomists to carry certain elements of the tradition[29] and that Jeremiah's absence from the stories about the organization and life under Gedaliah gave rise to the account of Jeremiah's royal imprisonment?[30]

Is there a single text that offers irrefutable evidence about the prophet Jeremiah? Until a short time ago most interpreters would have answered this question by pointing to the confessions, for in them one seems to encounter the outpourings of a sensitive individual. That consensus has eroded as a result of several analyses of these unusual poems. The unsettled nature of this question is reflected by the two essays on the so-called confessions in the volume which emerged from the Colloquium at Louvain. The traditional view was largely upheld by Franz D. Hubmann, who had earlier written a thorough study of the redaction of these texts,[31] while an opposing interpretation was offered by J. Vermeylen.[32] According to Vermeylen, it is preferable to call these texts *psalms* and to emphasize their place in the *book* bearing the name of Jeremiah rather than to view them as actually having derived from the prophet. Accordingly, each psalm represents the dramatic episodes during the exilic period, then those events associated with the second temple, and finally the sharp conflict between the postexilic community and the impious.

Of course this debate has engaged scholars for some time, but the contours of the argument have changed greatly from those arising out of Henning Graf Reventlow's claim that these texts are best explained in connection with a prophetic office in the cult.[33] Naturally, this thesis met stiff resistance, especially from John Berridge, John Bright, and Sheldon Blank.[34] Blank sought to characterize the poems as paradigms which Jeremiah himself provided for later generations who struggled to maintain faithfulness in the midst of adversity. Gerhard von Rad has proposed a sort of compromise,[35] for he believed the prophet Jeremiah took up his commission and internalized it in a manner that was wholly unprecedented. The result was a struggle within Jeremiah's soul that eventuated in no comforting resolution. Von Rad's remarks about a change in literary style as the result of this inner struggle have now been supplemented by Giorgio Buccellati,[36] whose observations about the lyric style appropriate to theodicy are surely applicable beyond the Mesopotamian texts which occupy the center of his attention.

The lyrical character of these soliloquies in the Book of Jeremiah poses an important question: Did ancient poets adapt their style to accord with the subject matter? Perhaps we need to ask whether certain types of material lend themselves more readily to prose than to poetry and vice versa. It may be that the radical distinction between poetry and prose is both arbitrary and misleading when applied to the matter of authenticity.

To return to the task of establishing the actual account of Jeremiah's life, we note a growing skepticism with regard to the traditional date of Jeremiah's call. In the face of such questioning of the biblical record, which represents the beginning of his ministry in 627 B.C., alternative dates have been suggested that remove the problems presented by the virtual absence of any oracles from a time prior to the death of Josiah in 609. Although Hyatt argued long and hard for the date 609, his view met stiff resistance. It has been championed recently by Holladay,[37] who believes Jeremiah was born in 627 and called to a prophetic vocation then (so 1:5), while his actual prophetic activity did not begin until the death of Josiah in 609. Holladay thinks the words in 1:4–11:6 were delivered between 609 and 601, and that some of the "confessions" emerged early in 600 in connection with a vocational crisis brought on by opposition prophets. Norbert Lohfink endeavors to combine both views; he thinks Jeremiah worked prior to 609 as a propagandist and poet for Josiah's court, but became a prophet in 605.[38] If the dramatic events of 609 and 605 radically affected the life of Jeremiah, can one conclude the same about the severe drought that devastated the country in 601? The latest examination of the liturgy associated with that drought (14:1–15:9) has yielded an affirmative answer to this question.[39]

By far the most devastating attack on the traditional view that we can discover the real Jeremiah has come from Robert Carroll. He writes: "The prophet behaves as a perfect deuteronomist because to the deuteronomists that is how a prophet working in Josiah's time should behave. Ideology shapes and creates the representation of the prophet, and helps to explain why the deuteronomists produced the Jeremiah tradition..."[40] In Carroll's view, the prophet who pronounced judgment gradually became in the hands of the traditionists a preacher of the community's well being. Similarly, the prophet preached repentance, failed, became more negative, and lost all hope; whereas the tradition then developed the motif of repentance into a dogma of repentance.[41] The deuteronomists also created the image of Jeremiah as intercessor and suffering just one.[42] Still Carroll recognizes the polyvalency of the Jeremianic materials, the wide latitude of interpretation that such texts evoke. Of the soliloquies he writes:

> ...it [this material] is the outpouring of Jeremiah's own confessions, it is the redactors' shaping of those confessions, it is the community's response to the tragedy, it is the laments of various sixth-century groups, it is a later presentation of the community's responses to grief under the image of the prophet, or it is even a theologization of the divine suffering brought about by the destruction of the people...[43]

While the general tone of Carroll's book is negative, here he approaches an appreciation for the contribution of the traditionists. Perhaps the words of Siegfried Herrmann provide the ablest corrective to the denigration of the activity of the Deuteronomists.

> What has been handed on to us is, in the best sense of the term, "living tradition," reminiscences which are unsimplified, restricted to a few lines, given uniformity by only a few witnesses. The text points to history, and has itself undergone a history. It is not insignificantly shaped for further historic effect.[44]

Herrmann goes on to describe the living tradition as a process by which the Word of God became visible to the community, a point which Nicholson has made most effectively.

V. Prophetic Conflict

The implications of extensive redactional activity behind the Book of Jeremiah are immense. If the prose sermons and biographical material, together with the soliloquies of the book, reveal a great deal about the exilic and postexilic Jewish community, can we trust the account that represents Jeremiah as a prophet standing alone over against a host of prophets who uttered a different word for the people? Do the stories of confrontation fall into the same category as other Deuteronomistic narratives whose purpose is essentially didactic (for instance, 1 Kings 13),[45] so that the issue of historical veracity was subsumed under an eminently greater purpose? Those scholars who have discussed the problem of prophetic conflict have by and large not addressed this issue, for they take it for granted that the stories are rooted in fact even though they often use stereotypical features.[46] There is one exception to this judgment, the study by Ivo Meyer.[47]

The thesis of this book is that in genuine oracles deriving from Jeremiah, other prophets opposed the people, not Jeremiah. Meyer does grant that prophets occasionally confronted Jeremiah (5:30–31; 6:9–15), and this fact gave the later redactors a polemical stance that they developed for all it was worth. In short, passages like 23:9–32 are comprised of a number of disparate elements. They are literary mosaics rather than historical accounts. In Meyer's view the polemic reflects the Deuteronomistic theology according to which the prophets played a decisive role in accomplishing the divine judgment against Jerusalem.

The disquieting feature of Meyer's monograph derives from its method rather than its conclusions. He makes absolute claims about genuine and spurious texts on the basis of various literary traits: tension within a unit; repetition; doubling of introductory formulae; linguistic affinities; colorless, superfluous, or characteristic vocabulary and the like. To be sure, these are judgments that most of us make to a greater or lesser extent. Yet I think Meyer says far more than can be known about a given text. What is at stake is the precise nature of poetry, the freedom to shock, to startle, to lull the audience to sleep by repeating what has already been said, and so on. In my judgment, we must begin to search for ways to recognize a poet's freedom of expression that departs from custom, both syntactic and grammatical.[48]

The essential truth in Meyer's thesis is the recognition that the conflict between Jeremiah and the other prophets functions in the book as a sort of theodicy. The collapse of the Judean state was interpreted as divine punishment for the villainous conduct of the professional leadership in Jerusalem. If Carroll's promised monograph[49] on the struggle among prophets in Jeremiah's day follows up this lead, which he has himself recognized and remarked upon again and again, we shall begin to understand better the texts concerning the prophets in the Book of Jeremiah.

In my analysis of prophetic conflict I characterized the history of prophetic research under three rubrics according to the emphasis of a given period. Those three foci were (1) the prophet, (2) the message, and (3) the audience. As I saw it, a decisive shift occurred from the great individual, the ethical monotheist, to the actual content of the prophetic word, especially its formal characteristics; and then yet another emphasis emerged, specifically the community within which prophets spoke their words. The three foci are integrally related, and our conclusions about one radically affect what we think about the other two.

If my earlier assessment of the situation is accurate, the next step in research requires a thorough examination of rhetoric, for one cannot attend to the audience without taking into account modes of speech that were shared by the prophet and those who heard the prophetic word. The art of persuasion was a point of contact between the two, prophet and people, just as it provides for us a means of access to the worlds of the prophet and the audience. It follows that sociological analysis is essential to this task of understanding the means of persuasion adopted by a given prophet. Although still in its infancy, this sort of approach has received impetus from at least two fronts. Robert R. Wilson has drawn heavily upon the ancient Near Eastern world of prophecy and mediation to clarify the issue of a "support group,"[50] while Thomas W. Overholt has turned to the native American scene in an effort to understand how groups determined authentic words when bogus messages were also falling on their ears in abundance.[51] Perhaps one should also mention in this connection Douglas A. Knight's study of moral consciousness as reflected in the Book of Jeremiah.[52]

Conclusion

Thus far we have asked five questions as a means of introducing some important studies about specific problems of interpreting the Book of Jeremiah. The lack of any adequate answers should occasion little surprise for the readers of this essay. The issues are by no means simple ones, for they concern the nature of religious language itself. The divine word cannot be isolated from human speech by resorting to a theory of poetics or syllable counting,[53] and stories do not necessarily connote secondary derivation. In a word, the later traditionist may be no less inspired than the original prophet; and the prose which confronts the exilic and postexilic community with a spiritual choice must surely be on par with enigmatic poetry. What we witness in the history of the text that bears the name "Jeremiah" is a living tradition, one that is absolutely essential to the spiritual health of a community. Indeed, that vital tradition is kept alive by those of us who read the Book of Jeremiah and endeavor to grasp its meaning in an age when the ancient faith stood in jeopardy. The threat to survival of cherished convictions fashioned a crucible from which emerged new words for the people. If in the process clear distinctions between fact and fiction disappeared, who can say that the end result was a mistake? The real error, in my view, is the dogged insistence that the words attributed to Jeremiah and the stories about him are understood correctly only on the "factual" level. What we have lost as the result of recognizing that the text gives us limited and debatable information about Jeremiah is more than compensated for by the emerging insight into the religious concerns of the later community.

Perhaps a final word about this "debatable" information is appropriate. While I think the emphasis on redactional activity in shaping the present form of the Book of Jeremiah is salutary, I do believe a caveat is necessary in the light of extreme conclusions of the sort Carroll advances.[54] Do we know enough about the circumstances of exilic and postexilic life to insist that certain stories and themes belong there rather than in Jeremiah's time? Are the circumstances of the communities so distinct that every line of continuity is severed? Could not some of the stories and theological expressions function in both contexts? This is the decisive issue; if theodicy, for example, was a burning question in both communities, in Jerusalem and in Babylonia, there was a line of continuity that later redactors wished to claim for their own time. Since Carroll believes the operative word is discontinuity, he remains consistent when insisting that Jeremiah has no word for us today, but grandly inconsistent as well: "Surely here is word from Jeremiah if any will receive it–yesterday's dogma is today's lie" and "To enshrine his tradition in the same way so that we revere it is to have learned nothing from his work."[55]

The point is well taken, but one does not have to enshrine or revere a tradition to appreciate it. Jeremiah's opposition to the dogma of his own day was grounded in an understanding of reality that had been transmitted to him from previous generations; in the same manner we can remain faithful to his legacy by weighing the traditions of the past and by using those which survive critical scrutiny in the struggle to forge a better world. Still, we have no assurance that we shall be any more successful in that endeavor than Jeremiah was; and we may be "torn and shattered by the sense of the apparent absence and neutrality of God."[56]

CHAPTER 16

Who Knows What YHWH Will Do?

The Character of God in the Book of Joel

The prophetic appeal for repentance in Joel 2:12–14 introduces a concept of deity incompatible with what has gone before. Nothing to this point supports the traditional attribution, which Joel may have derived from Exod 34:6 or any one of its many formulations,[1] that YHWH is "merciful and compassionate, patient and abundantly loyal." Such a confession flies in the face of reported facts, first a devastating invasion by locusts[2] that consumed the vegetation and threatened the survival of people and animals, and second, the ominous nearness of the day of YHWH.[3] Both threats directed against the Judean populace originated in its own deity, whose fury freely poured itself out. How then dare the prophet appeal to the very one bent on punishing his possession? What if Judah, like Job, is innocent of any wrongdoing? I propose to entertain the possibility that modern scholars have joined the ranks of Job's friends in being too quick to associate calamity with guilt in the book of Joel.[4] The ambiguity lies instead in the divine character as perceived by persons who attributed all events to divine causation.[5]

> The text of Joel's appeal for immediate turning is unproblematic. But even now–a divine oracle–return to me with your whole mind, with fasting, weeping, and mourning. Rend your inner disposition and not just your clothes, then return to YHWH your God; for merciful and compassionate is he, patient and abundantly loyal, repenting about punishment. Perhaps he will turn and relent, leaving a blessing in his wake, a cereal offering and libation for YHWH your God (Joel 2:12–14).

The adversative *wegam 'attâ*[6] acknowledges the lateness of the hour and radical boldness, like its use in Job 16:19a (*gam 'attâ hinnêh baššamayim 'ēdî*, "look, even now my witness is in heaven").[7] In each instance multiple signs pointed to the opposite conclusion; Judeans were buffeted by want and awesome portents of more to come, and Job bore the brunt of unsubstantiated charges of misconduct.[8] Whereas the poet has Job shift the point of view heavenwards by means of the particle *hinnēh*,[9] Joel calls upon a prophetic oracular formula, *ne'um-YHWH*, for this purpose.[10] The appeal to turn toward YHWH thus receives the highest possible legitimation,[11] one originating in the deity who for the moment is bent on destruction.

The unique occurrence of this expression in Joel indicates that the prophet did not wish to weaken its impact through indiscriminate use, unlike the prophets Haggai and Zechariah who peppered their speech with *ne'um YHWH* [*ṣebā'ôt*] and *kôh 'āmar YHWH ṣebā'ôt*.[12] In this respect Joel resembles Hosea, who found little use[13] for oracular formulae that mark prophetic utterance generally, except for the book of Habakkuk, where its literary form excluded such expressions.[14] The only other kindred feature in Joel is *kî YHWH dibbēr* in 4:8b, where the suggestion of divine authority reinforces an implausible promise that Judeans who were once sold into slavery will return to their native land and that their captors will assume the role of slaves in an unaccustomed environment. The suggestion that *wegam 'atta ne'um-YHWH* is a nominative sentence with an implicit predicate adjective ("but even now YHWH's word is valid")[15] does not take sufficiently into account the *waw* copulative on the verb *šûb*.[16]

This verb does not necessarily imply present guilt, although it frequently appears in contexts emphasizing habitual transgression as in Amos's liturgy of wasted opportunity using the refrain, *welō'-šabtem 'aday ne'um-YHWH* ("Still you did not return to me, says YHWH."[17] Deutero-Isaiah invites a pardoned nation to turn to its redeemer (*māḥîtî kā'āb pešā'ekā weke'ānān ḥaṭṭ'ō'tekā šûbâ 'ēlay kî ge'altîkā*, "I have obliterated your transgressions like a cloud and your sins like mist; turn unto me, for I have redeemed you," 44:22). The slate has been wiped clean and YHWH initiates a new relationship, for the guilt has been assuaged by excessive suffering, according to an earlier comment (40:2). In times of trouble, whether deserved or undeserved, turning to YHWH was the appropriate response inasmuch as he alone could remove the adversity. Joel's invitation therefore does not necessarily impute guilt to the unfortunate victims of circumstance. Perhaps the prophet's silence on this issue registers his own inability to pinpoint any culpability on the part of the Judeans commensurate with their misery. Hoping to fill the void left by Joel's silence, modern critics have been less hesitant than he. The charges against his contemporaries range from syncretistic worship[18] to hubris,[19] from emphasis on external ritual[20] to abdication of leadership,[21] from breach of covenant[22] to unwillingness to become identified with an impotent deity.[23] Naturally, any evidence supporting a particular version of Judah's guilt is deduced from what Joel says—or refrains from saying. The arguments from silence run something like this: (1) Joel's formulation of the invitation, "return to me," implies that the people were currently following after another deity; (2) the internalization of sorrow suggested by "rend your hearts" indicates pride that has not brought on genuine remorse; (3) the same expression in juxtaposition with ritualistic acts belies confidence in the efficacy of external behavior; (4) the necessity of commanding priests to mourn and intercede points to a failed leadership; (5) the calamity that has struck the covenant community demonstrates guilt, for the ancient treaty promised prosperity for faithfulness and adversity for breaking the conditions laid down at its ratification; and (6) mockery of the Judeans by foreigners issued in shame, which may even have driven YHWH's inheritance to another deity. Such unsubstantiated charges testify to the power exercised by a calculating morality and obscure the ambiguity of human existence that gave rise to a perceived ambiguity within the divine character.

The invitation attributed to YHWH displays no hint of displeasure with public ritual. To be sure, a resolute mind must precede the external manifestations of a more traditional kind. Affinities with Deuteronomy enable Joel to bring together the cognitive and affective dimensions of existence. According to Deut 4:30–31 dire circumstances will cause YHWH's people to return to him who is *raḥûm*,[24] and 30:2 reports that Israel will return with all its mind and being (*wešabtā 'ad-YHWH 'ĕlōheykā...bekōl-lebābkā ûbekol napšekā*). The compassion promised in 30:3 (*weriḥamekā*) by the same one enforcing the threats associated with the covenant resembles Joel's guarded optimism.

The triple manifestation of wholehearted remorse occurs elsewhere only once (*weṣôm ûbekî ûmispēd*, "fasting, weeping, and mourning"), although Joel's fourfold use of the preposition *be* contrasts markedly with the language in Esth 4:3. The emphasis on external ritual proves that Joel values visible expressions of an inner state.[25] Various texts from the postexilic period attest to uncertainty about the status of fasting, for example, whether over worthy causes like the fall of Jerusalem and the murder of Gedaliah (Zech 7:3,5)[26] or at the expense of good deeds (Isa 58:3–9). Both texts underline the self-interest of persons resorting to fasting and urge altruistic actions as something YHWH approves. The story about David's prayer for his sick child shows that the combination of fasting and tears, even when arising from genuine remorse, did not always result in the desired response (2 Sam 12:15b-23),[27] although it sometimes did (cf. 2 Chr 30:9b, *kî ḥannûn weraḥûm YHWH 'ĕlōhêkem welō'-yāsîr pānîm mikem 'im tāšûbû 'lāyw*, "for YHWH your God is gracious and compassionate and will not look away from you if you turn to him").[28] A rare comment in Mal 3:6a attributes constancy to YHWH (*kî 'anî YHWH lō' šānîtî*, "for I YHWH have not changed"), at the same time that the next verse promises reciprocal turning (*šûbû 'ēlay we'āšûbâ 'alēkem*, "return to me and I will turn to you").

The change in speakers apparent from third person address of the deity in v 13 seems to be a feature of a prophetic tendency to merge the identities of a messenger and the one commissioning the spokesperson.[29] The *waw* links the divine imperative and its human exposition. Joel's adoption of symbolic language (*weqir'û lebabkem*, "and rend your heart") follows ancient precedent recorded in Deut 10:16 and Jer 4:4 for circumcising the foreskin of the heart.[30] In light of the threefold expression of distress mentioned in YHWH's oracle, Joel's additional remark, *we'al-bigdêkem*, should be rendered, "and not just your garments." The shift from *'ad* to *'el* (*'āday* in v 12, *'el-YHWH 'elōhêkem* in v 13) also marks a shift in person from first to third and prepares the way for a doxological attribution.

The search for the source of this confessional statement has led to Exod 34:6,[31] although Joel's version differs appreciably from the full expression of YHWH's nature in vv 6–7. Indeed, the sequence *ḥannûn weraḥûm* accords with that in Exod 33:19, but not the verbal form.[32] Moreover, Joel does not mention *we'emet* nor a single attribute from v 7. Even the four attributes in common appear in entirely different syntax,[33] and a novel element concludes Joel's statement, *weniḥam 'al-hārā'â* ("and repents of evil"). For this expression in connection with the other four attributes from Joel 2:13 one must look to Jonah 4:2, the only difference being the direct address *'attâ-'ēl* ("you, God"). This affinity between the two texts becomes all the more striking when one compares the next verse in Joel, *mî yôdēa' yāšûb weniḥām* with Jonah 3:9, which is exactly the same except for the addition of *hā'elōhîm*.[34]

Does Joel cite these texts from Exodus and Jonah? Some remarkable correspondences between the text of Joel and the covenant formulary in Exod 32–34 cannot be denied: the words *berākā* (32:29), *nôrā'* (34:10), the reference to mockery (32:12), and the acknowledgment that YHWH changed his mind about evil (32:14).[35] Decisive differences in the context and function of these affinities suggest caution, for the blessing results from priestly slaughter of idolatrous Israelites and the mockery has God as object rather than Judeans as in Joel 2:17. Although Joel may indeed draw on the memory of the traditional account of the exodus for language about the locust plague and its unprecedented nature, that is quite different from saying that he consciously reinterprets scripture.

That a few expressions in the book of Joel can be identified elsewhere in the canon does not make him a compiler of anthologies.[36] No single text that he shares in common with another prophet can be shown to derive from a written source, for they belong to the religious vocabulary of ancient Israel and Judah. Even when Joel uses an expression that also occurs in another prophetic book, he often gives it a peculiar stamp, even turning on its head the old tradition about beating one's swords into plowtips and spears into pruning hooks (4:10[3:10]). One need not assume that the prophet sat down and pored over written texts of his predecessors, gleaning useful citations and priding himself on the astute manner in which he couched inner-biblical allusions. In my judgment the bookish direction of much contemporary research[37] conceals a fundamental assumption that ancient Israelites had ready access to written scripture. That is, in my judgment, highly unlikely.[38] Instead, much religious teaching was transmitted orally, and this spoken word is the probable source of Joel's language that occasionally coincides with something another prophet or psalmist also happened to say. The average person today who says, "I have a dream," has never read Martin

Luther King, Jr.'s speech, for that statement has become part of normal discourse in the same way quotations from Shakespeare have entered our daily conversation.

The addition of psalmist in the sentence above draws attention to religious language that probably informed the thinking of many leaders. Not surprisingly, the ancient doxology came to expression in various combinations within the psalter and in similar confessional prayer (e.g., Ps 86:15; 103:8; 111:4; 112:4; 145:8; Neh 9:17,31).[39] Occasionally, additional attributes found their way into the confession, particularly *ṣaddîq* (Ps 112:4),[40] perhaps an acknowledgment that divine mercy was balanced by justice as in Exod 34:6–7. The sole instance of a vindictive application of an attribute from the confession, *'erek 'appayim*, occurs in Nah 1:3 with Nineveh as the unfortunate object of divine zeal, although Jonah uses a longer formulation to accuse YHWH of injustice. The struggle between those who emphasized divine compassion and others who stressed YHWH's justice has left its trail in the bible, demonstrating both the tenacity of tradition and the versatility of its transmitters.[41]

Perhaps that controversy explains Joel's rhetorical question in the wake of a confession of YHWH's readiness to shower kindness on those who turn to him. Divine freedom must also be affirmed. Hence the open-ended question, in itself an assertion. "Who knows whether or not he will turn and relent, leaving a blessing behind, cereal offering and libation for YHWH your God?" In short, no one knows how the deity will react, as the few uses of *mî yôdēa'* in the Bible demonstrate (2 Sam 12:22; Joel 2:14; Jonah 3:9; Ps 90:11; Qoh 2:19; 3:21; 8:1; Esth 4:14).[42] Joel's use of the adverb *'aḥarāyw* echoes his earlier reference to scarred fields left behind by locusts (2:3) and provides an effective contrast between YHWH's previous conduct and that following the people's turning.

The threefold use of the verb *šûb* in these three verses, spoken once by YHWH and twice by the prophet, each with a different referent, is matched by two uses of the verb *niḥam*, both with reference to YHWH. Their essential meaning in 2:14 may be clarified by Exod 32:12, *šûb mēḥarôn 'appekā wehinnāḥem 'al-hārā'â le'ammekā* ("turn from your intense fury and repent concerning the harm [planned] for your people"). The result of such turning will be prosperity,[43] here signified *pars pro toto* by cereal offering and libation, a well-being that also benefits YHWH, as the awkward *laYHWH 'elōhêkem* concedes.

This interrelationship between the well-being of the people and their deity energizes the language of a shorter version of the old confession, Num 14:18. Here Moses persuades YHWH to forgive his people lest Egyptians conclude that he lacked power to bring them safely into the land of promise.[44] As further incentive Moses reminds YHWH of his own self-description: *YHWH 'erek 'appayim werab-ḥesed nōśē' 'āwōn wāpāša' wenaqqēh lō' yenaqqeh pōqēd 'awōn 'ābôt 'al-bānîm 'al-šillēšîm we'al-ribbē'îm* ("YHWH patient and abundantly loyal, forgiving iniquity and sin, but by no means clearing the guilty, visiting the iniquity of parents on children to the third and fourth generation"). The last verse in the book of Joel may echo this language of revenge against offenders, *weniqqêtî dāmām lō' niqqêtî* ("I will by no means clear the guilty of their blood that I have not avenged").[45]

Like most of the Hebrew Bible, Joel's normal discourse about the deity focuses on the realm of actions.[46] Locusts are dispatched against the Judean countryside by YHWH, who uses them to wreak havoc like invincible soldiers. This invasion is the harbinger of an army that will inaugurate the dreaded day of YHWH amidst heavenly portents and awesome signs. That accomplished, this same YHWH promises an outpouring of divine vitality on all Judeans, disposing them to conduct themselves as prophets with total disregard for customary distinctions based on age, gender, or social status.[47] Then YHWH will move to settle the score with traditional enemies of Judeans and to sit in judgment on all nations before acting to secure his sacred precincts and taking up residence in Zion. The motive for the abrupt change in YHWH's treatment of his inheritance and land is said to be zeal and pity.

In describing YHWH's actions Joel often uses traditional motifs grounded in ancient theophanies,[48] the day of YHWH,[49] the enemy from the north,[50] the sacred mountain,[51] the outpouring of the spirit,[52] the formula of acknowledgment of YHWH,[53] and the nations' mocking of YHWH's people.[54] Moreover, the prophet attributes to YHWH the control of rain[55] and thus nature's productivity. In his view, this mastery of history and nature entitled YHWH to the claim of uniqueness.[56] Therein lay the problem with which Joel, like so many others in ancient Israel, struggled mightily. Experience failed to confirm traditional belief. Faced with discontinuity between confessional statements about divine compassion and the circumstances confronting Judeans in his day, Joel valiantly strove to hold together competing views of YHWH's nature. Honesty compelled him, nevertheless, to remain silent when he saw no evidence that his compatriots deserved their sorry lot. At the same time, he boldly placed his trust in YHWH's heralded compassion, which he believed would surely rectify current events. The unknown author of the satirical treatment of the prophet Jonah used the same statement about YHWH's compassionate nature to condemn the deity for unprincipled conduct in sparing repentant foreigners.[57] It thus follows that even by excising the old confession's emphasis on justice as a counterbalance to mercy, the resulting statement remains sufficiently ambiguous to evoke both a particularistic and a universalistic reading.[58] Historical events inevitably complicated faith for religious thinkers who believed in divine power and goodness. Justice and mercy make strange bedfellows, which explains the tradition's readiness to separate them. Who knows whether Joel's dream–or Jonah's–accorded with reality?

CHAPTER 17

Freeing the Imagination

The Conclusion to the Book of Joel

The last five verses in Joel give voice to fundamental human aspirations to live in security, to experience prosperity, to look on justice, and to attain permanence. The language by which these modest hopes achieve expression resonates with other utopian dreams scattered throughout the Hebrew Bible, leaving the impression of ideological affinity if not outright literary dependence. Still, the restraint in Joel 4:17–21 [English Versions, 3:17–21] contrasts markedly with the imagistic exuberance characterizing much of the book. In this essay I wish to examine this extraordinary conclusion to the prophetic book of Joel in the light of alternative descriptions of imagined bliss and to explore the relationship between 4:17–21 and 1:1–4:16.

4:17 And you will know that I Yahweh your God
reside in Zion[1] my sacred mountain;
Jerusalem will be holy,
and strangers will not pass through it any more.
4:18 And on that day
Mountains will drip sweet wine, hills will ooze milk,
and all water sources of Judah will overflow.
A stream will flow from Yahweh's house,
watering the valley of Shittim.[2]
4:19 Egypt will be a desolation,
Edom a wilderness waste,
Because of violence against Judeans[3]
When they spilled innocent blood in their land.[4]
4:20 But Judah will be inhabited for a long time,
Jerusalem for many generations.
4:21 Truly I will consider their blood innocent
that I have not considered innocent,[5]
And Yahweh will reside in Zion.

The Concluding Section and the Rest of the Book

I have departed from something approaching scholarly consensus by including verse 17 in the final unit (Wolff: 74, 82–84; Allen: 122–26; Hubbard: 81–84; Prinsloo: 113–21; Kapelrud: 169; Ahlström: 134; Robinson and Horst: 69, who argue for a chiastic arrangement; Rudolph: 1971). My reasons for doing so are far from arbitrary. To begin with, virtually all interpreters recognize close kinship between this verse (v. 17) and its sequel, which seems to elaborate upon it. At the very least, verse 17 functions as a threshold point, marking off the boundary between two distinct sections but also serving as a means of entry from one to the other.[6] For me, the inclusio[7] in 4:17 and 4:21, specifically "Yahweh resides in Zion," offsets the illusion that the formula "On that day"[8] introduces a new unit. The statement of recognition in 2:27 and 4:17 ("And you will know that I am in the midst of Israel; truly I am Yahweh your God and there is no other" // "And you will know that I Yahweh your God reside in Zion, my holy mountain") serves as an inclusion for the entire book.[9] Hence my use of this stylistic device accords with ancient predilection either at the authorial level or at the redactional one.

Taking 4:17 as the beginning of a unit does not deprive the previous section of an appropriate ending. Ominous portents notwithstanding, Yahweh turns toward Israelites as a refuge and fortress while terrifying the nations with unnatural events and supernatural manifestations of divine fury. If v. 17 really functions as a threshold, the reference to foreigners who will never again desecrate the sanctuary may designate the nations who are summoned to judgment in 4:9–16, as well as Egypt and Edom in 4:19.

This transitional role of 4:17 explains why so many scholars connect the verse to what precedes. Actually, the unity of the concluding verses is by no means self-evident, and their sequence appears strained (Bewer: 143). Two things seem to disturb the harmony of the larger unit: the shift from first to third person address in 4:21 ("Truly I will consider...and Yahweh will reside..."); and the separation of 4:19b and 4:21a ("When they spilled innocent blood...Truly I will consider their blood innocent") by sentiment that otherwise provides a smooth ending to 4:19a ("Egypt will be...Edom...But Judah...Jerusalem"). The natural conclusion for 4:20, is therefore, 4:21b ("And Yahweh will reside in Zion"). Lacking supporting textual evidence for such an original, and refusing to believe that redactors had so little grasp of stylistic subtlety, I choose to interpret the present text and to assume that its apparent flaws have some other explanation.[10]

I. Sitting in the Rubble (1:1–2:11)

I turn now to the task of understanding the concluding section of the book in terms of what goes before it. In 1:1–2:11 a description of past disaster, a locust plague, fades into a report of this attack in images of fire and an invading army. A devastating drought complicates matters further, threatening both humans and animals. A virtual garden of Eden is quickly transformed into a desert waste (2:3). A single impression rises above the vivid account of extreme want–the land is so dry that fire races across the stubble, leaving a blackened earth as if to mock the wilted twigs discarded by the locust horde and to indicate the hopelessness signified by water sources that have become dry. The contrast in 4:17–21 could hardly be sharper; Judah's mountains and hills drip a constant supply of liquid, water sources flow freely, and a river extends from the sanctuary to a valley beyond. This picture of abundant water, milk, and new wine exists alongside another that transfers the desolation from Judeans to bitter enemies, Egyptians and Edomites. A single phrase, "Zion my holy mountain," gives continuity to the earlier description of calamity and the later promise (2:1; 4:17).

Only the threat against Judeans specifies its audience, whereas the combined promise of weal for Judah and woe for its enemies offers a lone clue about the audience, the personal pronoun "you." Those addressed directly in 1:1–2:11 are to a large extent functions of the narrative: elderly citizens who alone can verify the unprecedented nature of the locust plague; drunkards, who feel most personally the burden of a failed grape harvest; farmers and vintners, who watch their labor come to naught; priests, who stand before the sacred altar with empty hands because the ingredients for cereal and libation offerings have vanished. Together these groups comprise the audience of both sections, establishing the personal dimension lying behind the pronoun "you." On one occasion, the vocabulary becomes expansive, addressing "all inhabitants of the land" (1:12), but like the broad designation "Israelites" this reference restricts itself to Judeans.

The language of 1:1–2:1 betrays extraordinary interest in religious personnel associated with the cult and in priestly functions such as proclaiming fasts and sounding the alarm that summoned the populace for religious instruction. Three different designations exalt the priestly order as "ministers of the altar" (1:13), "ministers of Yahweh" (1:9–2:17), and "ministers of my God" (1:13). Likewise, three expressions occur for the act of celebration now missing from daily life: joy" (1:12), "rejoicing" (1:16), and "exultation" (1:16). A joyless society suffers the misfortunes sent by its Lord. The divine promise in 4:17–21 does not elevate priestly personnel, although it assures the purity of Jerusalem and the permanent presence of deity.

What kind of community is reflected in these literary units? All signs point to a struggling agrarian society desperately trying to eke out subsistence against overwhelming odds. Locusts have devastated the grain and destroyed grape vines, figs, olive trees, fruit trees, dates and pomegranates. Even the cattle add their bewilderment to the grief felt by human owners. The text mentions no professional class beyond priests and agriculturalists,[11] but these are precisely the ones necessitated by the events themselves. Silence may therefore not reveal anything about the makeup of the threatened Judean society, which may very well have had various crafts and professional guilds. Nevertheless, the implication that a locust plague brought virtual ruin can scarcely be denied, and that acknowledgement leads to the conclusion that agriculture was the community's primary means of subsistence.

The further silence about other professional groups who would be endangered by the day of Yahweh, the second metaphor for the threat to the community, reinforces this conclusion. The text is ambiguous about whether or not that terrible day has actually arrived, juxtaposing a statement that the day has come with a qualifier, "It is near" (2:16). Unlike Israelites addressed by Amos, these Judeans harbored no illusions that this day would bring victory over their enemies. The ominous features of the day, which Amos emphasized in graphic detail (Amos 5:18–20), are intensified in Joel's description. Amos' account of that dark day depicts one-on-one danger. A person fleeing from a lion meets a bear, but escaping both, is bitten by a serpent in the deceptive safety of home. Joel, however, describes a mighty army of locusts whose coming obscures sun, moon, and stars, so that the only appropriate adjectives are *nôrā' mᵉ'od*, exceedingly awesome)" and *mî yᵉkîlennû* (irresistible) (2:11b). Just as fire devours dry stubble, this army marches relentlessly, scales the city wall, and enters windows like a thief. Here the text strings together three sources of terror: soldiers, fire, and thieves. The first is highly organized, the second random, and the third extraordinarily furtive. Like Amos, Joel envisions no escape from the devastation (2:3c). How, then, did the community secure the divine assurances nestled in 4:17–21?

II. Looking for a Way Out (2:12–27)

Deliverance from the ravages of Yahweh's punitive agents came through sincere repentance, expressed here in the metaphor of rending hearts rather than garments. The text introduces the remote possibility that Yahweh would relent even at this late stage ("Yet even now," 2:12). It does so in the strongest manner possible–through use of a solemn oracular formula, "whisper of Yahweh" (Vetter: 2–3)[12] This stylistic device accompanied by fasting, weeping, and remorse is possible because of Yahweh's character declared to Moses. Just like other canonical texts that appeal to the ancient confession in Ex 34:6–7 (Crenshaw, 1984:9), this one concentrates solely on Yahweh's positive attributes. Joel describes God as merciful, compassionate, long-suffering, abundantly loyal, and repentant of causing harm (2:13b). To be sure, Joel remembers divine freedom as well,[13] and this memory prompts him to shape the conclusion in the form of a rhetorical question functioning as a denial, "who knows?"(Crenshaw, 1986:274–88). He may turn, repent, and leave a blessing–cereal offering and libation for Yahweh your God?" (2:14).

The text recounts in considerable detail the preparation for a ceremony of penitence involving everyone, even suckling infants and newlyweds. The prophet encourages the appropriate officials in language far from economical: blow the shofar in Zion, sanctify a fast, call a solemn assembly, and gather a congregation. Such lavish summoning of the populace functions to prevent any absentees from marring the event and frustrating its goal. As religious leaders of the gathered community, priests are instructed to enter the holy place and to implore Yahweh to have pity on one and all. The people of God thus seek to avoid the religious dilemma forced on them by disaster. In their misfortune they offer conclusive evidence in the eyes of foreigners that Yahweh has either abandoned them or does not really exist (Buber: 199–210). Nehemiah, the governor of Judah under Persian hegemony, individualizes this plea, using the rare verb *ḥûsāh* (pity) also and relying on Yahweh's abundant loyalty, *kᵉrōb ḥasdekā* (Neh 13:22).

The desire to escape mockery at the expense of foreign frivolity has left its mark on several biblical texts. Psalm 79 complains that foreigners ask, "Where is their God?" (v. 10) and that the taunters have defiled the sanctuary by spilling blood like water (79:1,3). The result of such cruelty is that foreigners reproach the victims (cf. Joel 2:17). The same question is embedded in Ps. 42:4,11 (E.V., 42:3,10), but the mocker may this instance actually be a member of the Israelite community. Elihu's use of this question is both hypothetical ("None asks, 'Where is God my maker who gives songs in the night?'" Job 35:10) and antithetical (that is, it emphasizes Yahweh's kindness rather than absence). Psalm 115 associates the question with foreigners but also stresses Yahweh's loyalty and faithfulness (vv. 1–2). This mocking question appears in prophetic literature (Mic 7:10 and Mal 2:17), although issuing from the lips of a personal enemy in the former case, and denying divine justice in the latter.

The decisive turning point of the book takes place at 2:18, which declares that Yahweh had compassion on land and people. The rest of chapter two announces the reversal of Judah's misfortune, and promises an abundance of the foodstuffs devoured by locusts. In addition to satisfying physical hunger, Yahweh recognizes the psychological impact of mockery, vowing never again to submit the people to such reproach. Indeed, the Lord goes one step further, promising to drive out the northerners, a term that seems to conjure up every kind of fear lurking in the psyche of Judeans.[14] Likewise, Yahweh determines to quench thirst and to banish desolation beyond the eastern or western seas.

Using an ancient expression for allaying anxiety in God's presence (Stähli:765–78), Joel urges land and animals not to fear and proposes joyous exultation in its place. In the wake of a return of herbage and fruit, Judeans happily celebrate Yahweh's name. Point for point the deity promises a complete reversal of everything that the locusts destroyed. The ancient recognition formula concludes Yahweh's promise, but this expression of certainty is flanked front and back by a solemn declaration that these humiliated Judeans will never again be subjected to shame (2:26b-27).[15] Armed with divine promises, the Judean community can once more confidently face the future.

III. Dreaming of Another Day (3:1–4:16)

Egalitarian interests occasionally erupted in Israelite society where religious functionaries enjoyed special privilege. Priestly groups, obliged to defend their fee structure,[16] argued that as a tribal entity they had given up all claim to territorial inheritance when the land was allocated to the several family units. In their view, this voluntary renunciation of an inheritance entitled priests to demand special payment from the populace for services rendered. Cultic prophets also enjoyed a lifestyle made possible partly by the fees they levied and partly by royal patronage.[17] Their possession of the spirit, or more accurately, the spirit's possession of them, more than once seems to have occasioned flights of fantasy. An example of wishful thinking survives in the story about Elad and Medad, who prophesied in the Israelite camp and encountered Joshua's opposition until Moses defended their zeal with the following words: "Are you jealous on my behalf? I wish all Yahweh's people were prophets and that the Lord would put his spirit in all of them" (Num 11:29).

The prophetic designation, "man of the spirit," indicates the importance of possession by the spirit, and at least one prophet felt constrained to boast about the full measure of divine spirit empowering his message (Mic 3:8). Other prophets stressed the visionary dimension of their vocation, one that resulted in two technical terms, *rō'eh* and *ḥōzeh* (seer). Still other prophetic figures emphasized the word, which they interpreted as divine authorization; this dimension of prophecy gave rise to the common designation *nābî'* (the called one). It appears that the representatives of these three different ways of viewing prophecy competed for recognition by the populace,[18] although at least one historiographer, the Deuteronomist, insists on continuity between diviner and *nābî'* (1 Sam 9:9).

Each mode of intermediation encountered difficulty of one sort or another. The *spirit* generated excessive behavior and could not always be trusted, according to the story about Micaiah ben Imlah's confrontation with court prophets loyal to King Ahab (1 Kgs 22). *Visionaries* suffered from a bad press in the episode featuring Balaam, and subsequent endorsement of visions by Amos failed to dissuade others like Jeremiah who felt threatened by prophets with opposing views arising from what he took to be bogus dreams and visions. The *word* also posed a problem, for its enigmatic quality necessitated interpretation and, according to Num 12:6–8, only Moses received unambiguous messages from Yahweh. All other prophets encountered the divine word as obscure riddles, and the resulting rival interpretations did little to encourage the people, who relied on prophets for spiritual guidance, to put their trust in anyone (Crenshaw, 1971).

Moses' spoken wish that all God's people were prophets lingered in the minds of pious Judeans until the prophet Joel once more gave it currency. He cautiously locates such a wondrous phenomenon in the future;[19] the only time frame he provides is the adverb "afterwards." In the context of the book this temporal designation harks back to the divine promise that disaster will be replaced by its opposite. Like Moses' wish, Joel's articulation of divine intent is limited to Judeans, despite the appearance of universalism in the expression "all flesh." The restrictive nature of the outpouring of the spirit gives way in one significant regard, for slaves, both male and female, will experience the power of god's spirit in the same way as do free Judeans. The rushing spirit manifests itself differently in its recipients, bringing harmony where opposition once reigned. Children will proclaim the divine word; their elders will dream; and young people will have visions. Such a religious community will not confront the perennial problem of testing intermediaries (Wilson, 1980), for in this ideal situation everyone has direct access to the divine will.

Pneumatic theology was deficient in one respect, for it did not convince outsiders, in Joel's case, foreigners. Hence from the speaker's point of view (Berlin: 43–82; Sternberg: 129–52; Bar-Efrat:13–45; Alter, 1981; Bal, 1985), the addition of astrological phenomena seems intended for external consumption. Yahweh threatens to inaugurate signs and portents–blood, fire, and ominous cloud–in the sky and on earth. These forebodings of apocalyptic thought stop short of pondering about a fiery holocaust.[20] Instead, they focus on a solar eclipse and a blood-red moon as harbingers of a far more dreadful event, the dawn of Yahweh's day. Two adjectives, *haggādōl* (great) and *wᵉhannôrā'* (awesome), suffice to release pent-up emotions associated with suppressed anxiety.

In contrast to other biblical texts in which emphasis falls on the total absence of any escape, this one takes a different form. Invocation of Yahweh's name opens an avenue of escape, particularly if it takes place in the holy city. Joel bases such assurance on divine promises from the past. What about Jews who had the misfortune of residing outside Zion? Does any hope exist for them? The reference to survivors, which gives the impression of an afterthought,[21] may allude to captives of earlier wars who have managed to endure the hardships associated with transported subjects. In their case, Yahweh does the calling.

The bold thought of survivors beyond the Judean hills triggers additional wanderings of the imagination. After all, cosmic portents imply universal rule on Yahweh's part, and this significant reality should translate into rescue for people who call upon the deity. The tables will be turned on Judah's conquerors, for judgment on the nations has been delayed too long.

This day of judgment will be located in the valley of Jehoshaphat, probably an imaginary place.[22] Chosen for its symbolic value, the name affirms that Yahweh will judge. These guilty nations have offended both Yahweh's inheritance, Israel, and the land apportioned to them. Joel specifies the particular crimes for which the nations must pay: casting lots over the people of God, selling a boy for the price of a harlot and a girl for the cost of wine *which they drank*. The final verb in Hebrew, *wayyištû* (and they drank it) registers the prophet's utter contempt for the conduct of these victorious soldiers.[23] For this act of greed Tyre, Sidon, and Philistines will be judged. Not content with valuables of this kind, they entered into a thriving slave trade, selling Judeans to Greeks, who relocated them in a faraway place. For their cruelty these sea-loving peoples will watch their own children being sold by the Judeans to Sabeans, who live in the desert.[24] This punishment is an appropriate one, for Judeans, who had no love for the sea, had been sold to sea-faring people.

The positioning of the two oracular formulas in the book of Joel suggests that the prophet recognized the fantastic dimension within such announcements. Once more Joel introduces divine authority for his own description of final retribution against the enemies at whose hands Judeans suffered humiliation and physical abuse. "For Yahweh has spoken"–this simple statement prevents Joel's audience from dismissing everything as idle speculation or wishful thinking. Now the hearers must reckon with a claim that the promises are grounded in Yahweh's integrity.[25]

Martial imagery bristles in what follows. Whereas Judeans were instructed to sanctify a fast, the nations are commanded to do likewise to a battle. Reversing ancient tradition about an era of peace, Joel urges the nations to beat their plowshares into swords and their pruning hooks into spears. Even their weaklings are told to boast of military valor. The description of Yahweh entering into judgment in the valley of Jehoshaphat betrays its origins within an agrarian community. The sickle will fell the harvest and the treader will extract juice from grapes. The language itself signifies the gravity of the offense; repetition of the word *hamônîm* (4:14) heightens the emotional intensity in the face of utter confusion in the valley of decision. The dreaded day of Yahweh has drawn near at last. In addition to the astrological portents here repeated, the day witnesses Yahweh's self-manifestation and an accompanying earthquake. Joel uses the same language that opens the book of Amos: "Yahweh roars from Zion and utters his voice from Jerusalem" (Joel 4:16a; Amos 1:2a).[26] Safely hidden in Yahweh, a refuge and fortress, God's people, Judeans and Israelites, escape the judgment finally directed against the nations.

Utopian Visions Outside the Book of Joel

Thus far I have examined the relationship between 4:17–21 and what precedes this concluding section. I wish now to consider the dominant ideas within comparable descriptions of a better day. I shall concentrate on the following biblical texts: Amos 9:11–15; Mic 4:1–4; Isa 2:2–4; 11:6–9; Ezek 47:1–12; Zech 14:1–21; Mal 3:19–21 [E.V. 4:1–3] and Gen 49:10–12.

At least three macro-themes stand out in these texts:

1. nature's transformation;
2. the restoration of the greatness of the Davidic dynasty;
3. the inauguration of an era of peace.

The absence of any allusion in Joel 4:17–21 to the Davidic dynasty may result from the position of the priests in the Judean community which the prophet addressed. If one assumes a date for the book in the fifth or fourth centuries,[27] recent precedent from the period of Haggai and Zechariah would provide an object lesson against an active messianism (see Meyers and Meyers: 336–75). The tightly governed Ptolemaic era did not countenance political unrest in the name of restoring Davidic rule. If Joel actually draws on Amos 9:11–15 and Gen 49:10–12, the book does so selectively. From the latter may come the mention of milk in the depiction of fertility, although this idea may derive from the ancient tradition about Canaan as a land of milk and honey; and from Amos 9:11–15 comes the reference to the bountiful flow of sweet wine from the mountains. Both Amos and Ezekiel surpass Joel 4:17–21 in the scope of fertility, with overlapping sowing and reaping, on the one hand, and prolific plants that mature in a month, on the other hand. Curiously, the picture of fertility in Hos 14:5–7 [4–7] does not appear to have influenced Joel 4:17–21.

Joel's reference to the nations' journey to Judean territory has nothing comparable to the pilgrimage for religious instruction in Mic 4:1–4 and Isa 2:2–4. Nevertheless, Joel uses the concept of Yahweh's judgment of the nations, which ushers in an era of peace. At the same time, he reverses the wonderful sentiment about beating swords into plowshares and spears into pruning hooks, applying the new version to a doomed army. The notion of healing in Ezek 47:1–12 and Mal 4:1–3 does not appear in Joel's account, whereas the life-giving stream does. This river that flows from the sanctuary in Jerusalem plays an important role in Ezek 47:1–12 and Zech 14:1–21, in the latter of which streams flow to the east and to the west. It follows that the closest affinities exist between Joel 4:17–21 and Ezek 47:1–12 and Zech 14:1–21. These three themes and virtual silence with respect to the exquisite imagery in Hos 14:5–7; Isa 11:6–9, 9:1–7; and Mic 4:1–4/Isa 2:2–4 must surely indicate priestly preferences of the author responsible for Joel 4:17–21.

Perhaps the most striking feature of Joel's description of a better day is its restraint. If one is going to dream, why not dream big? It remains a mystery why this unusual text modestly envisions nothing more than Yahweh's presence to assure a holy place, an ample supply of wine, milk, and water, revenge on enemies for the spilling of innocent blood, and a permanent title to the Judean hills. Other dreamers certainly set their sights higher, if one can judge from their robust language. The beauty of Joel 4:17–21 lies in its response to the suffering occasioned by calamity and the resultant soul-searching. Small wonder the inclusio in this unit focuses on Yahweh's residence in Zion. This author believed that Yahweh's abode in Jerusalem guarantees security for those who take refuge there. In a very real sense, this inclusio corresponds to the ecstatic shout with which Ezekiel concludes: "*Yahweh šammāh*," ("Yahweh is there!"). Where Yahweh resides, one need not fear locust plagues, drought, fire, or armies. That message in Joel 4:17–21 provides an effective conclusion to a book in which ominous threats play such a prominent role.

Works Consulted

Ahlström, G. W. *Joel and the Temple Cult of Jerusalem.* VTS 21. Leiden: Brill, 1971.

Allen, Leslie, C. *The Books of Joel, Obadiah, Jonah and Micah.* Grand Rapids: Eerdmans, 1976.

Alter, R. *The Art of Biblical Narrative.* New York: Basic Books, 1981.

Bal, M. *Narratology.* Toronto: University of Toronto, 1985.

Bar-Efrat, S. *Narrative Art in the Bible.* Sheffield: Academic Press, 2004.

Berlin, A. *Poetics and Interpretation of Biblical Narrative.* Sheffield: Almond, 1983.

Bewer, J. A. *A Critical and Exegetical Commentary on Obadiah and Joel.* ICC. Edinburgh: Edinburgh: T. & T. Clark, 1911.

Bourke, J. "Le jour de Yahvé dans Joël." RB 66:5–31, 191–212.

Buber, M. *On the Bible.* New York: Schocken, 1968.

Buccellati, G. "Wisdom and Not: The Case of Mesopotamia." JAOS 101:35–47.

Collins, J. J. The Apocalyptic Imagination. 2d edition. The Biblical Resources Series. Grand Rapids: Eerdmans, 1998.

Crenshaw, J. L. "Amos and the Theophanic Tradition." ZAW 80:203–15.

_____. *Prophetic Conflict.* BZAW 124. Berlin and New York: de Gruyter, 1971.

_____. *A Whirlpool of Torment.* Philadelphia: Fortress, 1984.

_____. "The expression *mî yôdea'* in the Hebrew Bible." VT 36:274–88.
_____. "Literature, Bible as." Pp. 515–19 in *Mercer Dictionary of the Bible*, ed. Watson E. Mills. Macon: Mercer University, 1990, 515–19.
Hoffmann, Y. "The Day of the Lord as a Concept and a Term in The Prophetic Literature." ZAW 93:37–50.
Hubbard, D. A. *Joel and Amos.* Downers Grove: Inter-Varsity, 1989.
Kapelrud, A. S. *Joel Studies.* Uppsala: Lundequistska, 1948.
Loader, J. A. *Polar Structures in the Book of Qohelet.* BZAW 152. Berlin and New York: de Gruyter, 1979.
Meyers, C. L., and E. M. Meyers *Haggai, Zechariah* 1–8. AB 25B. Garden City: Doubleday, 1987.
Mowinckel. S. "The 'Spirit' and the 'Word' in the Pre-exilic Reforming Prophets." JBL 53: 199–227.
Myers, J. M. "Some Considerations Bearing on the Date of Joel." ZAW 74:177–95.
Prinsloo, W. S. *The Theology of the Book of Joel.* BZAW 163. Berlin and New York: de Gruyter, 1985.
Robinson, T. and F. Horst. *Die Zwölf Kleinen Propheten.* 3d edition HAT 14. Tübingen: Mohr, 1964.
Rudolph, W. "Wann wirkte Joel?" In *Das ferne und Nahe Wort,* BZAW 105. Berlin: A. Töpelmar 1967: 193–98.
_____. *Joel, Amos, Obadiah, Jonah.* KAT 13, 2. Gütersloh: Mohn, 1971.
Sellin, E. *Das Zwölfprophetenbuch.* KAT 12. Leipzig: Deichertsche, 1922.
Smith, J. Z. "Wisdom and Apocalyptic." *Religious Syncretism in Antiquity*, ed. Birger Pearson. Missoula: Scholars Press, 1975: 131–56.
Stähli, H. P. "yr' fürchten." *Theologisches Handwörterbuch zum Alten Testament I*, ed. E. Jenni and C. Westermann. München: Kaiser, 1984, 1, 765–781.
Sternberg, M. *The Poetics of Biblical Narrative.* Bloomington: Indiana University, 1985.
Stoltz, F. "*bôš* zuschanden werden." *Theologisches Handwörterbuch zum Alten Testament,* ed. E. Jenni and C. Westermann. München: Kaiser, 1984, 1, 269–272.
VanderKam, J. C. *Enoch and the Growth of an Apocalyptic Tradition.* CBQMS 16. Washington D.C.: The Catholic Biblical Association, 1984.
Vetter, D. "*ne'ūm* Ausspruch." *Theologisches Handwörterbuch zum Alten Testament,* ed. E. Jenni and C. Westermann. München: Kaiser, 1984, 2, 2–3.
Wilson, R. *Prophecy and Society in Ancient Israel.* Philadelphia: Fortress, 1984.
Wolff, H. W. *Joel and Amos.* Hermeneia. Philadelphia: Fortress, 1972.
Zimmerli, W. *Ezekiel.* Hermeneia. 2 vols. Philadelphia: Fortress, 1979, 1982.

CHAPTER 18

Joel's Silence and Interpreters' Readiness to Indict the Innocent

The pervasive presence of a world view in which retributive justice functions with a vengeance makes it necessary to state the obvious. Not every misfortune issues from a sinful act. That elemental truth seems to have eluded interpreters of the book of Joel, which describes an unprecedented calamity in Judah without once pointing an accusing finger at the victims. Indeed, the agent of destruction stands out for special censure, having acted reprehensibly, perhaps like the Assyrian rod of divine anger overstepping its commission in Isa 10:5–19, but not a word of opprobrium falls on the Judeans.

This silence contrasts also with explicit indictment of foreigners, specifically the Phoenicians, Philistines, Edomites, and Egyptians. Here the charges become precise: the citizens of Tyre, Sidon, and Philistia entered into negotiations with Ionians, selling Judean boys and girls into the lucrative slave market, confiscating some of the land of Judah and plundering its sacred treasures. The Edomites and Egyptians slaughtered innocent Judeans as they fled from an attacking Babylonian army. In addition, foreigners taunted the defeated Judean populace, heightening their shame and disgrace by emphasizing their deity's impotence when confronted with a world power.

The designation of Judeans as innocent–hardly appropriate from Jeremiah's perspective–and the implicit innocence of the boys and girls who have been launched against their will on a career of prostitution place in perspective Joel's earlier silence about any sins that might have brought on the agricultural disaster. This juxtaposition of innocents and rapacious sinners demonstrates the prevalence of a calculating morality here no less than that permeating the Deuteronomistic history. In the eyes of the prophet Joel, foreigners who taunted Judeans have finally paid for their indiscretion, completing the slow process of revenge and vindication.

The prophet's reticence in accusing Judeans remains consistent when promising restoration of all losses from voracious locusts and an equally harsh drought. Nowhere does he utter the consoling assurance that sins have been pardoned. The return of divine favor comes without any mention of guilt, human or divine. How differently Deutero-Isaiah and a host of other prophets assessed disaster and deliverance.

Admittedly, Joel issues an invitation to turn to the Lord, demonstrating genuine piety along with customary ritual. What does the verb *šûb* imply? Its use by Job's friends to urge him to admit fault proves that such language can be wrongly applied, in that both the narrator and deity declare him innocent. Even prophetic use of *šûb* may imply nothing more than turning to the Lord in times of distress. The expression does not necessarily suggest previous abandonment of the deity, only a present turning with a resolute mind, although the verb *šûb* often does convey the sense of "returning," for example in Amos 4:6–11 with its haunting refrain, *welō' šabtem 'adai*.[1]

Do the parallels between the books of Joel and Jonah demand a supposition of guilt in both? Not necessarily, for the freedom of the Lord apropos creedal confession activates this discussion in quite distinct contexts. Ninevites, guilty as charged, acknowledge their violence and place their hope in the one who somehow balances justice and mercy, although as elsewhere Jonah's citation stops with Exod 34:6.[2] The condemned king and his people leave everything to divine freedom, contenting themselves with *mî yôdēa'*.[3] Likewise Joel restricts his characterization of deity to the compassionate traits, pausing also to assert divine freedom. In both texts the possibility of divine repentance furnishes the basis for hope. In Joel both Judeans and God turn, but only with reference to deity does the word repent (*niḥām*) occur.

Why, then, the persistent tendency to attach blame where none exists? Ancient historiography has bequeathed a dubious legacy, one that pervades modern thinking just as it did reflection in a bygone era. Grounded in human longing for order and predictability, this surrender to the persuasive logic of retributive justice endures every attack, be it in the name of justice like Job or honest pessimism like Qoheleth, as well as their sequels Golgotha and the Holocaust. This pervasive concept obscures the true nature of causality and misconstrues human nature, possibly also the divine.

What if, like Job, the Judeans of Joel's day were blameless? While writing the Anchor Bible commentary on Joel,[4] that thought struck me as worthy of pursuing, since none thus far has seemed so inclined. Such an understanding of the book would render erroneous the constant refrain echoing from the pages of modern commentaries. The merit of this proposal rests in its refusal to tread where the author of the book refused to go. Where is that?

In his definitive study of Joel and the cult G. W. Ahlström[5] located the fault in syncretistic worship. Growing indications that ancient Israelite worship lacked pristine purity make his theory plausible, although the specific evidence he adduces lacks cogency: the imagery of fire, signifying drought; lamentation over a fallen husband; the linguistic expression *šûbû 'aday* as opposed to *šûbû 'elay*; the frequent use of the verb *hālal*; and the reference to *hammôreh liṣdāqâ*. The semantic affinities with Ugaritic texts, fully explored by O. Loretz,[6] do not make Joel's contemporaries Canaanite any more than Hosea's use of naturalistic imagery identifies him as a follower of Baal. The additional argument previously advanced by A. S. Kapelrud[7]–above all, the cultic use of acacia wood–must be viewed in light of his own admission that the book was composed in the late seventh or early sixth century, not exactly the high period of Canaanite influence.

H. W. Wolff's[8] puzzlement over the meaning of *šûbû* in 2:12 prompts him to admit that "not the slightest touch of casuistry and moral criticism can be felt." What, then, does "returning" mean? In his words, "To reckon with the God who *has been* proclaimed as the one who *is* to come, to see the goal of God's ways not in the functioning cultus of Jerusalem" but to await the coming lord of history. This dancing around the sense of the imperative *šûbû* does not prevent him from detecting an element of *hybris* among the Judean populace. He seems not to have asked whether or not people in such miserable circumstances had occasion to exercise pride. Not a shred of evidence suggests that these suffering people harbored pride in their bosoms.

Perhaps their offense had something to do with the functioning cultus, dismissed by Wolff as irrelevant to the deity. G. Wanke[9] raises this possibility, blaming Judeans for elevating external ritual above inner devotion. But does not Joel encourage fasting and lamenting in solemn assembly, even promising divine blessing in the form of cereal and wine offering? Clearly, this prophet has no brief with ritual when accompanied by sincere piety, and nothing suggests that the people's religious lives are characterized by duplicity.

What about priestly leadership? Have the priests relinquished their duties, withholding cereal and wine for their own consumption rather than offering them to the deity? That is the scenario drawn by P. L. Redditt,[10] who accuses the priests of abdicating their posts under duress. Yet the text states that they join the people in remorse, and the prophet fully expects them to carry out their intercessory role. In a world where someone must be blamed for calamity, priests readily come to mind, in the same way as that which they preside over, the cultus, does. The sharp rebuke of priestly leaders in the book of Malachi encourages such pointing of an accusing finger.

Perchance the unfortunate Judeans violated covenantal relations between them and their deity, forgetting the dire threats accompanying the ratification of a bond. L. C. Allen[11] adopts this tact, assuming that treaty curses have been unleashed against a rebellious people. Unfortunately, Joel never appeals to an operative covenant, although he does have the Lord express ownership over land and people. Breach of covenant, no minor offense, would surely have elicited comment had Joel possessed an inkling that it had occurred.

The virtue of R. Simkins'[12] hypothesis is that it takes seriously the economic privation in which Judeans found themselves. In his view, they succumbed to despair, throwing up their hands in desperation over the defeat of their deity and the practical demonstration of his inability to compete with the gods of the Babylonians. Refusing to serve an impotent deity, and to submit to the consequent disgrace, they abandoned the Lord.

Undoubtedly, ancient Judeans wrestled with the dilemma posed by defeat on the battlefield, but religious people possess remarkable resilience in addressing cognitive dissonance. Various solutions present themselves, not all of which require human perfidy. Furthermore, Psalm 137 portrays a wholly different possibility in the face of defeat–dogged insistence on remaining faithful to the deity regardless of the circumstances. In the book of Daniel the response of the three Hebrews facing the prospects of a fiery furnace suggests still another rhetorical stance: Our God can save us, but come what may, we will not shift our allegiance to another.

This momentary glimpse at a fictional account lodged within an apocalyptic text raises yet another possibility. Did Joel break precedent with respect to indicting the guilty because of the self-fulfiling nature of prophetic accusations, culminating in the crippling pessimism of apocalyptic? M. Greenberg's[13] recent reflections on apocalyptic imply that well-intentioned religious leaders can unwittingly sever the nerve. Promises that never materialize can eventually transform vital faith into inertia devoid of hope. Can this situation explain Joel's silence as an unwillingness to lessen Judean self-esteem? Not really, for he actually joins the ranks of those who promise eventual rectification on a global scale.

Having accompanied these interpreters along heavily traveled paths and found them leading to no credible destination, I am convinced that modern critics would do well to follow Joel, remaining quiet where he has nothing to say.[14]

CHAPTER 19

Transmitting Prophecy across Generations

According to Mikhail Bakhtin, every utterance arises as a response to something that has preceded it. To the extent that this observation accords with reality, the task of interpretation entails the discovery of the earlier word evoking a reply, which in turn necessitates getting back to its social context. Such a search is severely compromised by an axiom in critical scholarship, specifically that biblical prophets addressed their own historical community to announce divine judgment, to stimulate repentant action in the face of anticipated calamity, and to encourage the downtrodden by pointing beyond their misery to improved conditions in the near future.[1]

Because this principle of interpretation fails to take into consideration the transmission of prophetic traditions across generations, it must be judged inadequate. Why would anyone be inclined to preserve prophetic teachings if they only addressed the immediate audience? A purely antiquarian interest hardly explains this phenomenon; other motives must have inspired individuals to keep the prophetic words alive in changing social circumstances.[2] Visions and oracles were thought to have possessed lasting value irrespective of the historical situation in which they initially burst on the scene.[3]

A comparison with wisdom literature may be instructive.[4] The sages preserved the teachings of predecessors primarily because of their pedagogic worth, whether in the form of short sayings, instructions, sustained dialogue, or monologue. The intrinsic value of such assessments of the human situation transcended space and time, partly because they lacked anything pertaining to a specific group or historical era, and partly because they focussed on humankind in general.[5] Although originating in specific times and places, the sapiential traditions give the impression of timelessness. The teachings of the eighth century were just as compelling in the second century; otherwise Ben Sira could not have made free use of the book of Proverbs, both as a model and as a source of material.[6]

The preservation of familial instruction and professional debate about life's meaning makes sense. In the interest of shaping character in youth,[7] parents needed an arsenal that had been tested over the years and that could effectively combat the twin foes of lust and laziness. Furthermore, those who trained advanced scribes also needed classic examples of intellectual engagement with mind-stretching questions. Institutional necessity thus led to the transmission of wisdom literature from one generation to the next. The family[8] and the scribal guild, perhaps eventually also the school,[9] gave impetus to the collection and maintenance of prized teachings.

With the collapse of the monarchy and temple cult in Judah, what social institution provided refuge for prophetic traditions? That question motivates this exploration into the preservation of oracles and stories about prophets. Every attempt to locate a group responsible for transmitting prophetic traditions comes up against a formidable claim that prophecy fell into disrepute for some reason in the view of those responsible for Zech 13:2–6, which goes beyond the attempt in Deut 18:15–22 to regulate prophecy and endeavors to stamp it out completely, or at least one type of prophecy.[10] Moreover, the form in which traditions were transmitted, whether oral or written, complicates the picture. Recent examinations of the persistence of orality as late as Ben Sira[11] and of the meager evidence of literacy[12] suggest that older paradigms may need to be replaced.

Similar reassessment has already begun in regard to the reliability of the biblical record pertaining to the prophets.[13] The recognition that texts bear witness first and foremost to the time of their composition, together with growing awareness that most of the prophetic canon achieved literary expression in exilic and post-exilic times, places a huge question mark before every reading of events prior to 587 B.C.E. To what extent did later editors retroject their own culture into descriptions of earlier events? Modern interpreters, ranging from minimalists to maximalists, adopt varying positions on this issue. The paucity of non-biblical evidence does little to settle this debate (e.g., the three types of prophets at Mari,[14] the ecstatic prophet mentioned in the Egyptian Tale of Wen Amun, and the reference to a prophet in the Lachish letters whose behavior resembles that of Jeremiah).

The position one takes on this issue determines the historical focus of discussion about the manner in which prophetic texts were "read." If an interpreter refuses to accept as reliable any information about pre-exilic prophets, the time-span of transmission is shortened by several centuries. In that case, an interpreter focuses on the social circumstances in the province of Judah during Persian and Hellenistic times. Those who adopt a less stringent attitude to the traditions take into consideration the two centuries before the exiled Judeans returned to the land from which they had been taken when Babylonian soldiers sacked Jerusalem.

An Inner Circle of Followers ("Disciples")

Perhaps a starting point for either analysis can be found in the immediate followers of holy persons. The last of the poems designated by Bernhard Duhm as Servant Songs (Isa 52:13–53:12) implies devoted disciples,[15] and this exilic text may lend credence to a similar phenomenon in earlier times, although one could argue that the socio-economic context of Deutero-Isaiah's era has been read back into the stories about followers of Elijah and Elisha.[16] The same applies to Isa 8:16, which refers to the practice of preserving prophetic testimony among those who have been instructed, a sealing up of the divine word communicated through the prophet until it comes to fruition.[17] Similarly, the deity tells Habakkuk to write the visionary prediction on tablets in clear letters for ease of reading, but also as a sign that the vision will definitely become reality.[18] The principle underlying this practice comes to expression in Isa 55:10–11, which asserts that YHWH's word is no less reliable than fructifying rain and snow.[19]

These texts both provide a plausible social location for the transmission of prophetic teachings and identify the most likely motive for such preservation. The immediate followers of prophets had a vested interest in authenticating a message and assuring faithfulness in its transmission. In addition, they may have wanted to supply fresh interpretation in light of changing circumstances, confident that they were acting in the spirit of their teacher. In their view, predictions that seemed to have gone awry, for some unknown reason, retained their power, making it necessary to wrest their hidden meaning by hook or crook.[20] Daniel's use of Jeremiah's prediction about the lapse of seventy years between exile and return (9:1–27; cf. Jer 25:11–12; 29:10) offers a specific instance of this practice.[21]

To some extent, the essential nature of prophetic mediation enhanced its durability, if one can trust the hint in Num 12:6–8. In that author's view, Moses alone received clear messages from YHWH, whereas all other prophets experienced the divine word as enigma (*beḥidot*). This elusive, and allusive, feature of intermediation infused the word with multivalence, leaving it completely open-ended.[22] Six components seem to characterize the activity of prophets from the reception of a message to its proclamation: (1) the putative revelatory moment during which an enigmatic vision or word captures the imagination; (2) a period of reflection about the meaning of this captivating message; (3) the articulation of the message in terms of a religious tradition deemed authoritative; (4) the refining of that word or vision by means of poetic language and/or rhetorical style; (5) the addition of supportive arguments, either threatening or comforting; and (6) the actual proclamation, complete with gestures and tone of voice, and occasionally accompanied by symbolic actions.[23]

As I have argued elsewhere,[24] that enigmatic feature also contributed to prophecy's decline, for it encouraged differing interpretations that placed prophets in conflict with one another. Discerning the divine will in a given situation could not be divorced from the principles by which a prophet lived, or the understanding of history/metahistory that seemed to be at work. Moreover, unprincipled charlatans may also have complicated the situation, although base motives could easily be concealed as various confrontations between prophets demonstrate and different views within the prophetic literature attest.

Competing understandings of divine intention increased the need for institutional backing. Those prophets whose reading of history placed them at odds with the Davidic dynasty and its theo-political agenda were thrust to the perimeter, forcing them to become outsiders fending for themselves. Their opposites found favor in high places and enjoyed a central position in society, which carried both prestige and power.[25] Neither type of prophetic activity was devoid of risk, for royal interests did not always correspond to prophetic proclamation.

The sometimes hot, sometimes cold, relationship between a given prophet and king in the biblical record has a ring of authenticity, for rulers would probably have wished for divine protection in perilous confrontations–as ample testimony from ancient Near Eastern texts demonstrates.[26] Similarly, prophets may have wanted to influence policy and transform society from above. Such a favorable assessment of this gravitation toward the places of power may also be supported by the assumption that higher ethical expectations apply to the upper class than to peasants (cf. Jer 5:4–5).[27] If these observations have any basis in reality, the charge that prophets courted royal favor for selfish reasons may miss the mark completely.

What social group had a vested interest in promoting the well-being of a small conclave of prophetic disciples?[28] The temple cult? The institutionalization of prophecy must surely have been problematic, for a definite anti-cultic bias permeates the oracles attributed to such individuals as Amos, Isaiah, and Jeremiah.[29] Its presence would have discouraged sponsors from priestly circles, who could find considerable opinion in this prophetic literature with which to take issue. They may have been persuaded to overlook this polemic, however, because of compensating features favorable to the king, under whose beneficence they themselves found shelter.

This ambivalent attitude could explain the presence of glosses in various prophetic books that employ language usually attributed to the Deuteronomist.[30] The lofty ethical ideals of this book rest comfortably with those articulated by eighth and seventh century prophets.[31] If the thesis has merit that a levitical hand can be detected behind Deuteronomy,[32] then a link between prophecy and torah may exist. Traditions that associate certain prophets, particularly Jeremiah and Ezekiel, with priests may not be easily dismissed, given the affinities between priests and the post-exilic prophets, Zechariah, Joel, and the unknown author of Malachi.[33] Moreover, the prophetic attack against cultic ritual may not be absolute, functioning rather to purify the cult by elevating ethics above ritual (cf. the juxtaposition of ritual language and its rejection in Psalm 51).[34]

Was sponsorship by an institution necessary for the survival of prophetic oracles? The marginal existence of prophetic bands associated with Elijah and Elisha does not encourage such speculation about their survival. The less-dire social circumstances of later classical prophets make it possible to imagine a self-sustaining group of followers bent on preserving the teachings of their leader. Such a collection of avid disciples could even have persisted without institutionalization, given the extent of their devotion and the scope of their vision.[35] Caught up in a view of meta-history and anticipating decisive divine action in the near future, they could certainly have kept the dream alive for generations.

Oral or Written Transmission?

In what form was the prophetic tradition transmitted across generations, oral or written? That question has returned to the forefront of discussion, thanks to recent research on literacy in the ancient Near East. Susan Niditch's efforts to isolate oral features within the biblical canon and to contrast them with characteristics of literary production illustrate the complexity of this problem,[36] and Michael Fishbane's magisterial analysis of innercanonical interpretation[37] shows indirectly how pressing the issue has become. What if the *traditum* existed in oral form? How different things would look from the description he has provided! My own study of education in ancient Israel[38] suggests that Fishbane's approach to the dynamic process within the canon of interacting with earlier views rests on the highly dubious assumption of widespread literacy and ready access to written materials. Such convenient texts for consultation strike me as a figment of the imagination, given the agrarian society of Yehud and the limited population of Jerusalem in the Persian period.[39]

Sparsely populated villages had little need for literate persons, and the scribal guild zealously guarded its monopoly on writing.[40] In such an oral culture, written words (icons) shimmered with the power of the sacred,[41] and religious figures used popular awe to their own advantage.[42] That is why one detects a growing emphasis on heavenly books, a registry for the names of those destined for life,[43] as well as mystical language of swallowing scrolls[44] and visions about a huge scroll in the sky.[45] In this realm of discourse, divine scribal activity is thinkable,[46] ranging from incising texts in stone (Exod 31:18) to writing on the human heart (Jer 31:33), or even forming ominous letters of the alphabet on a wall while humans revel in drunken debauchery (Dan 5:5).[47]

To be sure, certain indications of literacy exist within prophetic texts, but all these must be examined on their own merit. Apart from permanent testimonials to authenticate memorable predictive oracles, such reports may be retrojections of a later culture. If writing played a minimal role among the Israelite sages, is it likely that things were different in prophetic circles? Never does a wisdom teacher in Israel advise anyone to consult a written text; instead young men are urged to observe what transpires before their eyes and to listen eagerly to intelligent people.[48] That is how one acquired knowledge. To go a step further and gain wisdom, the student had to embody that information in the context of religious devotion.

Oral transmission of valued teachings has a distinct advantage, one recognized by Plato, who observed that a written text cannot choose its readers. Once put in writing, a text is subject to manipulation by literate interpreters.[49] While the same is true to some extent of orally transmitted teachings, access can be controlled to a greater degree. The person who wishes to pass along vital lore can choose those deemed worthy of receiving it. Even though accuracy of transmission may not have been a hard and fast rule, reformulation within an acceptable realm of discourse would have been a desideratum. In such circumstances, limited circulation among a fictive family of select disciples makes good sense. Did prophetic circles isolate particular ideas for further reflection by subsequent generations?

Thematic Emphases

Those who preserved biblical prophecy underlined the significance of several themes by various means. They frequently cited an ancient credo, often in new and bold associations (Exod 34:6–7);[50] they developed an idea in increasingly complex ways (the day of YHWH);[51] they reflected on mythic adumbrations of familiar notions (YHWH's garden or vineyard);[52] they elevated the linguistic register to the lyrical (utopian visions of Zion);[53] they stoutly resisted apparent empirical disconfirmations (the growing body of oracles against foreign nations); and they developed a form of lively debate (an end of suffering at YHWH's hand). Whether or not these thematic emphases correspond to the unresolved social issues of colonial Judah such as status, inclusion, and theodicy will need to be investigated.

By pondering these themes and developing them further, the successors to the prophets both honored their predecessors and kept the vision alive in new circumstances. Even though persuaded that their own insights were largely derivative, these descendants of YHWH's servants the prophets contributed to the prophetic tradition in important ways. The dynamic process of testing ancient words by the standards of their own age and making necessary changes inaugurated a movement that persists to this day. Nevertheless, a decisive difference has taken place; that process has become two-pronged, with one group transmitting the *traditum* from within the circle and with another group standing aloof and evaluating it from afar. The interaction of both approaches to the prophetic literature holds enormous potential, for it balances very distinct passions, subjective involvement with attempted scholarly detachment.[54]

CHAPTER 20

Theodicy in the Book of the Twelve

Because some historic events defy rationality, they append a huge question mark to fixed belief, transforming a society accustomed to affirmation into one plagued with interrogatives. The twentieth century alone witnessed several such transformative events beginning with World War I and concluding with the AIDS epidemic that continues to claim millions of lives in the new millennium. For many historians, the singular event of a century captivated by ethnic consciousness took the lives of over six million Jews and others targeted for elimination or condemned by association. Response to the Shoah has varied from a type of muscular Judaism aimed at defeating Hitler's ultimate goal (Emil Fackenheim) to an abandoning of theism altogether in favor of voluntarism determined to establish a safe haven for the Jewish people in the modern state of Israel (Arthur A. Cohen). Between these extremes, others have given up the long-standing conviction that God works within history, rewarding virtue and punishing sin, and blessing a chosen people (Irving Greenberg); they have opted for cyclical repetitiveness of nature (Richard Rubenstein); or they have stressed ultimate mystery and, ironically, the necessity of silence in the face of the unspeakable (Elie Wiesel). Victims have been viewed as martyrs, their suffering construed as vicarious, or they have been considered the ugly consequence of freedom bestowed on humankind by a deity who has hidden the divine face.[1] Consequently, the relationship between creator and sentient creature, once thought crystal clear, has become clouded with mystery. Two previously held convictions have become problematic: that God controls history and is compassionate, just, and powerful. Perhaps a third assurance has also fallen by the way: that God *is.*

Christian theology, unexplainably less touched by the Shoah, has nonetheless taken a direct hit, particularly liberalism's optimism, its belief in progress, and its exalted view of human nature. Here, too, extreme responses occurred, ranging from Neo-Orthodoxy's ringing re-affirmation of traditional beliefs to the announcement that God is dead. The phenomenon of fundamentalism flourishes as believers refuse to be overwhelmed by the *anomie* that characterizes modern existence.[2] Divine favoritism, once widely extolled, has become an embarrassment, except to those who consider themselves God's chosen, and the historical paradigm associated with the idea of an elect people has lost its appeal in a global society where competing religious claims must be taken into account.[3] In such a context, the question of God's character has assumed center stage for theists, and with it, the issue of theodicy in its purest sense, specifically a defense of divine justice.[4] Eighteenth and nineteenth century understandings of theodicy as (1) attempts to show that belief in a deity can coincide with belief in a mechanistic universe and (2) to demonstrate the intellectual credibility of an infinite being or power differ markedly from theodicy as manifest in the Bible and in its ancient Near Eastern context. Such post-Enlightenment efforts to buttress faith have come under attack recently, for valid reasons,[5] but earlier discussions of divine justice are not vulnerable to these criticisms. Like modern ones, however, biblical theodicy, although remote from purely intellectual exercises, arises from the anomalies of existence and endeavors to make sense of reality in the light of the prevailing world view.[6]

Theodicy in the Bible and Parallel Literature

Wisdom and Apocalyptic

Within the Bible, theodicy finds its purest expression in the book of Job, usually linked with the wisdom books of Proverbs, Ecclesiastes, Sirach, and Wisdom of Solomon.[7] The deutero-canonical Second Esdras, an apocalyptic masterpiece, rivals the biblical book of Job in posing the question of divine justice. Together these books raise the issue as it pertains to an individual and to humanity at large. Whereas the book of Job focuses on divine abuse of a faithful servant, Second Esdras nationalizes the issue, indeed comes close to universalizing it. An exquisite Psalm, the seventy-third, transforms a personal experience of wrestling with theodicy into a communal occasion for openly facing doubt without loss of trust in divine goodness.[8] Parallels to these texts dealing with Yahweh's justice have much in common with them: a brief section in the Egyptian Admonition of Ipuwer, the Sumerian parallel to Job, the Babylonian I Will Praise the Lord of Wisdom, and Theodicy. Less directly, but nonetheless related, are Ecclesiastes and its parallel, A Dialogue between a Master and his Slave, possibly also the Ugaritic Epics of Kirtu and Dan'el. The answers provided in this literature, less profound than the vetting of the issue, range from blaming the gods for creating perverse humans to condemning people as guilty, from acknowledging ignorance in the face of ultimate mystery to assurance that obedient worship will bring divine favor once more, from despair to hope. Because the sages responsible for this remarkable literature belonged to the intellectual elites[9] of society, their reflections on life's deepest mysteries occasion no surprise.

Popular Sentiment

Neither does the hue and cry of the less cerebreal among the populace, ordinary women and men who faced adversity and were unable to accommodate calamity with ancestral beliefs transmitted over the generations.[10] Their openness to doubt, forced on them by episodic and rampant evil, grew out of the inadequacy of a religion founded on calculatable morality once individualism surged to dominance. In addition, the conviction that Israel and Judah enjoyed the status of a favored nation plunged precipitously as successive empires from Assyria and Babylon wreaked havoc on the two kingdoms. Judging from complaints within the Psalter, the loss of honor that accompanied these defeats and the painful mockery heaped on Yahwists evoked a profound theological crisis. The question, "Where is your God?", yielded no easy answer. Religious pragmatism, encouraged by the dogma of reward and retribution, more often than not led to abandonment of traditional belief, particularly in a culture with no really dominant belief-system. With faith up for grabs, the prominence of theodicy in popular sentiment makes sense.

Prophecy

Where such questioning of divine justice seems out of place, however, is within biblical prophecy. By its very nature, prophecy conveys a divine message to society's leaders and ultimately to the populace in general, whom it also represents to the deity. This intermediary role implies a unique relationship between prophets and their divine commissioner, one based on a calling to service and implying affinity of intellect and affect. The titles associated with biblical prophets emphasize their unique relationship, a bond resulting from having been summoned, from the actual task of speaking on behalf of the deity (*nābî'*), or from possession (*'îš ha'elōhîm, 'îš hārûaḥ*). Alternatively, they stress either the prophet's access to divine secrets through special insight, usually called clairvoyance, or divinatory technique (*ḥōzeh, rō'eh).* Given the bond linking prophet and deity, and the peculiar vocation of the former, one hardly expects theodicy to come into play. That seems the case in extra-biblical prophecy as preserved in ancient Mari and in Neo-Assyrian texts from the seventh century, where ecstatics (*muḫḫum*), diviners (*sabru, sailu, apilum*), and proclaimers (*raggimu*) communicate messages from various deities, especially Adad and Ishtar, to ruling authorities–Zimri-Lim at Mari, Esarhaddon and Ashurbanipal in Nineveh.[11]

Biblical prophets distance themselves from Yahweh long enough to ponder the anomalies of history and their impact on the divine character, particularly the aspect of justice. They do so from a sense of personal affront and from a perception that the forces of chaos have gained the upper hand. Yahweh's failure to honor his promises to a loyal prophet like Jeremiah and to Moses and King David in regard to Israel and Zion reflected negatively on the divine character, just as the argument about the natural order of things and the causal nexus of sin and its consequences grew increasingly more problematic. Above all, liturgical renderings of events in terms of instrumental purpose, even when that goal meant catastrophe for those who saw themselves as the elect, introduced theodicy into the act of worship itself. The inexplicable fall of Jerusalem despite belief in its inviolability and razing of Yahweh's residence demanded a prophetic response that answered the charge of divine impotence or malice.[12]

In Ezekiel's case, a persistent attack on divine justice by the people exacerbated the issue and resulted in a virtual shouting match venting more fury than insight. When calm prevailed, he caught a glimpse of a deeper meaning in Yahweh's departure to Babylon, symbolized by the *kābôd*, and perceived the utter nothingness of idols.[13] His closing shout, reaffirming divine presence in a restored Zion, now made idyllic, stands in stark contrast to the lonely descent into despair attributed to Jeremiah in the so-called confessions. The empty affirmation of Yahweh's justice (12:1a) slipped precipitously when Jeremiah dared to direct charges against the deity (20:7). Innocence, the forensic meaning of *ṣaddîq*, quickly changed to its opposite, guilt.

The Minor Prophets

The Minor Prophets differ little from Isaiah, Jeremiah, and Ezekiel in this regard. For some of them, Isaiah's near-silence about theodicy becomes normative; for others, the examples of Ezekiel and Jeremiah prevail. The only investigation into the problem of theodicy within the entire Book of the Twelve of which I have any knowledge advances the argument that the issue never surfaced in genuine prophecy but was inserted into the text by scribal editors who wished to shape the reading of prophetic literature in a desired direction.[14] This interpretation of the facts avoids the difficulty discussed above–the possibility that individuals commissioned by Yahweh could question the justice of the one in whose service they proclaimed a divine word–but misconstrues the actual religio-historical context of prophecy.[15]

Modalities of Thinking

In a given society some people continue to believe what they have been taught about the deity regardless of historical circumstances. Others abandon traditional teachings at the drop of a hat. However one explains these dispositions to question everything or to accept things without reservation, they introduce a distinct dynamic into a religious community. The resulting struggle for dominance frequently overlooks the positive contribution of such tension. Each view represents a partial truth. Many, if not most, traditional beliefs have stood the test of time and will probably survive the present crisis. Therefore, its detractors need a reminder that considerable time and energy have been invested in the teaching. Nevertheless, not all beliefs can pass muster when confronting major shifts in cultural assumptions.[16] The inadequacy of these features of the belief-system are thus exposed to full view, opening its adherents to mockery. Occasionally, the imperative mood carries the day as a result of subjecting the declarative to the interrogative, and authority-figures issue the great demands that, if obeyed, keep the tradition intact. We can see all three perspectives at work in the Book of the Twelve.

Denial

When this tension eases, a religious community tends to abandon the tradition altogether or to pretend that no problem exists. The latter approach occurs in Zeph 3:1–5, which denies the mere possibility of divine injustice.

> Ah, soiled, defiled, oppressing city!
> It has listened to no voice;
>   it has accepted no correction.
> It has not trusted in the Lord;
>   it has not drawn near to its God.
> The officials within it are roaring lions;
> its judges are evening wolves
> that leave nothing until the morning.
> Its prophets are reckless, faithless persons;
>   its priests have profaned what is sacred,
>   they have done violence to the law.
> The Lord within it is righteous (*ṣaddîq*);
>   he does no wrong (*'awlâ*).
> Every morning he renders his judgment,
>   each dawn without fail;
>   but the unjust knows no shame.[17]

The exuberant confidence of the prophet Zephaniah matches that exemplified in Psalm 92, which envisions a just society with God unfailingly rewarding the righteous and finally crushing the wicked. The psalmist acknowledges the mystery of momentary success on the part of evildoers but attributes lack of understanding to human laziness and divine profundity (92:5–6). In this Lord who causes the righteous to flourish like a well watered palm the psalmist can detect no sign of injustice. The prophet Zephaniah suffers no delusions as to the extent of corruption in the holy city, but this moral laxity contrasts with the deity's perfection. Human leaders, without exception, are judged to be guilty–officials, judges, prophets, and priests. For them, the usual deterrent to ravenous conduct, a wish to avoid the slightest hint of shame, has lost its power, leaving them bereft of honor. Over against this perfidy stands a divine incapacity to do wrong, at least as the prophet sees things. Others may berate Yahweh for failing to keep times of judgment, but Zephaniah detects no such dereliction of duty.[18]

A similar passage in Ezek 22:23–31, an oracle attributed to the deity, lacks the assertion of divine justice but has the negative assessment of Judah's leaders. The behavior of its princes is likened to roaring lions; its priests have violated the teaching with respect to the sacred and the profane; its officials act like hungry wolves; its prophets invent visions and proclaim lies; and the people of the land commit extortion and robbery against the powerless. The expansionist nature of this text when compared with Zeph 3:1–5 makes it difficult to determine the precise relationship between the two, but the resemblances are too close to be accidental. Zephaniah's oracle about the defiled city and its leaders does not stop with this negative assessment but shifts to divine speech announcing a purging of the citizens, leaving a few humble people incapable of wrongdoing (3:6–13). Ezekiel mentions nothing beyond the outpouring of divine indignation, although the prophet will have more to say later about the restoration of Israel and Judah. An eschatological dimension seems to hover over Zephaniah's words, with the gathering of nations for judgment and invocation of the Lord recalling Joel's remarkable look into the future.[19]

> The gloss that concludes the book of Hosea also denies that divine
> injustice exists.
> Those who are wise understand these things;
> those who are discerning know them.
> For the ways of the Lord are right (*yešārîm*),
> and the upright (*ṣaddiqîm*) walk in them,
> but transgressors stumble on them (Hos 14:10).

The difference between this affirmation and Zephaniah's is noteworthy. Whereas Zephaniah characterizes Yahweh as *ṣaddîq*, indeed incapable of doing *'awlâ*, the gloss in Hosea refers to divine activity, rather than the deity's nature, uses a word indicating straight dealings, and reserves the adjective *ṣaddiqîm* for obedient people.[20]

Questioning the Traditional Affirmation That Virtuous People Prosper

The book of Malachi represents the opposite perspective from Zephaniah, for the issue of theodicy occupies a prominent place in the heated discussion between prophet and detractors.[21] Indeed, the divine character opens itself to a charge of favoritism at the very beginning (1:2–5), a preference for Jacob over Esau expressed in terms of love and hate. Like the gloss in Hos 14:10, Malachi's opponents concentrate on Yahweh's activity, or lack of it.

> You have wearied the Lord with your words. Yet you say, "How have we wearied him?" By saying, "All who do evil are good in the sight of the Lord, and he delights in them." Or by asking, "Where is the God of justice?" (Mal 2:17)

The prophet prefers silence to the relentless pursuit of answers, relegating into oblivion the problem of delayed recompense for evil and reward for virtue. His detractors possess too much integrity to remain silent; their disappointment in Yahweh takes extreme form–the idea that the deity actually delights in wickedness. Small wonder they inquire about the whereabouts of a God who values *mišpāṭ*. The deity smarts from the intensity of attack.

> You have spoken harsh words against me, says the Lord. Yet you say, "How have we spoken against you?" You have said, "It is vain to serve God. What do we profit by keeping his command or by going about as mourners before the Lord of hosts? Now we count the arrogant happy; evildoers not only prosper, but when they put God to the test they escape." (Mal 2:13–15)

Here we encounter the age-old problem of a misfit between the comforting belief that a principle of reward and retribution governs the universe and life as it is actually experienced. Here, too, the author sacrifices present reality by gazing into the future when, he thinks, a heavenly book[22] will reveal the names of those who have trusted Yahweh in spite of everything and when justice will finally dawn on earth.

The vexing disparity between virtue and its reward lies at the heart of the circumstances that elicited disquieting remarks attributed to Habakkuk in 1:2–4. An endless cry for help has fallen on deaf ears, or so it appears, and injustice prevails as perverse judgments favor the wicked. The prophet's language suggests the extent of his exasperation; intercession on his part has met with stony silence rather than expected deliverance. Neither persistence, implied by *'ad 'ānâ*, nor extreme duress, suggested by the combined verb *'ez'aq* and noun *ḥāmās*,[23] has moved Yahweh to ameliorate the situation. Furthermore, Habakkuk expresses resentment at being forced by Yahweh to observe such total overturning of society's values. On the surface, at least, the facts hardly support traditional belief that Yahweh cares deeply about justice.

The divine response in 1:5–11 uses a common prophetic motif, foreigners as instruments of Yahweh's punishment, to open Habakkuk's eyes to a deeper dimension of the problem. The idea is presented as if unprecedented, something the prophet would have difficulty believing. The observation that the Babylonians decide what constitutes justice (1:7) stands in perfect harmony with the final statement that might makes right (1:11).[24]

Yahweh's Character

Obviously unsatisfied by this troublesome response that has redefined justice and deity, Habakkuk presses further by exploring the matter of the divine character. Having first settled the question of Yahweh's eternality in language so shocking to later scribes that they altered its sense ("You shall not die" becomes "we shall not die"), Habakkuk wonders about the inconsistency between divine purity and an evil eye that seems to wink at the grossest malice possible.

> Your eyes are too pure to behold evil,
> and you cannot look on wrongdoings.
> Why do you look on the treacherous,
> and are silent when the wicked swallow
> those more righteous than they? (1:13).

This accusation of divine instability or hypocrisy illustrates the confusion resulting from continued belief in Yahweh's justice regardless of the evidence undercutting such conviction. The assertions, "You cannot" yet "you do" cancel each other out, although Habakkuk refuses to reach this obvious conclusion.

In another oracle Habakkuk receives a vision that instructs him to write the divine word as a testimony to its veracity and to proclaim it abroad, but also to trust it in the face of possible delay (2:1–4). This vision ends with the much-discussed word about the righteous living by their faith or faithfulness.

The likely object of *be'emûnātô*, the prophetic vision, is described as truthful but directed toward a specific time.[25] Moreover, it possesses an internal contradiction; it may seem to tarry but will not delay. With this curious language the prophet endeavors to protect himself in the event that expectations generated by the vision are not met with immediate gratification. The closing hymn in chapter 3 acknowledges the uncertainty of grand promises, even when originating above, and conveys the prophet's determination to remain faithful in unpromising circumstances. These sentiments usher the reader into the company of others who cherish divine presence above presents, especially the unknown author of the majestic seventy-third psalm.

Although a putative historical event figures prominently in the book of Jonah, specifically the sparing of Nineveh, the issue of theodicy arises from reflection on the deity's nature as proclaimed to Moses in Exod 34:6–7.[26] Because Jonah understands Yahweh to be compassionate, he shrinks from carrying out the mission entrusted to him by the Lord, and when compelled by circumstances to finish the original task, Jonah explains his reluctance to become a pawn in the divine game of chess.

> O Lord! Is not this what I said while I was still in my own country? That is why I fled to Tarshish at the beginning; for I knew that you are a gracious God and merciful, slow to anger and abounding in steadfast love, and ready to relent from punishing (4:2).

Having experienced Yahweh's readiness to forgive even a wayward messenger, Jonah resents this same compassion being extended to a city guilty of horrific malice directed at his own people. Rather than unleashing divine wrath against a disobedient prophet, Yahweh demonstrates the patience announced in the ancient confession and provides an object lesson intended to persuade Jonah that truly repentant creatures deserve a second chance, regardless of their ethnicity or pedigree.

Jonah has a point. Should guilty individuals escape responsibility for the calamities they have brought to others? Should repentance, even if genuine, remove the punishment demanded by their atrocities?[27] Where is the justice in letting guilty people escape the recompense due them? Who wants to live in a world devoid of justice, one in which evildoers can sin with impunity? The operative word here is evildoers, not foreigners, for elsewhere the book describes foreign sailors in admirable terms. Readers of the book would probably have known that Nineveh eventually fell to Babylonian soldiers, making Jonah's objection a moot point. The overturning of the hated city, whether by repentance or by subsequent invasion,[28] served as a *māšāl* of divine solicitude.

Jonah's legitimate objection therefore pales before the astonishing illustration of Yahweh's concern for the wellbeing of all creatures. Dogma, however revered, means less to the author of this book than divine compassion. After all, the belief in justice stands in tension with mercy, and when the two come into conflict mercy will prevail.[29] This message stands out in a conflicted medium, one freely employing irony, humor, and satire. Has the author faced theodicy and rendered it impotent? If so, Jonah's petulance in the open-ended tale must be judged unseemly. His protest becomes even more telling when we move from fiction to stark reality long enough to ponder the fact that divine compassion was not sufficiently strong to spare that great city and its inhabitants. In the end, theoretical treatments of theodicy do not suffice, for concepts of God that do not accord with reality, however inspiring, amount to little more than proverbial whistling in the dark.

Jonah was not alone in trying to reconcile the characterization of Yahweh as preserved in Exod 34:6–7 with everyday experience. The prophets Joel, Nahum, and Micah join Jonah in this arduous endeavor. Affinities between the texts of Joel and Jonah go beyond coincidence, but lacking valid criteria for dating the two books we cannot detect the line of dependence. The problem confronting Joel differs profoundly from that of Jonah; no evidence of guilt on the part of an afflicted people surfaces in the biblical text, although modern interpreters, like Job's friends, have labored long and hard to indict the innocent.[30] To them it seems obvious that sin has brought punishment in the form of a plague of locusts and drought. Joel urges the community to turn to Yahweh in supplication, relying on the deity's character as specified in Exod 34:6. His confidence is rewarded and Yahweh has compassion on the people (Joel 2:12–27). Elsewhere Joel insists on an exact measure for measure when Yahweh finally gets around to punishing foreign kingdoms for implementing slave trade and other atrocities against Israel and Judah. Like Joel, the prophet Obadiah envisions an exact retribution against the Edomites (v 15). The doxological conclusion to Micah reaffirms Yahweh's compassionate nature and views this readiness to exalt mercy over justice as unique (Mic 7:18–20)–like Nahum's application of the negative aspects of Yahweh's character to Nineveh (Nah 1:2–3). Without exception, the other uses of the creedal affirmation in Exod 34:6–7 stop short of mentioning Yahweh's exacting punishment, for they appeal to the compassionate side, hoping for pity. Nahum, however, has revenge in mind, and he does not hesitate to recall Yahweh's penchant for justice. Like Jonah, Nahum insists on exact retribution against a hated enemy, for in Nineveh's collapse, here graphically depicted, he recognizes an act of divine justice.

Liturgy

The liturgical function of the confession about Yahweh's essential nature corresponds to specific texts in the book of Amos with destructive acts affecting an elect nation. The people's fondness for proclaiming Yahweh's salvific acts (*ṣidqôt*) prompts Amos to mimic such liturgical moments. Looking back over the remembered past, he calls to mind devastating events–famine, drought, infestation of crops, pestilence, unspecified calamity like that at Sodom and Gomorrah–and explains them as Yahweh's discipline (Amos 4:6–12). In effect, the prophet constructs a liturgy of wasted opportunity,[31] concluding each segment with Yahweh's haunting words, "Yet you did not return to me." The prophet offers a theodicy in which misfortune is viewed instrumentally; suffering comes from God to stimulate repentance.

Its lack of success leads to an even more alarming tactic, which has been described as doxology of judgment. Three hymnic fragments, scattered throughout the book, announce destruction while lauding Yahweh's justice in sending such calamity (Amos 4:13; 5:8–9; 9:5–6). The hymn celebrates Yahweh's creative accomplishments, his control over nature itself, and his use of torrential rain as judgment. The contexts of the fragments high-light human guilt, justifying a final act of destruction. In this theodicy, Yahweh's attempt to educate a rebellious people does not find expression; indeed, the time has come for retribution.[32]

Nature

The shift from history to the realm of nature figures prominently in Amos 3:3–8, where the prophet argues from cause to effect. A series of logical deductions relating to causal events culminates in the attribution of evil to Yahweh. Just as one can deduce from a lion's roar that it has captured prey and from the sound of alarm that fear has been generated in the populace, the incidence of misfortune indicates divine activity. In this theodicy Yahweh assumes full responsibility for evil, as in Deut 32:39 and Isa 45:7. The harshness of this type of theodicy is softened by a gloss in Amos 3:8 suggesting that Yahweh never acts destructively without alerting prophetic messengers, who will then, it is implied, make intercession for an endangered people.[33]

Conclusion

The Minor Prophets, like Jeremiah and Ezekiel, experienced an intolerable discrepancy between the anomalies of life and theological belief. They felt this defect most acutely as a result of historical events that threatened what they held most dear, as a consequence of personal interaction with Yahweh that constituted an affront, and as a challenge to their understanding of the deity's essential character. While some prophets denied the problem altogether, others acknowledged its persistence and tried to grasp its fundamental nature and to construct a valid response. Caught in the tension between justice and compassion, they refused to relinquish either one. Hosea's terrible announcement that compassion is hidden from Yahweh's eyes (13:14) alternates with a proclamation of divine courtship (2:14–15 [2:16–17]), but the prophet comes short of saying that Yahweh's abandonment is momentary whereas compassion lasts forever (cf. Isa 54:7–8; Ps 30:5). Like faithful believers today, Israel's prophets learned the hard fact that life has a way of forcing them to walk the razor's edge between doubt and trust. Their integrity demanded that they pose the issue of theodicy to the very one into whose service they had been called.

CHAPTER 21

Theodicy and Prophetic Literature

Within the biblical canon the Former Prophets constitute a monumental theodicy,[1] an almost heroic attempt to exonerate the deity for permitting the defeat of Jerusalem and the exportation of a large number of Judeans to Babylonia. In the view of the authors of the Deuteronomistic History,[2] this core event resulted from repeated acts of disloyalty on the part of a covenanted people, not from weakness on YHWH's part.[3] The rebellious conduct is described as nothing less than a cycle of sin, punishment, repentance, and deliverance. The cumulative effect of such human wilfulness brought on a final calamity, the unthinkable razing of the cultic site believed to be the residence of the deity YHWH.[4] The fault, insofar as one can assess blame in matters of this kind, did not lie with the deity but rested on human shoulders, or so the books of Joshua, Judges, Samuel, and Kings suggest. This extraordinary historiography lays claim to prophecy in that the books feature prophetic figures[5] and interpret events in terms of human deeds and divine response to them.

The last book in the Latter Prophets continues to wrestle with the problem of theodicy, now intensified by the apparent prosperity of the wicked and exacerbated by stark pragmatism. The author of the book of Malachi considered the guarantor of justice guilty of dereliction of duty, which merely encourages evildoers to question the usefulness of religious allegiance.

> You have wearied YHWH with your words,
> But you ask, 'How'?
> By saying, 'YHWH favors and delights in the reprobate',
> or 'Where is the God of justice'? (2:17)

> 'You have directed sharp criticism at me', says YHWH,
> but you ask, 'How have we accused you'?

'Serving God is useless', you say,
'and what do we gain from YHWH of Hosts
by observing his statutes
or by going about as mourners?
Now we deem the arrogant happy;
the reprobate both thrive and escape
when they test God'. (3:13–15)[6]

The pragmatists undergoing close scrutiny here understand religion as barter (*quid pro quo*); they operate on a principle of giving in order to receive (*do ut des*). To some extent, all religion depends on reciprocity, mutual giving and receiving. When that principle becomes paramount and permits skeptics to extrapolate from its apparent failure to conclusions about fidelity, as Job's friends do, it is both malicious and counterproductive. In the instance above, pressing the principle of reciprocity threatens the relationship itself by denying divine justice on the basis of random samples of experience.

Every effort to provide a theodicy fails precisely at this point, for mortals naturally lack a global perspective.[7] All attempts to justify divine activity, or to indict it, suffer from temporal and spatial limitations, in addition to the inevitable weaknesses of intellect, moral insight, and worldview. That is why the comment directed at Lot by residents of Sodom, the condemned city in Genesis 19 ('Stand back; this one came as a sojourner and now would actually act the judge' [Gen.19:9a]) functions paradigmatically.[8] A stranger residing temporarily in a village exhibits exceptional chutzpah when submitting others to a different ethical code from the one which governs their society. Similarly, presuming to know the appropriate standard to apply to the deity amounts to extreme arrogance.[9] Without such boldness, however, theological discourse easily becomes dishonest because it does not take the enigmas of existence seriously enough.[10]

What difference does it make whether or not a given community believes its deity acts justly? Even within a polytheistic worldview encumbered by an uneasy balance between benevolent and malevolent gods, people can endure the anomalies that befall them, although an unexpected tilt toward demonic deities brings considerable unease. Over time, the shift in the metaphors from the natural realm through the royal to the familial[11] was accompanied by increased dependability, if also a certain dullness, on the part of the gods. The social construction of a worldview, the crystalizing of ideals, ethics, and warrants, was the occasion for shaping religious values. A vital feature of this task, the imaging of deity, included both language and artifact. An elaborate cultic apparatus, including a priestly ministry and sacred objects, attests to the importance of this dimension of life in the ancient world. People constructed their gods in accord with their values, foremost of which was authority that wielded power justly.[12]

That concern finds expression in the popularity of myths about a deity's combat with a fierce champion of chaos.[13] An untamed element threatened existence until defeated by a god, who subsequently established order in the universe. Although chaos was believed to have been overcome, the memory of its awesome power lingered, surfacing during unstable times. Belief in gods who dispensed justice unfailingly, and eventually in a single just deity, therefore arose as a corollary to the various stories chronicling divine battles against formidable foes. The prophetic literature in the Bible acknowledges the threat from chaos and attributes victory over the mythic beast to YHWH. Jeremiah entertains the horrendous possibility of a return to the chaotic state prior to the establishing of order as recorded in Genesis 1.

> I saw the earth–waste and void,
>   the heavens–devoid of light;
> I saw the mountains–quaking,
>   every hill–rocking;
> I saw–no human,
>   and every bird–vanished...(Jer. 4:23–25)[14]

Deutero-Isaiah understands the divine agenda quite differently; the mythic battle, now historicized and applied to Israel's experience in departing from Egypt, will be overshadowed by an even greater miracle, YHWH's deliverance of exiled Judeans (Isa. 51:9–11). The prophet's conviction that justice will be achieved on earth freely employs earlier traditions relating to the original ordering of society. Given no such memory, calamities like the exile would extinguish the spirit.

Biblical prophets like Jeremiah and Deutero-Isaiah inherited an ambiguous conception of deity. On the one hand, YHWH was believed to have been a guarantor of justice, a sovereign who as champion of widows and orphans responded favorably to pleas for redressing wrongs. On the other hand, a harsh demeanor frequently presented itself, according to collective memory as preserved in sacred traditions, which told of rash attacks for no apparent reason, monstrous tests[15] of loyal servants, ethnic cleansing, favoritism, braggadocia, bellicosity, and other malicious traits.[16] Such behavior, tolerable in an era of multiple deities, grew more troublesome with the emergence of monotheism.[17] The centrality of justice in this process of stamping out polytheism has left an indelible mark on Psalm 82, which condemns the gods to death for failing to ensure justice among the nations entrusted to them.[18] Modern theologians have taken comfort in the concept of *deus revelatus et absconditus*, using it almost like a mantra[19] when coming face to face with the inexplicable in divine conduct.

The legacy bequeathed to the prophets had its own dynamic, depending on the traditions informing a given individual. Mosaic emphases competed with Davidic, exodus with Zion, priestly with lay. From this rich treasure, each prophet shaped a concept of deity and together they constructed a worldview to which they held Israel and Judah accountable. Meanwhile, some of the people also constructed a worldview, one frequently at odds with the prophetic over the issue of divine justice.[20] Sometimes an embattled and embittered prophet lent a voice to this popular dissent.

Who were these ancient prophets? The picture slowly emerging as a result of approximately one hundred and forty ancient Near Eastern attestations of prophetic activity outside the Bible indicates remarkable durability over a millennium and a half.[21] Whether at Mari during the reign of Zimri Lim, or at Nineveh under Esarhaddon and Assurbanipal, or in scattered areas throughout the Near East, intermediaries presented themselves to kings and ordinary citizens as authoritative interpreters of the divine will, just as they did in Israel and Judah. This extraordinary phenomenon from several locales shared a similar understanding of prophecy and a special discourse; worked outside the cult as well as within it; made use of written delivery and oral presentation; took the initiative but also responded to requests for advice. Above all, prophets claimed to be spokespersons for a given deity who had communicated with them directly or by means of dreams. Their impact varied, depending on whether or not they played a central or peripheral role in society,[22] often determined by which deity they represented.

The rhetoric, rich in formulaic expressions and graphic imagery, drew heavily from royal protocol, for kings were believed to represent divine sovereignty on earth. Prophets therefore endeavored to impose lofty values on terrestrial rulers; this royal ideology placed widows, orphans, and the poor under the protection of kings. In doing so, the intermediaries often blurred the distinction between messenger and source, the prophetic ego merging with the deity in speech. This perceived unity between sender and messenger, itself an artifice of royal diplomacy, did not always contribute to a healthy relationship but occasionally, as in the case of Jeremiah, produced rancor in one who felt betrayed.

Unlike sages in Israel and Mesopotamia, who developed a unique genre, the philosophical dialogue, to explore the question of divine justice,[23] prophets were less original, unless the book of Jonah, a satiric exemplary *māšāl*, falls into this category of fresh thinking.[24] In general, prophetic discussions of theodicy treat the national entity rather than single individuals, the focus in wisdom literature. Prophets employ an argumentative mode based on consensus, appeal to personal authority, wax eloquent with lyrical praise, and imitate liturgical recitation of a pedagogical nature. Extra-Israelite prophetic texts do not appear to have pressed the issue of divine justice to the extent that canonical literature does.

Like their counterparts in Mari and Nineveh, biblical prophets did not come from a single mold. The different titles for their activity (*maḫḫu, raggimu, apilum*) suggest distinct understandings of prophecy: ecstatic proclamation, visionary, cultic respondent. Corresponding to the ecstatic *maḫḫu* were certain *nebi'îm* associated with King Saul, Elijah and Elisha, and the hypothetical prophets depicted in Zech. 13:1–6. As one especially called by YHWH, a *nābî'* spoke words entrusted to him or her. Visionaries, variably labeled either a *ḥōzeh* or a *rō'eh*, were thought to have possessed clairvoyancy, an ability to see things hidden from ordinary sight. Cultic functionaries seem not to have had a distinct title, unlike the *apilum* elsewhere. The confusion of nomenclature is evident from the observation in 1 Sam. 9:9b ('Today's *nābî'* was formerly called a *rō'eh*) and from such additional designations as man of God and man of the spirit.

Ancient Near Eastern prophets addressed both king and commoner, but their frequent indictments of royalty indicate that they acknowledged a higher allegiance than an earthly ruler. Individuals risked life and limb to communicate what they believed to be divine will, sometimes paying dearly for their boldness. Royal toleration of prophetic interference probably varied with the political situation, but unstable circumstances demanded a reliable system of control, making it possible to punish those whose words stirred up sedition. This clear reminder of the king's authority, ranging from collecting samples of hair and clothing at Mari to priestly censure of highly-charged political dissent in Amos 7:10–15, to the torture and imprisonment of Jeremiah, and to the murder of Uriah (Jer. 26:20–23), was counteracted by an intense sense of divine constraint. For persons willing to risk everything to secure their own integrity, the transition to questioning the deity for apparent injustice may have been less dramatic than one might think.

Belief in direct access to a deity's intention did not carry with it persuasive demonstration of the reliability of such conviction. This situation, hardly visible so long as prophets spoke univocally, became troublesome the moment their messages clashed.[25] Competing traditions and varying interpretations of reality produced contradictory understandings of the social, political, and religious scene. Champions of alternative ideologies perceived the divine will through different lenses, and audiences chose authentic representatives of their views over disseminators of lies, from their perspective. One should therefore expect to encounter various attitudes toward theodicy in prophetic literature. In general, however, they fall into five categories: (1) personal affront; (2) the divine character; (3) the interpretation of history; (4) liturgical readings of historical events and (5) the natural order of things.

Personal Affront

Biblical prophecy makes an outrageous claim: that it mediates YHWH's words to a covenantal people. To perform this function effectively, prophets believed that they participated in the divine council, and to do this they had to be in a right relationship with the deity. This conviction encouraged intimacy between messenger and sender, a profound trust rooted in commonality of purpose. Nowhere does this mutual involvement in a unified goal find better expression than in the laments attributed to Jeremiah, where the prophet expresses carnal pleasure over the bond uniting him with the one reputed to be a fountain of living waters, a union comparable to marriage reportedly denied him by this object of spiritual desire.[26]

In marriage, high expectations are frequently crushed by unexpected conduct; a similar dashing of hopes evokes in Jeremiah a crescendo of troubled thoughts pertaining to the deity's justice. The traditional claim retains residual power over him, forcing the accuser to concede too much at the outset:

> You are 'not guilty,' YHWH,
>   when I press charges against you.
>   nevertheless, I will read the indictment.[27]
> Why do evildoers prosper,
>   the treacherous thrive?

You plant them, they take root,
flourish and bear fruit;
You are near in their speech
but distant from their hearts...
For they say, 'He [God] cannot see our ways'; (Jer. 12:1–2, 4b β).

Torn between an intense desire to give YHWH the benefit of the doubt, Jeremiah feels the equal force of brutal reality, events that challenge his worldview. Violent people succeed without the anticipated punishment from above, thus encouraging popular questioning of the principle of reward and retribution undergirding religion itself.

The ambivalence persists, despite a sense of having been abandoned to enemies at his most vulnerable moment, one generated both by the discovery of YHWH's words and their enthusiastic consumption, issuing in a feeling of utter joy, and by the soothing memory of being personally claimed by the deity. That ecstasy gives way, however, to a different kind of consumption, a sickness enveloping body and soul.

Why is my pain constant,
my affliction terminal,
rejecting a cure?
Truly, you are like a deceitful stream to me,
like unreliable waters (Jer. 15:18).

In his own mind, the prophet believes that YHWH rules over a topsy-turvy world, one in which deeds of kindness are met with acts of hatred (Jer. 18:20a).

At last Jeremiah's ambivalence spills over into outright distrust born of perceived betrayal by YHWH. The language leaves little unspoken.

You have seduced me, YHWH, and I have been raped;
You have seized me and prevailed (20:7a).
Cursed be the day
on which I was born (20:14a).

No greater personal affront can be imagined than rape. Jeremiah thinks of himself as naïve, an innocent taken advantage of by an accomplished rake. He no longer wishes to inhabit such a world. Justice has failed, and with it a relationship. It makes little difference whether we envision this experience as authentic to the prophet or as a later redactional fiction. In either instance, it describes a perceived betrayal of trust by none other than the deity. The guarantor of justice has become a violator of the most sacred relationship known to mortals.

The Divine Character

This suspicion of personal affront carries in its wake an even more vexing one, puzzlement over the divine character. Other prophets came to share the point of view attributed to Jeremiah, most notably the reluctant Jonah, but similar observations surface in unexpected places within the books of Ezekiel and Isaiah. Resembling Jeremiah's charge of rape is the sobering declaration credited to Ezekiel and placed in YHWH's mouth: 'Furthermore, I gave them bad statutes, requirements devoid of life; I defiled them through their offerings when they offered up their firstborn, so as to horrify them and to convince them that I am YHWH' (Ezek. 20:25–26; cf. Exod. 22:29–30). Such a shocking revelation of sadism on the deity's part–a malevolence exceeding YHWH's interference with human wills to prevent discernment glimpsed by Isaiah (Isa. 6:9–13)–seems not to have dampened Ezekiel's enthusiasm for divine justice, which he defends in the face of opposing views among the people. Indeed, their repeated attacks on YHWH's justice pushes Ezekiel to an extraordinary position, the rejection of transgenerational punishment, but one that arguably crosses over the boundary separating corporate and individual retribution. In the end, we witness little more than a shouting match with prophet pitted against a group of people, each persuaded by its own rhetoric. 'YHWH is unjust,' they insist, only to be met with Ezekiel's confident, 'YHWH is just' (Ezek. 18)[28]

The divine character moves to center stage in the exchange between Jonah and the deity who pressed him into service against his better judgment. Indeed, the angry prophet justifies his flight from the commissioned task precisely by appealing to YHWH's reputation for bountiful pardon, which seemed altogether inappropriate when applied universally. True, Jonah himself had experienced the divine long-suffering proclaimed again and again in Israel's liturgical tradition (Exod. 34:6–7),[29] but he did not possess bloody hands like the people of Nineveh. It seemed to him a gross miscarriage of justice for YHWH to turn away from the deafening cry of spilled blood and to pardon a guilty multitude of hated foreigners. Jonah's petulance is matched by divine forbearance, an eagerness to spare without limit. The irony of the exchange would not have been missed by readers familiar with Nineveh's actual overturn in 612 BCE.

The prophetic book of Joel also places the spotlight on YHWH's character as revealed to Moses by a hiding deity. An unexplained calamity has left the stricken community in dire need, although no guilt is specified. Joel urges the Judeans to turn to YHWH, whose merciful character everyone knows, in the hope that rescue will follow. Like Amos before him, Joel recognizes divine freedom, the necessity for a 'perhaps' and 'who knows?' even when dealing with a compassionate deity (Joel 2:12–14). Elsewhere, however, Joel envisions an exact measure for measure when YHWH will finally avenge Israel and Judah, a retribution replete with irony for seafaring peoples driven into the desert and semi-nomads forced to venture forth on dangerous waters.[30] Traditionists' reluctance to cite the negative attributes of the ancient confessional statement in Exod. 34:6–7 is balanced by an eagerness to apply them, at least to enemies. The prophets who probed the divine character searched in vain for assurance that YHWH could be trusted to act justly in relating to sentient creatures of flesh and blood.

The Interpretation of History

Historical events, never as simple as biblical literature implies, frequently took perplexing turns that defied systematization.[31] The rigid application of a theory based on a strict principle of reward and retribution by the Deuteronomistic historian and the author of the Mesha stela[32] was destined to fail in the face of historical anomalies. Josiah's death must have rendered speechless all who thought they had discovered a definitive historiography grounded in religious conviction.[33] The widespread belief in the ancient Near East that the gods shaped political events was doubly flawed, first because it downplayed human involvement, and second because the gods waxed and waned in direct proportion to their devotees' success on the battlefield.

Habakkuk's distress over rampant injustice calls forth a response, presumably divine, grounded in the principle that YHWH orchestrates international politics.

> How long, YHWH, must I cry
>   and you do not answer;
> I shout to you, 'Violence',
>   and you do not hear?
> Why do you observe perversity
>   and look on trouble?
> Destruction and violence beset me;
>   strife and contention rise up…
> Look among the nations and take note,
>   be astonished and perplexed.
> For I am executing a plan in your time
>   you would not believe if told (Hab. 1:2–3, 5).

The traditionist implicitly acknowledges the objections evoked by appealing to divine control over current events but pleads for a broadened vision. Local politics, so he argues, and present circumstances comprise too small a sample for measuring YHWH's adherence to the principle of justice.[34] The description of the Babylonians who worship their own power, reminiscent of the divine speeches in Job 38–41, only exacerbates the prophet's dismay.

> Are you not from ancient times, YHWH,
>   My God, my Holy One?
>   You will not die…[35]
> Your eyes are too pure to look at evil,
>   you can not observe trouble.
> Why do you see the treacherous
>   and remain silent
>   when the wicked swallow
>   those more righteous than they? (Hab. 1:12a, 13)

Habakkuk recoils at the thought of YHWH subjecting a covenant people to barbarous soldiers, whom the prophet likens to fishermen wielding nets that capture helpless Judah, no better than lowly fish. Here the issue differs from the one generated by Isaiah's comparable attribution of Assyrian aggression to YHWH, whom the invading soldiers arrogantly forgot. For Habakkuk, the merciless and endless swath of destruction defied rationality, as did divine mortality despite the contrary opinion in Ps. 82:7. Failure to ensure justice has placed YHWH perilously close to the gods mentioned in this psalm who are sentenced to die.[36]

Habakkuk's appeal to divine supervision of political events did not commend itself to Ezekiel, who tried an entirely different approach in dealing with the disaster in 587 BCE. Understanding the exile as YHWH's voluntary departure from a sinful people, Ezekiel viewed the later restoration as a parallel to the return of divine images in other cultures. In this way he avoided the embarrassment of thinking that YHWH had been defeated in battle. Idolatry, in Ezekiel's view, misrepresented divine presence, for the images were actually nothing.[37] For this reason, he never uses the word *'elōhîm* when referring to idols. For him, divine absence was altogether misleading. Needing no physical representation, YHWH could be present in exile in the form of *kābôd*, glory, even without a functioning cult.[38] In a sense, Ezekiel transforms earlier historiography by snatching victory from the jaws of defeat. After him, no one need worry about territorial limitations to YHWH's power or think that historical events demonstrate YHWH's impotency vis à vis other gods.

Perhaps Ezekiel has taken a giant step in the direction of monotheism; if true, he has introduced more problems for theodicy than were resolved by his brilliant strategy in confronting the events surrounding the destruction of Jerusalem. In any event, his bold strategy revitalized an exilic community burdened by a faulty interpretation of history, one that ignored such shaping factors as internal stability, strength of enemies, economic conditions, social inequities, competing parties, and so on.

Liturgical Readings of Historical Events

From Ezekiel's interpretation of the exile and restoration in light of an inoperative cult, it is but a short step to liturgical readings of current events. Traditionists responsible for the book of Amos have preserved the most notable examples of such attempts to interpret political anomalies in terms of cultic remembrance. The first instance, Amos 4:6–12, probably imitates a popular liturgy which celebrated specific victories believed to demonstrate divine favor, designated as *ṣidqôt YHWH*.[39] For Amos, however, the specific incidents attributed to YHWH's initiative were unrelentingly destructive. They include famine, drought, fungi and locusts, pestilence, warfare, and earthquake.

Five times a refrain concludes the divine report by indicting the hearers for squandering an opportunity to repent ('Yet you did not return to me–YHWH's oracle'). Such staggering events must have threatened belief in YHWH's ability to bestow favor on an elect people. One way to defuse such thinking has elsewhere assumed proverbial form: 'Whom God loves, God chastens.' Using the analogy of caring parents, who discipline children lest they become liable to more severe punishment, this approach to misfortune removes its sting. Here the onus falls on humans rather than the deity, for they have wasted an opportunity to repair their relationship with YHWH. Here, too, puzzling incidents fit readily in a worldview that features a providential ruler, and sacred litany becomes an instrument for transferring guilt from above to below. The mention of Sodom and Gomorrah in the last report of calamities, together with the image of a burning ember snatched from a fire, seriously compromises the dominant theme of paternal discipline, whose purpose is to shape character, not to destroy someone.

The other example of liturgical reading of historical events orients itself toward the future rather than the past, as in the first instance. Prefaced by a challenge to get ready to engage in battle, this hymnic fragment mixes various mythic concepts, especially creation, revelatory disclosure, extraordinary hiddenness, and theophanic victory (Amos 4:13).[40] In context, form and content clash; a doxology functions as an expression of judgment, and YHWH is exonerated for bringing destruction against the Israelites.

Two additional fragments, possibly from the same hymn from which the first was taken, have been placed in similar contexts announcing unprecedented ruin (Amos 5:8–9 and 9:5–6). The wide-ranging images suggest an expansive understanding of deity, all the more terrifying because of the announcement of total destruction introducing the last hymnic fragment. YHWH created well-known constellations, governs light and darkness, orchestrates universal destruction by controlling the source of water, initiates earthquakes, and fashions the universe. In the hands of the traditionist, normally benign descriptions of divine activity turn deadly. Lest anyone mistake these attributes as possessions of an alien deity, a refrain occurs three times to link them to YHWH. The traditionists' use of mythic features associated with stories of creation, when faced with the problem of theodicy, may be explained by the necessity for universalization. Divine justice was no local issue but crossed all conceivable boundaries.

How differently the author of Isaiah 40–55 treats mythic traditions, although within the perspective of liturgy like the materials from the book of Amos. Beginning with an assumption that double payment for all wrongs has been exacted from the exiles, Deutero-Isaiah proceeds to play down previous occasions for celebration, including the root experience of the exodus from Egypt, so as to place the announced new exodus from Babylon in a more favorable light. The departure from strict justice is balanced rhetorically by the excesses of divine favor. A desire for justice fades before such wonderful largesse, a divine extravagance worthy of the creator.[41] Nevertheless, extreme claims of uniqueness pose fresh reminders of a shadow-side to YHWH, originator of both weal and woe, and provide a matrix that produces the revolutionary concept of vicarious suffering.

The Natural Order of Things

Whereas the traditionists who preserved the liturgical interpretation of events emphasized the enigmas of nature and history, others viewed the natural order of things differently. After all, a definite rhythm is discernible in nature despite its idiosyncrasies. The sun does rise predictably, and darkness follows inevitably. Like the farmers implied in Isa. 28:23–29, people whose livelihood depends on such regularity arrange their activities accordingly. This brief glance at agricultural practice in the ancient Judean hills gives way at two significant junctures, each time pointing beyond the routine to make a theological statement. The first claim concerns the source of this knowledge about the optimum schedule for producing a desired harvest ('For they are taught accurately; their God instructs them', v 26). The second observation removes all possibility of restricting such pedagogy to deity in general, identifying the earlier *'elōhîm* with YHWH. This claim is reinforced by reiterating the original one ('This also issues from YHWH of hosts') and by introducing traditional epithets ('Counselor of wonder, greatly perceptive'). In short, the text uses one of the fixed realities, encountered daily, to defend a view of YHWH as both sagacious and powerful. This teacher, it asserts, does not apply an arbitrary standard but follows the rule of law (*lammišpāṭ*), even when executing a strange deed ('...to carry out a work–strange is his work–and to do a foreign deed–foreign is his deed', v 21b).

The argument from the orderliness of nature was not the only one of this kind employed by prophetic traditionists. In Amos 3:3–8 the principle of cause and effect reinforces a claim that nothing takes place apart from YHWH's knowledge and initiative. The sole source of misfortune, according to this text, is YHWH ('...or does evil beset a city and YHWH has not done it?' v 6b). Here, too, such a troubling concept is softened by assurance that the Lord will do nothing without mediating that plan to prophetic servants.[42]

In one way or another these two texts that presuppose nature's regularity and cold indifference place them under YHWH's sovereignty. Behind the mystery of nature rests one permanent reality, the texts assert, a divine teacher who communicates openly and clearly. The explicit use of arguments from nature in contexts of theodicy, found here in seed only, will germinate, flourish, and produce fruit in sapiential literature, particularly Sirach and Wisdom of Solomon.[43]

An anecdote purporting to involve Jeremiah during his enforced sojourn in Egypt reveals the potential for a different reading of natural events (Jer. 44:15–19). This text exposes a problem that crops up elsewhere in prophetic literature and Psalms, namely the careful study of deed and consequence that yields no confirmation that virtue is rewarded and vice punished. The speakers are persuaded that the worship of YHWH pays less dividend than service under the Queen of Heaven. Their reasoning, entirely pragmatic, resembles that of the rebels depicted in Isa. 29:15–16 who question the deity's ability to see them and consequently divine knowledge of their conduct. Their perspective on divine blindness may turn things upside down, as mockingly stated, but it can only arise when the anticipated rewards for serving YHWH are withheld.

Nowhere within prophetic literature does a wounded spirit lash out at the natural order with the velocity of Second Esdras,[44] but the prophets' sustained emphasis on human perversity paved the way for this trenchant critique of reality and its creator. This propensity for evil throws into question the created order itself; indeed, it would have been better, Ezra argues, if God had never made mortals. Because they lack the will to reject sin, they become subject to a curse, thus producing a condemned humanity, a *massa damnationis*. This grim prospect facing the human race presents a monumental challenge to the deity. Will mercy triumph over justice? That issue, recognized earlier by the prophet Hosea, was never fully resolved, either by traditionists responsible for the book by that name or by others who preserved prophetic literature from the southern kingdom. One fact is certain: Israel fell to Assyria, and Judah to Babylon. Is the rival claim any less real–that justice was done in those events? The difficulty of affirming divine justice in the face of such atrocities matches that confronted by sages who concentrated on individual miscarriages of justice.[45]

CHAPTER 22

The Sojourner Has Come to Play the Judge

Theodicy on Trial

The dramatic confrontation between Lot and the citizens of Sodom takes a turn for the worse when they accuse the sojourner of playing the role of judge (Gen 19:9).[1] Refusing his overtures of comradeship–the initial linking of himself with them as brothers and the subsequent offer of two virginous daughters for their pleasure–,[2] the men of Sodom threaten a worse fate for Lot than "sodomy."[3] The concept of judging[4] also lies at the center of the episode leading up to this story of conflicting wills, Abraham's intercession for Sodom and Gomorrah. In it, a sojourner par excellence utters the unimaginable, although stating it interrogatively: "Shall not the Judge of the whole earth act justly?" (Gen 18:25). No better paradigm exists for the effort to defend divine justice, theodicy, inasmuch as human beings are quintessentially sojourners.[5]

At least two things make such "playing at judge" extraordinary. A sojourner brings a different perspective to bear on the situation, for other experiences and friendships have shaped that alien viewpoint than those responsible for the ethos prevailing in an adopted environment.[6] Moreover, anyone who has merely taken up residence among strangers but dares to pronounce judgment on their value system displays a high degree of chutzpah. When that shameless audacity extends to its ultimate expression, theodicy, the sole justification may rest in the existential fact of life's brevity. This sobering reality, the death sentence proclaimed over the entire human race, inspires courage in the face of awareness that a sojourner's understanding is different and that resident aliens lack authority.[7]

Indeed, the patriarch's venture in this realm comes as a result of the deity's initiative. Reflecting on the special relationship with Abraham and his vocation with respect to the nations, Yahweh ponders the advisability of informing him of the possibility, or probability, that the wickedness of the two cities signals their ruin. Like a true sojourner, Abraham approaches the Lord with empty pockets, but the lack of a bargaining chip does not deter Abraham from inventing one and imposing it on the sovereign visitor. Lying behind the poignant question, "Shall not the Judge of the whole earth do justly?" is the assumption that Yahweh must abide by a moral code of human devising.[8] Unless the deity acts in accord with the divine nature as moral, human beings have no reason to exercise justice. Abraham's argument implies that the deity should, at a minimum, aspire to the same level of morality as that achieved on earth.[9]

The decisive issue concerns indiscriminate sweeping away of the innocent alongside the guilty–the Dostoevskian concern for the tears of children–as if virtue means nothing. An earlier sweeping away, with which this text has remarkable similarities, was less inclusive, for Noah and his extended family escaped the Deluge. Hence the emphatic "indeed"–"Will you indeed sweep away the righteous with the wicked?" Will the same principle apply in this new irruption of divine judgment? Abraham's bold overture mixes an accusatory tone with self-effacing language: e.g., "Far be it from you"..."I who am dust and ashes"..."Let not the Lord be angry if I speak just once more."[10]

Stung–or pleased–by the sojourner's perspective, Yahweh accedes to his wishes. The principle of a minority functioning to save the majority has been established through a combination of human and divine solicitousness. "For the sake of fifty, I will forgive the entire population" (Gen 18:26). Now it falls to Abraham to ascertain the limits of such forbearance, and he proceeds by gradations of five, then ten, until arriving at the point at which a group dissolves into individuals.[11] From the perspective adopted thus far in this analysis, the narrator's concluding words in this episode carry double force: "and Abraham returned to his place." The sojourner-judge reverts to the status of alien resident while simultaneously going home. The wheels of justice begin to grind more rapidly, at least for the city of Sodom.

Lot's munificence as host failed to rival that of his uncle–until pressed by extenuating circumstances. Both sojourners demonstrated a determination to abide by the existing moral code, specifically the requirement of hospitality.[12] Having demonstrated a willingness to entertain a new principle of justice, the deity acts on the basis of an old one, already in effect on the occasion of the Deluge. Still, none who heard about the destruction of the cities could accuse Yahweh of sweeping away the innocent with the guilty. Neither the exact accounting, spelled out with rational exactitude by the prophets Jeremiah (18:8–11) and Ezekiel (14:12–20;18), nor the newly-won principle of a saving minority comes into play here, unless the sparing of the little village of Zoar–and of Lot's daughters–qualifies as the latter. The narrator assiduously avoids any specific identification of Lot as righteous.[13]

We may surmise that the calamity befalling the cities of the plain in persistent memory served paradigmatically for the similar fates of Samaria and Jerusalem. The haunting question, "If there, why not here?" must have burned itself into the minds of thinking people. Why had Yahweh acted to spare the only individuals in Sodom with the slightest claim to goodness while sweeping away the righteous with the wicked in the case of a chosen people?[14] If any comfort is to be had, it must come from a firm conviction that the Lord does not desire the death of anyone, to quote Ezekiel. Abraham the sojourner had elicited that concession at considerable risk.

Another link between the two episodes in Genesis 18 and 19 illustrates the danger when sojourners treat the divine word lightly. From a place of apparent concealment, Sarah laughed on hearing that she would once more "find pleasure" and conceive a son, and Lot's future(?) sons in law considered his dire warning a mere jest.[15] Whoever dares to sit in judgment over divine ways does well to ponder the implications of a vantage point accessible only to deity, before whom every lying protest comes to light and every belittling of serious warning issues in disaster–if, that is, the deity bows before the moral law. The story reckons, however, with randomness, an ignoring of human merit, or lack of it, that allows the wicked to escape, for nothing suggests that everyone in Zoar was blameless. Perhaps the unspoken answer to Yahweh's question, "Is anything too hard for the Lord?" is "yes." Holding together the qualities of mercy and justice comes to mind.[16]

In the patriarch's intercession for condemned cities the reader encounters a rare feature within ancient Near Eastern theodicies.[17] The complaint of the human sojourner takes the form of direct address to the culpable(?) deity. Normally, such accusation assumes a less confrontative mode, the speaker taking shelter in descriptive narrative. The aggrieved one complains about the deity, or deities, rather than engaging in dialogue with the originator of physical, intellectual, and religious dismay. A pharaoh observes that the shepherd has neglected the sheep, demonstrating reckless disdain for life and social order;[18] an innocent sufferer accuses the creators of concealing their will,[19] and another tells a faithful friend that the gods gave deception to human beings.[20] These critics of the gods acknowledge a measure of human fault, but they deny that it is met with commensurate punishment. The gods have stacked the deck, as it were, making it impossible to ensure a life of well-being by adhering to a moral code.[21]

Biblical critics of Yahweh complain to the deity, as if face to face, sometimes in language just short of irreverent. "How long?" and "why?" ring out from prophetic challengers of humans and God. Jeremiah goes farthest of all, accusing Yahweh of spiritual seduction and rape,[22] whereas Habakkuk soberly reminds the Lord of moral standards regulating human society.[23] Sometimes the accuser appeals to an ideal past as a basis for complaining about the disagreeable present. The judge Gideon reminds Yahweh's messenger that the hardships of the moment create a cloud of disbelief over cherished stories about more favorable treatment by the deity. Similarly, Job contrasted earlier days of divine favor with his daily misery at eventide.[24] When the occasion arises for him to challenge Yahweh face to face, however, his earlier courage fades–or his trust triumphs–and issues in silence.[25]

Some accusers of Yahweh refuse to pull their punches, having completely departed from belief in providence. Their voices usually reach us indirectly, either by way of a prophet's citation of their view only to refute it,[26] or concealed within liturgical condemnation of unacceptable religious talk. On one occasion the doubting thoughts comprise a stage in a psalmist's spiritual journey from envying the prosperous people devoid of ethics to a new awareness of what constitutes the goodness of the Lord.[27] Others speak freely because they enjoy a buffer zone provided by an angel, who zealously defends Yahweh's actions even when they fall in the realm of the imponderable. Thus Ezra takes the Lord to task for inaugurating the whole process that we may loosely call the human experiment, since the rules of the game condemn most inhabitants of the earth to eternal damnation.[28]

In light of such boldness, persons eager to defend Yahweh's justice seize every available opportunity to do so, oblivious to the implications for a biblical anthropology. The Deuteronomistic history represents a monumental theodicy with a single message: the calamity that struck the people of the Lord came as punishment for the nation's wickedness only after persistent prophetic warning and divine forbearance. Impatient with dissenting views, the prophet Ezekiel engages in a shouting match with those who rejected Yahweh's justice, insisting that they, not he, lied.[29] Even radical changes in world view presaged by a growing emphasis on the individual rather than the group did not deter this prophet from maintaining traditional dogma in new circumstances regardless of the gyrations forced on him.

Contemporary interpreters of this ancient literature belong to the category of sojourners in a twofold manner. Besides being temporary residents on earth, they try to imagine life as it unfolded millennia ago. Then they sit in judgment on the deity, the writers, and a society about which they know very little. As one of these critics, I readily acknowledge this fact, at the same time refusing to concede that the guild's approach to theodicy is flawed from the outset.[30] That charge of neglecting the social dimension comes from a scholar wielding enormous influence and merits serious consideration.

The three categories of evil (natural, moral, and religious) can by no stretch of the imagination be rejected as inadequate because they leave out the social dimension. What else does moral evil mean? If by religious evil one refers to the vertical relationship, moral evil must surely cover the horizontal dimension of life in society. That is why I could write about two types of theodicy, one for the oppressed and another for the oppressor.[31] This survival technique on the part of widely different groups has profound social implications. Rulers devise a theodicy to justify their power and status, and to encourage subjects to submit to this view of reality; the powerless invent quite different arguments, often based on revolutionary or eschatological concepts.

Furthermore, corporate solidarity in early Israel excluded individualistic morality by definition. The rise of a wealthy class and urban culture seriously compromised the older sense of a family that linked the larger nation, but the emerging idea of vicarious suffering held in tension the new individualism and the waning solidarity. This balancing of competing notions continues in Psalm 73, which begins by focusing on the social dimensions of theodicy and concludes by concentrating on the existential realities connecting the individual worshiper with the Transcendent One.

The choice of the three categories did not arise from any desire to cover up social processes, nor did it constitute a sort of social contrivance.[32] Because the actual causes of human misery–Philistines, Canaanites, Assyrians, Babylonians, land-grabbing Israelites, corrupt religious and political figures in Judah–were so obvious that stating it seemed unnecessary,[33] the social context may not have received its due. That neglect, however, resulted from conviction that modern interpreters know next to nothing about social factors governing ancient Israel, despite the voluminous speculation prompting a single question, "Where is the proof?" Form critics have long sought to recognize the social location of each particular literary type, with minimal results. Modesty in this endeavor strikes me as essential in the wake of elaborate hypotheses based largely on cultural anthropology or political theory.

The accusation of supernaturalism[34] rests on a misunderstanding of descriptive analyses of biblical texts. These may give the impression of supernaturalism, for they accept the imaginary world of the authors, who definitely believed in an interventionalist deity. By no means does that openness to an alien world view suggest personal acceptance of it. Israelites naturally attributed everything to divine initiative, and discussions of theodicy were no exception. Even when Job goes from pariah to his former status, the narrator attributes the change to Yahweh before going on to credit relatives and friends with the restoration. Interpreters have not been blind to this latter feature of the story; instead, they have struggled to integrate such an epilogue into the larger literary context.[35]

The suggestion that interpreters have ignored social processes because they belong to the "haves" rather than the "have nots"[36] takes up an argument leveled against the foreign sage Agur.[37] This curious view assumes that all affluent people lack compassion for those less fortunate than they, which is palpably untrue. Anyone who hazards a guess about an author's social status on the basis of attitudes to rich and poor ignores the remarkable diversity at all levels of society. Moreover, some contemporary scholars who fall into the category of "haves" remember vividly earlier days of impoverishment. Past experience has taught them compassion for the "have nots."

What about the essential brief with members of the guild? Are they guilty of stressing *theos* rather than *dike*?[38] The first thing that comes to mind concerns the meaning of theodicy. The word must have primary reference to *theos*, and that has guided interpreters in their treatments of the problem. The other half of the word, *dike*, also refers to divine action. The insistence that it be restricted to social processes has no linguistic basis. To be sure, biblical writers understood the evil repercussions of certain social processes, and these frequently provoked theodicies, but the blame fell on Yahweh as supreme ruler and shepherd. In the view of the writers, the Lord was ultimately responsible for social processes. The more sophisticated biblical authors may have realized that individuals make their own choices, but they still attributed actions to Yahweh.

Modern interpreters understand events differently, but they err when projecting their own views on biblical texts. The ancients believed that Yahweh provided the impetus of social process, acting as its norm and as the agent for its transformation.[39] They may even have been comfortable with the claim that Yahweh guided the process through human instruments.

The changing of the question from "Why do the innocent suffer?' to, "How does history work?"[40] solves nothing as long as Yahweh is thought to orchestrate human events.[41] The interpreter may concentrate on the deity's malfeasance or on human social processes, but theodicy requires that one pronounce judgment on Yahweh, whatever else may be said about societal responsibility.

In short, the enthusiasm generated by recent sociological interpretations of the Bible should be tempered by an awareness of our profound ignorance. When did individualistic thinking first surface, and when did it reach the point that it forced thinkers to offer a theodicy exonerating Yahweh for apparent injustices? What periods of history made this issue one that could not be ignored? When did the question become abstract, a matter for erudite speculation rather than a struggle to maintain religious faith?[42] At what time did someone first entertain the thought that Yahweh was either immoral or impotent? When did biblical thinkers begin to take refuge in the belief that Yahweh concealed the truth while revealing limited insights to humans?[43] What enticed biblical thinkers to attribute fault to human beings rather than assailing the deity? Why did later sages internalize the signs of divine retribution?[44] In response to these and similar questions, a stinging *kî tēdā'* shimmers with irony.

If the unknown poet responsible for Deutero-Isaiah correctly perceived the vast chasm separating divine and human ways, as well as thoughts, every effort at theodicy may indeed be an arrogant exercise in futility. Nevertheless, stories like those concerning Abraham's intercession for Sodom and its sequel encourage the attempt. As sojourners we lift our voices in protest when society fails to implement justice. We may put the blame on the ultimate source of authority, but that does not overlook human transgression, which evoked the complaint in the first place. Theodicy may indeed be on trial today, but not because its practitioners have overlooked the social dimension. Rather, modern society's self-absorption has eroded the transcendent dimension of reality, condemning the present world to a single option, the secular, and in the process erasing *theos*.[45] In such a world, theodicy has indeed shifted to anthropodicy.[46]

Notes

Chapter 1: Flirting with the Language of Prayer

[1]"The Book of Job," *NIB* vol. IV (Nashville: Abingdon Press, 1996). On the language of prayer in wisdom literature, see "The Restraint of Reason, the Humility of Prayer," 206–222 in James L. Crenshaw, *Urgent Advice and Probing Questions* (Macon: Mercer University Press, 1995). Job's reluctance to adopt the stance of prayer occasions little surprise in the light of the sages' virtual silence in this regard. Only three prayers appear in canonical wisdom: Prov 30.7–9; Sir 22.27–23.6; and 36.1–22. The subject of prayer in ancient Israel has been examined in some detail by Samuel E. Balentine, *Prayer in the Hebrew Bible* (Minneapolis: Fortress Press, 1993). See also Moshe Greenberg, *Biblical Prose Prayer as a Window to the Popular Religion of Ancient Israel* (Berkeley, Los Angeles, London; University of California Press, 1983). Recognizing true prayers is difficult (cf. Job 13.20–22 and Prov 3.70).

[2]Each of Job's speeches in the first cycle ends with an address to the deity (7.7–21; 10.2–22; 13.20–14.22). After that, only 17.3–4 (and possibly 16.7–8), 30.20–23, 40.3–5, and 42.1–6 do so. The dominant concept now appears to be forensic; Job increasingly voices a concern to face the deity in a "courtroom." Vindication has replaced reconciliation as Job's goal.

[3]The harsh treatment of faithful Jews by the Seleucid authorities during the Maccabean revolt gave rise to the anticipation of divine redress for some, punishment for others (Dan 12.2). The martyrology surrounding 2 Macc 7.9 was precipitated by the same calamity. The exact circumstances evoking a similar belief in resurrection expressed in Isa 26.19 cannot be established, but the allusion to the power of dew to bestow life on the dead reappears in the story about Isaac's resuscitation in the garden of Eden following Abraham's actual sacrifice of his son. One can make a strong case for viewing Ps 73.24 as an expression of the conviction that profound intimacy with God will survive death's ravages.

[4]The translation avoids gender-specific renderings when the Hebrew text implies both male and female. Hence the plural "mortals." In other instances, it omits a notable feature of Hebrew style, the frequent use of "and" to connect lines in parallelism.

[5]In 13.20–22 Job pleads for the deity to enable him to enter into litigation with his frightening opponent. Only when God removes the oppression and Job's terror can he stand a chance in a trial. Then the deity can call and Job will respond. He desperately needs an arbiter, a champion of his cause (9.32–34), but he has discarded such a possibility as unlikely. He returns to this idea in 19.25–27, but the terrible state of the text renders its meaning uncertain.

[6]Job has already accused the deity of loathing the work of divine hands (10.3); now Job imagines a different emotion, an instinctual affection for one's progeny. The verb *kāsap* denotes powerful inner feelings of both animals and humans.

[7]The modern idea that time's passage alters the conception of justice was not entirely unknown in ancient Israel. This willingness to pardon debtors after the lapse of a specified number of years may have more to do with compassion for the needy than with the Jubilee year, which had as its primary purpose the preservation of family land-holdings.

[8]Here he shifts from posing a universal question, "If mortals die, will they live again?" to asking a purely personal one. The injustice surrounding his own case prompts this way of putting the question. Job thinks that the cruel circumstances of his own life merit exceptional treatment, if not in this life then beyond the grave. This depiction of existence in Sheol differs sharply from his earlier account (3.17–19). In Norman C. Habel's view, vv 13–17 function as a pivotal text, a radically new dream that synthesizes earlier speeches (*The Book of Job* [Philadelphia: Westminster Press, 1985] 238).

[9]The expression for observing one's steps seems always to carry a hostile meaning. The author may have Job reverse this use as part of his wholesale attack on traditional belief. The book teems with irony, on which see above all Yair Hoffman, *A Blemished Perfection. The Book of Job in Context* (JSOTSup 213. Sheffield: Academic Press, 1996).

[10]The primary sense of *ṣb'* is enforced service (A. S. van der Woude, "*ṣᵉba'* army," 1041 in Ernst Jenni and Claus Westermann, *Theological Lexicon of the Old Testament*, vol. 2 [Peabody: Hendrickson Publishers, Inc., 1997]). That involuntary service may take the form

of corvée labor on administrative projects or on any one of many lesser tasks. Leo G. Perdue, *Wisdom in Revolt* (JSOTSup 112. Sheffield: The Almond Press, 1991) understands the term in 14.14 as slavery. He finds a comparable use in Isa 40.2 with reference to the exile in Babylon.

[11]Referring to 7.1 where Job compares daily existence to service in the military, Habel writes that Job now finds such service endurable under the new rules he has just outlined (*The Book of Job*, 243). In the end such speculation proves unproductive, for he does not believe that the deity will act in this kindly manner toward him.

[12]This conviction that YHWH preserved the life of the faithful, even gathering every tear, finds expression in the concept of a heavenly scroll in which were inscribed the names of those designated for life (cf. Exod 32.33, Ps 139.16, and Dan 12.1). On this belief in the ancient Near East, see Shalom M. Paul, "Heavenly Tablets and the Book of Life," *JANESCU* 5 (1973) 345–53.

[13]A. L. Oppenheim, "On an Operational Device in Mesopotamian Bureaucracy," *JNES* 18 (1959) 121–28. For an account of the earliest form of keeping records, see Denise Schmandt-Besserat, "Record Keeping Before Writing," 2097–2106 in *Civilizations of the Ancient Near East*, ed. Jack M. Sasson, vol. IV (New York: Charles Scribner's Sons, 1995). She traces a development from clay tokens to envelopes for holding them and ultimately to written tablets.

[14]N. H. Tur-Sinai (Torczyner), *The Book of Job, A New Commentary* (Jerusalem: Kiryath Sepher, 1957) adopts this explanation and reproduces an illustration from Emil G. Kraeling, *The Brooklyn Museum Aramaic Papyri* (New Haven: Yale University Press, 1953), plate 21. The picture shows a bundle of written documents with the wax seal intact.

[15]The Hebrew word for serpent, *hannāḥāš*, is otherwise used of ordinary snakes, but in Amos' mind it functions in an extraordinary way as an agent of divine punishment. The usual designations for the chaos-monster (Leviathan, Tannin, Rahab) belong to poetic texts in Isaiah, Psalms, and Job. In them, the fearful creature is either conquered and destroyed, like its prototype Tiamat, or its activity is severely restricted.

[16]The personification of the sword as an agent ready to perform YHWH's command occurs also in prophetic texts, for example Jer 15.3 (along with dogs, birds, and beasts).

[17]The vindictive spirit at the end of this exquisite psalm troubles those who believe one should have compassion on all, even enemies. For an effort to understand the religious dynamic of such psalms, see Erich Zenger, *A God of Vengeance?* (Louisville: Westminster John Knox, 1996).

[18]Neil Gillman, *The Death of Death* (Woodstock, Vermont: Jewish Lights Publishing, 1997) shows how competing views about the future life–resurrection and immortality of the soul–have fared through the centuries in Jewish circles. His discussion ranges widely, beginning with biblical and rabbinic sources and tracing the canonization of a doctrine. His insights on Maimonides' teachings and those of mystic Jews provide a useful background for his analysis of modern prayer books compiled by the four branches of Judaism in the United States. Gillman does not belong to those persons excoriated in Ernest Becker's *The Denial of Death* (New York: Free Press, 1973), but neither does he believe that death has the final word.

[19]Michael Kolarcik, *The Ambiguity of Death in the Book of Wisdom 1–6* (Roma: Editrice Pontificio Istituto Biblico, 1991) 163, 174 recognizes the complexity of death in this book. He argues that three distinct yet related perceptions of death occur here: mortality, physical death as punishment, and ultimate death.

[20]Pieter van der Lugt, *Rhetorical Criticism and the Poetry of the Book of Job* (Leiden: E. J. Brill, 1995), 171 identifies two cantos (vv 1–12, 13–22) and four canticles (vv 1–6, 7–12, 13–17, 18–22). Because the first word begins with *'alep* and the last with *tau*, and because the canticle has twenty-two lines, he labels it alphabetic. According to Habel, the elegy on the human condition moves from proverbial to formulaic tradition in question form to probing question to blunt accusation (vv 1, 10, 14, 19; *The Book of Job*, 237). Edwin M. Good, *In Turns of Tempest* (Stanford: Stanford University Press, 1990) connects 14.1–6 with what immediately precedes, 13.23–28, and considers this section cross-examination. He then links 14.7–22 together and calls it Job's pondering of life and death, permanence and ephemerality, hypothetical hope and actual decay (237).

[21]James L. Crenshaw, *Ecclesiastes* (Philadelphia: Westminster Press, 1987) opts for "ephemeral" and "futile" as the usual meanings, whereas Michael V. Fox, *Qohelet and his Contradictions* (JSOTSup 71; Sheffield: Almond Press, 1989) prefers "absurdity". Choon

Leong Seow, *Ecclesiastes* (Garden City: Doubleday, 1997) retains the traditional translation, "vanity".

[22]In the Hebrew Bible the phrase *yelûd 'iššâ,* occurs only in Job (15.14, 25.4 besides 14.1), but it also appears outside the canon in Sir 10.18, 1 QS 11.21, 1 QH 13.17, 18.12–13, 16.23–24. "A person born of woman" includes everybody (A. de Wilde, *Das Buch Hiob* [Leiden: E. J. Brill, 1981] 172–3). If v 4 represents a cultic rather than a forensic view, it may comprise a gloss on a misunderstanding of v 1 as a reference to the impurity of women during specific periods.

[23]Jon D. Levenson, *Creation and the Persistence of Evil* (San Francisco: Harper & Row Publishers, 1988) examines the motif of a chaos-monster in the Hebrew Bible and the ancient Near East, tracing the development of the traditions relating to this mythical figure in ancient cosmologies. Gisela Fuchs, *Mythos und Hiobdichtung* (Stuttgart, Berlin, Köln: Verlag W. Kohlhammer, 1993), although more comprehensive, throws considerable light on the myth as employed in the book of Job.

[24]The author of Psalm 1 restricts the comparison of mortals to a tree, limiting its applicability to the righteous and likening the wicked to wind-driven chaff. The sages viewed wisdom as a tree of life; in contrast to the other tree of mythic lore, this one had no guardian cherubim and no flaming sword to prevent access. Within Jewish apocalyptic, a mighty king can be symbolized by a majestic tree, and its stump represents the survival of the dynasty (Daniel 4).

[25]Laments within the Bible frequently picture the speaker as already sinking into Sheol, its raging waters engulfing the helpless supplicant. Sickness was understood as transporting its victim into the realm of the dead. The rhetoric easily lends itself to misunderstanding, so the modern interpreter needs to exercise caution.

[26]Some critics interpret this comment about disappearing streams as an ironic statement of the impossible, e.g. Edouard Dhorme, *A Commentary on the Book of Job* (London: Thomas Nelson and Sons, 1967), 200.

[27]The expansive vocabulary (awake, rise, rouse from slumber) echoes that found in Isa 26.19 (rise) and Dan 12.2 (awake). John E. Hartley thinks the choice of several verbs reflects a period devoid of technical language for resurrection (*The Book of Job* [Grand Rapids: William Eerdmans, 1988] 235).

[28]Note the structure of the verse, specifically the centering of the personal reference in each colon (*'ālāyw*). He feels only *his own* flesh; he mourns *his own* self (14.22). On suffering as a theological problem, see James L. Crenshaw, "Suffering", 718–19 in *The Oxford Companion to the Bible*, eds. Bruce M. Metzger and Michael D. Coogan (New York & Oxford: Oxford University Press, 1993). Jonathan Lamb, *The Rhetoric of Suffering* (Oxford: Clarendon Press, 1995) treats the manner in which the literati read the book of Job in the eighteenth century, and David Kraemer, *Responses to Suffering in Classical Rabbinic Literature* (New York & Oxford: Oxford University Press, 1995) looks at a much earlier time.

[29]The location of v 22 presents a problem. Unlike Uralu in Mesopotamian lore, Sheol was not a place of punishment, with a single canonical exception (Isa 66.24; cf. Jdt 16.17). Newsom solves this difficulty by projecting the time of v 22 to the experience of death rather than viewing it as postmortem pain (*The Book of Job,* 443).

[30]On various responses to the problem of perceived injustice by the deity, see Crenshaw, *Urgent Advice and Probing Questions,* 141–221.

[31]"'*iyyôb* has definitely become '*ôyeb*" (Good, *In Turns of Tempest*, 241). In this unit, the order of references to water, dust, and hope is the reverse of the sequence in vv 7–9.

[32]Perdue, *Wisdom in Revolt*, 157–62 examines the two trajectories represented by (1) "The Death of Gilgamesh" and "Gilgamesh, Enkidu, and the Netherworld", and (2) "Gilgamesh, Inanna, and the Bull of Heaven" and "Gilgamesh, Enkidu, and the Netherworld", as well as their combination in "The Gilgamesh Epic." The two traditions celebrate a hero who marries and appropriates the powers of fertility and a powerful king who conquers all enemies.

Chapter 2: Wisdom and the Sage

[1]G. von Rad, *Wisdom in Israel*, 1972, 97–110.

[2]J. S. Bruner, *On Knowing*, 1966, 132–37.

[3]S. N. Kramer, *The Sumerians,* 1963; M. Lichtheim, *Ancient Egyptian Literature,* I–III, 1973;'76,'80; *Late Egyptian Wisdom Literature in the International Context,* 1983.

[4]C. A. Newsom, "Woman and the Discourse of Patriarchal Wisdom: A Study of Proverbs 1–9," 142–60 in *Gender and Difference in Ancient Israel*, ed. P. L. Day, 1989.

[5]J. Blenkinsopp, "The Social Context of the 'Outsider Woman' in Proverbs 1–9," *Bib* 72 (1991) 457–73.

[6]J. L. Crenshaw, "Education in Ancient Israel," *JBL* 104 (1985) 601–15; M. Haran, "On the Diffusion of Literacy and Schools in Ancient Israel," 81–95 in *VTSup* XL (Congress Volume, Jerusalem, 1988).

[7]P. W. Skehan and A. A. DiLella, *The Wisdom of Ben Sira*, 1987, 193 and J. G. Snaith, *Ecclesiasticus*, 1974, 39.

[8]M. Lichtheim, *Ancient Egyptian Literature*, I, 131.

Chapter 3: The Primacy of Listening in Ben Sira's Pedagogy

[1]Two examinations of research on Sirach indicate the scope of scholarly interest in the second half of the twentieth century: Johannes Marböck, "Sirachliteratur seit 1966: Ein Überblick, *TRev* 71 (1975) 177–84 and Daniel J. Harrington, "Sirach Research since 1965: Progress and Questions," 164–76 in *Pursuing the Text: Studies in Honor of Ben Zion Wacholder on the Occasion of his Seventieth Birthday*, eds. John C. Reeves and John Kampen (JSOTSup 184; Sheffield: Academic Press, 1994). An assessment of the evidence can also be found in "Introduction," "The Book of Sirach," NIB V, 603-40.

[2]John D. Sawyer, "Was Jeshua ben Sira a Priest?" *Proceedings of the Eighth World Congress of Jewish Studies* (Jerusalem, 1982) 65–71 answers the question affirmatively, pointing to (1) the author's positive attitude to the priesthood, (2) the large number of later *ḥakāmîm* who were priests, and (3) his Zadokite name. Saul M. Olyan, "Ben Sira's Relationship to the Priesthood," *JTR* 80 (1987) 261–86 reaches the same conclusion, as does Helga Stadelmann, *Ben Sira als Schriftgelehrter* (WUNT 6; Tübingen: J. C. B. Mohr-Paul Siebeck, 1980). J. G. Snaith, "Ben Sira's Supposed Love of Liturgy," *VT* 25 (1975) 167–74 finds no evidence in Sirach for enthusiastic support of the priesthood.

[3]Peter Höffken, "Warum schwieg Jesus Sirach über Esra?" *ZAW* 87 (1975) 184–202 explains the silence about Ezra in terms of Ben Sira's ideological difference with levitical priests, whereas Christopher Begg, "Ben Sira's Non-mention of Ezra," *BN* 42 (1988) 14–18 thinks Ben Sira concentrates on those persons involved in building projects involving the city and temple.

[4]J. L. Koole," Die Bibel des Ben-Sira," *OTS* 14 (1965) 374–96.

[5]According to W. C. Trenchard, *Ben Sira's View of Women: A Literary Analysis* (BJS 38; Chico, CA: Scholars Press, 1982), misogynism correctly describes Ben Sira's attitude to women. A much more nuanced interpretation appears in Claudia V. Camp, "Understanding a Patriarchy: Women in Second Century Judaism through the Eyes of Ben Sira," 1–39 in "*Women Like This*": *New Perspectives on Jewish Women in the Greco-Roman World*, ed. Amy-Jill Levine (Atlanta: Scholars Press, 1991).

[6]The single exception of interpretation dealing with the philosophy of education is chapter ten, "Erziehung und Bildung," 174–200 in Oda Wischmeyer, *Die Kultur des Buches Jesus Sirach* (BZNW 77; Berlin & New York: Walter de Gruyter, 1995).

[7]My fuller analysis of education, literacy, and epistemology in ancient Israel appears in *Education in Ancient Israel: Across the Deadening Silence* ; Anchor Bible Reference Library (New York: Doubleday, 1998).

[8]On the history and scope of the discoveries of Hebrew manuscripts, see the discussion in Patrick Skehan/Alexander A. DiLella, *The Wisdom of Ben Sira* (AB 39; New York: Doubleday, 1987) 51–62.

[9]J. Ziegler, *Sapientia Iesu Filii Sirach* (Septuaginta 12/2; Göttingen: Vandenhoeck & Ruprecht, 1965).

[10]Dominique Barthélemy and Otto Rickenbacher, *Konkordanz zum hebräischen Sirach mit syrisch-hebräischen Index* (Göttingen: Vandenhoeck & Ruprecht, 1973) and *The Book of Ben Sira, Text, Concordance and an Analysis of the Vocabulary* (Jerusalem: Academy of the Hebrew Language and the Shrine of the Book, 1973).

[11]Hans Peter Rüger, *Text und Textform in hebräischen Sirach. Untersuchungen zu Textgeschichte und Textkritik der hebräischen Sirachfragmente aus der Kairoer Geniza* (BZAW 112; Berlin: Walter de Gruyter, 1970); Tadeusz Penar, *Northwest Semitic Philology and the Hebrew Fragments of Ben Sira* (Bib Or 28; Rome: Biblical Institute Press, 1975), and Friedrich Vincent

Reiterer, *'Urtext' und Übersetzungen. Sprachstudie über Sir 44:16–45:26 als Beitrag zur Siraforschung* (AzTuSAT, 12; St. Ottilien: EOS-Verlag, 1980).

[12]Milward D. Nelson, *The Syriac Version of the Wisdom of Ben Sira Compared to the Greek and Hebrew Materials* (SBLDS 107; Atlanta: Scholars Press, 1988).

[13]Francesco Vattioni, *Ecclesiastico-Testo ebraico con apparato critico e versioni greca, latina e siriaca* (Testi 1; Naples: Instituto Orientale di Napoli, 1968).

[14]Theophil Middendorp, *Die Stellung Jesu Ben Siras zwischen Judentum und Hellenismus* (Leiden: E. J. Brill, 1973) thinks Ben Sira drew extensively from anthologies of Greek texts while also relying heavily on canonical Jewish literature.

[15]Volker Kieweler, *Ben Sira zwischen Judentum und Hellenismus. Eine Auseinandersetzung mit Th. Middendorp* (BzEATuAJ 30; Frankfurt: Peter Lang, 1992) recognizes the considerable variety within both Hellenism and Judaism at the time of Ben Sira and understands his response as one brought on by an aggressive Greek culture.

[16]Rudolf Smend, *Die Weisheit des Jesus Sirach* (Berlin: Verlag von Georg Reimer, 1906) xxiii declares that in selecting the earlier motto, "the fear or the Lord is the beginning (its inner essence) of wisdom," "formuluiert er die Kriegserklärung des Judentums gegen den Hellenismus").

[17]Martin Hengel, *Judaism and Hellenism: Studies in their Encounter in Palestine during the Early Hellenistic Period,* 2 vols. (Philadelphia: Fortress Press, 1974), especially 131–53 for Ben Sira.

[18]Jack T. Sanders, *Ben Sira and Demotic Wisdom* (SBL MS 28; Chico, CA: Scholars Press, 1983).

[19]David Winston, "Theodicy in Ben Sira and Stoic Philosophy," 239–49 in *Of Scholars, Savants, and their Texts: Studies in Philosophy and Religious Thought, Essays in Honor of Arthur Hyman,* ed. Ruth Link-Salinger (New York et. al: Peter Lang, 1989), but see Raymond Pautrel, "Ben Sira et le Stoicisme," *RSR* 51 (1963) 535–49.

[20]Wolfgang Roth, "Sirach: The First Graded Curriculum," *The Bible Today* 29 (1991) 298–302 and "On the Gnomic-Discursive Wisdom of Jesus Ben Sirach," *Semeia* 7 (1980) 59–79. Roth thinks Ben Sira began with elementary ethical considerations, then moved to advanced theological issues, finally to his own creative reflections that go beyond the tradition he inherited. The work resulted from several stages, according to Roth. An original book (1:1–23:27; 51:1–30) in four sections was thematically arranged on the basis of words beginning with the letters of the alphabet in sequence, and three times Ben Sira felt compelled to add further reflections to this original book.

[21]Skehan/DiLella, *The Wisdom of Ben Sira,* adopt such a reading, emphasizing the introductory praise of wisdom in several units.

[22]Burton Mack, *Wisdom and the Hebrew Epic: Ben Sira's Hymn in Praise of the Fathers* (Chicago/London: University of Chicago Press, 1985) emphasizes the historical understanding of Ben Sira in forging national consciousness and thinks the priestly scribe is transformed via Hellenism into the office of teacher-sage, "a *novum* indeed" (107).

[23]Thomas Lee, *Studies in the Form of Sirach 44–50* (SBLDS 75; Atlanta: Scholars Press, 1986).

[24]Chris A. Rollston, *The Non-Encomiastic Features of Ben Sira 44–50,* M. A. Thesis, Emmanuel School of Religion, 1992. Rollston's critique reveals the considerable freedom with which Ben Sira treated Greek encomia, if he actually adapted them for rhetorical use.

[25]On genres in biblical wisdom, see James L. Crenshaw, "Wisdom," 225–64 in *Old Testament Form Criticism,* ed. John Hayes (Trinity University Monograph 2; San Antonio: Trinity University Press, 1974; reprinted in James L. Crenshaw, *Urgent Advice and Probing Questions: Collected Writings on Old Testament Wisdom* [Macon: Mercer University Press, 1996, 45–77]) and Roland E. Murphy, *Wisdom Literature* (FOTL 13; Grand Rapids: William B. Eerdmans Publishing Company, 1981).

[26]Johann Marböck, *Weisheit im Wandel. Untersuchungen zur Weisheitstheologie bei Ben Sira* (BBB 37; Bonn: Peter Hanstein Verlag, 1971) teems with valuable insights into the literary and theological significance of Sirach.

[27]Josef Haspecker, *Gottesfurcht bei Jesus Sirach. Ihre religiöse Struktur und ihre literarische und doctrinäre Bedeutung* (An Bib 30; Rome: Biblical Institute Press, 1967).

[28]Jean Hadot, *Penchant mauvais et volonté libre dans la Sagesse de Ben Sira (L'Ecclésiastique)* (Brussels: Presses Universitaires de Bruxelles, 1970) answers the question in the affirmative.

[29]Gian Luigi Prato, *Il problema della teodicea in Ben Sira* (An Bib 65; Rome: Biblical Institute Press, 1975) and James L. Crenshaw, "The Problem of Theodicy in Sirach: On Human Bondage," *JBL* 94 (1975) 49–64 = *Urgent Advice and Probing Questions*, 155–74.

[30]Reinhold Bohlen, *Die Ehrung der Eltern bei Ben Sira: Studien zur Motivation und Interpretation eines familienethischen Grundwertes in frühhellenistischer Zeit* (TTSt 51; Trier: Paulinus Verlag, 1991).

[31]James L. Crenshaw, "The Restraint of Reason, The Humility of Prayer," 206–21 in *Urgent Advice and Probing Questions*; Johannes Marböck, "Das Gebet um die Rettung Zions Sir 36, 1-22 (G:33, 1-13a; 36:16b-22) im Zusammenhang der Geschichtsschau Ben Siras," *Memoria Jerusalem*, ed. J. B. Bauer (Jerusalem/Graz: Akademische Druck und Verlagsanstalt, 1977) 93–116; and P. C. Beentjes, "Sirach 22:27–236 in zijn Context," *Bijdragen* 39 (1978) 144–51.

[32]Lutz Schrader, *Leiden und Gerechtigkeit: Studien zu Theologie und Textgeschichte des Sirachbuches* (BBEuT 27; Frankfurt am Main et. al.: Peter Lang, 1994).

[33]James D. Martin, "Ben Sira's Hymn to the Fathers: A Messianic Perspective," *Crises and Perspectives* (Leiden: E. J. Brill, 1986) 107–23.

[34]Emile Puech, "Ben Sira 48:11 et la resurrection," 81–90 in *Of Scribes and Scrolls: Studies on the Hebrew Bible, Intertestamental Judaism, and Christian Origins Presented to John Strugnell on the Occasion of his Sixtieth Birthday,* ed. Harold W. Attridge et al (Lonham, MD: University Press of America, 1990).

[35]Luis Alonso-Schökel, *Proverbios y Eclesiastico. Los libros sagrados* (Madrid: Christiandad, 1968) and Skehan/DiLella, *The Wisdom of Ben Sira.*

[36]Crenshaw, *Sirach*, *NIB*, V, 641-867.

[37]André Lemaire, *Les Écoles et la formation de la Bible dans l'ancien Israël* (OrBibOr 39; Fribourg: Éditions Universitaires and Göttingen: Vandenhoeck & Ruprecht, 1981). Lemaire speculates on the basis of epigraphic evidence that schools dotted the landscape, marking the whole spectrum of education from elementary to advanced professional training. He also understands the canonical process as the direct result of these educational institutions.

[38]James L. Crenshaw, "Education in Ancient Israel," *JBL* 104 (1985) 601–15 = *Urgent Advice and Probing Questions*, 235–49; Stuart Weeks, *Early Israelite Wisdom* (Oxford: Clarendon Press, 1994) 132–56; Graham I. Davies, "Were There Schools in Ancient Israel?" 199–211 in *Wisdom in Ancient Israel*, eds. John Day, Robert P. Gordon, and H.G.M. Williamson (Cambridge: University Press, 1995); and Friedemann Golka, "Die israelitische Weisheitsschule oder 'des Kaisers neue Kleider'," *VT* 33 (1983) 257–70.

[39]Susan Niditch, *Oral World and Written Word: Ancient Israelite Literature* (Louisville: Westminster/John Knox Press, 1996). The difficulty of finding the right criteria by which to determine oral tradition remains, despite Niditch's powerful defense of the persistence of orality in Israel until quite late. Her comparison of creation myths in Genesis 1 and 2 with Ezekiel 28 graphically illustrates the problem, for precisely those characteristics in the latter text that she takes to be literary strike me as signs of orality–"its erudite use of synonyms for sin and its list of gem-quality materials" (38).

[40]Norbert Lohfink, "Gab es eine deuteronomistische Bewegung?" *Jeremia und die "deuteronomistische Bewegung,"* ed. Walter Gross (BBB 98; Athenaum: Beltz, 1995) 313–83, especially 341–2 mentions over one thousand exemplars, including 33 of the Psalter, 27 of Deuteronomy, 20 of Isaiah, 16 of Jubilees, and many others, in addition to sectarian writings.

[41]The term is used by John Bains," Literacy and Ancient Egyptian Society," *Man* 18 (1983) 577.

[42]Aaron Demsky, "Literacy," *The Oxford Encyclopedia of Archaeology in the Near East*, ed. Eric Meyers (New York & Oxford: Oxford University Press, 1997) 367 "It [Aramaic] became the *Reichsprach*, a most unusual example of a conquered people's language becoming an instrument of the conqueror in empire building").

[43]Merikare mentions written texts which the student is told to copy, advises against killing "one with whom you have recited the writings," and refers to reading in the Sipu-book. Anii reminds his son of his mother's support of his education, for she enrolled him in school where he was taught to write. The much later Ankhsheshanky urges readers to teach sons to write–along with plowing, fowling, and hunting.

[44]This conclusion is based on the glossary in James M. Lindenberger, *The Aramaic Proverbs of Ahiqar* (Baltimore and London: The Johns Hopkins University Press, 1983).

[45]Khonshotep found himself in a moral dilemma; while approving the teachings of his father and admiring him for embodying them, the son believed himself unable to live up to such noble deeds.

[46]A. Wolters, "*Sôpiyyâ* (Prov 31:27) as Hymnic Participle and Play on *Sophia*," *JBL* 104 (1985) 577–87.

[47]Charles F. Whitley, *Koheleth: His Language and Thought* (BZAW 148; Berlin & New York: Walter de Gruyter, 1979) 102 translates as follows: "and he listened and considered the arrangement of many proverbs."

[48]Niditch, *Oral World and Written Word*, 117–29 offers four different models in evaluating the degrees of orality and literacy in a given text.

[49]This assessment of the matter comes closer to the view represented by Claus Westermann, *Wurzeln der Weisheit: Die altesten Sprüche Israels und anderer Völker* (Göttingen: Vandenhoeck & Ruprecht, 1990) than to that of Michael V. Fox, "The Social Location of the Book of Proverbs," 227–39 in *Texts, Temples, and Traditions: A Tribute to Menahem Haran*, eds. Fox et al (Winona Lake: Eisenbrauns, 1996).

[50]On foreign wisdom in the book of Proverbs, see James L. Crenshaw, *Urgent Advice and Probing Questions*, 371–95.

[51]Nili Shupak, *Where Can Wisdom Be Found: The Sage's Language in the Bible and in Ancient Egyptian Literature* (OrBib etOr, 130; Fribourg: University Press and Göttingen: Vandenhoeck & Ruprecht, 1993) provides an exhaustive comparison between the vocabularies of wisdom in the Bible and in Egypt.

[52]Alan Millard, "An Assessment of the Evidence for Writing in Ancient Israel," *Biblical Archaeology Today. Proceedings of the International Congress of Biblical Archaeology, Jerusalem, 1984* (Jerusalem: Israel Exploration Society, 1985), as well as "The Knowledge of Writing in Late Bronze Age Palestine," *TB* 46 (1995), 207-17 and "The Knowledge of Writing in Iron Age Palestine" in *Lasset und Brücken bauen . . .": Collected Coummnications to the XVth Congress of the Organization for the Study of the Old Testament, Cambridge, 1995* (BEATAJ 42; Frankfurt am Main/Berlin: Lang, 1998), 33-39.

[53]Wischmeyer, *Die Kultur des Buches Jesus Sirach*.

[54]The understanding of these references to a place of instruction as symbolizing the book of Sirach loses force because of the verb "lodge" rather than "meditate."

[55]James D. Martin, "Ben Sira–A Child of His Time," *A Word in Season: Essays in Honor of William McKane*, ed. J. D. Martin & P. R. Davies (JSOTS 42; Sheffield: JSOT Press, 1986) 141–61 and Burton L. Mack, "Wisdom Makes a Difference: Alternatives to 'Messianic' Configurations," 15–48 in *Judaisms and their Messiahs at the Turn of the Christian Era*, eds. Jacob Neusner, William Scott Green, & Ernest S. Frerichs (Cambridge: Cambridge University Press, 1987).

[56]Norbert Lohfink, "Poverty in the Laws of the Ancient Near East and of the Bible," *TS* 52 (1991) 34–50.

[57]Even the Egyptian hieroglyph for instruction (*sb3*) reinforces this cruel reality; it depicts an arm raised in a threatening manner, poised to whip errant boys (Shupak, *Where Can Wisdom Be Found?*, 31).

[58]As occupant of the office that Roland Murphy graced during his years at Duke University, I cannot escape his spirit in life and in work–nor do I wish to do so. I shall always cherish his friendship.

Chapter 4: Qoheleth's Understanding of Intellectual Inquiry

[1]Michael V. Fox, *Qohelet and His Contradictions* (JSOT SS 71), Sheffield, 1989: 79–120. He writes that "Qohelet constantly interposes his consciousness between the reality observed and the reader" (p. 93). Fox's remarkable description of Qoheleth's epistemology provides the understanding of intellectual inquiry that I shall be questioning in the remarks that follow. Although agreeing with him in many respects, I cannot concur in some essentials. At the same time, I consider his analysis of Qoheleth's epistemology indispensable reading.

[2]The identification of the speaker as a woman who warns young men against a dangerous person of her own gender is hardly justified by appealing to the motif of a woman at the window or by conceding that women can criticize other women. The usual speaking voice in the book of Proverbs, the authorial persona, is masculine, an authoritative father, but he occasionally alludes to maternal instruction, one example of which appears

in 31:1–9. Viewing the speaker of 7:6–27 as feminine has modern heuristic value, as Meike Heijerman demonstrates in "Who Would Blame Her? The 'Strange' Woman of Proverbs 7," *A Feminist Companion to Wisdom Literature*, ed. Athalya Brenner, Sheffield, 1995: 100–109.

[3]The verb *'ābar* links the two accounts, 7:6–27 and 24:30–34 but in the former the young man in peril is the subject whereas the speaker passes by in the latter. The lesson derived from observation sometimes arises from what is missing from sight, as in Ps 37:25 (cf. R. N. Whybray, *Proverbs*, Grand Rapids, 1994, p. 356).

[4]My views about Ben Sira appear in *Sirach* (NIB, Nashville, 1997).

[5]Peter Höffken, "Das Ego des Weisen," *ThZ* 4 (1985) 121–135 focuses attention on sapiential self-consciousness, the extent to which the ego functioned as a criterion for assessing reality, particularly in Job and Qoheleth. Ben Sira refers to himself repeatedly (e.g., 24:30–34; 33:16–18; 34:9–12; 39:12, 32–35; 50:25–29; 51:13–30). Recognizing his place at the end of a long tradition, he lays claim to inspired utterance and to having labored on behalf of others.

[6]Israelite sages did not rush to capitalize on erotic imagery for describing the intellectual quest, possibly because of the negative connotations of Wisdom's rival, Folly. Gradually, however, they embraced the idea of scholarly ardor. An acrostic poem in Sir 51:13–30 (vv 13–20a of which appear on 11QPs[a]) may represent such early daring, but the imagination threw off restraint in another poem from Qumran, 4Q184, which John Allegro entitled "The Wiles of the Wicked Woman." This text is informed by the description of the foreign/strange woman in the book of Proverbs, and erotic features, although exaggerated initially, are certainly discernible. Curiously, Qoheleth refused to spice up his teachings by emphasizing the sexual symbolism of intellectual pursuits, choosing rather to encourage actual sensual delights with one's lover (cf. Plato's erotic understanding of knowledge in *Symposium*).

[7]Crenshaw, "Clanging Symbols," pp. 371–382 in *Urgent Advice and Probing Questions: Collected Writings on Old Testament Wisdom*, Macon, 1995 (originally published in *Justice and the Holy*, eds. D. A. Knight and P. J. Paris, Philadelphia, 1989: 51–64).

[8]Current preoccupation with literary theory has rejuvenated biblical scholarship in many respects, despite hostile reception in some quarters. That hostility arises partly from a perception that the approach represents soft scholarship and partly from intrinsic notions that a historical method alone has legitimacy in the Academy. In some circles, the loss of a "single right answer" and the literary critic's substitution of "multiple possibilities" has eroded a perceived certainty in an era when all absolutes have come under attack.

[9]Fox, *Qohelet and His Contradictions*, pp. 311–329 develops the notion of persona as a means of explaining the several voices in the book. In this view, an author projects a particular persona, perhaps fictional, and different voices address readers from various levels. Although a provocative interpretation, this approach overstresses the book's unity and downplays efforts to bring Qoheleth's teachings under the umbrella of traditional views about the central place of obedience to torah.

[10]Crenshaw, *Ecclesiastes*, Philadelphia: Fortress, 1987: 189–192.

[11]I thank C. F. Melchert for calling my attention to this quotation (*Wise Teaching: Biblical Wisdom and Educational Ministry*, Philadelphia, 1998).

[12]In my survey of research on Qoheleth, four explanations for contradictions within the book come to prominence: (1) redactional comments; (2) citations of traditional wisdom; (3) indications of life's ambiguities and time's passage; and (4) an endeavor to embrace the entirety of experience ("Qoheleth in Current Research," pp. 520–529 in *Urgent Advice and Probing Questions* [originally published in *HAR* 7:1984, pp. 41–56]).

[13]Loretz, O. "Poetry and Prose in the Book of Qoheleth (1:1–3:22; 7:23–8:1; 9:6–10; 12:8–14)," pp. 155–189 in *Verse in Ancient Near Eastern Prose*, eds. Johannes C. de Moor and Wilfred G. E. Watson, Neukirchen/Vluyn, 1993; "Anfänge jüdischer Philosophie nach Qohelet 1, 1–11 und 3, 1–15," *UR* 23 (1991): 223–244; and "Frau' und griechisch-jüdische Philosophie im Buch Qohelet (Qoh 7, 23–8, 1 und 6, 6=10)," *UF* 23 (1991): 245–264. A. P. Hayman, "Qohelet and the Book of Creation," *JSOT* 50 (1991) 93–111 stresses the empirical methodology that attains philosophical character in subsequent reflection about creation in *Sefer Yesira*.

[14]Robert Gordis, *Koheleth-The Man and His World*, 1968, pp. 88–94 remarks on Qoheleth's efforts to shape the Hebrew language in a form suitable for philosophical discourse. Gordis calls Qoheleth a linguistic pioneer (p. 88).

[15]The debate over the appropriateness of labeling the imagery in Qoheleth's concluding description of old age and death (in Fox's view, a funeral) rages, with the extent of such symbolism dwindling more and more in recent commentaries. Daniel F. Fredericks thinks the imagery depicts a raging storm: "Life's Storms and Structural Unity in Qoheleth 11:1–12:8," *JSOT* 52 (1991): 95–114. On the scope of this poem, see Norbert Lohfink, "Grenzen und Einbindung des Kohelet-Schlussgedichts," pp. 33–46 in *Altes Testament Forschung und Wirkung. Festschrift für Henning Graf Reventlow*, eds. Peter Mommer und Winfried Thiel, Frankfurt am Main et. al., 1994.

[16]Martin Hengel, *Judaism and Hellenism*, Vols I-II, Philadelphia, 1974 remains the standard work on the relationship between the two cultures.

[17]Peter Machinist, "Fate, *miqreh*, and Reason: Some Reflections on Qoheleth and Biblical Thought," pp. 159–174 in *Solving Riddles and Untying Knots: Biblical, Epigraphic, and Semitic Studies in Honor of Jonas C. Greenfield*, eds. Ziony Zevit, Seymour Gitin, and Michael Sokoloff, Winona Lake: Eisenbraun's, 1995. Machinist argues that Qoheleth moves toward a more explicit conceptualization and abstraction than earlier understandings of fate. He finds this tendency in three expressions for patterned time, *ḥešbôn*, *ma'aśeh*, and *'ôlām*, as well as in *miqreh*. He writes: "Put another way, what is significant in Qohelet is not simply the concern with the subject matter on which human reason focuses and the conclusions it yields, but an awareness of, a reflection on the reasoning process itself" (p. 173).

[18]Norbert Lohfink, *Kohelet*, Stuttgart, 1980 has made a strong case for Greek influence on Qoheleth, even apart from his hypothesis that the structure of the book comprises a palindrome.

[19]Fredericks, *Qoheleth's Language: Re-evaluating its Nature and Date* (ANETS 3), Lewiston, 1988. An insightful assessment of this book has come from Antoon Schoors in *JBL* 108 [1989] pp. 698–700 and *The Preacher Sought to Find Pleasing Words* (OLA 41). Louvain, 1992, pp. 14–15.

[20]C. L. Seow, "Linguistic Evidence and the Dating of Qoheleth," *JBL* 115 (1996): 643-666.

[21]Seow, "The Socioeconomic Context of 'The Preacher's' Hermeneutic," *The Princeton Seminary Bulletin*, 1996, pp. 168–195, and *Ecclesiastes*, AB 18c (New York: Doubleday, 1997).

[22]Elias Bickermann, *Four Strange Books of the Bible*, New York, 1967, pp. 158–167 emphasizes Qoheleth's preoccupation with wealth; Frank Crüsemann, "Die unveränderbare Welt. Überlegungen fur 'Krisis der Weisheit' beim Prediger (Kohelet)," pp. 80–104 in *Der Gott der kleinen Leute*, ed. Willi Schotroff and Wolfgang Stegemann, Munich, 1979 (ET, *The God of the Lowly*, Maryknoll, N.Y. 1984).

[23]Seow's interpretation depends on the unique aspect of Persian rule, features that were not duplicated in the later Ptolemaic period. Such a claim is difficult, if not impossible, to substantiate.

[24]C. Robert Harrison, *Qoheleth in Social-historical Perspective*, Ph.D. Dissertation, Duke University, 1991 explores the Zenon papyri in placing Qoheleth within the period of the Ptolemies. Stephan de Jong, "Qoheleth and the Ambitious Spirit of the Ptolemaic Period," *JSOT* 61 (1994): 85–96 concentrates on a psychological characteristic of the era.

[25]Joseph Blenkinsopp, "Ecclesiastes 3.1–15: Another Interpretation," *JSOT* 66 (1995): 55–64. For a feminist reading of this text, see Athalya Brenner, "M Text Authority in Biblical Love Lyrics: The Case of Qoheleth 3.1–9 and its Textual Relatives," pp. 133–164 in *On Gendering Texts: Female and Male Voices in the Hebrew Bible*, eds. A. Brenner and Fokkelien Van Dijk Hemmes (Leiden/New York/Koln, 1993).

[26]Hartmut Gese, "Die Krisis der Weisheit bei Kohelet," pp. 139–151 in *Les sagesses du Proche-Orient ancien: Colloque de Strasbourg, 1962*, Paris, 1963. Roland E. Murphy, *The Tree of Life: An Exploration of Biblical Wisdom Literature*, 2nd edition, Grand Rapids: Eerdmans, 1996, p. 212 and *Ecclesiastes* (Dallas: Word, 1992), pp. 140–143 cautions against such language.

[27]Rüdiger Lux, "Der 'Lebenskompromiss'–ein Wesenszug im Denken Kohelets? Zur Auslegung von Koh 7, 15–18," pp. 267–278 in *Alttestamentlicher Glaube und Biblische Theologie* (FS H.D. Preuss), eds. Jutta Hausmann and Hans-Jürgen Zobel, Stuttgart/Berlin/Köln, 1992 emphasizes the positive aspects of acknowledging conflicts between transmitted teachings and one's actual experiences.

[28]Eric Weil, "What Is a Breakthrough in History?" *Daedalus* (Wisdom, Revelation, and Doubt: Perspectives on the First Millennium), Spring, 1975: 21–36 observes that the

moments we consider breakthroughs are part of our own intellectual and political autobiography (p. 22), but breakthroughs imply breakdowns.

[29]Carol A. Newsom, *The Book of Job* (NIB), Nashville, 1996, *passim* throws dazzling light on the text's irony; from quite another perspective, so does Yair Hoffman, *A Blemished Perfection: The Book of Job in Context* (JSOT SS 213), Sheffield, 1996.

[30]Theophany occurs nowhere else in biblical wisdom; the presence of this genre in the book of Job is not easily explained (Crenshaw, "When Form and Content Clash: The Theology of Job 38:1–40:5," pp. 455–467 in *Urgent Advice and Probing Questions* (originally published in *Creation in the Biblical Tradition*, ed. R. J. Clifford and J. J. Collins [CBQMS 24], 1992).

[31]Fox, Qohelet and His Contradictions, pp. 85–100.

[32]Norbert Lohfink, "Qoheleth 5:17–19–Revelation by Joy," *CBQ* 52 (1990); 625–635 thinks God uses joy as a medium of revelation. Otto Kaiser, "Die Botschaft des Buches Kohelet," *ETL* 76 (1995): 48–70 also stresses the positive side of Qoheleth's message, as does Martin A. Klopfenstein, "Kohelet und die Freude am Dasein," *ThZ* 47 (1991): 97–107.

[33]Niditch, *Oral World and Written Word*, Louisville, Ky.:Westminster/John Knox, 1996.

[34]James L. Crenshaw, "The Primacy of Listening in Ben Sira's Pedagogy," 172–187 in chapter 3 above, originally published in *Wisdom, You Are My Sister. Studies in Honor of Roland E. Murphy, O. Carm., on the Occasion of His Eightieth Birthday*, ed. Michael L. Barré (CBQMS 29; Washington, D.C.: The Catholic Biblical Association of America, 1997.

[35]To understand the context within which such fresh insights first became one component among many in the process of transmission, one needs to learn more about the Israelite family. The recent publication edited by Leo G. Perdue, *Families in Ancient Israel* (Louisville: Westminster/John Knox, 1997) contains valuable essays by Carol Meyers ("The Family in Early Israel"), Joseph Blenkinsopp ("The family in First Temple Israel"), and John J. Collins ("Marriage, Divorce, and Family in Second Temple Judaism"), to which the editor adds a summary of their findings and theological reflections. The changes within society with respect to the family probably impacted heavily both on the content of sapiential instruction and on its form, but few traces of this adjustment have survived. The central role of parents in the small villages of the early period, the extraordinary demands on the whole family to survive in an agrarian economy of subsistence largely on grain, grapes, oil, and olives, and the importance of the clan began to slip during the monarchy, with its concerted effort to centralize power in the capital, its assertion of control over citizens' lives and possessions, and its usurpation of religious authority. The emerging disparity between the wealthy and the poor, with loss of land belonging to individual families and the exilic experience of being a resident alien, a feeling that continued in a sense during post-exilic times because of foreign rule, must surely have contributed to skeptical interpretations of reality. On the relevance of village life to the origin of the sayings in the book of Proverbs, see Claus Westermann, *Roots of Wisdom: The Oldest Proverbs of Israel and Other Peoples*, Louisville: Westminster/John Knox, 1995.

[36]Fox, Qohelet and His Contradictions, p. 91.

[37]Klein, *Kohelet und die Weisheit Israels: Eine formgeschichtliche Studie* (BWANT 132), Stuttgart/Berlin/Köln, 1994.

[38]Otto Kaiser, "Beiträge zur Kohelet-Forschung: Eine Nachlese," *ThR* 60 (1995): 1–31 and 233–253. Two recent investigations of the book's structure are indicative: A. Fischer, "Beobachtungen zur Komposition von Kohelet 1,3–3,15," *ZAW* 103 (1991) 72–86 and Stephan de Jong, "A Book on Labour: The Structuring Principles and the Main Theme of the Book of Qohelet," *JSOT* 54 (1992) 107–116.

[39]Nili Shupak, *Where Can Wisdom Be Found? The Sage's Language in the Bible and in Ancient Egyptian literature* (OBO 130), Fribourg and Göttingen, 1993 approaches the topic from a different perspective than that employed here, but she reaches similar conclusions where our interests overlap. My fuller discussion appears in *Education in Ancient Israel: Across the Deadening Silence;* ABRL (New York: Doubleday, 1998.

[40]Despite the passive rendering in the Septuagint, strong textual evidence supports an active verb. One could object to an argument based on Qoheleth's linguistic practice, for the Epilogue derives from someone other than the author of the rest of the book.

[41]Peter Machinist, "Fate, *miqreh*, and Reason: Some Reflections on Qohelet and Biblical Thought," pp. 159–175.

[42]By understanding v 26 as a quotation with which Qoheleth takes issue, several recent interpreters have endeavored to rid him of the charge of misogyny: Norbert Lohfink, "War

Kohelet ein Frauenfeind?" 259–287 in *La Sagesse de l'Ancien Testament*; A. Schoors, "Bitterden dan de Dood is de Vrouw (Koh 7, 26)," *Bij* 54 (1993): 121–140; F. J. Backhaus, "*Denn Zeit und Zufall trifft sie alle: "Studien zur Komposition und Gottesbild im Buch Qohelet* (BBB 83), Frankfurt, 1993. See also Thomas Krüger, "'Frau Weisheit' in Koh 7, 26?," *Bib* 73 (1992): 394–403, who introduces the notion of personified Wisdom here.

[43]The unusual word for interpretation, *pešer*, may be an audial pun on the previous *yāšar*. It would then indicate the meaning of searching for the sum of things, hence the verse would not be intrusive.

[44]The rhetorical question, "Who knows?", implies that no one does, on which see my article entitled "The Expression *mî yôdēa'* in the Hebrew Bible," pp. 279–291 in *Urgent Advice and Probing Questions*) originally published in *VT* 36 [1986] 274–288.

[45]I examine this difficult verse at length in "The Eternal Gospel (Ecclesiastes 3:11)," pp. 548–572 in *Urgent Advice and Probing Questions* (originally published in *Essays in Old Testament Ethics*, eds. J. L. Crenshaw and John T. Willis [New York], 1974).

[46]"*ḥāqar, ḥeqer; meḥqar*," *Theological Dictionary of the Old Testament*, Vol. 5, eds. G. Johannes Botterweck and Helmer Ringgren, Grand Rapids, 1986), p. 150.

[47]Author's translation.

[48]James L. Crenshaw, "The Problem of Theodicy in Sirach: On Human Bondage," pp. 155–174 in *Urgent Advice and Probing Questions* (originally published in *JBL* 94 [1975] 49–64).

Chapter 6: Unresolved Issues in Wisdom Literature

[1]Among contributions by feminist scholars, certain works stand out, notably Claudia V. Camp, *Wisdom and the Feminine in the Book of Proverbs* (BLS 11; Sheffield: Almond Press, 1985), Carole R. Fontaine, *Traditional Sayings in the Old Testament* (BLS 5; Sheffield: Almond Press, 1982), and Carol A. Newsom, "Woman and the Discourse of Patriarchal Wisdom: A Study of Proverbs 1–9," 142–60 in *Gender and Difference in Ancient Israel*, ed. Peggy L. Day (Minneapolis: Fortress Press, 1989). Athalya Brenner, ed. *A Feminist Companion to Wisdom Literature* (Sheffield: Sheffield Academic Press, 1995) also includes some important essays on various topics. Women interpreters at the front ranks of sapiential scholarship include Miriam Lichtheim and Nili Shupak in Egyptian studies, Helga Stadelmann and Oda Wischmeyer on Sirach, Dorothea Sitzler and Katherine J. Dell on the book of Job, and Jutta Hausmann and Gerlinde Baumann on Proverbs.

[2]The minimal interest shown by liberation scholars (Gustavo Gutiérrez being the exception) is puzzling, although the themes from Exodus and the prophetic conscience naturally offer much more easily recognizable points of contact.

[3]R. N. Whybray, *The Intellectual Tradition in the Old Testament* (BZAW 135; Berlin & New York: Walter de Gruyter Verlag, 1974) and Stuart Weeks, *Early Israelite Wisdom* (OThM; Oxford: Clarendon Press, 1994). Whybray later revised his views, largely because an intellectual tradition needs trained guardians other than people who have large estates.

[4]Claus Westermann, *Der Aufbau des Buches Hiob* (Stuttgart: Calwer Verlag, 1977) and *Roots of Wisdom* (Louisville, KY: Westminster John Knox Press, 1995). On formal grounds, Westermann excludes the book of Job from wisdom literature.

[5]The impact of critical theory has been felt acutely where interpreters using tools of literary analysis have sought to demonstrate the integrity of texts that on other presuppositions have seemed totally disjointed. Irony has come to the forefront in analyses of the book of Job, especially by Carol A. Newsom, "The Book of Job," *NIB* (Nashville: Abingdon Press, 1996) and Yair Hoffman, *A Blemished Perfection: The Book of Job in Context* (JSOT SS 213; Sheffield: Academic Press, 1996).

[6]Katharine J. Dell, "On the Development of Wisdom in Israel," *VTSup* LXVI; Congress Volume Cambridge 1995 (Leiden: E. J. Brill, 1997), 135–51.

[7]Michael V. Fox, "Ideas of Wisdom in Proverbs 1–9," *JBL* 116 (1997), 613–33.

[8]A growing restlessness over this practice is detectable, particularly in Miriam Lichtheim, *Moral Values in Ancient Egypt* (OBO 155; Göttingen: Vandenhoeck & Ruprecht, 1997).

[9]Onomastica, once thought to signify sapiential activity, have been shown to belong to the wider community of intellectual productivity. See Michael V. Fox, "Egyptian Onomastica and Biblical Wisdom," *VT* 36 (1986), 302–10.

[10]W. Lee Humphreys, "The Motif of the Wise Courtier in the Book of Proverbs," 177–90 in *Israelite Wisdom: Theological and Literary Essays in Honor of Samuel Terrien*,

ed. John G. Gammie et. al. (Missoula, Mont.: Scholars Press, 1978) could find very little evidence of court wisdom in the Bible.

[11]Friedemann Golka, *The Leopard's Spots* (Edinburgh: T. & T. Clark, 1992) makes this point with telling effect.

[12]A suitable explanation for the overlap of texts from the Bible with other literature from the ancient Near East has yet to appear. Can one really imagine this phenomenon apart from trained sages utilizing similar literature from neighboring cultures?

[13]Westermann, *Roots of Wisdom*, argues that the book of Proverbs originated in tiny villages and reflects the intimacy of family life.

[14]The problem is twofold: at what point, if ever, did the Hebrew words for father and son assume a metaphorical sense, and how can one detect the moment when such metaphors lost vitality.

[15]Susan Niditch, *Oral World and Written Word: Ancient Israelite Literature* (LAI; Louisville: Westminster John Knox, 1996), and James L. Crenshaw, "The Primacy of Listening in Ben Sira's Pedagogy," in chapter 3 above, originally published in *Wisdom, You Are My Sister. Studies in Honor of Roland E. Murphy, O. Carm., on the Occasion of His Eightieth Birthday*, ed. Michael L. Barré (CBQMS 29; Washington, D.C.: The Catholic Biblical Association of America, 1997), 172–187.

[16]Why have no scribal texts with teacher's corrections survived in ancient Israel? Why do books such as Proverbs and Sirach lack specific features of didactic technique?

[17]An advanced level of cognition is presupposed by the books of Job and Ecclesiastes. It is remotely possible that the gnomic expressions in the book of Proverbs belong to a similar setting, for serious philosophical thinking can take the form of epigrams (Pascal, Wittgenstein).

[18]The technical use of *ḥakāmîm* cannot be proven beyond a doubt, but the evidence seems to favor such use in the epilogue to Ecclesiastes, and Ben Sira seems to presuppose it (James L. Crenshaw, "Sirach," *NIB*, vol. V, 1997).

[19]William P. Brown, *Character in Crisis: A Fresh Approach to the Wisdom Literature of the Old Testament* (Grand Rapids: Eerdmans, 1996).

[20]Christa Maier, *Die 'fremde Frau" in Proverbien 1–9* (OBO 144; Fribourg: Universitätsverlag, 1995) and Bernard Lang, *Wisdom and the Book of Proverbs: An Israelite Goddess Redefined* (New York: Pilgrim Press, 1986).

[21]Weeks, *Early Israelite Wisdom.*

[22]James L. Crenshaw, "Method in Determining Wisdom Influence on 'Historical' Literature," *JBL* 88 (1969), 129–42 (312–25 in *idem*, *Urgent Advice and Probing Questions: Collected Writings on Old Testament Wisdom* (Macon: Mercer University Press, 1995).

[23]The necessity for a more sophisticated approach to classification has claimed the attention of Giorgio Buccellati, "Wisdom and Not: The Case of Mesopotamia," *JAOS* 101 (1981), 35–47.

[24]On Psalm 73, see James L. Crenshaw, *A Whirlpool of Torment* (OBTh; Philadelphia: Fortress Press, 1982), 93–109.

[25]The problem also surfaces in the book of Genesis, on which see James L. Crenshaw, "The Sojourner Has Come to Play the Judge: Theodicy on Trial," chapter 22 in this volume, originally published in *God in the Fray: A Tribute to Walter Brueggemann*, eds. Tod Linafelt and Timothy K. Beal (Minneapolis: Fortress, 1998), 83–92.

[26]Gerhard von Rad's attempt to explain the Joseph narrative as a type of wisdom literature has increasingly come under attack ("The Joseph Narrative and Ancient Wisdom," 292–300 in *The Problem of the Hexateuch and Other Essays* [Oxford: Blackwells, 1966]). Moshe Weinfeld, *Deuteronomy and the Deuteronomic School* (Oxford: Clarendon Press, 1972) has failed to convince many readers.

[27]Roland E. Murphy, *The Tree of Life: An Exploration of Biblical Wisdom Literature* (Grand Rapids: Eerdmans, 1996, 2nd ed) has made this point repeatedly.

[28]Horst-Dietrich Preuss, *Einführung in die alttestamentliche Weisheitsliteratur* (UT 383; Stuttgart: Kohlhammer Verlag, 1987); his view was vigorously opposed by Franz-Josef Steiert, *Die Weisheit Israels–ein Fremdkörfer im Alten Testament?* (FThSt; Freiburg: Herder Verlag, 1990).

[29]John J. Collins, *Jewish Wisdom in the Hellenistic Age* (OTL; Louisville, Ky.: Westminster John Knox), 1997.

[30]The character of God in this book comes closer to the classic *Urgott*, a distant creator deity, than to the biblical Yahweh.

[31]An intrinsic connection between law and wisdom has been associated with the period of the clan (Erhard Gerstenberger, *Wesen und Herkunft des "apodiktischen Rechts"* [WMANT 20; Neukirchen: Neukirchener Verlag, 1965]).

[32]Only when a given word has a unique sense in wisdom literature can one reasonably assume exclusive use, but even this instance may be purely accidental.

[33]David L. Petersen, "Rethinking the Nature of Prophetic Literature," 23–40 in *Prophecy and Prophets*, Yehoshua Gitay, ed. (SBLSyms; Atlanta: Scholars Press, 1997).

[34]Simo Parpola, *Assyrian Prophecies* and Marti Nissinen, *References to Prophecy in Neo-Assyrian Sources*, vols. IX and VII respectively in State Archives of Assyria (Helsinki: Helsinki University Press, 1997 and 1998).

[35]Anthologizing is not unique to Israelite wisdom, for it also plays a significant role in prophetic books, particularly Isaiah.

[36]Hoffman, *A Blemished Perfection*.

[37]Michael V. Fox, *Qohelet and His Contradictions* (JSOTSup 71; BLS 18; Sheffield: Almond Press, 1989 (a major revision will appear shortly under the auspices of Eerdmans Publishing Company).

[38]Armin Schmitt, *Weisheit* (Würzburg: Echter, 1989) and David Winston, *The Wisdom of Solomon* (AB 43; Garden City, N.Y.: Doubleday, 1979).

[39]R. N. Whybray, "The Identification and Use of Quotations in Qoheleth," *VTSup* 32. *Congress Volume Vienna 1980* (Leiden: E. J. Brill, 1981), 435–51.

[40]Gerald F. Sheppard, "The Epilogue to Qoheleth as Theological Commentary, *CBQ* 39 (1977), 183–89 and *idem*, *Wisdom as a Hermeneutical Construct* (BZAW 151; Berlin & New York: Walter de Gruyter Verlag, 1980).

[41]On this poem, see above all Stephen A. Geller, "Where Is Wisdom? A Literary Study of Job 28 in Its Setting," 169–75 in *Judaic Perspectives on Ancient Israel*, ed. Jacob Neusner, Baruch Levine, and E. S. Frerichs (Philadelphia: Fortress Press, 1987).

[42]Besides the Joban parallels, one thinks of The Aramaic Sayings of Ahikar and The Instruction of Onkhsheshonqy.

[43]James L. Crenshaw, *Ecclesiastes* (OTL; Philadelphia: Westminster Press, 1987); Fox, *Qohelet and His Contradictions*, Roland E. Murphy, *Ecclesiastes* (WBC 19a; Dallas: Word, 1988), and Choon-Leong Seow, *Ecclesiastes* (AB 18c; New York: Doubleday, 1997).

[44]Burton O. Mack, *Wisdom and the Hebrew Epic: Ben Sira's Hymn in Praise of the Fathers* (Chicago & London: University of Chicago Press, 1985).

[45]Michael Kolarcik, *The Ambiguity of Death in the Book of Wisdom 1–6: A Study of Literary Structure and Interpretation*. AnBib 127; Rome: Editrice Pontificio Instituto Biblico, 1991).

[46]Dell, "On the Development of Wisdom in Israel." Curiously, she uses my introductory study of wisdom to describe views that she considers in need of revising but in several important instances she acknowledges that I do not share the view she rejects. Her interpretation needs considerable nuancing to show how I have consistently challenged operative assumptions in the discipline. See the revision of the above work (*Old Testament Wisdom: An Introduction, Revised and Enlarged* [Louisville, Ky.: Westminster John Knox, 1998]).

[47]The reader will recognize Walther Zimmerli's well-known dictum from 1964 ("Wisdom thinks resolutely within the framework of a theology of creation," 148 in "The Place and Limit of Wisdom in the Framework of Old Testament Theology," *SJTh* 17 [1964] 146–58).

[48]Leo G. Perdue, *Wisdom in Revolt* (JSOTSup 112; Sheffield: Almond Press, 1991).

[49]Hans-Heinrich Schmid, *Wesen und Geschichte der Weisheit* (BZAW 101; Berlin & New York: Walter de Gruyter, 1966).

[50]Hence the sharp differences among interpreters regarding the date of the book (mid-third century according to most critics, much earlier in the views of Seow and Daniel C. Fredericks, *Qoheleth's Language: Re-evaluating Its Nature and Date* (ANETS 3; Lewistown, N.Y.: Mellen Publishers, 1988), but see Antoon Schoors, *The Preacher Sought to Find Pleasing Words: A Study of the Language of Qoheleth* (Leuwen: University Press, 1995).

[51]James L. Crenshaw, *Education in Ancient Israel: Across the Deadening Silence* (ABRL; New York: Doubleday, 1998).

[52]Even Ben Sira's reference to a house of study has been read as a metaphor referring to the book itself, Oda Wischmeyer, *Die Kultur des Buches Jesus Sirach* (BZNW 77; Berlin & New York: Walter de Gruyter Verlag, 1994), 175–76.

[53]See James L. Crenshaw, "Qoheleth's Understanding of Intellectual Inquiry," 205–24, chapter 4 above, originally published in *Qohelet in the Context of Wisdom* (BETL 136;

Leuwen: University Press, 1998) and Oswald Loretz, "Anfänge jüdischer Philosophie nach Qohelet 1, 1–11 und 3, 1–15," *UF* 23 (1991), 223–44 and *idem*, "'Frau' und griechisch-jüdische Philosophie im Buch Qohelet (Qoh 7, 23–8, 1 und 5, 6–10"), *UF* 23 (1991), 245–64.

Chapter 7: A Proverb in the Mouth of a Fool

[1]Translation is from Miriam Lichtheim, *Ancient Egyptian Literature* (3 vols.; Berkeley: University of California Press, 1971–80) 1:142. The probability that the theme of national distress became a literary topos in the ancient Near East complicates every attempt to explain such texts as products of social crises.

[2]Lichtheim, *Ancient Egyptian Literature*, 1:208. The poem goes on to say that anyone who consorts with the sea does not harvest grain, which remotely resembles Qoh 11:1 and 4, where bread is associated with the sea and it is said that "whoever observes the wind will not sow, and whoever watches the clouds will not reap."

[3]See the stimulating analysis of ethics by Miriam Lichtheim, *Moral Values in Ancient Egypt* (OBO 155; Fribourg: University Press; Göttingen: Vandenhoeck & Ruprecht, 1997). She identifies three sources of the Egyptian's moral code: his self-esteem, his sense of interconnectedness with others, and his recognition of an underlying right order, *maat* (p. 13).

[4]In these verses, access to one's daily bread, but nothing in excess, staves off the profanation of the deity, either from dire need or from a feeling of self-sufficiency.

[5]The author nevertheless holds the thief responsible, noting that a sevenfold repayment will be exacted if he is caught. Here is an example of case law that failed to keep up with moral sentiment (only here and in the Greek text of 2 Sam 12:6 does sevenfold payment occur). Some interpreters read Prov 6:30 as a rhetorical question, but this understanding weakens the contrast in the larger unit, vv. 20–35, between prostitution and adultery, money and life. On the text, see Michael V. Fox, *Proverbs 1–9* (AB 18A; New York: Doubleday, 2000) 234–37. He notes a similar leniency in the Egyptian "Tale of the Eloquent Peasant": "Stealing by a thief is the misdeed of one who is needy. He should not be blamed, for this is just a matter of seeking (necessities) for himself" (p. 234, citing Lichtheim, *Ancient Egyptian Literature*, 1:174).

[6]The observation that even exuberant praise of the gods cannot bring birds to the desert stands in stark contrast with the biblical story of divine succor in the wilderness by means of quail.

[7]See Lichtheim, *Ancient Egyptian Literature*, 1:215. This proverbial saying is also discussed by Antonio Loprieno, "Theodicy in Ancient Egyptian Texts," in *Theodicy in the World of the Bible* (ed. Antti Laato and Johannes C. de Moor; Leiden: Brill, 2003) 46–47.

[8]Benjamin R. Foster, *From Distant Days: Myths, Tales, and Poetry of Ancient Mesopotamia* (Bethesda, Md.: CDL, 1995) 206.

[9]"Like the good moral character traits, the intellectual qualities were understood as innate dispositions which grew with age, training, and experience." Lichtheim, *Moral Values in Ancient Egypt*, 84.

[10]Foster, *From Distant Days*, 213 and William L. Moran, "New Evidence from Mari on the History of Prophecy," in *The Most Magic Word* (ed. Ronald S. Hendel; CBQMS 35; Washington, D.C.: Catholic Biblical Association of America, 2002) 136–37.

[11]Harry A. Hoffner Jr., "Theodicy in Hittite Texts," in *Theodicy in the World of the Bible*, 100.

[12]Jerome F. D. Creach, *Yahweh as Refuge and the Editing of the Hebrew Psalter* (JSOTSup 217; Sheffield: Sheffield Academic Press, 1996) and P. Hugger, *Jahwe meine Zuflucht: Gestalt und Theologie des 91. Psalms* (Münsterschwarzacher Studien 13; Würzburg: Vier-Türme-Verlag, 1971). William P. Brown, *Seeing the Psalms: A Theology of Metaphor* (Louisville: Westminster John Knox, 2002) surveys the wide range of metaphors in the Psalms.

[13]Thorkild Jacobsen, *The Harps That Once...: Sumerian Poetry in Translation* (New Haven: Yale University Press, 1987) 192.

[14]Further examples may be found in Foster, *From Distant Days*, 389–90, William W. Hallo, "Proverbs Quoted in Epic," in *Lingering over Words: Studies in Ancient Near Eastern Literature in Honor of William L. Moran* (ed. Tzvi Abusch, John Huehnergard, and Piotr Steinkeller; Atlanta: Scholars Press, 1990) 203–17, and Gary Beckman, "Proverbs and Proverbial Allusions in Hittite," *JNES* 45 (1986) 19–30.

[15]The older work by Otto Eissfeldt, *Der Maschal im Alten Testament* (BZAW 24; Giessen: Alfred Töpelmann, 1913) has been supplanted by the broader cultural setting in the work of Carole R. Fontaine, *Traditional Sayings in the Old Testament* (BLS 5; Sheffield: Almond, 1982).

[16]The operative word in the narrative is "pretend." Similar language occurs in the story about Jonadab, who used his intelligence to help Amnon rape his half-sister Tamar. Curiously, no one to my knowledge has insisted that he was a professional sage. This fact alone casts suspicion on all attempts to show that the woman of Tekoa belonged to the *ḥākām* 'wise'. After all, the adjective *ḥākām* is attributed to both individuals. In the case of Jonadab, it is even reinforced by *me'od* 'exceptionally' (2 Sam 13:3).

[17]For views of the afterlife in the ancient Near East, see J. Edward Wright, *The Early History of Heaven* (Oxford: Oxford University Press, 2000).

[18]Although several biblical narratives emphasize the important psychological influence of rhetoric on the enemy (for example, the confrontation between David and Goliath [1 Sam 17:43–47], the dissimulating speech of Hushai that won precious time for a fleeing David [2 Sam 17:7–13], and the mocking taunts of the Rabshakeh against Hezekiah and the people of Jerusalem [Isa 36:4–10, 13–20 and parallels in 2 Kgs 18:19–25, 28–35; 2 Chr 32:10–15]), it is Wisdom of Solomon that first introduces psychology as a central theme in divine retribution.

[19]On this formula and its significance for theodicy, see James L. Crenshaw, *Defending God: Biblical Responses to the Problem of Evil* (New York: Oxford University Press, 2005).

[20]Laato and de Moor, *Theodicy in the World of the Bible.*

[21]"The bitch in its haste gave birth to blind puppies"; "An ant if disturbed bites the hand that disturbs it"; "One cannot snatch a dead body from the jaws of a roaring lion; where one is raging another cannot advise him"; "Evil deeds proceed from evil people" (1 Sam 24:14[13]). In the last instance, the saying is identified as a *māšāl*. When such designation is absent, a proverb can be recognized by other indications: its apparent incongruity in context, a remark that people regularly say it, or its presence in a list of proverbs (Hallo, "Proverbs Quoted in Epic," 212–13).

[22]It seems that proverbs functioned in the ancient world the way sound bites do in modern society, summing up a distinct view of things in a brief, catchy phrase. Seldom, however, do sound bites carry authority.

[23]This reading is preferred in REB and NRSV. The late use of the verb *'ālâ* ('go up, ascend' followed by the preposition *b*– 'with'–has this meaning, on which see William McKane, *Proverbs: A New Approach* (Philadelphia: Westminster, 1970) 598–99 and W. E. Oesterley, *The Book of Proverbs* (London: Methuven, 1929) 232–33. Richard J. Clifford, *Proverbs* (Louisville: Westminster John Knox, 1999) 232 thinks this interpretation "strains the meaning of the verb."

[24]Oesterley, *Book of Proverbs*, 232.

[25]Feminist scholars have thrown considerable light on the background and function of personified wisdom (and folly). See especially Sylvia Schroer, *Wisdom Has Built Her House: Studies on the Figure of Sophia in the Bible* (Collegeville, Minn.: Liturgical Press, 2000), Judith E. McKinlay, *Gendering Wisdom the Host: Biblical Invitations to Eat and Drink* (Sheffield: Sheffield Academic Press, 1996), Christl Maier, *Die "Fremde Frau" in Proverbien 1-9* (OBO 144; Fribourg and Göttingen: Vandenhoeck & Ruprecht, 1995), Claudia V. Camp, *Wisdom and the Feminine in the Book of Proverbs* (BLS 11; Sheffield: Almond, 1985), and Gerlinde Baumann, *Die Weisheitsgestalt in Proverbien 1-9* (FAT 16; Tübingen: Mohr Siebeck, 1996).

[26]Claus Westermann, *Roots of Wisdom* (Louisville: Westminster John Knox, 1995).

[27]See the careful analysis of words for wisdom and folly by Michael V. Fox, "Words for Wisdom," *ZAH* 6 (1993) 149–69 and "Words for Folly," *ZAH* 10 (1997) 1–12, as well as *Proverbs*, 28–43.

[28]I have led this charge, beginning with "The Influence of the Wise upon Amos," *ZAW* 79 (1967) 42–52, which by coincidence was partly directed against Terrien's views, and culminating in wholesale questioning of the utility of the category "wisdom psalms" (*The Psalms: An Introduction* [Grand Rapids: Eerdmans, 2001] 87–95), with a much-cited article in between ("Method in Determining Wisdom Influence upon 'Historical' Literature," *JBL* 88 [1969] 129–42 [= *Urgent Advice and Probing Questions* (Macon, Ga.: Mercer University Press, 1995) 312–25]).

[29]The design of the book of Psalms has evoked fresh approaches that rival earlier form criticism, as recent analyses of interpretation demonstrate, above all James L. Crenshaw,

"Foreword: The Book of Psalms and Its Interpreters," chapter 12 in this volume, originally published in Sigmund Mowinckel, *The Psalms in Israel's Worship* (Grand Rapids: Eerdmans, 2004), Erich Zenger, "Psalmenforschung nach Hermann Gunkel und Sigmund Mowinckel," in *Congress Volume: Oslo, 1998* (ed. André Lemaire and Magne Saebo; VTSup 80; Leiden and Boston: Brill, 2000) 399–435 and Manfred Oeming, "An der Quelle des Gebets: Neuere Untersuchungen zu den Psalmen," *TLZ* 127 (2002) 367–84.

[30]Samuel Terrien, *The Psalms: Strophic Structure and Theological Commentary* (Grand Rapids: Eerdmans, 2003) finds possible sapiential influence in numerous psalms (see pp. 22–24, 43, 57, 71, 73, 85–86, 98–99, 104, 122, 131–32, 143, 145, 164, 166, 172, 179, 193, 201, 215–16, 254, 294, 300, 305, 320–21, 326, 331, 339, 388, 412, 458, 526, 534, 554, 564–65, 589, 630, 635, 638, 643, 645, 655–56, 664, 693–94, 717–18, 740, 800, 805, 811, 822, 851, 854, 875, 877, 881, 896, 909–10).

[31]The seminal essay is that by Walther Zimmerli, "The Place and Limit of the Wisdom in the Framework of the Old Testament Theology," in *Studies in Ancient Israelite Wisdom* (ed. James L. Crenshaw; New York: Ktav, 1976) 314–26 (…"Wisdom thinks resolutely within the framework of a theology of creation," p. 316). See also Leo G. Perdue, *Wisdom and Creation: The Theology of Wisdom Literature* (Nashville: Abingdon, 1994).

[32]On practical atheism as one response among many to divine injustice, see Crenshaw, *Defending God*, ch. 1.

[33]Terrien is not alone in this aversion to theodicy. He is joined by, among others, Terrence W. Tilley, *The Evils of Theodicy* (Eugene, Ore.: Wipf & Stock, 2000). Ancient peoples were less hesitant to raise the question of divine justice than many modern theologians. Marcel Sarot, "Theodicy and Modernity: An Inquiry into the Historicity of Theodicy," in *Theodicy in the World of the Bible*, 1–26 addresses the modern philosophical issue of defining theodicy and opts for a broad definition similar to that of the ancients.

[34]In his stimulating book *The Elusive Presence: Toward a New Biblical Theology* (San Francisco: Harper & Row, 1978), the adjective "elusive" scarcely functions, so powerful is the sense of divine presence.

[35]Language of individual retribution permeated the entire social fabric of the ancient world; it is therefore natural to expect commonalities of expression between Deuteronomy, Jeremiah, and Psalms. Such sentiment does not derive from sages.

[36]"Such confessions of confidential introspection belong generally to the sapiential circles (Job 9:27; 29:18; Eccl 2:1; but see Jer 5:40; cf. also Ps 119:8, 17, 34, 44, 55, 88, 101, 134, 146)." Terrien, *Psalms*, 331.

[37]The contrast between Qoheleth and the orthodox epilogist who added Qoh 12:13–14 could hardly be greater. Qoheleth may well have counseled others to fear the deity, that is, to tremble before divine presence, but that has little if anything to do with revering God and keeping the commandments.

[38]Terrien, *Psalms*, 645. For an assessment of this claim, see James L. Crenshaw, *Education in Ancient Israel: Across the Deadening Silence* (New York: Doubleday, 1998).

[39]Friedemann Golka, *The Leopard's Spots: Biblical and African Wisdom in Proverbs* (Edinburgh: T. & T. Clark, 1993).

[40]R. N. Whybray, *Wealth and Poverty in the Book of Proverbs* (JSOTSup 99; Sheffield: JSOT Press, 1990). Whybray detects four types of social milieu: the court, educated urban society, prosperous farmers, and farmers with limited land earning a precarious living (116).

[41]Rainer Albertz, "Der sozialgeschichtliche hintergrund des Hiobbuches und der 'Babylonischen Theodizee,'" in *Die Botschaft und die Boten* (ed. Jörg Jeremias and Lothar Perlitt; Neukirchen-Vluyn: Neukirchener, 1981) 349–72.

[42]Oda Wischmeyer, *Die Kultur des Buches Jesus Sirach* (BZNW 77; Berlin and New York: de Gruyter, 1995) and James L. Crenshaw, "The Book of Sirach," *NIB*, vol. 5 (1997) 603–867.

[43]See the judicious study of the linguistic evidence by Avi Hurwitz, "Wisdom Vocabulary in the Hebrew Psalter: A Contribution to the Study of 'Wisdom Psalms,'" *VT* 38 (1988) 41–51. James L. Crenshaw, "Wisdom Psalms?" *CurBS* 8 (2000) 9–17 and "Gold Dust or Nuggets? A Brief Response to J. Kenneth Kuntz," *CurBR* 12 (2003) 155–58 and J. Kenneth Kuntz, "Reclaiming Biblical Psalms: A Response to Crenshaw," *CurBR* 12 (2003) 145–54 present opposite interpretations of the data.

[44]The mystery of pregnancy evoked comments in Israel and in Egypt (Qoh 11:5 and "The Hymn to the Aten." The latter text reads, "Who makes seed grow in women, who creates people from sperm; who feeds the son in his mother's womb, who soothes him to still his tears…When the chick in the egg speaks in the shell, You give him breath within to

sustain him." Lichtheim, *Ancient Egyptian Literature*, 2:97–98). This idea was not alien to Egyptian sages, however; see Papyrus Insinger 32,7–9 ("He created the breath in the egg though there is no access to it. He created birth in every womb from the semen which they receive. He created sinews and bones out of the same semen." Lichtheim, *Ancient Egyptian Literature*, 3:210).

[45] It is a pleasure to present this essay as a token of my gratitude to Michael Fox, from whom I have learned much and whose friendship I cherish.

I would like to express my appreciation to Carol Shoun for assisting me with the final form of this essay.

Chapter 8: From the Mundane to the Sublime

[1]Rarely does the author of a canonical text reflect on the bare essentials for survival beyond such formulations as "Human beings cannot live by bread alone," which functions as a summons to recognize the importance of spiritual reality. Ben Sira is an exception in this regard. In Sir 29:21 he lists life's necessities as water, bread, clothes, and lodging. Elsewhere, in a less Spartan mood, he increases that short list to include fire for warmth and cooking, iron for weapons and tools, salt, milk, honey, wine, and oil (Sir 39:26). Curiously, this expansion of basic necessities omits a place to lay one's head at night. One may compare Ben Sira's four essentials to Qoheleth's exhortation in 9:7–10, which includes bread, wine, clothing, oil, and a woman (perhaps toil also). Later rabbinic speculation about the divine gifts to humans at creation, grain and flax, stresses human participation in the ongoing creation of basic necessities, food and clothes.

[2]The importance of solar imagery in Qoheleth has been examined in a recent Ph.D. dissertation by Jacobus Wilhelm Gericke entitled *Possible Allusions to ancient Near Eastern Solar Mythology in Qohelet. A Comprehensive Enquiry.* The University of Pretoria, 2002. For Qoheleth, the phrase "under the sun" covers the entire world inhabited by humans, and seeing the sun was one of the characteristics of existence. Light therefore has positive connotations, in contrast to darkness. Wisdom illuminates both face and feet (Qoh 8:1; 2:13–14), but it has only relative advantage over folly, which is never praised by Qoheleth.

[3]Qoheleth's view of the deity has been the subject of special studies by L. Gorssen (1970: 282–324), Diethelm Michel (1973/4: 87–100), Hans Peter Müller (1968: 238–64; 1986:1–19), Stefan de Jong (1997: 154–67), Schoors (2002: 251–70; 2003: 375–409), and Crenshaw (1995: 191–205.) Above all, Qoheleth complained about the random nature of divine gifts, that is, their lack of correspondence with meritorious conduct, and about the veil of secrecy that obscured the deity's activity and disposition from human observation. The empirical basis of Qoheleth's epistemology has been championed by Michael V. Fox (1987: 137–55; 1998: 225–38) but contested by Crenshaw (1998b: 205–24). See now Annette Schellenberg (2002).

[4]Those interpreters who emphasize Qoheleth's seven exhortations to enjoy life (2:24a; 3:12; 3:22a; 5:17; 8:15a; 9:7–9a; 11:7–12:1a) naturally dissent from this skeptical view (Roger N. Whybray, 1982: 87–98; Lohfink, 1990: 625–35). Their failure to acknowledge the serious qualification of such optimism in three of the seven texts (2:26b, "This also is futile and shepherding the wind"; 9:9, "all the days of your futile existence" [2x], and 12:1b-7 [oncoming old age and death]), as well as the profound implication of 1:2 and 12:8, renders the optimism suspect. Such exhortations to seize the day grow out of the grim prospects of a futile existence under death's shadow (Crenshaw, 1995: 573–85). Qoheleth is a realist; he describes life as he experiences it, and that reality is far from pretty. To those capable of grabbing moments of pleasure, he issues words of encouragement, but such diversions cannot compensate for the fact that everything is futile.

[5]The precise meaning of *hebel* in Qoheleth is the subject of intense debate, with near consensus on nuances of futility/absurdity, transience, and vapor/breath (Fox, 1986: 409–27; Aarre Lauha, 1983: 19–25; Graham S. Ogden, 1987: 301–7; Timothy Polk, 1976: 3–17; Lohfink, 1998: 215–58; Konrad Ehlich, 1996: 49–65; John E. McKenna, 1992: 19–28; Ethan Dor-Shaw, 2004: 67–87). The clear instances where *hebel* implies ephemerality rules out a single meaning such as absurd.

[6]By coded language I mean something entirely different from ironic discourse, which is undoubtedly present in Qoheleth, although not to the extent detected by Carolyn J. Sharp (2004: 37–68), especially in the epilogue and in the silence about covenantal relationship and its obligation on Israelites (see also Bernd Willmes 2000). I refer to

Qoheleth's use of ordinary language to connote Greek philosophical concepts (Peter Machinist, 1995: 159–75) and his use of daily vocabulary such as bread to convey something quite different from the product of grain.

[7]Biblical authors seldom meditate on the deity's role in shaping the fetus (cf. Job 10:8–12 and Ps 139: 13–18), and even then an echo of the primary myth of creation can be heard in the allusion to a return to dust. Striking, however, is the hint of a predestined sojourn below (Ps 139:16), the extent of which becomes an object of prayer in Ps 39:5–7, 12, a psalm with linguistic affinities with Qoheleth (*kol hebel, beṣelem, welō' yeda' mî 'ōsepām, 'ak hebel kol 'ādām*). The Great Hymn to the Aton also praises the deity for making seed grow in women, creating people from sperm, feeding a child in its mother's womb, and giving breath. This text extends divine creativity to include chicks in eggs (Miriam Lichtheim, 1976: 97–8).

[8]The clause that modifies "the days of darkness," *kî-harbeh yihyû*, probably refers to Sheol, since there is no assurance that any young man will have a long life. The concluding expression, *kōl- šebbā' habel*, reinforces this understanding of 11:8. Pleasure is therefore a diversion from the prospect of death (Fox, 1999: 317). A different interpretation of this verse as indicating either old age or the difficulties throughout life is advocated by Krüger (2004: 195–6) and Choon Leong Seow (1997: 348–9), both of whom find more optimism in Qoheleth than I detect.

[9]Neither 10:20 nor 11:1 has one of Qoheleth's markers for endings and beginnings (e.g., *hakkōl hebel ûre'ut rûaḥ, yāda'tî, weggam-zeh, hû' ra'yon rûaḥ, wehinneh gam-hû' hābel, gam zeh hābel hû'* etc. for endings; *'amārtî 'anî belibbî, wešābtî 'anî, rā'îtî 'anî* etc. for beginnings. His indiscriminate use of such markers, even within a coherent unit, explains the need to debate whether or not Qoheleth is a unified thematic treatment of a topic or a collection of unrelated observations in sentence form (Walther Zimmerli, 1974: 221–30).

[10]Affinities between the themes in Qoheleth and other ancient Near Eastern literature have been explored by Loretz (1964: 196–208; 1980: 267–78), who lists seventy-one topoi. The distinctive features of Qoheleth–his insistence that everything is *hebel*, that death renders all striving for profit both futile and absurd, that wisdom fails in the end to give its possessor assurance of success, that God does not guarantee a just order, that everything has its time, unknown to humans, that one ought to seize the moment that offers pleasure–are unmatched elsewhere, although the Babylonian Dialogue between a Master and his Slave approaches his skepticism, as do some of the Egyptian harper songs.

[11]In Wright's analysis, a numerological investigation following a clue in 1:2 yields two halves of the book, each with 111 verses (1:1–6:8; 6:10–12:14); while refrains set divisions apart as well: "all is vanity and a striving after wind" in part one, "not find out" and "do not know" in the second part. Although his interpretation of numerical values requires some manipulation of the facts, Wright's recognition of the significance of refrains in determining Qoheleth's structure is salutary.

[12]The shift away from the author to the text enhanced literary critics' appreciation of the artistry of a work through a strategy of close reading. In biblical studies, this love affair with new criticism came when secular theoreticians were moving away from the text to the reader. For an illuminating discussion of this development, see Phyllis Trible (1994: 1–87); a critique of new criticism and two companion approaches, structuralism and canonical criticism, can be found in John Barton (1984).

[13]Older studies by Rainer Braun (1973), Martin Hengel (1973), John G. Gammie (1985: 169–87) and Otto Kaiser (1985: 135–53) have been supplemented by Reinhold Bohlen (197: 249–73), an unpublished Ph.D. dissertation (C. Robert Harrison: 1991), and a study of Qoheleth in the context of the entire ancient Near East (Christoph Uehlinger, 1997: 155–247). The latter's proposal that symposiastic philosophy best describes Qoheleth merits consideration, perhaps also for Sirach.

[14]The brevity of the formally similar 11:1 and 2 (but not 6) contrasts with the wordy 11:3, 5, and 8. The first three consist of a sentence introduced by an imperative followed by a *kî* clause giving the rationale for action, while the second group of three verses displays little structural similarity. Verse 8 does incorporate a *kî* clause, although it is preceded by a *qal* imperfect verb and two *qal* jussives. Verses 4 and 7 bear little formal kinship with either group: participles followed by negated verbs in the *qal* (v 4) and noun clauses (v 7).

[15]Perhaps the qualifying adverb should be italicized, for it may be too much to expect total consistency in any author or in redactors responsible for the present arrangement of proverbial collections. In the book of Proverbs, the exceptions are 1:10 and 8:32, both of

which function emphatically, the first to underline the danger of violent gangs, the second to stress the importance of personified wisdom as the source of life. The possible exception in Qoh 12:12 can be explained as the actual introduction of the second epilogue if one takes *weyōtēr* in 12:9 and 12:12 as structural parallels introducing the two epilogues (12:9–11; 12:12–14). The few exceptions in Sirach (3:12, 38:9) may also reflect the teacher's desire to stress the topic under consideration.

[16]Given the author's preference for specific vocabulary, the limitations of the Hebrew language, and common themes, some repetition of vocabulary is likely. Most of the duplications here, however, do not fall into the category of Qoheleth's favorite topoi.

[17]No interpreter has emphasized the contradictions in Qoheleth's teachings more than Fox (1989), although the revision of his commentary softens that line (Fox: 1999).

[18]The contradictions were recognized quite early (Shabbat 30b; Megillah 7a) and are still unexplained. There may be some truth in each of the major explanations: (1) the biographical, which calls attention to life's messiness and lack of consistency; (2) the redational, which stresses the presence of later glosses aimed at easing the tensions; (3) and the dialogic, which identifies more than one voice engaged in the search for truth.

[19]Krüger has championed this particular understanding of the tensions within Qoheleth's thought, but he concedes that one must take a maximalist view of things, considering much more than the immediate contexts of given observations (Krüger, 2004:18). This procedure makes it possible to relativise every statement, but then the choice of "normative" sayings becomes absolutely crucial. By what objective standard can one judge this approach to be superior to the redactional one advocated recently by Alexander A. Fischer (1997). My objection may not be apropos, if one subscribes to Krüger's version of reader response, which requires that cooperative readers must follow Qoheleth's train of thought and notice where an idea has been temporarily introduced only to be dropped as inadequate.

[20]The importance of analogy based on the natural order lies at the heart of Gerhard von Rad's interpretation of Israelite wisdom (1972) and explains the frequent description of sapiential discourse as intimately associated with creation in secondary literature. That is why the concept of order similar to natural law in the modern realm of discourse has played so prominent a role in the discussion of biblical wisdom today. Ancient sages believed that lessons could be learned from close examination of nature and the animal kingdom. Analogy was central to the utilization of information acquired in this manner.

[21]Gen 8:21–22 credits the deity with resolve to guarantee the conditions essential to survival despite a realistic assessment of human malice. A text in the book of Isaiah describes an even more active involvement of the divine teacher who communicates to farmers the proper sequence for planting and sowing, together with the correct manner of performing daily chores (Isa 28:23–29). Even attentive listening, however, might be negated by a host of factors, as every worker of the soil knew well.

[22]Sociological investigations of wisdom literature have failed to reveal the exact setting of individual texts, whether the home, a school for scribes, or a general audience. The first epilogue appears to favor the latter option for Qoheleth (12:9, where *hāʿām* is said to have been the recipient of Qoheleth's instruction), while the expression "my house of instruction" in Sir 51:23 may favor the second option for Ben Sira–if it does not serve as a metaphor for the book itself (Oda Wischmeyer, 1994: 175–6). The older collections in the book of Proverbs (Prov 10–22:16; 25–29) point to a family setting (Claus Westermann: 1995). On teachers and students, as well as the function of instructional literature, see Crenshaw (1998).

[23]The sequence seven/eight occurs six times in Ugaritic and once in an incantation from Arslam Tash (KAI 27, 17–18). The texts from Ugarit are discussed by K. J. Cathcart (1968: 512–3).

[24]Cathcart observes that the Aramaic and Phoenician uses of the sequence seven/eight occur in incantations, that UT 52 is a magical text, and that 1 Aqht 42–43 is a curse (see also Schoors, 1992: 219).

[25]The biblical use of language pertaining to eating and drinking for sexual relations (cf. Prov 5:15–18; 30:20; Sir 26:12) emphasizes intimacy, whereas the metaphor of plowing a garden stresses passion, perhaps violence as well (cf. Jdg 14:14, 18 where both metaphors, eating and plowing, occur in a highly charged erotic setting). This language is widespread in the ancient world, on which see Crenshaw (1978: 112–20; cf. David M. Carr: 2003 for a general discussion of erotic discourse in the Bible and its environment).

[26]The association of *zera'* with progeny makes this symbolic interpretation credible, while morning and evening easily function as ciphers for opposite stages of life, youth and adulthood. This understanding of 11:6 provides a smooth transition to 11:8–12:7.

[27]The translation is from Lichtheim (1980: 174). Line 3 of the 19th section emphasizes the feeling of satisfaction derived from generosity, which is said to be sweeter than actually receiving a gift. The intervening lines (4–9), however, do not relate to charity, nor do those that follow (19:11–25), but such lack of relationship among collected aphorisms is typical. The translation by Hellmut Brunner (1988: 283) is different ("Do a good deed and throw it into the flood; when the water recedes, you will find it again").

[28]Elias Bickerman (1967: 139) coined the phrase "The philosophy of an acquisitive society" to characterize Qoheleth's teaching (cf. James Kugel, 1989: 32–49 and Franz Crüsemann, 1984: 57–77). In Qoheleth, the philosopher's exhortation to share wealth with others is replaced by the drive to enjoy wealth. The understanding of 11:1 as mercantile investments receives support from Isa 18:12 and Prov 31:14 (note the symbolic use of bread in *mimmerḥāq tābî' laḥmāh*).

[29]"Do not place all your possessions in bulbous ships; leave most of them at home; you may ship the smaller portion" (Hesiod, *Works and Days*, 689–90) expresses similar caution.

[30]The four possible interpretations of 11:1–2 are conveniently summarized by Fox (1999: 311–12). They are: (1) send your merchandise over the seas, but divide it among several boats for safety's sake; (2) take chances, even long shots, and in the future you may benefit from them, but protect yourself against unexpected misfortunes by spreading the risk around; (3) an unreflective, improvident deed may succeed while a prudent and cautious deed may fail; (4) do deeds of charity, not expecting a reward, but it will eventually come.

[31]Qoheleth is aware that nature runs its course, with predictable results. The sun rises in the east and sets in the west, the winds blow from appropriate directions, and the rivers flow into the ocean (1:4–11).

[32]Compare 2 Sam 22:15, where *ḥiṣṣîm* stands in parallelism with *bārāq* ("He [YHWH] released arrows, and dispersed them, lightening, and made them panic"). For this understanding of Qoh 11:3, however, *ḥēṣ* would have to be substituted for *hā'ēṣ*; as for the alternative reading, (seed of) a tree, arguments from ellipsis are always tenuous, and this one especially so.

[33]The participles underscore the durative aspect here (*šōmēr* and *rō'eh*). At issue is whether the farmer resorts to the persistent study of meterological phenomena as a magical pursuit or simply examines the weather in lieu of productive work.

[34]In the Bible *ḥokmâ* refers to skills with the hands and to intellectual pursuits.

[35]This interpretation of vv 1–4 as ironic differs markedly from the dominant hypothesis in current research.

[36]The causative sense of *ya'aśeh* extends the divine role beyond origins, dominant in 3:11, to ongoing events, *creatio continua*.

[37]On any reading of 11:1–2, 4 human striving, and failing to act, assumes center stage. Nature's ebb and flow comes to the forefront in 11:3, with humans merely taking note of the consequences of this movement. Verse 5 raises the discussion once more, moving from the wind to ultimate causation.

[38]Rarely do Israelite sages reflect on the beginning of life (cf. Job 10:11–12), but the composer of Ps 139:13–16 and the author of 2 Macc 7:22 wax eloquent when thinking about the deity's role in this mystery (cf. also the Egyptian Hymn to the Aton and Qoh Rab 5:10).

[39]The substantive use of *hammālē'â* may have originated as a pun on the verb *yimmālē'û* in verse 3, but it is also attested at Qumran and in Mishnaic Hebrew (Yebam.16:1).

[40]The particle of negation, *'ēn*, occurs 44 times in Qoheleth, in contrast with 16 uses of *yēš*, the particle of existence. For discussion of Qoheleth's quantitative language, see James L. Crenshaw, "Qoheleth's Quantitative Language," chapter 10 above, originally published in *The Language of Qoheleth in Context: Symposium in Honor of Antoon Schoors (Leuven: Peeters,* 2006), where the argument is that Qoheleth was influenced by Greek philosophical speculation about a unifying factor in the universe and by daily activity of scribes who were employed by wealthy clients to assist with entrepreneurial enterprises.

[41]The wind's invisibility to humans made it a powerful expression for the deity's activity; neither the wind nor the deity could be seen, but their effect was clearly visible. A sharp contrast between flesh and spirit in prophetic thought prepared the way for esoteric discussions such as that said to have taken place between Jesus and Nicodemus in John 3:2–15 [21?].

[42]The syntax of the verbs in 11:1–2, 6 differs appreciably from those in 11:3–5, less so from the jussives in 11:8; still the exhortation is implicit where nothing but observation occurs. Whoever hears the remark about observing the clouds is thereby warned against a course of action and implicitly urged to do something quite different. Nevertheless, instructions do differ formally from "sentences," as form critics have frequently observed. No clear course of action seems to lie behind 11:3 and 5.

[43]Martin Buber employed the word *Leitwörter* to draw attention to words that function thematically in a literary unit (e.g., *lēbāb* in Psalm 73). This idea, when used with stylistic features like inclusion, refrain, repetition, rhetorical question, acrostic, and so forth, has illuminated many texts, despite much indiscriminate use by interpreters.

[44]Qoheleth's choice of *miqreh*, along with *ḥešbôn*, *maʿaśeh*, and *ʿôlām*, to imply reflection on the rational process itself has been underlined by Machinist (1995: 159–75). He understands *miqreh* as a close approximation of the Greek notion of fate, but with this difference: *miqreh* indicates both the rational process and a reflection on what rationality consists of, a kind of second order thinking.

[45]An emphasis on divine revelation, whether oracular or otherwise, has given canonical texts a decidedly aural stamp. For this reason, the title of a recent monograph on Psalms by William P. Brown stands out (*Seeing the Psalms*), as does the iconographic research of Othmar Keel (1997).

[46]I refer, of course, to the well-known allegory about the human predicament, in short, clinging to a vine while suspended over an abyss as white and black rats, signifying day and night, nibble away at the fragile lifeline.

[47]Although the biblical concept of Sheol lacked the idea of eternal punishment, with the possible exception of Isa 66:24, Sheol was far from an attractive place. Its inhabitants were thought to be only shadowy figures possessing no semblance of the power or honor that existed before death. Only slowly did YHWH's dominion reach into Sheol, perhaps because of fear that such an extension of his rule would threaten the belief that a deep chasm separated the biblical deity from the gods of other peoples. For a fresh examination of the emergence of belief in heaven see J. Edward Wright (2000).

[48]The meaning of *kōl šebbāʾ hābel*, like so much else in Qoheleth, is unclear. It may refer to all coming generations of people (Seow: 348–9), old age (Krüger 2004: 196), or death (Fox, 1999: 317). If one chooses the first interpretation, *hebel* can have the sense of transience. The other two understandings of the assertion imply a different nuance for *hebel*, absurdity or futility. Even then it has been understood positively (enjoy life now because there will be numerous dark days) or negatively (you cannot escape the darkness of death and Sheol).

[49]Qoheleth's indiscriminate use of days and years weakens the case for interpreting 11:8bB with reference to the present life. It does not necessarily follow that *yemê* indicates a shorter duration and therefore refers to old age and other difficulties.

[50]The prominence of death in Qoheleth, long recognized, (Crenshaw: 1978b, 205–16) has been highlighted by Shannon Burkes' examination of Egyptian biographies (1999).

[51]The view of Qoh 12:1–7 as a description of individual deterioration and ultimate death (whether symbolized by the destruction of the body or of a house) has given way to emphasis on an apocalyptic calamity (Seow: 1997, 372–82). A mediating position, according to which Qoheleth deconstructs such notions by removing the fear and reducing the hope associated with apocalypticism can be found in Krüger (2004: 198–205). He writes: "Thus an eschatology oriented on the end of the world and judgment of the world is critically 'deconstructed' in 12:1–7 in a way similar to that in 1:9–11" (p. 204). The complexity of the symbols is best demonstrated by Fox (1999: 333–49).

[52]The many instances of the *lamed* with the first person pronominal suffix *î* (eight times in 2:4–9) in the royal experiment (1:12–2:26) can be attributed to the genre, but even in the one instance where his individualism threatens to give way, Qoh 4:9–12, self-interest finally dominates. Qoheleth's self absorption in 1:12–2:26, has been highlighted by Peter Höffken (1984: 121–35).

[53]See Robert Gordis (1939/40: 123–47; 1949: 157–210), Fox (1980: 416–31), and Whybray (1980: 435–51). The ease with which such a theory removes tensions within Qoheleth's thought renders it suspect, even when the presence of a citation is plausible, as in 7:28b, on which see especially Lohfink (1979: 259–87), Krüger (1992: 394–403), Fox (1978: 26–38), and Schoors (1992b: 121–40).

Chapter 9: Deceitful Minds and Theological Dogma

[1]A sweeping generalization about innate perversity can alternate with admissions that exceptions do occur, as in Gen 6:5–6 and 6:8. The first text offers a fleeting glimpse into the creator's dismay over having made humankind, while the second reports that one person, righteous Noah, brought pleasure to YHWH. Even texts that appear to suggest that the entire human community is corrupt to the core tend to qualify the scope of the negative judgment. For example, Psalm 14 (=53 with minor differences) castigates the entire populace in the words "They are corrupt and abominable; no one does the good" (Ps 14:1b), then goes on to assert that "They all have turned away, they are entirely loathsome; no one does the good, not even one" (Ps 14:3). This negative assessment stands alongside the comforting assurance that "Elohim is with the generation of the righteous" (Ps 14:5b). It would seem, therefore, to be incumbent on interpreters of such texts to recognize hyperbole in the service of polemics, in this instance against practical atheists. The Apostle Paul fails to make this distinction when citing from Psalm 14 to support his theology of fallen humanity (Rom 3:10–12). The capacity of the intellect to juggle opposing views is nowhere so transparent as when religious people submit to the deity with blind faith while hedging their bets by rational means. A fine example comes from ancient Lydia. Wishing to attack Cyrus, king of Persia, Lydia's king Croesus first inquired of all the famous oracles known to him. Only two of these, Delphic Apollo and Amphiaraus, successfully passed the test put to them (to describe Croesus' actions one hundred days after envoys had left his court). This tale of "comparison shopping," to use the language of Sarah Iles Johnston, ed. (*Religions of the Ancient World* [Cambridge: Harvard University Press, 2004, ix and xiv) relies on ambiguity of the divine word ("A great empire will fall"). Exactly which empire would fall remained to be seen.

[2]Leiden: Brill, 1978.

[3]I discuss several features of biblical utopian hopes in "Freeing the Imagination: The Conclusion to the Book of Joel," chapter 17 in this volume, originally published in Yehoshua Gitay, ed. *Prophecy and Prophets: The Diversity of Contemporary Issues in Scholarship* (SBL SS; Atlanta: Scholars Press, 1997), 129–47. It is not necessary to assume that such views grew out of disappointment. One can just as easily understand the grand ideas as the natural outgrowth of religious intimacy similar to the breakthrough achieved in Psalm 73 through consciousness of divine presence that even death could not destroy. In my view, both a sense of betrayal by the deity and a perception of providential love gave birth to apocalyptic retreat from this world into a realm of fantasy.

[4]That is, in such a world human beings will have no needs, since all evil will have been overcome, and petition will vanish. Prayer as praise will remain, however, as if in defiance of Feuerbach. For him, humans created a deity to meet their own selfish desires.

[5]Without opposition, which is usually understood as evil, there would be no stimulus to resist temptation and no growth toward emotional and religious maturity. Pirke Abot 3:17 cites Jer 17:6 and 8 to describe persons whose wisdom is more abundant than their works, and vice versa.

[6]This type of reasoning was also capable of salutary spiritual insights, as the slightest familiarity with Second Esdras and Second Baruch will reveal. The struggle to draw the deity into a circle of compassion for the entire human race is what makes the heroes, Ezra and Baruch, unforgettable.

[7]For detailed discussion, see James L. Crenshaw, *Old Testament Wisdom* (Louisville: Westminster John Knox, 1998), John J. Collins, *Jewish Wisdom in the Hellenistic Age* (Louisville: Westminster John Knox, 1997), and Gerhard von Rad, *Wisdom in Israel* (Nashville: Abingdon, 1972). Because of wisdom's universalism, Horst-Dietrich Preuss, *Einfuhrung in die alttestamentliche Weisheitsliteratur* (UT 383; Stuttgart: Kohlhammer, 1987) dubiously compares it to paganism, denying its revelatory power.

[8]Scholars usually place the three representatives of canonical wisdom–Proverbs, Job, Ecclesiastes–on a spectrum beginning with dogmatism and evolving into challenge and

ultimate rejection of such a neat understanding of reality. This reading of the texts can be challenged because none of these books has a unified perspective throughout.

[9]F. Stolz, "לֵב *lēb* heart," *TLOT,* vol. 2: 638–42.

[10]Erhard Gerstenberger, "בטח *bṭḥ* to trust," *TLOT,* vol. 1: 226–30.

[11]Debate rages over whether the designation *'ar'ar* indicates a shrub or an individual, although parallelism with *'ēṣ* seems to favor the first interpretation. Psalm 102:18 uses *hā'ar'ār* to indicate destitute people whose prayer is heard by YHWH.

[12]*Ancient Egyptian Literature,* vol. 2 (Berkeley: University of California Press, 1976), 150–51.

[13]Perhaps this feature of the comparison hints at the early demise of the heated person, in contrast to the death of the silent individual at the appropriate time.

[14]For a thorough analysis of sapiential vocabulary in Egypt and cognates in Israel, see Nili Shupak, *Where Can Wisdom Be Found? The Sage's Language in the Bible and in Ancient Egyptian Literature* (OBO 130; Göttingen: Vandenhoeck & Ruprecht, 1993).

[15]Shalom M. Paul, *Amos* (Minneapolis: Fortress Press, 1991), 292–3 emphasizes the widespread nature of such hope in the ancient Near East.

[16]Amos Hakham, *The Bible. Psalms with the Jerusalem Commentary,* Vol. 1 (Jerusalem: Mosad Harav Kook, 2003), 5 understands *to'bēd* as the destruction of the wicked *and* their teachings/practices. Samuel Terrien, *The Psalms: Stophic Structure and Theological Commentary* (Grand Rapids: Eerdmans, 2003), 75 writes that "the way of the ungodly simply loses itself in the sand (Job 6:15–20)."

[17]Important questions remain: who transmitted the Egyptian teachings to the biblical author and how different were the two social contexts, Egyptian and Israelite? Harold C. Washington, *Wealth and Poverty in the Instruction of Amenemope and the Hebrew Proverbs* (SBL DS 142; Atlanta: Scholars Press, 1994) explores the latter issue in depth.

[18]Glendon E. Bryce, *A Legacy of Wisdom: The Egyptian Contribution to the Wisdom of Israel* (Lewisburg: Bucknell University Press, 1979) attends to the ways by which foreign concepts were adapted for an entirely different environment.

[19]The minimal role of wisdom literature in John Barton's analysis of Israelite ethics is noteworthy (*Understanding Old Testament Ethics: Approaches and Explorations* [Louisville: Westminster John Knox, 2003]). The comparable volume by Miriam Lichtheim, *Moral Values in Ancient Egypt* (OBO 155; Göttingen: Vandenhoeck & Ruprecht, 1997) restores the balance. She discerns three sources of the Egyptian's understanding of right and wrong: (1) self-esteem; (2) a sense of interconnectedness with other persons; and (3) a recognition of an underlying right order (p. 13). Friedrich Junge, *Die Lehre Ptahhoteps und die Tugenden der Ägyptischen Welt* (OBO 193; Schweiz: Universitätsverlag and Freiburg/Göttingen: Vandenhoeck & Ruprecht, 2003) argues that the Instruction of Ptahhotep represents an early form of a rationalistic ethic possessing its own theory of knowledge and a secular understanding of economic relations. Junge emphasizes the inner connection of reason, self-control, self-esteem, and regard for others. He views the ethical system as grounded in the order of the cosmos, as in Plato. Corresponding to this cosmic ontology is, in Junge's thinking, an attention to the inner person, the body, spirit, and soul. The goal of this secular ethical instruction is to provide a model for the elite in Egypt.

[20]Of the many recent studies devoted to the personification of wisdom and its rich symbolism, the most provocative is Silvia Schroer, *Wisdom Has Built her House: Studies on the Figure of Sophia in the* Bible (Collegeville: The Liturgical Press, 2000). She writes that "*Ḥokmā* is the God of Israel in the image of a woman and in the language of the goddesses" (p. 29).

[21]*From Distant Days: Myths, Tales, and Poetry of Ancient Mesopotamia* (Bethesda, Maryland: CLD Press, 1995).

[22]*The Harps that Once...: Sumerian Poetry in Translation* (New Haven: Yale University Press, 1987).

[23]This understanding of the Hebrew *'āqōb* is possible from an extended sense of unfathomable (Wilhelm Rudolph, *Jeremia* [HAT 12; Tübingen: J. C. B. Mohr [Paul Siebeck, 1958]), 106.

[24]The rhetorical question, "Who can find it?", functions like *mî yôdēa'* ("No one can know"). Those interpreters who understand *'anî* in 8:2 as the answer to *mî yôdēa'* in 8:1 ignore this linguistic fact. The inability to discover various mysteries, especially divine secrets, becomes a topos in wisdom literature, beginning with Prov 30:1–4 and the divine questions put to Job.

[25]Tsvi Novick,"עָקֹב הַלֵּב מִכֹּל וְאָנֻשׁ הוּא מִי יֵדָעֶנּוּ," *JBL* 123 (2004), 531–35 emphasizes unfathomability rather than perversity. He does so by reading מכל as an infinitive form of the verb *kûl* meaning deep, profound (in a symbolic sense) instead of the preposition *min* with *kōl*.

[26]Symmachus' translation removes the parallelism between *'āqōb* and *we'ānuš*, although it has been preferred by some interpreters (for example, Paul Volz, *Der Prophet Jeremia* (KAT X; Leipzig/Erlangen: A. Deichertsche Verlagsbuchhandlung Dr. Werner Scholl, 1992), 185.

[27]Stolz, "לֵב lēb heart," 638.

[28]James L. Crenshaw, "The Expression *mî yôdēa'* in the Hebrew Bible," *VT* 36 (1986): 274–88 (=*Urgent Advice and Probing Questions*, 279–91).

[29]Ernst Jenni, "בחן *bḥn* to test," *TLOT*, vol. 1: 207–09. On the cognitive function of *bḥn* and *ḥqr*, see chapter 4 above; originally published as James L. Crenshaw, "Qoheleth's Understanding of Intellectual Inquiry," 205–24 in Antoon Schoors, ed. *Qohelet in the Context of Wisdom* (BETL cxxxvi; Leuven: University Press, 1998).

[30]Similarly, the participle of *bāṭaḥ* occurs in formulae from prayer and song, as well as in curses and blessings, especially in the Psalter (Gerstenberger, "בטח bṭḥ to trust," 226–30.

[31]William McKane, *Jeremiah* (Edinburgh: T. & T. Clark, 1986), 388–402 provides the most penetrating analysis of Jer 17:5–11 of the many commentaries consulted. See also Jack R. Lundbom, *Jeremiah* (AB 21A; New York: Doubleday, 1999) and William L. Holladay, *Jeremiah,* vol. 1 (Minneapolis: Fortress Press, 1989).

[32]Marvin A. Sweeney's notes to Jeremiah in *The Jewish Study Bible* (New York: Oxford University Press, 2004) emphasize the sin of idolatry as the primary interest of Jer 17:5–8, 11.

[33]Patrick D. Miller, "The Book of Jeremiah," *NIB*, vol. 6, 2001: 709.

[34]Some interpreters understand *ṭōb* and ḥō*m* strictly in terms of rain and its absence, whereas others broaden the concept to include various types of beneficial and malevolent forces.

[35]McKane stresses this reading of the text in accord with his desire to make ancient views less objectionable to the modern mind. Belief in divine sheltering of virtuous people from all harm existed in the ancient world, despite plenty of evidence to the contrary. On the problem such dogma presented for some people, see James L. Crenshaw, *Defending God: Biblical Responses to the Problem of Evil* (New York: Oxford University Press, 2005).

[36]The text may expose a deep chasm in the social fabric of the Judean society: competing claims about the roles of faith and the intellect.

[37]There appears to have been increasing awareness of divine mystery during the late Greco-Roman period. Ben Sira goes so far as to warn against tackling intellectual tasks that might be too difficult (Sir 3:21–24) and the Qumran community turned the concept of a "mystery yet to be revealed" into a familiar saying (Daniel J. Harrington, S. J., *Wisdom Texts from Qumran* [London & New York: Routledge, 1996], 40–59, 70–74).

[38]Crenshaw, *Defending God*, chapter 9.

[39]*Ibid.*, chapter 1.

Chapter 10: Qoheleth's Quantitative Language

[1]C. R. Harrison, *Qoheleth in Social-historical Perspective* (Ph.D. Dissertation, Duke University, 1991) examines the context of Qoheleth in the light of the Zenon archives from Egypt during the Ptolemaic period (cf. also Harrison, "Hellenization in Syria–Palestine: The Case of Judea in the Third Century BCE," *BA* 57 [1994]: 94–108, and "Qoheleth among the Sociologists," *Bib Int* 5 [1997]: 160–82).

[2]J. L. Kugel, "Qohelet and Money," *CBQ* 51 (1989): 32–49; F. Crüsemann, "The Unchangeable World: The 'Crisis of Wisdom' in Koheleth," 57–77 in *The God of the Lowly*, eds. W. Schottroff and W. Stegemann (Maryknoll, N.Y.: Orbis, 1984); M. Dahood, "The Phoenician Background of Qoheleth," *Bib* 47 (1966): 264–82; C. W. Reines, "Koheleth on Wisdom and Wealth," *JJS* 5 (1954): 80–84; and E. Bickerman, *Four Strange Books of the Bible* (New York: Schocken, 1967).

[3]O. Wischmeyer, *Die Kultur des Buches Jesus Sirach* (BZNTW 77; Berlin and New York: de Gruyter, 1995) has provided a comprehensive analysis of Ben Sira's culture. A comparable examination of Ecclesiastes is a desideratum, although complicated by several

factors, not the least of which is the book's ambiguity, but also the unsettled question of the date of the author and the editorial process which the book has undergone.

[4]R. N. Whybray, "Qoheleth, Preacher of Joy," *JSOT* 23 (1982): 87–98 and N. Lohfink, "Qoheleth 5:17–19–Revelation by Joy," *CBQ* 52 (1990): 625–35 and *Qoheleth* (Minneapolis: Fortress, 2003), and L. Schweinhorst-Schönberger, "Gottes Antwort in der Freude: Zur Theologie göttlicher Gegenwart im Buch Kohelet," *BK* 54 (1999): 156–63 emphasize the positive aspects of Qoheleth's teachings where others find the overwhelming mood to be grim. Few would contest the claim that he looked at traditional views with critical skepticism, questioning the power of wisdom to enable one to guarantee the good life. The crucial difference between Qoheleth and earlier sages was his starting point, the reality of death as the common fate of all and therefore as the determining factor of epistemology. Death was certain for everyone, he insisted, but joy was only a possibility for a lucky few, in his language, those whom the deity favored. Regrettably, there was no positive correspondence between piety and divine favor, a presupposition of the authors of Proverbs. For a stimulating analysis of the problem, see H. P. Müller, "Theonome Skepsis und Lebensfreude zu Koh 1, 12–3, 15" *BZ* 30 (1986): 1–19.

[5]The emphatic position of the direct object reinforces the exaggeration inherent to *hakkōl*, while the ambiguity of the adjective qualifying Qoheleth's existence tinges with irony, invoking both brevity and futility. He has crammed a lot of experience into a short span of days, but the acquired knowledge partakes of a single nature, uselessness. In the long run its practicality is zero.

[6]The several investigations into the meaning of *hebel* have illuminated its polyvalency, but none of them has succeeded in isolating a single meaning that can apply in every instance. The transitory sense of its etymology lingers in some instances; in the remaining cases, the nuance seems to oscillate between futility and absurdity. Of the numerous studies, see especially M.V. Fox, "The Meaning of *Hebel* for Qoheleth," *JBL* 105 (1986): 409–27; N. Lohfink, "Zu הבל im Buch Kohelet," *Studien zu Kohelet* (SBA, AT 26; Stuttgart; Katholisches Bibelwerk, 1998), 215–58; A. Lauha, "Omnia Vanitas: Die Bedeutung von *hbl* bei Kohelet," 19–25 in *Glaube und Gerechtigkeit: Festschrift für R. Gyllenberg*, ed. J. Kulunen, et. al (SFEG 38; Helsinki: Suomen Eksegeetisen Seura, 1983); and K. Ehlich,"הבל–Metaphern der Nichtigkeit," 49–64 in *"Jedes Ding hat seine Zeit..." Studien zur israelitschen und altorientalischen Weisheit*, ed. A. A. Diesel et. al (BZAW 241; Berlin/New York: de Gruyter, 1996).

[7]H. Gese, "The Crisis of Wisdom in Koheleth," 141–53 in *Theodicy in the Old Testament*, ed. J. L. Crenshaw (IRT, 4; Philadelphia/London: Fortress/SPCK, 1983). Perhaps interpreters have overused the word "crisis" when discussing Qoheleth's teachings. The book of Job seems to be a response to the collapse of a world view that must have precipitated a genuine crisis of belief in a just deity. Qoheleth stood on this side of that failure in traditional views, being able to learn from earlier responses to a sea-change that must have shaken the very foundations of existence for many. His intellectualization of the changed perspective lacks the intimate fervor of the Joban debate and is characterized by a distancing from the dangerous deity who had, according to the narrative, brought calamity to Job's household.

[8]Pages 375–409 in *Theodicy in the World of the Bible*, ed. A. Laato and J. C. de Moor (Leiden-Boston: Brill, 2003). See also A. Schoors, "God in Qoheleth," *Schöpfungsplan und Heilsgeschichte. Festschrift für Ernest Haag* (Rome: Paulinus, 2002), 251–70.

[9]Y. Amir, "Doch ein griechischer Einfluss auf das Buch Kohelet?" 35–50 in Amir, *Studien zum antiken Judentum* (BEAT 2; Frankfurt am Main: Lang, 1985 (originally in *Beth Miqra* 10 [1965]: 36–42) and N. Lohfink, "Koh 1, 2 'Alles ist Windhauch'..universale oder authropologische Aussage?" *Studien zu Kohelet*, 125–42 (originally 201–16 in *Der Weg zum Menschen. Zur philosophischen und theologischen Anthropologie,* ed. R. Mosis and L. Ruppert (Freiburg: Herder, 1989).

[10]Most interpreters concur that these verses form an inclusio that articulates the motto of the book, but the agreement does not extend to the origin of the bold claim asserted there. The repetition of the verse in 12:8 stands as a cogent argument against those who think this assertion is subsequently relativized. Its recurrence in 12:8 means that, at least for the editor responsible for the motto, Qoheleth never abandoned the position that everything was futile. Those interpreters who distinguish between Qoheleth and a narrator in the frame narrative have found a way to neutralize the skepticism (cf. M. V. Fox, *A Time to Tear Down & a Time to Build Up* [Grand Rapids: Eerdmans, 1999], E. S. Christianson, *A*

Time to Tell: Narrative Strategies in Ecclesiastes (JSOTSup 280; Sheffield: Sheffield Academic Press, 1998), and T. Longman III, *The Book of Ecclesiastes* (Grand Rapids: Eerdmans, 1998).

[11]On the similarities between Qoheleth and the Cynic Monimus, see Lohfink, "Koh 1, 2 'alles ist Windhauch'–universale oder anthropologische Aussage?" 126–28 and T. Krüger, *Qoheleth* (Minneapolis: Fortress Press, 2004), 43, n. 8.

[12]Indeed, Lohfink writes that readers' inability to break free of the prejudice generated by negative feeling toward "the eternal return of the same" prevents them from recognizing the praise of the "cosmos as glorious and eternal in this image of cyclic return" (*Qoheleth*, 40). See also Lohfink, "Koh 1, 2 'alles ist Windhauch'–universale order anthropologische Aussage?" 142, where he writes: "Galte 1, 2 namlich kosmologisch oder grundsätzlich von allem Seiendem, dann müssten die Kreislaufaussagen dieses Gedichts Orchesterklange eines letzten kosmischen Pessimissmus sein."

[13]Christianson, *A Time to Tell*, 88–91. "The lack of antecedent is obvious with 1.2 and 12.8 (cf. 11:8, כָּל-שֶׁבָּא הָבֶל 'all that comes is absurd'). There could, however, possibly be a referent for הַכֹּל at 3:19 if we take it there to mean 'everyone' (all animals and humans; so 3:20,x3). It seems more likely, however, that Qoheleth reflected that (כִּי) everything is absurd (הַכֹּל הָבֶל 3:19b) *as a result* of comparing the circumstance of animals to that of humans (3.18–21) and that הַכֹּל at 3:19 is therefore more generalized and abstract" (88). Christianson goes on to say that the referents of 1:14, 2:11, and 17 are less evident. He concludes: "Because of the all-encompassing referents for הַכֹּל, הָבֶל must, it seems, be applied to all things without exception, including knowledge, wisdom, and even the frame narrator's quite different epistemological priorities (see Chapter 4.3)" (89).

[14]P. Machinist, "Fate, *miqreh*, and Reason: Some Reflections on Qohelet and Biblical Thought,"159–75 in *Solving Riddles and Untying Knots. Biblical, Epigraphic, and Semitic Studies in Honor of Jonas C. Greenfield*, ed. Z. Zevit, S. Gitin, and M. Sokoloff (Winona Lake, Indiana: Eisenbrauns, 1995) argues that Qohelet's understanding of *miqreh* closely resembles the Greek notion of fate and, together with the related words *ḥešbôn*, *ma'aśeh*, and *'ōlām*, indicates an awareness of and reflection on the reasoning process itself. Still, Machinist is cautious about Greek influence, which "may reside not so much in the use of *miqreh* for fate per se, as in the ability to write about *miqreh* in a way that indicates both a rational process at work and, even more, a reflection on what rationality consists of. We have here, in short, a concern for 'second-order' thinking such as marked Greek thought from the pre-Socratics onward and that otherwise is hardly noticed in the written remains of the pre-Hellenistic Near East" (174).

[15]These first two conclusions arise from the dual sense of *dābār*, word and thing (cf. Eccl 1:8, "All words, or things, are wearisome; a person is unable to speak [them]").

[16]C. L. Seow, *Ecclesiastes* (AB 18c; New York: Doubleday, 1997), 298 opts for a human referent on the basis of *gam gam* in 9:6, but Lohfink, *Qoheleth*, 111 thinks the reference pertains to divine emotions, as does Fox, *A Time to Tear Down & A Time to Build Up*, 291. Krüger, *Qoheleth*, 168–9 retains the ambiguity and suggests that by this means Qoheleth undercuts the connection between deed and result in that people cannot know either their own psychology or the deity's disposition, on which see B. Janowski, "Die Tat kehrt zum Tater zurück: Offene Fragen im Umkreis des 'Ergehen-Zusammenhangs," *ZThK* 91 (1994): 247–71.

[17]In support of this interpretation are the Septuagint, Symmachus, and Syriac. The precise meaning of *lipnehem* is unclear, whether spatial or temporal. Moreover, the suffix may allude to *ha'ādām*, to love and hate, or to the righteous and the wise (despite a difference in number for the first option and in gender for the second). The context favors a temporal understanding of *lipnehem*, the long stay in Sheol (vv 3 and 6). Fox, *A Time to Tear Down & A Time to Build Up*, 291 thinks *lipnehem* means "all that they see."

[18]G. Sauer, "כֹּל *kōl* totality," *TLOT* 2:615–16 writes: "Esp. when used abs. and with the article, *kōl* serves in some (exilic and post-exilic) theological statements to describe the entire creation, without becoming either a theological or a cosmological technical expression for 'universe' C. R. North, *IDB* 4:847b, id., *Second Isaiah* [1964], 145f.)"

[19]In Isa 44:24b the last two words in the Kethib, LXX, and Vulgate and many manuscripts read "Who was with me?"

[20]On the personal pronoun *hû'*, see B. K. Waltke and M. O'Connor, *An Introduction to Biblical Hebrew Syntax* (Winona Lake, Indiana: Eisenbrauns, 1990), 292–301.

[21]Exod 29:24; Lev 1:9 (cf. however 2 Sam 1:9).

[22]Indeed, S. Terrien, *The Psalms: Strophic Structure and Theological Commentary* (Grand Rapids: Eerdmans, 2003), 792 translates the verse as follows: "Days stand by thy appointment/For the universe is thy servant."

[23]N. Calduch-Benages, 'God, Creator of All (Sir 43:27–33)," 79–99, especially 89–91 in *Treasures of Wisdom: Studies in Ben Sira and the Book of Wisdom* (FS M. Gilbert, ed. N. Calduch-Benages and J. Vermeylen; BETL 143; Leuwen: Peeters, 1999).

[24]On the relationship between Ben Sira and Stoic philosophy, see O. Kaiser, "Die Rezeption der stoischen Providenz bei Ben Sira," *JNSL* 124 (1998): 41–54; S. L. Mattila, "Ben Sira and the Stoics: A Re-examination of the Evidence," *JBL* 119 (2000): 473–501, and U. Wicke-Reuter, *Göttliche Providenz und menschliche Verantwortung bei Ben Sira und in der Frühen Stoa* (BZAW 298; Berlin/New York: de Gruyter, 2000).

[25]The view that deity penetrates the whole universe in such a way that the two are identical threatened divine freedom and uniqueness, and for this reason was resisted in Jewish circles. Too sharp a distinction between the deity and the created world, however, ran the risk of a gnostic perception of reality, where materiality was denigrated.

[26]Seow, *Ecclesiastes*, 390. See also A. Hurwitz, " רֹאשׁ-דָּבָר and סוֹף-דָּבָר: Reflexes of two Scribal Terms imported into Biblical Hebrew from the Imperial Aramaic Formulary," 281–86 in *Hamlet on a Hill. Semitic and Greek Studies Presented to Professor T. Muraoka on the Occasion of his sixty-Fifth Birthday*, ed. M. F. J. Baasten and W. T. Van Peursen (OLA 118; Leuven: Peeters, 2003).

[27]The text on which this translation is based is that of P. C. Beentjes, *The Book of Ben Sira in Hebrew. A Text Edition of all Extant Hebrew Manuscripts and Synopsis of all Parallel Hebrew Ben Sira Texts* (Leiden: Brill, 1997).

[28]On the hymnic quality of Sirach, see Johannes Marböck, *Weisheit im Wandel: Untersuchungen zur Weisheitstheologie bei Ben Sira* (BBB 37; Bonn: Hanstein, 1971). Compare also Calduch-Benages, "God, Creator of All (Sir 43:27–33)," 91–93 and M. Gilbert, "God, Sin and Mercy: Sirach 15:11–18:14," 118–35, especially 129–32 in *Treasures of Wisdom.*

[29]J. L. Crenshaw, "The Problem of Theodicy in Sirach," *JBL* 94 (1975): 59–64 = idem, *Urgent Advice and Probing Questions: Collected Writings on Old Testament Wisdom* (Macon: Mercer University Press, 1995), 155–74; G. L. Prato, *Il problema della teodicea in Ben Sira. Composizione dei contrari e richiamo alle origini* (An Bib 65; Rome: Pontifical Biblical Institute, 1975); D. Winston, "Theodicy in Ben Sira and Stoic Philosophy," 239–49 in *Of Scholars, Savants, and Their Texts: Essays in Honor of Arthur Hyman*, ed. R. Link-Salinger (New York: Peter Lang, 1989); and M. McGlynn, *Divine Judgment and Divine Benevolence in the Book of Wisdom* (WUNT, 2. Reihe 139 (Tübingen: Mohr Siebeck, 2001).

[30]New York: Oxford Univesity Press, 2005. My earlier thoughts on this subject appear in *Urgent Advice and Probing Questions*, 141–221; "The Reification of Divine Evil," 327–32 in *Perspectives in Religious Studies* 28 (2001); "Theodicy in the Book of the Twelve," chapter 20 above, originally published in *Thematic Threads in the Book of the Twelve*, ed. P. L. Redditt and A. Schart (BZAW 325; Berlin/New York: de Gruyter, 2003), 175–191; and "Theodicy and Prophetic Literature," chapter 21 in this volume, originally published in *Theodicy in the World of the Bible*, ed. A. Laato and C. de Moor (Leiden: Brill, 2003), 236–55.

[31]J. Fichtner, *Die altorientalische Weisheit in ihrer israelitisch-jüdischen Ausprägung* (Giessen: Töpelmann, 1933), 97–105 treats this difficult topic resulting from the incomplete Hebrew text.

[32]J. L. Crenshaw, "Sirach," *NIB*, vol. V (Nashville: Abingdon, 1997), 603–867, especially 624–26 and P. W. Skehan and A. A. di Lella, *The Wisdom of Ben Sira* (AB 39; New York: Doubleday, 1987); and M. Hengel, *Judaism and Hellenism* (Philadelphia: Fortress, 1974), 131–53.

[33]Crenshaw, "The Eternal Gospel (Ecclesiastes 3:11)," 548–72 in *Urgent Advice and Probing Questions* (originally 23–55 in *Essays in Old Testament Ethics*, ed. J. L. Crenshaw and J. T. Willis (New York: Ktav, 1974) and Crenshaw, *Ecclesiastes.*

[34]M. V. Fox, "Qoheleth's Epistemology," *HUCA* 58 (1987): 137–55 and "The Inner Structure of Qohelet's Thought," 225–38 in Qo*helet in the Context of Wisdom*, ed. A. Schoors (BETL CXXXVI; Leuven: University Press, 1998) emphasizes empiricism, but James L. Crenshaw, "Qoheleth's Understanding of Intellectual Inquiry," 205–24, chapter 4 above, originally published in *Qohelet in the Context of Wisdom* (BETL CXXXVI; Leuwen: University Press, 1998), questions the extent to which Qoheleth's epistemology is grounded in experience. The debate continues in A. Schellenberg, *Erkenntnis als Problem. Qohelet und*

die alttestamentliche Diskussion um das menschliche Erkennen (OBO 188; Göttingen: Vandenhoeck & Ruprecht, 2002).

[35]If the philosopher is correct that everything is mist and illusion, then his claim also falls into that category.

[36]The assertion that everything that the deity created was good seems to be called into question by the presence of human sin, just as Augustine's understanding of paradise prior to the fall leaves no place for rebellion. This flaw in the biblical explanation for evil arises from the attempt to posit perfection that vanished through a wilful act. The problem is obvious: why would a perfect being turn away from God.

[37]J. L. Crenshaw, "Deceitful Minds and Theological Dogma: Jeremiah 17:5–11," chapter 9 above, forthcoming in *Utopia and Dystopia in Prophetic Texts*, ed. E. Ben Zvi (Helsinki: Finnish Exegetical Society).

[38]That is, the repetition of the motto in 12:8 reinforces its impact in 1:2, coming as it does after the seven exhortations to enjoy life insofar as possible. That is why I find it impossible to accept the view of some interpreters that Qoheleth gradually abandons his early pessimism.

[39]Qoheleth thinks of the universe as ordered in such a way that everything is appropriate *in its time*. That much is certain, regardless of how one understands the difficult *ha'ōlām* (duration, mystery; or if emended to *ha'āmāl*, toil).

[40]The attribution of everything to divine causation results in a huge problem: does free will exist, or are humans mere puppets whose destiny is fixed for them? M. Gilbert, "God, Sin and Mercy: Sirach 15:11–18:14," provides a scintillating treatment of this issue (see also H. Brünner, "Der freie Wille Gottes in der Ägyptischen Weisheit," 103–20 in *Les Sagesses du Proche-Orient ancien* [Paris: Presses Universitiares de France, 1963]).

[41]H. P. Müller, "Wie sprach Qohälät von Gott?" *VT* 18 (1968): 507–21 underlines the significance of the verb *natan* for Qoheleth. The problem with the deity's generosity, as Qoheleth viewed it, was the lack of connection between morality and divine favor.

[42]On the text, see J. L. Crenshaw, "Flirting with the Language of Prayer (Job 14.13–17)," chapter 1 above; originally published in *Worship and the Hebrew Bible: Essays in Honor of John T. Willis*, ed. M. P. Graham, R. R. Marrs, and S. L. McKenzie (JSOTSup 284; Sheffield: Academic Press, 1999), 110–23.

[43]*The Preacher Sought to Find Pleasing Words*, 151–2 (cf. Bo Isaksson, *Studies in the Language of Qoheleth with Special Emphasis on the Verbal System* [Acta Universitatis Uppsaliensis 10; Uppsala: Almqvist & Wiksell International, 1987], 172–4 who observes that in 1:10 and 2:21 *yeš* has a conditional nuance, while its frequent employment is in "exemplifying" function). One could argue that the negative particle falls outside the present discussion of quantitative language, for it denies that any quantity exists. The mere expression of denial, nevertheless, assumes a quantity that is said not to exist. For that reason, it is discussed here.

[44]J. L. Crenshaw, *Old Testament Wisdom. An Introduction* (Louisville: Westminster John Knox, 1998), 120–and 136, no. 20.

[45]In Ps 135:17b *'ayin* precedes *yēš* (*'ap 'ayin-yēš-ruaḥ bepîhem*).

[46]*The Preacher Sought to Find Pleasing Words*, 152 [cf. Isaksson, *Studies in the Language of Qoheleth*, 174–5 [non-existence 30 times, once in absolute state)..

[47]On the mystery of birth alluded to in this verse, see J. L. Crenshaw, "From the Mundane to the Sublime (Reflections on Qoh 11:1–8)," chapter 8 above, originally published in *From Babel to Babylon: Essays in Honor of Brian Peckham*, ed. Joyce Rillett Wood and John E. Harvey (Sheffield: Sheffield Academic Press) and James L. Crenshaw, "Beginnings, Endings, and Life's Necessities in Biblical Wisdom," chapter 11 above, forthcoming in *Mesopotamian Wisdom Literature*, ed. R. J. Clifford and Peter Machinist (Atlanta: Society of Biblical Literature).

[48]"Fate, *miqreh*, and Reason: Some Reflections on Qohelet and Biblical Thought," 170–71.

[49]G. Sauer, "אחד *'eḥād* one," *TLOT* vol. 1:78–80 lists Mal 2:10; Job 31:15; Jer 32:39; Ezek 34:22; 37:22; Hos 2:2; and Zeph 3:9.

[50]"Das Ego des Weisen," *TZ* (1984): 121–35.

[51]Interpreters generally characterize the authors of wisdom literature as self-centered, given their primary interest in looking out for number one. Occasional exceptions do occur, although the assumption underlying the book of Proverbs is that the deity rewards virtuous acts with the good things in life. Lazy people and the wicked do not, in the sages' view, deserve charity. Ben Sira encourages compassionate acts toward the needy, but he also

recognizes the significance of divine mercy. In both of these attitudes, he differs greatly from older wisdom. For discussion, see J. L. Crenshaw, "The Concept of God in Old Testament Wisdom," 191–205 in *Urgent Advice and Probing Questions* (originally 1–18 in *In Search of Wisdom*, ed. L. G. Perdue, B. B. Scott, and W. J. Wiseman [Louisville: Westminster/John Knox, 1993]).

[52]C. Uehlinger, "Qohelet im Horizont mesopotamischer, levantinischer und agyptischer Weisheitsliteratur der persischen und hellenistischen Zeit," 181–82 in L. Schwienhorst-Schönberger, ed. *Das Buch Kohelet: Studien zur Struktur, Geschichte, Rezeption und Theologie* (BZAW 254; Berlin/New York, 1997).

[53]W. M. W. Roth, *Numerical Sayings in the Old Testament: A Form-Critical Study* (VTSup; Leiden: Brill, 1965) and G. Sauer, *Die Sprüche Agurs: Untersuchungen zur Herkunft, Verbreitung und Bedeutung einer biblischer Stilform unter besonderer Berucksichtigung von Proverbia c. 30* (BWANT 84; Stuttgart: Kohlhammer, 1963).

[54]J. L. Berquist, *Judaism in Persia's Shadow: A Social and Historical Approach* (Minneapolis: Fortress, 1995).

[55]A variety of views about this text is found in N. Lohfink, "War Kohelet ein Frauenfeind? Ein Versuch, die Logik und den Gegenstand von Koh., 7, 23–8, 1a herauszufinden," *Studien zu Kohelet*, 31–69 (originally 259–87, 417–20 in *La Sagesse de l'Ancien Testament*, ed. M. Gilbert [BETL 51; Leuven: University Press, 1979); J. Y. S. Pahk, "The Significance of אֲשֶׁר in Qoh 7, 26: More bitter than death is the woman, *if* she is a snare," 373–83 in *Qohelet in the Context of Wisdom*; T. Krüger, "'Frau Weisheit' in Koh 7, 26?" *Bib* 73 (1992): 394–403 (Krüger, 121–30 in *Kritische Weisheit: Studien zur weisheitslichen Traditionskritik im Alten Testament* (Zurich: Pano, 1997); K. Baltzer, "Women and War in Qohelet 7:23–8:1a," *HTR* 80 (1987): 127–32; M. V. Fox, "Unsought Discoveries: Qoheleth 7:23–8:1a," *HS* 19 (1978); 26–38; D. Rudman, "Woman as Divine Agent in Ecclesiastes," *JBL* 116 (1997): 411–27; A. Schoors, "Bitterder dan de Dood is de Vrouw: (Koh 7, 26)," *Bijdr* 54 (1992): 121–40; and C. R. Fontaine, "'Many Devices' (Qoheleth 7, 23–81, 1): Qoheleth, Misogyny and the Malleus Maleficarum," 137–68 in *Wisdom and Psalms*, ed. A. Brenner and C. R. Fontaine (FCB 2/2; Sheffield: Sheffield Academic Press, 1998).

[56]Ben Sira's innovative teaching falls short of the extreme view expressed by Wisdom of Solomon, where we read "For Blessed is the barren woman who is undefiled, who has not entered into a sinful union...blessed also is the eunuch whose hands have done no lawless deed...Better then is childlessness with virtue..." (3:13–14, 4:1).

[57]The ambiguous language of the short anecdote has given rise to opposite views about the event. Some interpreters stress the potential for delivery that went untapped, while others emphasize the ingratitude of people who were actually saved from disaster.

[58]The participle *meḥelqôt* recalls the prominence of *ḥeleq* in Qoheleth's vocabulary.

[59]The link between piety and ethics in Ben Sira's teaching is an intimate one in which observance of torah goes hand in hand with mundane activities involving issues of integrity and justice.

[60]For Qoheleth, fear of the deity involved an element of the numinous, justifying the translation "dread" (E. Pfeiffer, "Die Gottesfurcht im Buche Kohelet," 133–58 in *Gottes Wort und Gottes Land. Festschrift für H. W. Hertzberg*, ed. H. G. Reventlow (Göttingen: Vandenhoeck & Ruprecht, 1965).

[61]If one follows HALOT in taking *we'izzēn* as II piel "balance" derived from *môzenayîm*, this word would also need to be taken into consideration when tabulating quantitative vocabulary.

[62]Zenon was chief administrative officer of Apollonius, the minister of finance for Ptolemy II Philadelphius. For details, see P. W. Pestmann, *A Guide to the Zenon Papyri* (Papyrologica Lugundo-Batava 21 A-B; Leiden: Brill, 1981); and M. Rostovtzeff, *A Large Estate in Egypt in the Third Century B.C.: A Study in Economic History* (University of Wisconsin Studies in the Social Sciences and History 6; Madison: University of Wisconsin, 1922).

[63]On the basis of similarities between the Egyptian Instruction of Duauf and Sir 38:24–30, it may be inadvisable to move from the literary topos to historicity. Ben Sira's account is less satirical and much more appreciative of manual labor, even when setting scribes apart as an elite intelligentsia.

[64]W. Zimmerli's assessment of wisdom has been accepted by many interpreters: the endeavor to master reality by the intellect for human benefit ("Ort und Grenze der Weisheit im Rahmen der alttestamentlichen Theologie," *Les Sagesses du Proche-Orient Ancien*, ET, "The Place and Limit of the Wisdom in the Framework of the Old Testament Theology," [SJTh

17, 1964]: 146–58 and 175–207 in *Studies in Ancient Israelite Wisdom*, ed. J. L. Crenshaw, [New York: Ktav, 1976]).

[65]C. Klein, *Kohelet und die Weisheit Israels. Eine formgeschichtliche Studie* (BWANT 12; Stuttgart/Berlin/Koln: Kohlhammer, 1994), 168–204.

[66]For Qohelet's understanding of God, see A. Schoors, "God in Qohelet,"; L. Gorssen, "Le cohérence de la conception de Dieu dans l'Ecclésiaste," *TThL* 46 (1970): 282–324; S. de Jong, "God in the Book of Qohelet: A Reappraisal of Qohelet's Place in Old Testament Theology," *VT* 47 (1997): 154–67; D. Michel, "Gott bei Kohelet: Anmerkungen zu Kohelets Reden von Gott," *BK 45* (1990): 32–36; and H. P. Müller, "Wie sprach Qohälät von Gott?," *VT* 18 (1968): 507–21.

[67]*Biblical Myth and Rabbinic Mythmaking* (Oxford: Oxford University Press, 2003).

[68] B. Lang, *Wisdom and the Book of Proverbs: An Israelite Goddess Redefined* (New York: Pilgrim, 1986); J. E. McKinlay, *Gendering Wisdom the Host: Biblical Invitations to Eat and Drink* (JSOTSup 216; Sheffield: Sheffield Academic Press, 1996); G. Baumann, Die Weisheitsgestalt in Proverbien 1–9 (FAT 16; Tübingen: Mohr [Paul Siebeck], 1996); and S. Schroer, *Wisdom Has Built her House: Studies on the Figure of Sophia in the Bible* (Collegeville, Minnesota: The Liturgical Press, 2000).

[69]Several texts from Qumran mention "the mystery that is to come," especially *The Book of Mysteries and Sapiential Work A.* A natural outgrowth of an acknowledgment that the intellect cannot comprehend the deity, this emphasis on the unfathomable nature of God and divine activity was very much at home in a culture where mystery religions flourished.

[70]M. E. Stone, *Fourth Ezra* (Minneapolis: Fortress, 1990). See also J. E. Wright, *Baruch Ben Neriah. From Biblical Scribe to Apocalyptic Seer* (Columbia: University of South Carolina Press, 2003) for discussion of a related text, Second Baruch, and the traditions associated with the scribe by that name.

[71]B. E. Daley, "Is Patristic Exegesis Still Usable? Some Reflections on Early Christian Interpretation of the Psalms," 69–88 in *The Art of Reading Scripture*, ed. E. F. Davis and R. B. Hays (Grand Rapids: Eerdmans, 2003) asks some probing questions about the Postmodern age and its subjectivism, while at the same time insisting that the gains of historical criticism ought not be given up, even when interpreters utilize insights from patristic exegesis, a "hermeneutic of piety."

[72]Christianson, *A Time to Tell;* G. D. Salyer, *Vain Rhetoric: Private Insight and Public Debate in Ecclesiastes* (JSOTSup 327; Sheffield: Sheffield Academic Press, 2001); A. A. Fischer, *Skepsis oder Furcht Gottes? Studien zur Komposition und Theologie des Buches Kohelet* (BZAW 247; Berlin/New York: de Gruyter, 1997); C. G. Bartholomew, *Reading Ecclesiastes: Old Testament Exegesis and Hermeneutical Theory* (AnBib 139; Roma: Pontificio Istituto Biblico, 1998).

Chapter 11: Beginnings, Endings, and Life's Necessities in Biblical Wisdom

[1]For the processing of information, see James L. Crenshaw, "Qoheleth's Understanding of Intellectual Inquiry," in chapter 4 above; originally published in Antoon Schoors, ed. *Qohelet in the Context of Wisdom* (BETL cxxxvi; Leuven: University Press, 1998), 205–24; *Education in Ancient Israel* (ABRL; New York: Doubleday, 1998); and Michael V. Fox, "The Inner Structure of Qohelet's Thought," 225–38 in *Qohelet in the Context of Wisdom.* Further analysis of epistemology can be found in Peter Machinist, "Fate, *miqreh*, and Reason: Some Reflections on Qohelet and Biblical Thought," 159–74 in *Solving Riddles and Untying Knots (Fs. J. C. Greenfield)*, ed. Ziony Zevit et. al. (Winona Lake: Eisenbrauns, 1995) and Annette Schellenberg, *Erkenntnis als Problem. Qohelet und die alttestamentliche Diskussion um das menschliche Erkennen* (OBO 188; Göttingen: Vandenhoeck & Ruprecht, 2002).

[2]Gerhard von Rad, *Wisdom in Israel* (Nashville and New York: Abingdon, 1972) emphasizes the importance of analogical thinking in the sages' repertoire, while William P. Brown, *Character in Crisis. A Fresh Approach to the Wisdom Literature of the Old Testament* (Grand Rapids: Eerdmans, 1996) stresses the formation of character.

[3]Translations in this article are by the author unless otherwise indicated.

[4]Maurice Gilbert, *La Critique des dieux dans le livre de la Sagesse* (An Bib 53; Rome: Pontifical Biblical Institute Press, 1973) offers a thorough analysis of the attitude to idolatry in Wisdom of Solomon. Along with the worship of distant emperors and grief over a dead son, pride in artistic craft completes the three explanations for worshipping something

finite. John F. Kutsko, *Between Heaven and Earth. Divine Presence and Absence in the Book of Ezekiel* (BJSt, 7; Winona Lake: Eisenbrauns, 2000) relates theodicy and the prophetic understanding of the worship of "non-gods."

[5]J. Vollmer, " עשׂה *'śh* to make, do," *TLOT*, vol. 2 (Peabody: Hendrickson, 1997), 944–51.

[6]Carol A. Newsom, "The Book of Job," *NIB*, vol. 4 (Nashville: Abingdon, 1996), 414 refers to Eduard Dhorme, *A Commentary on the Book of Job* (London: Nelson, 1967), 149–50 for parallels from later literature.

[7]Samson's response to Delilah's badgering in Jdg 16:13 employs an imperfect form of *'ārag* together with a noun from *nāsak* II with the meaning "web." The imperfect verbal form in Job 10:11 to indicate intricate weaving is from *sākak*.

[8]The initial *kî* is taken as emphatic here.

[9]Literally, "kidneys."

[10]The verb is *tesukkēnî*, as in Job 10:11 (*tesōkkēnî*).

[11]This word *golmî* (embryo) evoked considerable speculation in later Judaism.

[12]On this idea, see Shalom M. Paul, "Heavenly Tablets and the Book of Life," *JANESCU* 5 (1973): 345–53.

[13]Samuel Terrien, *The Psalms. Strophic Structure and Theological Commentary* (Grand Rapids: Eerdmans, 2003), 876–8. "The poet rebels against a doting father who dictates every move and word of his adored child. Now surprise! This harassed child asks for more 'divine examination, scrutiny, and search'" (p. 878).

[14]James L. Crenshaw, *The Psalms. An Introduction* (Grand Rapids: Eerdmans, 2001), 109–27.

[15]Similar language is used in Agur's opening remarks (Prov 30:1) to indicate incapacity and in Jeremiah's lament in 20:7 where it lacks the negation because the referent is Yahweh. The result is the same, human impotence.

[16]Three psalms, 10, 14, and 54, stand out as expressions of this attitude, which is linked with fools. I treat each of these psalms in *Defending God: Biblical Responses to the Problem of Evil* (New York: Oxford University, 2005).

[17]Shalom M. Paul, *Amos* (Minneapolis: Fortress, 1991), 277 notes the presence of pentads here (five conditional sentences highlighted by a fivefold repetition of *miššām* "from there") and in the earlier refrain, *welō' šabtem 'adai ne'um-yhwh* (4:6–11), and five visions. Paul's exemplary treatment of Amos 9:2–4 draws on ancient Near Eastern parallels while being attentive to literary and theological features of the Hebrew text.

[18]Terrien, *The Psalms*, 877. He writes: "Nevertheless, the poet does not stumble under the threat of metaphysical hubris." Elsewhere Terrien admires this poet's "skill, finesse, and force, as if he were a religious acrobat who dances on the high wire without a safety net" while exclaiming, "All my ways are known to thee, Lord" (p. 879).

[19]James C. VanderKam, *Enoch: A Man for All Generations* (Columbia: University of South Carolina, 1995).

[20]John J. Collins, *The Apocalyptic Imagination. An Introduction to the Jewish Matrix of Christianity* (New York: Crossroad, 1984) and "Early Jewish Apocalypticism," *ABD*, vol. 1 (New York: Doubleday, 1992) 281–88.

[21]Raymond C. Van Leeuwen, "The Background to Proverbs 30:4a," 102–21 in Michael L. Barré, S. S. ed., *Wisdom, You Are My Sister. Studies in Honor of Roland E. Murphy, O. Carm., on the Occasion of His Eightieth Birthday* (CBQMS 29; Washington, D.C.: The Catholic Biblical Association of America, 1995). For the larger text Prov 30:1–14, see James L. Crenshaw, "Clanging Symbols," 371–82 in *Urgent Advice and Probing Questions. Collected Writings on Old Testament Wisdom* (Macon: Mercer University, 1995, originally 51–64 in *Justice and the Holy*, ed. D. A. Knight and P. J. Paris, [Philadelphia: Fortress, 1989]). Karel van der Toorn, "Sources in Heaven: Revelation as a Scholarly Construct in Second Temple Judaism," 265–77 in *Kein Land für sich allein. Studien zum Kulturkontakt in Kanaan, Israel/Palästina und Ebirnâri für Manfred Weippert zum 65. Geburtstag*, ed. Ulrich Hübner und Ernst Axel Knauf (OBO 186; Göttingen: Vandenhoeck & Ruprecht, 2002) stresses the emergence of the concept of revelation to replace earlier human wisdom in Mesopotamia and Israel. He views the first millennium version of the Myth of Adapa in this light, for Adapa returned from heaven with the revealed secrets of heaven, knowledge hidden from ordinary mortals (p. 274).

[22]F. Stolz, "לֵב *lēb* heart,'*TLOT*, vol. 2 (Peabody: Hendrickson, 1997), 638–42. "In addition to *kābēd* 'liver' (>*kbd*), particular reference should be made to *kelāyôt* 'kidneys'

which often parallels 'heart,' indicating the most private, hidden being of a person, accessible only to God..."(p. 640).

[23]Amos Hakham, *The Bible, Psalms with The Jerusalem Commentary*, vol. 3 (Jerusalem: Mosad Harav Kook, 2003), 400–411 is a perceptive analysis of the entire psalm.

[24]J. L. Crenshaw, "From the Mundane to the Sublime (Reflections on Qoh 11:1–8)," chapter 8 above, originally published in *From Babel to Babylon: Essays in Honor of Brian Peckham*, ed. Joyce Rillett Wood and John E. Harvey (Sheffield: Sheffield Academic Press) The midrash Qoheleth Rabbah includes this mystery of birth in the seven great mysteries. The others are the day of one's death; the timing of the messianic consolation; the profundity of divine judgment; the source from which one will profit; the precise thought or feeling in a friend's heart; and the exact time that the kingdom of Edom (=Rome) will fall.

[25]Antti Laato and Johannes C. de Moor, ed. *Theodicy in the World of the Bible* (Leiden: Brill, 2003), and James L. Crenshaw, *Defending God*, and "Theodicy in the Book of the Twelve," chapter 20 above, originally published in *Thematic Threads in the Book of the Twelve*, ed. P. L. Redditt and A. Schart (BZAW 325; Berlin/New York: de Gruyter, 2003), 175–191 attest the powerful attraction of this vexing problem, brought to public attention once more by the devastating Tsunami of December, 2004.

[26]Hugh Anderson, "4 Maccabees," 531–64 in James H. Charlesworth, ed. *The Old Testament Pseudepigrapha* (New York: Doubleday, 1985). Strongly influenced by Stoic philosophers, the author of 4 Maccabees departs from them in the belief that reason controls the passions instead of extirpating them (n.e, p. 546).

[27]No one has emphasized the collapse of belief in order throughout the ancient Near East as decisively as Hans Heinrich Schmid, *Wesen und Geschichte der Weisheit* (BZAW 101; Berlin: Töpelmann, 1966). Questioning the significance of order is Roland E. Murphy, on which see James L. Crenshaw, "Murphy's Axiom: Every Gnomic Saying Needs a Balancing Corrective," 344–54 in *Urgent Advice and Probing Questions.*

[28]James L. Crenshaw, "The Shadow of Death in Qoheleth," 573–85 in *Urgent Advice and Probing Questions* and Shannon Burkes, *Death in Qoheleth and Egyptian Biographies of the Late Period* (SBLDS 170; Atlanta: Society of Biblical Literature, 1999).

[29]J. L. Crenshaw, "Flirting with the Language of Prayer (Job 14.13–17)," chapter 1 above; originally published in *Worship and the Hebrew Bible: Essays in Honor of John T. Willis*, ed. M. P. Graham, R. R. Marrs, and S. L. McKenzie (JSOTSup 284; Sheffield: Academic Press, 1999), 110–23.

[30]James L. Crenshaw, "Love is Stronger than Death (Intimations of Life Beyond the Grave)" in *Resurrection*, ed. James Charlesworth (New York: T. & T. Clark, 2006), 53–78.

[31]Martin Hengel, *Judaism and Hellenism* (Philadelphia: Fortress, 1974), 107–53; Otto Kaiser, *Gottes und der Menschen Weisheit. Gesammelte Aufsätze* (BZAW 261; Berlin and New York: de Gruyter, 1998); S. L. Mattila, "Ben Sira and the Stoics: A Re-examination of the Evidence," *JBL* 119 (2000): 473–501; U. Wicke-Reuter, *Göttliche Providenz und menschliche Verantwortung bei Ben Sira und in der Frühen Stoa* (BZAW 298; Berlin and New York: de Gruyter, 2000), and Reinhold Bohlen, "Kohelet im Kontext hellenistischer Kultur," 249–73 in L. Schwienhorst-Schönberger, ed. *Das Buch Kohelet: Studien zur Kultur, Geschichte, Rezeption, und Theologie* (BZAW 254; Berlin and New York: de Gruyter, 1997).

[32]David Winston, *The Wisdom of Solomon* (AB 43; Garden City: Doubleday, 1979).

[33]Michael Kolarcik, *The Ambiguity of Death in the Book of Wisdom 1–6. A Study of Literary Structure and Interpretation* (AnBib 127; Rome: Editrice Pontificio Istituto Biblico, 1991).

[34]I follow the text as produced in Pancratius C. Beentjes, *The Book of Ben Sira in Hebrew. A Text Edition of all Extant Hebrew Manuscripts and Synopsis of all Parallel Hebrew Ben Sira Texts* (Leiden: Brill, 1997).

[35]Georg Sauer, *Jesus Sirach/Ben Sira* (ATD Apokryphen Band 1; Göttingen: Vandenhoeck & Ruprecht, 2000) writes: "Eine kleine Kulturgeschichte kann an dieser Aufzählung abgelesen werden, vgl. auch Sir 29, 21 und Dtn 32:13f." (p. 274).

[36]Pancratius C. Beentjes, "Theodicy in the Wisdom of Ben Sira," 509–24 in *Theodicy in the World of the Bible*, and John J. Collins, *Jewish Wisdom in the Hellenistic Age* (OTL; Louisville: Westminster, 1997), 80–96 supplement my earlier article, "The Problem of Theodicy in Sirach. On Human Bondage,"*JBL* 94 (1975): 49–64 (=155–74 in *Urgent Advice and Probing Questions*).

[37]Patrick W. Skehan and Alexander A. DiLella, *The Wisdom of Ben Sira* (AB 39; New York: Doubleday, 1987), 457–61.

[38]Skehan/DiLella list the following biblical references, among others: Gen 49:11 (grain and wine), Hos 2:10, Jer 31:12, Neh 10:38 [actually it is 39], (oil), Exod 3:8; 13:5; 33:3; Lev 20:24 (milk and honey).

[39]On writing as enculturation, see David M. Carr, *Writing on the Tablet of the Heart. Origins of Scripture and Literature* (New York: Oxford University Press, 2005).

[40]James L. Crenshaw, "The Restraint of Reason, the Humility of Prayer," 206–21 in *Urgent Advice and Probing Questions* examines the place of prayer in sapiential literature.

[41]Oda Wischmeyer, *Die Kultur des Buches Jesus Sirach* (BZNTW 77; Berlin and New York: de Gruyter, 1994).

[42]The remarkable similarities between the two texts could be explained without reference to literary influence. It would then be an instance of polygenesis, the spontaneous emergence of similar ideas in separate locations. It is much more likely, however, that the story about Gilgamesh was known to Qoheleth, given its wide distribution in the ancient Near East.

[43]The irony of Qoheleth's recognition of the necessity for companionship to the good life, insofar as it could be achieved, should not escape notice, particularly in light of his egoism, on which Peter Höffken has written astutely ("Das Ego des Weisen," *TZ* 4 [1985]: 121–35).

[44]Qoheleth's use of the verb *'ānâ* in different senses has made it difficult to understand one verse in particular, 5:19. Does *ma'aneh* imply affliction, preoccupation, or answer? Norbert Lohfink, "Qoheleth 5:17–19–Revelation by Joy," *CBQ* 52 (1990): 625–35 and Ludger Schwienhorst-Schönberger, "Gottes Antwort in der Freude: Zur Theologie göttlicher Gegenwart im Buch Kohelet," *BK* 54 (1999): 156–63 prefer the last meaning, thus a positive interpretation of the text.

[45]Avi Hurvitz, "רֹאשׁ-דָּבָר and סוֹף-דָּבָר : Reflexes of two Scribal Terms imported into Biblical Hebrew from the Imperial Aramaic Formulary," 281–86 in *Hamlet on a Hill. Semitic and Greek Studies Presented to Professor T. Muraoka on the Occasion of his Sixty-Fifth Birthday*, ed. M. F. J. Baasten and W. Th. Van Peursen (OLA 118; Leuven: Peeters, 2003) writes that *rō'š* and *sôp* represent semantic mirror images. In Qoheleth and Psalm 119 *rō'š-dābār* and *sôp-dābār* denote "the beginning of the matter" and "the end of the matter," not the scribal "beginning/end of a[written] word (=text)."

[46]One could profitably extend this discussion of beginnings and endings to the difficult problem of delineating textual units, as well as to prologues, epilogues, and thematic statements. Norbert Lohfink, "Jeder Weisheitslehre Quintessenz. Zu Koh 12, 13," 195–205 in Irmtraud Fischer, Ursula Rapp, und Johannes Schiller, ed. *Auf den Spuren der schriftgelehrten Weisen. Festschrift für Johannes Marböck* (BZAW 331; Berlin and New York: de Gruyter, 2003) and "Zu einigen Satzeröffnungen im Epilog des Koheletbuches," 131–47 in "*Jedes Ding hat seine* Zeit...," ed. A. A. Diesel, R. G. Lehrmann, E. Otto, und A. Wagner (BZAW 241; Berlin/New York: de Gruyter, 1996) has initiated such an investigation. The language of origins attributed to Wisdom in Prov 8:22–31 could also be studied fruitfully in this connection, but that would extend the scope of this paper to unacceptable lengths. The initiative for such analysis has been taken by Michaela Bauks/Gerlinde Baumann, "Im Anfang war...? Gen 1, 1ff und Prov 8, 22–31 in Vergleich," *BN* 71 (1994): 24–53.

Chapter 12: The Book of Psalms and Its Interpreters

[1]James Limburg, "Psalms, Book of," *ABD* vol. V (New York: Doubleday, 1992), 522–36; James L. Crenshaw, "Psalms, Book of," *Eerdmans Dictionary of the Bible*, ed. David Noel Freedman (Grand Rapids: Eerdmans, 2000), 1093–95, Erich Zenger, "Psalmenforschung nach Hermann Gunkel und Sigmund Mowinckel," *Congress Volume Oslo 1998*, eds. André Lemaire and Magne Saebo (VT Sup 80; Leiden/Boston: Brill, 2000), 399–435, and Manfred Oeming, "An der Quelle des Gebets: Neuere Untersuchungen zu den Psalmen," *TLS* 127 (2002): 367–84. Earlier surveys can be found in D. J. A. Clines, "Psalms Research Since 1955: I. The Psalms and the Cult," *Tyndale Bulletin* 18 (1967): 103–25; "Psalms Research Since 1955: II. The Literary Genres," *Tyndale Bulletin* 20 (1969): 105–25; B. Feininger, "A Decade of German Psalm-Criticism," *JSOT* 20 (1981): 91–103; Audrey R. Johnson, "The Psalms," pages 162–209 in H. H. Rowley, ed., *The Old Testament and Modern Study* (Oxford: Clarendon, 1951); A. S. Kapelrud, "Scandinavian Research in the Psalms after Mowinckel, " *ASThI* 4 (1965): 74–90; J. J. Stamm, "Ein Vierteljahrhundert Psalmenforschung," *ThR* 23 (1955); 1–68.

[2]David Weiss Halivni, *Peshat & Derash: Plain and Applied Meaning in Rabbinic Exegesis* (New York and Oxford: Oxford University Press, 1991) presses this controversial point. He writes that the time of Ezra was "the end of prophecy" and the "end of idolatry." "Interpretation took the place of revelation" (p. vi). He adds: "Only with the cessation of prophecy did the text become indispensable and, therefore, textual solicitude imperative and urgent" (136). Innerbiblical exegesis is examined in magisterial fashion by Michael Fishbane, *Biblical Interpretation in Ancient Israel* (Oxford: Clarendon Press, 1985).

[3]The following statistics are taken from Klaus Seybold, *Introducing the Psalms* (Edinburgh: T. & T. Clark, 1990), 6 and 10. See also P. W. Flint, "The Book of Psalms in the Light of the Dead Sea Scrolls," *VT* 48 (1998): 453–72.

[4]The Psalms of Solomon show a similar predilection toward viewing personal conflict in eschatological terms. On these psalms see Kenneth Atkinson, "Theodicy in the Psalms of Solomon," pages 546–75 in *Theodicy in the World of the Bible*, eds. Antti Laato and Johannes C. de Moor (Leiden: Brill, 2003).

[5]William L. Holladay, *The Psalms through Three Thousand Years: Prayerbook of a Cloud of Witnesses* (Minneapolis: Fortress, 1993), 162.

[6]This discussion of Jewish scholars draws upon Uriel Simon, *Four Approaches to the Book of Psalms: From Saadiah Gaon to Abraham Ibn Ezra* (Albany, N.Y.: SUNY Press, 1991) and Joshua Baker and Ernest W. Nicholson, *The Commentary of Rabbi David Kimhi on Psalms CXX-CL* (Cambridge: Cambridge University Press, 1973).

[7]Abraham Ibn Ezra comes to his defense, accusing the accusers of lack of knowledge.

[8]These interpretive approaches involve the substitution of different letters of the alphabet for the ones in the text, for example, the final letter for the first, the next to last letter for the second, and so forth.

[9]Moses Buttenwieser, *The Psalms* (Chicago: The University of Chicago Press, 1938), 18.

[10]Buttenwieser's introduction to the commentary (pages 1–18 in particular) summarizes his conclusions, which are defended at great length and in intricate detail later in the book (29–874).

[11]Gunkel did not live long enough to complete his introduction to the Psalms, which became the task of his student Joachim Begrich, who drew on copious notes left by the teacher. The published work is now available in English translation by James D. Nogalski (Hermann Gunkel and Joachim Begrich, *An Introduction to the Psalms* [Macon, Ga.: Mercer University Press, 1998]).

[12]See his monumental volume, *He that Cometh* (Oxford: Basil Blackwell, 1959).

[13]Zenger, "Psalmenforschung nach Hermann Gunkel und Sigmund Mowinckel," 409–35 identifies five inadequacies of the form critical approach represented by Gunkel and Mowinckel and a like number of current adjustments to their interpretation. The limitations: the rich variety in the main genres, the leveling of individuality, the overlooking of the esthetic and theological value of mixed genres, the imprecision of actual social contexts, and the absence of any interest in the book of Psalms as a whole. The new interests: the study of adjacent psalms, psalm groups, macrostructural composition, inner and extrabiblical analogies, and Psalms as a popular composition unrelated to the temple. Zenger provides extensive bibliography for this modern research and labels Psalms a linguistic temple that enables worshippers to enthrone YHWH through prayer (Ps 22:4).

[14]Cross, F. M. Jr, and Freedman, D. N. *Studies in Ancient Yahwistic Poetry.* SBLDS 21. Missoula: Scholars Press, 1975.

[15]A revised edition of the 1963 work by Luis Alonso-Schökel, *Estudio de poetica hebrea* (Barcelona: Juan Flors) has appeared in English under the title, *A Manual of Hebrew Poetics* [Subsidia Biblica, 11; Rome: Pontifical Biblical Institute, 1988]). Meir Weiss, *The Bible from Within: The Method of Total Interpretation* (Jerusalem: Magnes Press, 1984) goes beyond his earlier articles and offers a good introduction to holistic reading of the Bible.

[16]James Muilenburg, "Form Criticism and Beyond," *JBL* 88 (1969): 1–18. For his impact, see Phyllis Trible, *Rhetorical Criticism: Context, Method, and the Book of Jonah* (Minneapolis: Fortress Press, 1994).

[17]Robert Alter, *The Art of Biblical Narrative* (New York: Basic Books, 1981); Meir Sternberg, *The Poetics of Biblical Narrative* (Bloomington, Ind.: Indiana University Press, 1985); Adele Berlin, *Poetics and Interpretation of Biblical Narrative* (Sheffield: The Almond Press, 1983). Less influential, but in many ways more stimulating, is Herbert Chanan Brichto, *Toward a Grammar of Biblical Poetics. Tales of the Prophets* (New York and Oxford: Oxford University Press, 1992).

[18]*The Poets' Book of Psalms: The Complete Psalter as Rendered by Twenty-Five Poets from the Sixteenth to the Twentieth Centuries,* ed. Laurance Wieder (New York & Oxford: Oxford University Press,), 1995.

[19]S. E. Gillingham, *The Poems and Psalms of the Hebrew Bible* (Oxford: University Press, 1994), 173–89 traces historical-critical interpretation of Psalms in five stages: (1) psalmists as individual poets; (2) psalmists as poets serving the community; (3) psalmists as liturgical poets serving the cultic community; (4) psalmists as liturgical poets serving a private cultus; and (5) psalmists as poets of life. She relates the first stage to Romanticism of the 1820s, the second to emerging national consciousness beginning in the 1880s, the third to the influence of the History of Religions School in the 1920s and the Myth and Ritual School in the 1930s, the fourth to sociological emphases beginning in the 1960s, and the fifth to a contemporary life-centered interest.

Chapter 13: The Deuteronomist and the Writings

[1]"Method in Determining Wisdom Influence upon 'Historical' Literature," *JBL* 88 (1969) 129–42, reprinted in Crenshaw, *Urgent Advice and Probing Questions: Collected Writings on Old Testament Wisdom* (Macon: Mercer University Press, 1995) 312–25. Scott L. Harris, *Proverbs 1-9: A Study of Inner-Biblical Interpretation* (SBLDS 150; Atlanta: Scholars Press, 1995) has reversed the process, arguing on the basis of Prov 1:8–19; 1:20–33; and 6:1–19 that the author used the Joseph narrative and Jeremiah, among other earlier canonical texts. Harris relies on "the transposition of words from another context, the anthological combination of vocabulary adapted to a new sapiential context, key words and phrases, virtual citations, and allusive language" (p. 22) to relate biblical texts to one another. One must be careful, however, not to seize upon accidental similarities in language resulting from a limited vocabulary and common topics as evidence of actual reflection on a given canonical text.

[2]See the discussions in Richard Coggins, "What Does 'Deuteronomistic' Mean?" *Words Remembered, Texts Renewed: Essays in Honor of John F. A. Sawyer*, eds. Jon Davies, Graham Harvey, and Wilfred G. E. Watson (JSOT SS 195. Sheffield: Academic Press, 1995) 135–48 and Norbert Lohfink, "Gab es ein deuteronomistische Bewegnung?" *Jeremia und die 'deuteronomistische' Bewegnung,* ed. Walter Gross (Weinheim: BELTZ Athenaum, 1995) 313–82.

[3]Lohfink, "Gab es ein deuteronomistische Bewegnung?" recognizes the problems involved in ascertaining the extent of literacy in post-exilic Yehud. Jews in exile had seen the importance of written texts in the Babylonian culture, but on returning to Yehud they possessed limited resources and met with considerable difficulty, both politically and economically.

[4]Coggins, "What Does 'Deuteronomistic' Mean?" 135–48 asks a significant question: who were these Deuteronomists? He lists the different responses within scholarly literature: Levites (von Rad), heirs to the prophetic tradition (E. Nicholson), wisdom schools (Weinfeld), and reformers (R. Clements). Perhaps one should also inquire as to the meaning of school, which is preceded by the adjective Deuteronomistic. Presumably, the reference is to a particular kind of thinking based on the book of Deuteronomy rather than an institution consisting of professional teachers and students.

[5]Patricia Dutcher-Walls, "The Social Location of the Deuteronomist: A Sociological Study of Factional Politics in Late Pre-Exilic Judah," *JSOT* 52 (1991) 77–94 uses the research of Gerhard Lenski and T. F. Carney on related agrarian societies in her effort to understand the social tiers and conflicts in Israel. Consciously ignoring apologetic or polemic in Deuteronomistic texts, she hopes to arrive at unbiased description, itself problematic. Deuteronomists, in her view, cut across the various social groupings and roles making up the highest class of society in Yehud. They comprised "a mixed elite grouping of priests, prophets, scribes, court officials and gentry" (p. 93). Specific groups within North American society illustrate the manner in which discourse comes to be specific to a particular segment of the population. Athletes, for example, talk of "making history" through breaking a record of victories or the like; they speak about "coming to play" and "giving one hundred and ten percent" of effort to the game. Frequently, athletes speak of themselves in the third person, hardly a sign of humility, which seems directly opposed to their arrogance/cockiness.

[6]*Deuteronomy and the Deuteronomic School* (Oxford: University Press, 1972, reprint Eisenbrauns, 1992).

[7]Weinfeld considers the Sayings of Agur in Prov 30:1–14 to be early, but a virtual scholarly consensus has placed this text at the end of the compositional process in the book of Proverbs. Its meaning continues to baffle interpreters, who cannot agree on its length and sense. Raymond C. van Leeuwen, "The Background to Proverbs 30:4a ," in *Wisdom, You Are My Sister. Studies in Honor of Roland E. Murphy, O. Carm., on the Occasion of His Eightieth Birthday*, ed. Michael L. Barre (CBQMS 29; Washington, D.C.: The Catholic Biblical Association of America, 1997) 102–21 is the latest in a long line of investigations into the meaning of this difficult text. He emphasizes the antiquity of the topos about heavenly ascent and descent by gods and quasi-divine figures. R. N. Whybray, *The Book of Proverbs. A Survey of Modern Study* (Leiden: E. J. Brill, 1995) 86–91 discusses the different scholarly views about the sayings of Agur.

[8]The belief in reward and retribution was widespread among various professionals–prophets, priests, sages–and probably represented the view of the populace at large. The claim that a sensitive or humane concern for the defenseless (whether animal, fowl, or human) was peculiarly sapiential begs the question. Presumably, sensitive persons belonged to most, if not all, ranks of life.

[9]Priestly and royal interests probably enlisted the service of most scribes. Sages did not restrict their activity to the written word. They taught and learned largely through oral pedagogy, and the verb "to write" occurs only five times (once in Sirach) in canonical wisdom. The oral nature of Israelite society has been highlighted by Susan Niditch, *Oral World and Written Word: Ancient Israelite Literature* (Louisville: Westminster/John Knox Press, 1996).

[10]Particularism, collections of laws, curses, narratives exalting the deity, and a host of similar features place Deuteronomy in a different world from wisdom literature.

[11]*Deuteronomy and the Deuteronomic School*, 320–65 (Appendix A). In the Preface, Weinfeld insists that this Appendix is "a vital part of the work, since style is the only objective criterion for determining whether a biblical passages is Deuteronomic or not." Just how objective the material really is remains questionable. The conclusions drawn from similarities in phraseology are highly subjective. Louis Stulman, *The Prose Sermons of the Book of Jeremiah. A Redescription of the Correspondences with Deuteronomistic Literature in the Light of Recent Text-Critical Research* (Atlanta: Scholars Press, 1986) 44 views the phrase *qr' welō' 'nh* as similar to Deuteronomic language although it never occurs in Deuteronomy! The expression appears in Prov 1:28 (*'az yiqrā'unnî welō' 'eʿeneh*).

[12]James L. Crenshaw, "Prohibitions in Proverbs and Qoheleth," 115–24 in *Priests, Prophets, and Scribes*, ed. E. Ulrich et. al. (Sheffield: JSOT Press, 1992) and *Urgent Advice and Probing Questions*, 417–25. On the sayings of Agur, see Crenshaw, "Clanging Symbols," 51–64 in *Justice and the Holy*, ed. D. A. Knight and P. J. Paris (Philadelphia: Fortress Press, 1989) and *Urgent Advice and Probing Questions*, 371–82.

[13]Weinfeld concedes this fact (*Deuteronomy and the Deuteronomic School*, 262). He claims that a new concept of wisdom emerged during the time of Hezekiah, "which marked the beginning of Deuteronomic literary activity" (p. 255). "The Deuteronomist no longer conceived of 'wisdom' as meaning cunning, pragmatic talent, or the possession of extraordinary knowledge, but held it to be synonymous with the knowledge and understanding of proper behaviour and with morality"). In Weinfeld's opinion, an ideological conflict resulted: human wisdom was no longer knowledge of nature and human nature but expressed itself in fear of God.

[14]See the perceptive remarks on colophons by Michael Fishbane, *Biblical Interpretation in Ancient Israel* (Oxford: Clarendon Press, 1985) 27–32.

[15]This translation assumes an original balanced parallelism of *'almānâ* and *yetômîm* (cf. the Instruction of Amenemopet 6).

[16]Michael Fishbane, *Biblical Interpretation in Ancient Israel, passim*, has shown how extraordinarily gifted editors were in handling older traditions, but such practice obscures relationships between texts. With minimal affinities between a supposed original and its adaptation, one comes up against the strong possibility that the overlap in expression is purely accidental.

[17]Amenemopet 6 ("Do not carry off the landmark at the boundaries of the arable land, Nor disturb the position of the measuring-cord; Be not greedy after a cubit of land, Nor encroach upon the boundaries of a widow," *ANET*, 422).

[18]Instructions from ancient Egypt use the expression, "an abomination of the gods," quite freely (cf. Amenemopet 13, "Do not confuse a man with a pen upon papyrus–the

abomination of the god," "Amenemopet 10, "Do not talk with a man falsely–the abomination of the god," *ANET*, 423).

[19]One difference between Egyptian wisdom and similar texts in Mesopotamia and the Bible is noteworthy: the address, "my son," occurs at the beginning, with a single exception. Sumerian and biblical sages intersperse the expression, "my son," throughout the teaching.

[20]Here I disagree with Weinfeld, *Deuteronomy and the Deuteronomic School*, 244–81.

[21]The importance of land to anyone in Israel during the biblical period seems obvious, inasmuch as most people's survival depended on its yield. They harvested grain, grapes, olives, figs, cucumbers, and similar crops, and their small cattle (sheep and goats) required enough land to survive the hostile environment. On the role of various members of an Israelite family, see Leo G. Perdue et. al. *Families in Ancient Israel* (Louisville: Westminster/John Knox, 1997). The contributors to this volume are Joseph Blenkinsopp, John J. Collins, Carol Meyers, and Perdue.

[22]Weinfeld, *Deuteronomy and the Deuteronomic School*, 274–81 (fear of God), 316–19 (theodicy), 307–13 (reward).

[23]Weinfeld, *Deuteronomy and the Deuteronomic School*, 274–5 acknowledges that the concept of fear of the god has no national limitations.

[24]James L. Crenshaw, ed., *Theodicy in the Old Testament* (Philadelphia & London: Fortress Press & SPCK, 1983). The importance of this concept to the author of Genesis 18 has recently claimed my attention. See "The Sojourner Has Come to Play the Judge: Theodicy on Trial," chapter 22 in this volume, originally published in *God in the Fray: A Tribute to Walter Brueggemann*, eds. Tod Linafelt and Timoty K. Beal (Minneapolis: Fortress Press, 1998), 83-92.

[25]The presence of harsh discipline in pedagogical settings makes a saying like, "Without love there can be no instruction" stand out all the more. It is not clear precisely what this Egyptian saying implies: That learning requires love for the subject matter, love for the student, love for the teacher, or all the above. Mutuality of interest must surely be present before learning takes place.

[26]Qoheleth represents a distancing from the deity, both with respect to the designation for God (Elohim in Qoheleth, Yahweh in Deuteronomy) and in the avoidance of a personal pronoun attached to the word for deity. On the text, see James L. Crenshaw, *Ecclesiastes* (Philadelphia: The Westminster Press, 1987) 116–7.

[27]Gerald T. Sheppard, "The Epilogue to Qoheleth as Theological Commentary," *CBQ* 39 (1977) 182–9 and *Wisdom as a Hermeneutical Construct* (*BZAW* 151; Berlin & New York: Walter de Gruyter, 1980). Choon-Leon Seow, "'Beyond Them, My Son, Be Warned': The Epilogue of Qoheleth Revisited," 125–41 in *Wisdom, You Are My Sister*, does not consider the epilogue to be alien to the teachings of the rest of the book ("Only vv 13b-14 may be regarded as secondary, but like vv 9–13a, the content of these verses is not contrary to the rest of the book," p. 141). The perspective is not far different, Seow writes, from that expressed in Deut 4:6.

[28]John Bright, *Jeremiah* (Garden City, N.Y: Doubleday, 1965) and Artur Weiser, *The Psalms* (Philadelphia: Westminster Press, 1962) have rightly recognized the presence of a liturgical mode of discourse in the time of Jeremiah and later, a style that resembles didactic expressions in Deuteronomy. If they are right, one need not assume that a biblical book, specifically Deuteronomy, shaped the language and style.

[29]Weinfeld, *Deuteronomy and the Deuteronomic School,* passim.

[30]James L. Crenshaw, "The Restraint of Reason, the Humility of Prayer," *Urgent Advice and Probing Questions*, 206–21 traces the development of prayer in sapiential circles, particularly in Sirach.

[31]The ancestry of religious language in Deutero-Isaiah probably includes royal boasts from Mesopotamia, as well as lyrical texts.

[32]Weinfeld, *Deuteronomy and the Deuteronomic School,* Appendix A.

[33]Space does not permit a detailed discussion of these biblical books.

[34]Raymond F. Person, *Second Zechariah and the Deuteronomic School* (JSOTSup 167; Sheffield: Academic Press, 1993) 146–75 thinks a Deuteronomic school continued in the exile, returning to Yehud with Zerubbabel and later becoming disenchanted with Ezra because of his ties with the Achaemenids. Person views the increase in eschatology as one result of their disappointment. He also senses a change in Deuteronomic language over the years (p. 98) and a vigorous interpretive community (p. 103).

[35]A sharper contrast with Deuteronomy's preoccupation with Yahweh's "hands-on" approach to governing the chosen people can scarcely be imagined.

[36]The choice of texts to annotate almost never expresses itself in such a way as to reveal the rationale behind it. Some texts seem to have cried out for editorial revision, but none occurred; others appear to have been dragged, kicking and screaming, through a process of virtual reformulation.

[37]World views may have clashed in this instance, as the scholarly discussion about the absence of any reference to God in the book of Esther indicates rather emphatically.

[38]Person, *Second Zechariah and the Deuteronomic School*, relies heavily on social setting and linguistic affinities.

[39]I examine the evidence for literacy in ancient Israel in *Education in Ancient Israel: Across the Deadening Silence;* Anchor Bible Reference Library (New York: Doubleday, 1998).

[40]Lohfink, "Gab es ein deuteronomistische Bewegnung?"

[41]The first Greek private library seems to date from the third century B.C.E.

[42]William V. Harris, *Ancient Literacy* (Cambridge: Harvard University Press, 1989) mentions the various factors that made literacy possible on a wider scale. These include the invention of the printing press, the availability of cheap paper, Protestantism's emphasis on reading the Bible, the invention of eye glasses, the industrial revolution with its need for literate supervisors, philanthropy, and density of population. An agricultural economy in Israel presented a natural hindrance to formal education, for children were needed to assist in the almost endless tasks associated with farming.

[43]The Instruction for Duauf (Satire of the Trades) from ancient Egypt offers an example of scribal elitism and disdain for other trades, whereas the similar text in Sirach 38:24–39:11 states that society cannot exist without the services of such workers.

[44]James L. Crenshaw, "The Primacy of Listening in Ben Sira's Pedagogy," in chapter 3 above, originally published in *Wisdom, You Are My Sister. Studies in Honor of Roland E. Murphy, O. Carm., on the Occasion of His Eightieth Birthday*, ed. Michael L. Barré (CBQMS 29; Washington, D.C.: The Catholic Biblical Association of America, 1997), 172–187.

[45]Lohfink, "Gab es ein deuteronomistiche Bewegnung?" states that, besides Essene writings, Qumran has yielded thirty three exemplars of the Psalter, twenty-seven of Deuteronomy, twenty of Isaiah, and sixteen of Jubilees.

[46]In Mesopotamia omen texts played a central role in predicting the future, and access to crucial documents belonged to a few knowledgeable scribes. Esotericism thrived in Jewish apocalyptic circles, and conscious efforts at concealing data by means of coded language came to prominence. In addition, apocalyptic authors wrote under the names of well-known figures from the distant past. For such deception to succeed, their followers claimed that the texts had been hidden among the faithful for generations.

[47]The sacred word was thought to have been invested with profound meaning that had to be interpreted by discerning students. Those who searched out the right interpretation (*pešer*) of a text became convinced of its awesome mystery (*raz*).

[48]Lutz Schrader, *Leiden und Gerechtigkeit. Studien zu Theologie und Textgeschichte des Sirachbuches* (BbETh 27; Frankfurt et. al.: Peter Lang, 1994) reckons with minor textual additions during the Maccabean era but does not find evidence of extensive redaction by Deuteronomistic scribes.

Chapter 15: A Living Tradition

[1]P. M. Bogaert, ed., *Le Livre de Jérémie* (Leuven: University Press, 1981).

[2]Siegfried Herrmann, "Forschung am Jeremiabuch," *ThLZ* 102 (1977) 482–90, and Georg Fohrer, "Neue Literatur zur alttestamentlichen Prophetie (1961–1970). VII. Jeremia," *ThR* 45 (1980) 109–21. See also T. R. Hobbs, "Some Remarks on the Composition and Structure of the Book of Jeremiah," *CBQ* 34 (1972) 257–75, esp. 261–67.

[3]Leo G. Perdue, "Jeremiah in Modern Research: Approaches and Issues," in Perdue and Brian W. Kovacs, eds., *A Prophet to the Nations: Essays in Jeremiah Studies* (Winona Lake, Ind.: Eisenbrauns, 1983). The following topics are discussed at length: (1) the date of Jeremiah's call, (2) Jeremiah and the Deuteronomic reform, (3) the foe from the north, (4) the text of the book, (5) the composition of the book, (6) the quest for the historical Jeremiah, and (7) new directions of research (rhetorical criticism, canonical shaping, and social dimensions).

[4]ICC (McKane); OTL (Carroll); New Century Bible (Jones); BKAT (Herrmann). John Thompson, *The Book of Jeremiah* (Grand Rapids: Wm. B. Eerdmans, 1980), provides a recent study of Jeremiah from the conservative perspective.

[5]*From Chaos to Covenant: Prophecy in the Book of Jeremiah* (New York: Crossroad, 1981), p. 11.

[6]William L. Holladay observes that there is no reason to doubt the accuracy of the account, in *The Architecture of Jeremiah 1–20* (Lewisburg and London: Bucknell University Press/ Associated University Presses, 1976), p. 174; others are not so sanguine.

[7]In this analysis Holladay differs from Claus Rietzschel, for whom the original scroll extends from 1:4 to 6:30 *(Das Problem der Urrolle: Ein Beitrag zur Redaktionsgeschichte des Jeremiabuches* [Gütersloh: Gerd Mohn, 1966]).

[8]*Jeremiah: A Study in Ancient Hebrew Rhetoric,* SBLDS 18 (Missoula, Mont.: Scholars Press, 1975).

[9]Carroll raises similar objections: "The way the chiasmus has been fractured by redaction or transmission makes one less impressed by the claims of Lundbom and Holladay for rhetorical criticism. It is an important approach to the text, but the redaction or transmission has been content to destroy the chiastic symmetry in order to incorporate into the statement a number of elements from the tradition" *(From Chaos to Covenant,* p. 294).

[10]*Die Prosareden des Jeremiabuches,* BZAW 132 (Berlin and New York: Walter de Gruyter, 1973), and "Der Beitrag ausserbiblischer Prophetentexte zum Verständnis der Prosareden des Jeremiabuches," in *Le Livre de Jérémie,* pp. 83–104.

[11]Holladay concurs in her judgment that the prose sermons go back to Jeremiah, but differs from her over Deuteronomic influence, which he thinks is very real. See "A Fresh Look at 'Source B' and 'Source C' in Jeremiah," *VT* 25 (1975) 394–412, esp. 409–12.

[12]"The Date of the Prose Sermons of Jeremiah," *JBL* 70 (1951) 15–35. See also *Jeremiah,* AB 2 (Garden City, N.Y: Doubleday & Co., 1965).

[13]"Here it is a matter of phraseology in public worship" (*The Old Testament: Its Formation and Development* [New York: Association Press, 1961], p. 217).

[14]A. Vanlier Hunter denies the view that prophets endeavored to call the people to repentance. In his opinion, the exhortations are subsumed under the larger sentence of a judgment that has already been established *(Seek the Lord! A Study of the Meaning and Function of the Exhortations in Amos, Hosea, Isaiah, Micah, and Zephaniah* [Baltimore: St. Mary's Seminary and University, 1982]). The issue is more complex than that in my judgment. I am not prepared to rule out altogether a summons to repentance as an intrinsic function of Israelite prophecy.

[15]"'Source B' and 'Source C' in Jeremiah," pp. 410–11.

[16]"Jeremiah and Deuteronomy," *JNES* 1 (1942) 156–73. See also "The Deuteronomic Edition of Jeremiah," *Vanderbilt Studies in the Humanities* 1 (1951) 71–95.

[17]*Preaching to the Exiles* (Oxford: Basil Blackwell, 1970).

[18]*Ibid.,* p. 134. See also E. Janssen, *Juda in der Exilzeit,* FRLANT 69 (Göttingen: Vandenhoeck und Ruprecht, 1956), p. 107.

[19]*Die deuteronomistische Redaktion von Jeremia 1–25,* WMANT 41 (Neukirchen-Vluyn: Neukirchener Verlag, 1973), and *Die deuteronomistische Redaktion von Jeremia 26–45,* WMANT 52 (Neukirchen-Vluyn: Neukirchener Verlag, 1981). William McKane has pointed to the various levels on which such statistical analyses as Thiel's and Weippert's function and has demonstrated the complexity of the problem by focusing upon two brief texts ("Relations Between Poetry and Prose in the Book of Jeremiah with Special Reference to Jeremiah III 6–11 and XII 14–17," VTSup, *Congress Volume, Vienna* [Leiden: E. J. Brill, 1981], pp. 220–37). I share McKane's caution with regard to such endeavors as those represented by Thiel and Weippert.

[20]*Untersuchungen zur sogenannten Baruchschrift,* BZAW 122 (New York and Berlin: Walter de Gruyter, 1971). See also Karl-Friedrich Pohlmann, who views certain texts, esp. 37–44, as fourth-century apologetic in behalf of the Babylonian exiles at the expense of those Jews who remained in Judah or who subsequently emigrated to Egypt (*Studien zum Jeremiabuch,* FRLANT 118 [Göttingen: Vandenhoeck und Ruprecht, 1978]).

[21]James Muilenburg, "It has been our contention that the so-called 'Deuteronomic additions' by no means represent a separate source, but conform to conventional scribal composition and are therefore to be assigned to Baruch" ("Baruch the Scribe," in John I.

Durham and J. R. Porter, eds., *Proclamation and Presence* [London: SCM Press, 1970], pp. 215–38; p. 237 cited).

[22]"Leidensgemeinschaft mit Gott im Alten Testament," *EvTh* 13 (1953) 122–40.

[23]*Old Testament Theology* (New York: Harper & Row, 1965), 2:206–8.

[24]*From Chaos to Covenant*, p. 210.

[25]"'Gathering and Return' in Jeremiah and Ezekiel," in *Le Livre de Jérémie*, pp. 119–42.

[26]J. Gerald Janzen, *Studies in the Text of Jeremiah*, HSM 6 (Cambridge: Harvard University Press, 1973).

[27]*From Chaos to Covenant*, p. 255.

[28]*Ibid.*, p. 25.

[29]*Ibid.*, p. 151.

[30]Ibid., p. 228.

[31]"Jer 18, 18–23 im Zusammenhang der Konfessionen," in *Le Livre de Jérémie*, pp. 271-96; and *Untersuchungen zu den Konfessionen Jer 11, 18–12, 2 und Jer 15, 10–21*, FzB 30 (Zurich: Echter Verlag, 1978).

[32]"Essai de Redaktionsgeschichte des 'Confessions de Jérémie,'" in *Le Livre de Jérémie*, pp. 239–70.

[33]*Liturgie und prophetisches Ich bei Jeremia* (Gütersloh: Gerd Mohn, 1963). Compare Erhard Gerstenberger, "Jeremiah's Complaints: Observations on Jeremiah 15:10–21," where it is argued that an older layer, vv. 10–11, was augmented in the tradition by 15–21, and still later by 13–14 (*JBL* 82 [1963] 393–408).

[34]Berridge, *Prophet, People, and the Word of Yahweh* (Zurich: EVZ Verlag, 1970); Bright, "Jeremiah's Complaints: Liturgy, or Expressions of Personal Distress?" in *Proclamation and Presence*, pp. 189–214; idem, "A Prophet's Lament and Its Answer: Jeremiah 15:10–21," *Int* 28 (1974) 59–74 ("His faith was neither serene nor unshakable; on the contrary, there were times when it crumbled beneath him and spilled him into the pit of despair," p. 69); and Blank, "The Prophet as Paradigm," in James L. Crenshaw and John T Willis, eds., *Essays in Old Testament Ethics* (New York: KTAV, 1974), pp. 111–30. See also Muilenburg, "The Terminology of Adversity in Jeremiah," in Harry Thomas Frank and William L. Reed, eds., *Translating and Understanding the Old Testament* (Nashville: Abingdon Press, 1970), pp. 42–63.

[35]"Die Konfessionen Jeremias," *EvTh* 3 (1936) 265–76, published in Eng. trans. in *Theodicy in the Old Testament* (Philadelphia: Fortress Press and London: SPCK, 1983).

[36]"Wisdom and Not: The Case of Mesopotamia," *JAOS* 101 (1981) 42–44.

[37]"A Coherent Chronology of Jeremiah's Early Career," in *Le Livre de Jérémie*, pp. 58–73.

[38]"Der junge Jeremia als Propagandist und Poet: Zum Grundstock von Jer 30–31," in *Le Livre de Jérémie*, pp. 351–68.

[39]W. A. M. Beuken and H. M. W. van Grol, "Jeremiah 14, 1–15, 9: A Situation of Distress and Its Hermeneutics. Unity and Diversity of Form–Dramatic Development," in *Le Livre de Jérémie*, pp. 297–342. While the emphasis falls on unity of structure and drama, the authors do think the text can derive from Jeremiah or nearly so. Holladay would seem to be even more convinced of the Jeremianic origin of this text, at least in nucleus (14:2–6; 15:5–9; *The Architecture of Jeremiah 1–20*, pp. 147–48).

[40]*From Chaos to Covenant*, p. 105.

[41]*Ibid.*, p. 77.

[42]*Ibid.*, pp. 115, 124.

[43]*Ibid.*, p. 261.

[44]"Forschung am Jeremiabuch," p. 488.

[45]For recent discussion of this fascinating text, see Werner E. Lemke, "The Way of Obedience: 1 Kings 13 and the Structure of the Deuteronomistic History," in Frank M. Cross, Werner E. Lemke, and Patrick D. Miller, eds., *Magnalia Dei: The Mighty Acts of God* (Garden City, N.Y: Doubleday & Co., 1976), pp. 301–26.

[46]For works prior to 1971, see my *Prophetic Conflict: Its Effect Upon Israelite Religion*, BZAW 124 (Berlin and New York: Walter de Gruyter, 1971). *A* more recent discussion of the problem is by James A. Sanders, "Hermeneutics in True and False Prophecy," in George W. Coats and Burke O. Long, eds., *Canon and Authority* (Philadelphia: Fortress Press, 1977), pp. 21–41.

[47]*Jeremia und die falschen Propheten, Orbis Biblicus et Orientalis* 13 (Freiburg: Universitätsverlag; Göttingen: Vandenhoeck und Ruprecht, 1977).

[48]I have tried to address this issue in several recent studies, the latest of which is "Wisdom and Authority: Sapiential Rhetoric and Its Warrants," VTSup, *Congress Volume,*

Vienna (1980), pp. 10–29. A recent analysis of a text in Jeremiah by Phyllis Trible is especially pertinent here: "The Gift of a Poem: A Rhetorical Study of Jeremiah 31:15–22," *ANQ* 17 (1977) 271–80.

[49]*From Chaos to Covenant,* p. 319.

[50]He argues that Jeremiah championed older Ephraimite traditions and was supported by certain Levitical groups and kinsmen. If the materials on which Wilson draws have undergone extensive editing, his historical conclusions become problematic *(Prophecy and Society in Ancient Israel* [Philadelphia: Fortress Press, 1980]).

[51]"The Ghost Dance of 1980 and the Nature of the Prophetic Process," *Ethnohistory* 21 (1974) 37–63. See also "Jeremiah and the Nature of the Prophetic Process," in *Scripture in History and Theology: Essays in Honor of J. Coert Rylaarsdam* (Pittsburgh: Pickwick Press, 1977), pp. 129–50.

[52]Two things dominate the discussion: the conditions of the moral agent (rationality, volition, affectivity, sociality, temporality, and historicality) and the ambiguity of hope. Knight concludes that Jeremiah adopted an equivocal position on the question of moral freedom ("Jeremiah and the Dimensions of the Moral Life," in James L. Crenshaw and Samuel Sandmel, eds., *The Divine Helmsman* [New York: KTAV, 1980], pp. 87–105, esp. pp. 100–101).

[53]I have reference here to David Noel Freedman's simplistic solution to the problem of determining authentic prophecy: "Pottery, Poetry, and Prophecy: An Essay on Biblical Poetry," *JBL* 96 (1977) 5–26, esp. 24–26.

[54]For an assessment of Carroll's book see Gordon H. Matties's review, *CBQ* 45/2 (1983): 276–80.

[55]*From Chaos to Covenant,* p. 278.

[56]Muilenburg, "The Terminology for Adversity in Jeremiah," in *Proclamation and Presence,* p. 62. Jeremiah 20:7 advances beyond an apparent absent or neutral God to one who seduces and overpowers innocent people. I intend to publish a monograph on this perception of God as "enemy" in the near future.

Chapter 16: Who Knows What YHWH Will Do?

[1]The longer form of this confessional statement, Exod 34:6–7, probably belongs together despite arguments to the contrary by J. Scharbert, "Formgeschichte und Exegese von Ex 34,6f. und seiner Parallelen," *Bib* 38 (1957) 130–50. Its unity is defended by R. C. Dentan, "The Literary Affinities of Exodus XXXIV 6f," *VT* 13 (1963) 34–41. Chastened Israelites had little inclination during prayer and praise to remind the deity of the negative attributes recorded in v. 7, hence later divine predications invariably concentrate on YHWH's compassionate nature, on which see P. Trible, *God and the Rhetoric of Sexuality* (OBT; Philadelphia: Fortress, 1978) 1–5; L. Schmidt, *"De Deo": Studien zur Literarkritik und Theologie des Buches Jona, des Gesprächs zwischen Abraham und Jahve in Gen. 18, 22ff. und von Hi 1* (BZAW 143; Berlin and New York: de Gruyter, 1976) 90–96; G. Vanoni, *Das Buch Jona* (St. Ottilien: Eos, 1978) 139–41; D. N. Freedman, "God Compassionate and Gracious," *Western Watch* 6 (1955) 6–24; T. B. Dozeman, "Inner-Biblical Interpretation of Yahweh's Gracious and Compassionate Character," *JBL* (1989) 207–23; and above all, M. Fishbane, *Biblical Interpretation in Ancient Israel* (Oxford: Clarendon, 1985) 335–50 for a more nuanced view.

[2]Considerable light has been shed on locust infestation in ancient Israel by J. A. Thompson, "Joel's Locusts in the Light of Near Eastern Parallels," *JNES* 14 (1955) 52–55; and R. Simkins, *Yahweh's Activity in History and Nature in the Book of Joel* (Ancient Near Eastern Texts and Studies 10; Lewiston et al.: Mellen, 1991). Popular fascination with this insect is beautifully illustrated by A. Taylor, "A Riddle for a Locust," in *Semitic and Oriental Studies: A Volume Presented to William Popper* (ed. W. J. Fischel; University of California Publications in Semitic Philology 11; Berkeley: University of California, 1951) 429–32.

[3]J. Bourke ("Le jour de Yahwe dans Joël," *RB* 66 [1959] 5–31, 191–212) concludes his exhaustive examination of the day of YHWH by isolating three principal themes in Joel (the day of YHWH combined with an army from afar, destruction and restoration of fertility, and an eschatological era) and three lines of tradition (the day of YHWH, the Deuteronomic school, and exilic and postexilic eschatology). In quite a different vein, F. E. Deist ("Parallels and Reinterpretation in the Book of Joel: A Theology of the Yom Yahweh," in *Text and Context: Old Testament and Semitic Studies for F. C. Fensham* [ed. W. Claassen; JSOTSup 48; Sheffield: JSOT, 1988] 63–79) understands the locusts and drought as purely literary metaphors for the horrors inaugurated by the day of YHWH. Deist thinks the book

of Joel has three or four interpretations of the day (anti-Canaanite [?], theophanic and judgmental, eschatological, and apocalyptic). Y. Hoffmann ("The Day of the Lord as a Concept and a Term in the Prophetic Literature," *ZAW* 93 [1981] 37–50) limits the expression to an eschatological sense (cf. K.-D. Schunck, "Strukturlinien in der Entwicklung der Vorstellung vom 'Tag Jahwes,'" *VT* 14 [1964] 319–30), thus rejecting the wide basis for analysis adopted by G. von Rad, "The Origin of the Concept of the Day of Yahweh," *JSS* 4 (1959) 97–108; M. Weiss, "The Origin of the Day of Yahweh, Reconsidered,' *HUCA* 37 (1966) 29–72; and A. J. Everson, "The Days of Yahweh," *JBL* 93 (1974) 329–37.

[4]D. W. Cotter's remark about Eliphaz's initial speech also applies to Bildad and Zophar ("There is, in fact, no word of sympathy in the whole poem. What there is is a succession of sixteen verbal punches, sixteen 'your's' as Eliphaz relentlessly separates himself from the sufferer"; *A Study of Job 4–5 in the Light of Contemporary Literary Theory* [SBLDS 124; Atlanta: Scholars, 1992] 239). The possibility that Job may be the object of parody or satire has been advanced by B. Zuckerman (*Job the Silent* [New York: Oxford University, 1991]) and K. J. Dell (*The Book of Job as Sceptical Literature* [BZAW 197; Berlin and New York: de Gruyter, 1991]), whose history of interpretation of Job complements that by N. N. Glatzer ("The Book of Job and its Interpreters," in *Biblical Motifs* [ed. A. Altmann; P. W. Lown Institute of Advanced Judaic Studies, Studies and Texts 3; Cambridge: Harvard University, 1966] 197–220).

[5]The exclusive emphasis on YHWH's control of historical events has receded in more recent studies, beginning with B. Albrektson, *History and the Gods* (ConBOT 1; Lund: Gleerup, 1967) and chronicled in R. Gnuse, *Heilsgeschichte as a Model for Biblical Theology* (College Theological Society Studies in Religion 4 [Lanham, New York, and London: University Press of America, 1989]). T. N. D. Mettinger (*In Search of God* [Philadelphia: Fortress, 1988] 175–200) brings this research into the realm of sapiential studies, on which see L. Boström, *The God of the Sages* (ConBOT 29; Stockholm: Almqvist & Wiksell International, 1990), and J. L. Crenshaw, "The Concept of God in Old Testament Wisdom," 3–18 in *In Search of Wisdom: Essays in Memory of John G. Gammie* (ed. L. G. Perdue, B. B. Scott, and W. J. Wiseman [Louisville, KY: Westminster/John Knox, 1993]).

[6]See E. Sellin, *Das Zwölfprophetenbuch* (KAT 12/1; Leipzig: A. Deichertsche...D. Werner Schoff, 1929); H. W. Wolff, *Joel and Amos* (trans. W. Janzen et al.; Hermeneia; Philadelphia: Fortress, 1977) 48; and H. A. Brongers, "Bemerken zum Gebrauch des adverbialen *wᵉʿattāh* im Alten Testament," *VT* 15 (1965) 289–99.

[7]Despite the difficulty presented by this extraordinary statement and laid out clearly by E. M. Good, *In Turns of Tempest* (Stanford: Stanford University, 1990) 248–50, one can make reasonable sense of it as a figure parallel to the Advocate, one who will "stir God to perform his *opus proprium*" (N. Habel, *The Book of Job* [OTL; Philadelphia: Westminster, 1985] 275). This view avoids the common interpretation of a schizophrenic deity and the alternative understanding of the witness as a rival tutelary deity. In this unknown witness Job hopes to find a mediator who will vouch for him in Eloah's presence.

[8]With the addition of *biśpātāyw* ("with his lips") to the narrator's denial that Job had sinned (2:10; cf. 1:22), the floodgates open wide for accusing him of rash thoughts "in the heart," as ancient interpreters quickly recognized. J. T. Wilcox (*The Bitterness of Job* [Ann Arbor: University of Michigan, 1989]) continues that tradition, now in a philosophical vein. In his view, Job cursed God by means of moral bitterness, being both ignorant and weak, and was reminded of nature's grandeur devoid of morality. This profoundly skeptical reading of the biblical book is marred by special pleading about weakened authorial powers whenever a text presents difficulty for Wilcox's thesis, a weakness not afflicting a similar denial of justice in the world by M. Tsevat, "The Meaning of the Book of Job," *HUCA* 37 (1966) 73–106.

[9]J. Fokkelman (*Narrative Art in Genesis* [Assen and Amsterdam: Van Gorcum, 1975] 50–51) recognizes that *hinnēh* often marks a shift in narrative point of view from third-person omniscience to that of the person involved in the story.

[10]See F. Baumgärtel, "Die Formel *ne'um Jahwe*," *ZAW* 73 (1961) 277–90; and D. Vetter, "*ne'um* Ausspruch," *THAT* 2.2–3.

[11]Unless an omniscient narrator is viewed as having the last word in any written text.

[12]On these prophets see C. L. and E. M. Meyers, *Haggai, Zechariah 1–8* (AB 25B; Garden City, NY: Doubleday, 1987); and D. L. Petersen, *Haggai and Zechariah 1–8* (OTL; Philadelphia: Westminster, 1984).

[13]Two of the three occurrences of *nĕ'um-YHWH* (2:16, 21) are in a section often denied to Hosea on other grounds: the reversal of the prophet's judgment on the nation, Israel. The other one is in 11:11, also a text indicating a date after YHWH's people had been driven into foreign lands.

[14]Dialogue between a prophet and the deity, on the one hand, and hymnic praise, on the other hand.

[15]See Wolff, *Joel and Amos*, 48; W. Rudolph, *Joel-Amos-Obadja-Jona* (KAT 13/2; Gütersloh: Mohn, 1971) 50.

[16]See W. S. Prinsloo, *The Theology of the Book of Joel* (BZAW 163; Berlin and New York: de Gruyter, 1985) 50.

[17]See J. L. Crenshaw, "A Liturgy of Wasted Opportunity: Am. 4:6–12; Isa 9:7–10:4," *Semitics* 1 (1971) 27–37. Lexical analysis of the verb *šûb* has been provided by W. L. Holladay, *The Root šûbh in the Old Testament* (Leiden: Brill, 1958), and a survey of research appears in J. M. Bracke, "*šûb šebut:* A Reappraisal," *ZAW* 97 (1985) 233–44. H. W. Wolff ("Das Theme 'Umkehr' in der alttestamentliche Prophetie," *ZTK* 49 [1951] 129–48) treats the general concept of returning, as does T. M. Raitt ("The Prophetic Summons to Repentance," *ZAW* 83 [1971] 30–49).

[18]G. W. Ahlström (*Joel and the Temple Cult of Jerusalem* [VTSup 21; Leiden: Brill, 1971] 26) argues from Joel's use of the stronger preposition *'āday* rather than *'ēlay* that the people have turned to worshiping other gods.

[19]Wolff (*Joel and Amos*, 48–53) locates the fault in the people's reliance on the fact that they were YHWH's inheritance, which seemed in their minds to guarantee divine favor. In Wolff's view, the issue is one of God's freedom, which Joel zealously guards.

[20]See G. Wanke, "Prophecy and Psalms in the Persian Period," in *The Cambridge History of Judaism* (ed. W. D. Davies and L. Finkelstein; Cambridge: Cambridge University, 1984) 177. Wanke writes that "the only suggestion of a criticism of the people of Jerusalem may be contained in 2:12f, where too intensive an orientation toward external ritual can dimly be perceived as a cause for lament."

[21]P. L. Redditt ("The Book of Joel and Peripheral Prophecy," *CBQ* 48 [1986] 225–40) claims that Joel's accusations against cultic leaders eventually pushed him and his followers to the periphery of society, thus limiting his effectiveness appreciably. The category of peripheral, as opposed to central, prophecy informs R. R. Wilson's study of biblical prophecy, *Prophecy and Society in Ancient Israel* (Philadelphia: Fortress, 1980).

[22]See L. C. Allen, *The Books of Joel, Obadiah, Jonah and Micah* (NICOT; Grand Rapids: Eerdmans, 1976) 77–84. Although he observes that the covenant people have "evidently strayed from their Shepherd, turning to their own way," Allen also writes that "it is evidently left to the people and priests to search their own hearts and habits for evidence of the sin that God's reaction proved to be there" (78–79). In Allen's view, Joel's interpretation of the locust plague presupposes serious sin, but he fails to use the normal place in the rhetoric of v. 12 to mention the people's sin.

[23]Simkins, *Yahweh's Activity*, 181–90.

[24]H. J. Stoebe, "*rḥm* pi. sich erbarmen," *THAT* 2.762–68.

[25]The inner attitude is matched by word and deed, the heart and tongue being motivated by turning to YHWH. According to T. Collins, "The Physiology of Tears in the Old Testament," *CBQ* 33 (1971) 18–38, 185–97, *bkh* ("weeping") comes from the mouth and voice, whereas *dm'* ("shedding tears") originates in the eyes (see also V. Hamp, "*bākâ*," TDOT 2.116–20, esp. 117). The verb *bākâ* is therefore often connected with the voice, *qōl*. Although YHWH may become angry (*k's*) and grieve (*'ṣb*), he is never described as weeping. Hamp has observed that "collective penitent weeping is typically biblical, and is just as foreign to Greek texts of lamentation as is the weeping of imploring and hoping in prayer" (119).

[26]The prophet uses four different verbs for weeping and fasting, *bkh* and *nzr* in 7:3, *ṣwm* and *spd* in 7:5. The combination of second person plural and infinitive absolute in 7:5 (*ṣamtem wĕsāpôd*) stresses interrelatedness and intensity, providing an absolute contrast with v. 6 (Meyers, *Haggai and Zechariah 1–8*, 388).

[27]Nor did such unconventional behavior by a monarch bring about a change in custom. G. A. Anderson (*A Time to Mourn, A Time to Dance* [University Park, PA: Pennsylvania State University, 1991] 2) emphasizes the performative elements of such epiphenomena as constitutive rather than ornamental. Accordingly, he understands expressions of grief and

joy as creators of emotion instead of the other way around, the grief producing signs of sorrow. In this regard he follows C. Geertz, who views religion as a powerful symbolic system that produces corresponding moods and motivations. In short, religions shape reality (5–9). On this reading, when David's penitential rite failed to produce the desired result, he naturally brought it to an end and resumed ordinary activities, particularly sexual joy (83–84).

[28]The story in 2 Kgs 20:1–11 interprets a reprieve in Hezekiah's illness as YHWH's favorable response to a tearful king who was able to call to divine memory a life characterized by faithfulness (*zĕkār-nāʾ ʾet ʾăšer hithallaktî lĕpāneykā beʾemet ûbĕlēbāb šālēm,* "remember that I have walked before you faithfully and with an undivided mind"). The shift from the verb *bkh* in v. 3 to *dmʿ* in v. 5 may focus attention on the total act of grief (*wayyēbĕkĕ ḥizqîyāhû bĕkî gādôl...rāʾîtî ʾet-dimʿātekā,* "Hezekiah wept mightily...I have seen your tears").

[29]A similar ambiguity marks the text in Exod 34:6, which can be translated as a proclamation by YHWH or by Moses. The Masoretic accentuation favors Moses as speaker: *wayyaʿabōr YHWH ʿal-pānāyw wayyiqrāʾ YHWH YHWH ʾēl raḥûm weḥannûn* ("YHWH passed by him and he called out, 'YHWH, YHWH, a compassionate and gracious God'"). One can ignore the conjunctive accent linking the two instances of the divine name and the disjunctive accent on the verb *qrʾ*, yielding "YHWH passed by him and YHWH called out, 'YHWH, a compassionate and gracious God."' The shorter version in Num 14:17–18 attributes the proclamation to the deity. On the divided views of modern scholars over the translation of Exod 34:6 see B. S. Childs, *The Book of Exodus* (OTL; Philadelphia: Westminster, 1974) 603–4.

[30]The larger context of this metaphor for inner transformation includes YHWH's invitation for the people to turn away from inappropriate conduct (*ʾim-tāšûb yiśrāʾēl nĕʾum YHWH ʾēlay tāšûb,* "If you want to return, Israel, return to me," Jer 4:1a).

[31]Dozeman ("Inner-Biblical Interpretation") argues that both Joel and Jonah offer conscious commentary on the implications of the covenant formulary, with completely opposite emphases. Whereas Joel concerns himself with showing how the divine attributes furnish a basis for belief in the eventual elevation of Judeans at the expense of the nations, the book of Jonah includes the worst foreign nation, Assyria, as an object of YHWH's gracious pity.

[32]Joel has *kî-ḥannûn wĕraḥûm hûʾ,* but first person speech characterizes Exod 33:19 (*wĕḥannōtî ʾet-ʾăšer ʾāḥōn wĕriḥamtî ʾet-ʾăšer ʾăraḥēm,* "I shall be gracious toward whom I wish to favor and I shall have compassion on whom I desire to be compassionate").

[33]YHWH YHWH *ʾēl raḥûm weḥannûn ʾerek ʾappayim werab-ḥesed weʾemet* (Exod 34:6) and *kî-ḥannûn wĕraḥûm hûʾ: ʾerek ʾappaʾyim wĕrab-ḥesed* (Joel 2:13bβ).

[34]J. Magonet (*Form and Meaning: Studies in Literary Techniques in the Book of Jonah* [Bible and Literature; Sheffield: Almond, 1983] 77) writes that "the coincidence of two such phrases, so clearly interrelated in each case, in such similar contexts (last opportunity for repentance before destruction comes), without some sort of mutual interrelationship is unlikely." He attributes priority to Jonah, who earlier had combined Exod 32:12 and 34:6. J. Sasson (*Jonah* [AB 24B; New York: Doubleday, 1990] 280–83) improves on Vanoni's chart of every formulation of the divine attributes; in doing so Sasson makes many astute observations about distinctive features and traits held in common among several of the seventeen texts he studies, for which he has twelve different columns.

[35]Dozeman ("Inner-Biblical Interpretation," 221–23) overlooks the expression *berākā,* while concentrating on the vocabulary for awesome deeds and the idea of mockery.

[36]S. Bergler (*Joel als Schriftinterpret* [Beiträge zur Erforschung des Alten Testaments und des antiken Judentums 16; Frankfurt-am-Main et al.: Peter Lang, 1988]) gives an exhaustive analysis of linguistic affinities between Joel and the rest of the Hebrew Bible. I cannot accept Bergler's assumptions about literary dependence, given the limited evidence and difficulty of establishing priority. Dozeman ("Inner-Biblical Interpretation," 207–9) thinks of Joel as a person who gathers allusions from a canon of sorts and arranges them into an anthology. The difficulty of demonstrating this hypothesis explains scholars' cool response to A. Robert's earlier efforts to apply such an approach to the Bible ("Littéraires, Genres," *DBSup* 5.405–21).

[37]Fishbane's *Biblical Interpretation in Ancient Israel* demonstrates the immense possibilities inherent to such an approach, but I am left with the suspicion that word choice in ancient Israel was often less dictated by intimate knowledge of written texts than by the accidents of religious language during a given era or geographical location. Can one really

imagine such scribal activity occurring in preexilic or even exilic times? The real value of Fishbane's synthesis of texts is the brilliant demonstration of the vitality of religious tradition and richness of the ancient imagination.

[38]I have described the ancient intellectual endeavor in an essay entitled "The Contemplative Life," scheduled to appear in a two-volume work on *Civilizations of the Ancient Near East,* ed. J. M. Sasson, to be published by Scribners.

[39]Fishbane *(Biblical Interpretation,* 349–50) extends the psalmic petitionary use of the attribute formulary to Mic 7:18–20. Fishbane calls it "an expression of gratitude which concludes a larger liturgical structure of lament, confession, and assurance of divine grace." The only similarities between this prophetic text and the other attributions discussed above are the name *'ēl,* the nouns *ḥesed* and *'emet,* and the verb *rḥm.*

[40]This adjective frequently conveys a forensic assessment of innocence on all charges. In Jer 12:1 the prophet concedes YHWH's innocence as a general principle before calling it into question in his special case (Jer 12:1a, *ṣaddiq 'attâ YHWH kî 'ārîb 'eleykā,* "You are innocent, YHWH, when I bring an accusation against you").

[41]The inevitable tension between justice and mercy, works and faith, law and gospel, human initiative and divine grace has invigorated Judeo-Christian theological discourse for over three millennia. Religious thinkers have emphasized one or other of the concepts, depending on the circumstances at the moment. A chastened people has sensed the need for the scales to tilt in favor of YHWH's mercy, and a proud, complacent religious community has generally evoked sterner descriptions of God from its spiritual leaders.

[42]I have examined these texts in "The Expression *mî yôdēa'* in the Hebrew Bible," *VT* 36 (1986) 274–88.

[43]Note the binary categories here, *hārā'â* in Joel 2:13 and *bĕrākâ* in the next verse. The macrostructure of the first two chapters exemplifies such binary thinking, for the restoration in Joel 2:18–27 matches in detail the things adversely affected by the invasion of locusts and accompanying drought.

[44]Simkins *(Yahweh's Activity,* 184–90) emphasizes the Mediterranean concepts of honor and shame as crucial to understanding the impact of mockery in the book of Joel. The taunt "Where is their God?" (2:17) brought dishonor to Judeans and their deity, who alone could remove their shame forever (2:26–27) and restore their former honorable status. See also M. A. Klopfenstein, *Scham und Schande nach dem Alten Testament* (ATANT 62; Zurich: Theologischer Verlag, 1972).

[45]The text of this difficult verse probably comments on *dām-nāqî* of v. 19. The Greek, Syriac, and Targumic renderings of the initial verb attest to a form of the verb *nqm,* "to avenge." The Greek translation of the second verb, *kai ou mē athōōsō* ("and I will not leave unpunished") has an imperfect verb rather than the perfect tense in Hebrew (*lō'-niqqêtî,* "I have not declared innocent"). A. S. Kapelrud (*Joel Studies* [Uppsala: A. B. Lundequistska, 1948] 175) sees *lō'* as an ancient *"la* asseverative."

[46]Schmidt *("De Deo")* concentrates on exceptions to this statement, specifically Abraham's dialogue with YHWH about the necessity of exemplifying justice to all peoples, the prologue in Job, and the characterization of YHWH in Jonah. Schmidt's outdated source criticism detracts from an important insight, which many theologians have ignored because of a bias toward divine actions.

[47]The language of this account echoes the three fundamental types of prophetic mediation: oracle, dream, and vision.

[48]See J. Jeremias, *Theophanie* (WMANT 10; Neukirchen-Vluyn: Neukirchener Verlag, 1965) and T. Hiebert, "Theophany," *ABD* 6.505–11.

[49]L. Cerny, *The Day of Yahweh and Some Relevant Problems* (Prague: Nákladem Filosofické Fakulty University Karlovy, 1948).

[50]B. S. Childs, "The Enemy from the North and the Chaos Tradition,"*JBL* 78 (1959) 187–98.

[51]See J. D. Levenson, *Sinai and Zion: An Entry into the Jewish Bible* (Minneapolis, Chicago, and New York: Winston, 1985); and R. J. Clifford, *The Cosmic Mountain in Canaan and the Old Testament* (HSM 4; Cambridge: Harvard University, 1972).

[52]See A. Kerrigan, "The 'sensus plenior' of Joel III,1–5 in Act II,14–36," in *Sacra Pagina* (ed. J. Coppens; BETL 13; Gembloux: Duculot, 1959] 295–313; and R. Albertz and C. Westermann, *Rûaḥ* Geist," *THAT* 2.726–53.

[53]W. Zimmerli, *I Am Yahweh* (trans. D. W. Stott; ed. W. Brueggemann; Atlanta: John Knox, 1982).

[54]The verb *mšl* has two different meanings, (1) to rule over and (2) to be like. The former sense would imply that Judeans deplore their subject status, whereas the second suggests that the enemies have turned the miserable circumstances of YHWH's people into a byword. The latter nuance seems the more probable one in context, although *mšl b* normally means "to rule over" and the versions translate it this way (LXX *katarxai,* Vulgate *dominentur*). Wolff (*Joel and Amos,* 52) argues for the usual meaning, "to rule over," but Simkins (*Yahweh's Activity,* 173–74) suggests that both senses may be intended, with "byword" as primary. Rudolph *(Joel-Amos-Obadja-Jona,* 53n.17) observes that "consensus of the versions is no guarantee of accuracy," for the context, especially YHWH's answer in 2:19, requires the meaning "taunt, mockery, byword." Marti *(Das Dodekapropheton* [KHCAT 13; Tübingen: Mohr/Siebeck, 1904] 130) appeals to Ezek 18:3 for translating *mšl b* as "mock" and to Jer 24:9 where *lĕḥerpâ ûlĕmāšāl* are juxtaposed as in Joel 2:17.

[55]On the meaning of 2:23, see G. W. Ahlström, *"Hămmōreh liṣdāqāh* in Joel II 23," *Congress Volume: Rome, 1968* (VTSup 17; Leiden: Brill, 1969) 25–36; idem, *Joel and the Temple Cult.* K. S. Nash ("The Palestinian Agricultural Year and the Book of Joel" [Ph.D. diss., Catholic University of America, 1989]) emphasizes changing weather patterns and a severe sirocco as the cause for dismay in the book of Joel, and O. Loretz *(Regenritual und Jahwetag im Joelbuch* [Ugaritisch-biblische Literatur 4; Altenberge: CIS, 1986]) sees the primary problem of the book as drought, to combat which the people undertake a ritual for producing rain.

[56]See C. J. Labuschagne, *The Incomparability of Yahweh in the Old Testament* (Pretoria Oriental Series 5; Leiden: Brill, 1966).

[57]Both Jeremiah and Ezekiel take up a popular proverb, accusing YHWH of acting without principle in transgenerational imputation of punishment for guilt, the essential point of Exod 34:7b (cf. Jer 31:26; Ezekiel 18).

[58]See Dozeman, "Inner-Biblical Interpretation," 221–23.

Chapter 17: Freeing the Imagination

[1]Alternatively, "And you will know that I am Yahweh, who resides in Zion..."

[2]I understand the phrase to be symbolic, like the valley of Jehoshaphat, rather than a literal valley of acacias. It therefore becomes meaningless to search for its location, whether to the west of Bethlehem in the modern Wādi-es-Sănt or to the east of Jerusalem in the Wādi-'en-Nār. My view also renders problematic Kapelrud's hypothesis about the importance of acacia wood in cultic use (170–71). Kapelrud, too, thinks the valley looks to the future. In this regard he concurs with Sellin (177), who writes that the valley (the name of which he emends to demons, *haššēdim*) is concerned with a geography of the end of the age.

[3]Context requires an objective accusative here; Judeans are victims of the crimes, not the perpetrators.

[4]Syntax favors the land of Judah rather than Egypt and Edom. Accordingly, Necho's murder of Josiah at Megiddo and Egyptian incursions by Sheshonq I and Osorkon I qualify, as do the attacks against Jehoshaphat by a coalition of Edomites, Ammonites, and Moabites. On the other hand, if "their land" refers to foreign territory, one thinks of Jeremiah and his compatriots from Mizpah who fled to Egypt and of the Jews at Elephantine, as well as Edom's harsh treatment of Judeans fleeing from Babylonians in 587.

[5]The Septuagint and the Syriac read *nqm,* avenge, in 21a while the MT reads *nqh.* I retain *nqh* in both instances of the verse, reading the first verb as a prophetic perfect.

[6]"A threshold is in fact a point of contact and of separation, the symbol of both an end and a beginning. It is static in that it marks a boundary; yet it is dynamic in that it is meant for crossing" (Buccellati: 35).

[7]Judicious use of the principle of inclusion often illuminates a text's structure, but excessive claims by some interpreters, e.g., Loader (1979) have rendered suspect any appeal to inclusion.

[8]On "bᵉyôm YHWH," see especially Hoffmann (37–50) and Bourke (5–31, 199–212).

[9]The formula combines features of recognition and self-introduction (Zimmerli: 36–40). Against my interpretation, one could argue that the statement of recognition concludes the two parts of the book, with 4:18–21 functioning as a supplementary unit.

[10]This tendency to concentrate on the final form of the text is one of the many contributions of literary interpretations of the Bible; I have discussed this approach in

(1990: 515–19) and have developed my own approach (1989: 51–64).

[11]Note the diversity of professions enumerated in Sir 38:23–34.

[12]The word *ne'um* occurs 365 times in the formula "whisper of" followed by a name for the deity. Only eleven occurrences are not connected in this way with divine speech.

[13]Not every liturgy of repentance achieved its desired result, for divine freedom sometimes asserted itself because of the burden borne by the deity. An example is Jer 14:1–15:9 (Crenshaw, 1984: 50–56).

[14]The enemy from the north in the book of Jeremiah evokes this same fear, one brought on by constant armies spilling over the land of Judah (and Israel) from Syria, most having originated elsewhere in Assyria and Babylonia.

[15]Consult Stolz: 1979. The term occurs frequently in prophetic texts, but also 34 times in Psalms.

[16]In contrast to Josh 14:3–4, which omits the tribe of Levi in allocating the land, Ezek 48:8–14 envisions a substantial territory being given to the priestly groups, Zadokites and Levites, in the midst of which stands the Temple.

[17]The story about Saul's search for lost asses throws light on ancient attitudes about consulting seers. According to 1 Sam 9:5–10, Saul recognized the need for some sort of gift when approaching a seer for counsel. Interestingly, a servant had a small piece of silver although Saul had brought along nothing of value.

[18]Sigmund Mowinckel's hypothesis (199–227) that early Israel's emphasis on the spirit suffered an eclipse during eighth century classical prophecy but enjoyed resurgency during the sixth century with Ezekiel, Haggai, and Zechariah offers a plausible explanation for curious gaps in some prophetic literature with respect to the spirit as a means of authorization.

[19]In this respect Luke's use of Joel's prophecy in describing the remarkable infusion of the spirit during Pentecost cannot be faulted (Acts 2:1–21). Luke's citing of Joel 3:1–5a has some interesting features: the addition of an oracular formula to identify the divine speaker; the location of the event "in the last days"; the inversion of references to young men and old men (does this shift correspond to a shift in attitude from honoring maturity of years to revering youthful athletes?); the possessive pronoun attached to the servants (they are God's property!); and the omission of 3:5b, the promise of survivors on Mt. Zion and beyond.

[20]Scholarly understanding of apocalyptic has changed remarkably in recent years. My own views have profited greatly from reading Collins (1984), Smith (131–56).

[21]BHS proposes to transpose "and in Jerusalem" from 3:5b to 3:c, thus arriving at the translation, "And in Jerusalem survivors whom Yahweh calls."

[22]The 'valley-plain of Jehoshaphat, 'just like 'the northener' in 2:20 and the 'valley of the acacias' in 4:18b, is a cipher; the use of such was quite popular in the emerging apocalypticism" (Wolff: 76); "...hence a theological symbol rather than a topographical one" (Prinsloo: 105); "this valley cannot be located on any map; it, too, belongs to the sphere of mythology" (Kapelrud: 147).

[23]The word *lehêklēkem* (4:5) may also refer to palaces; in all likelihood, some of the booty was confiscated by high ranking soldiers for their personal use–even if placing the valuable vessels in foreign sanctuaries heaped indignity on a defeated deity.

[24]Wolff (77–78) writes that slave trade between Greece and a coaltion of coastal peoples including Tyre, Sidon, and Philistines flourished from the fifth century until 343 BCE, but he adds that during the fourth century Phoenicia was subject to strong Greek influences.

[25]Readers of sacred texts often forget that truth claims are not self-validating. Even the formula of recognition, which might carry an element of legal proof, hardly persuades anyone who is not already committed to belief. The reverse-side of proof from stupendous events is equally cogent; failure of the deity to act decisively can be read as weakness, at the least, and non-existence at the extreme.

[26]Whereas Amos localizes the repercussions of the divine appearance, Joel universalizes its effects. I have discussed Amos' use of theophanic language; see Crenshaw (1968: 203–15).

[27]I do not place much confidence in our ability to determine dates for ancient texts, although I believe it essential to attempt to do so. A few facts seem to indicate a date after the building of the temple in 521–516 BCE under the leadership of Haggai and Zechariah: silence about a king of Judah; the reference to an active temple cult; the mention of a city wall; the allusion to slave trade between Greeks and Phoenicians; the reference to Sabeans

in this context as well; the character of the language; the stage of proto-apocalyptic thought in the book; the use of earlier canonical literature, especially Obadiah, Zephaniah, Ezekiel and Zechariah 14; and the absence of any reference to Assyrians and Babylonians. On the other hand, Rudolph (1967: 193–98) argues strongly for the late pre-exilic period, and Myers (177–95) prefers 521–516 BC.

Chapter 18: Joel's Silence and Interpreters' Readiness to Indict the Innocent

[1]J. L. Crenshaw, "A Liturgy of Wasted Opportunity: Am 4:6–12; Isa 9:7–10:4; 5:25–29," *Semitics 1* (1971) 27–37.

[2]J. L. Crenshaw, "Who Knows What Yahweh Will Do? The Character of God in the Book of Joel," chapter 16 in this volume, originally published in *Fortunate the Eyes That See. Essays in Honor of David Noel Freedman in Celebration of his Seventieth Birthday,* ed. A. H. Bartlett et al. (Grand Rapids: William B. Eerdmans Publishing Company, 1995), 197–209 examines the rich understanding of divine character reflected in Exod 34:6–7.

[3]J. L. Crenshaw, "The Expression *mî yôdēa'* in the Hebrew Bible," VT 36 (1986) 274–88.

[4]J. L. Crenshaw, *Joel* (New York: Doubleday, 1995).

[5]G. W. Ahlström, *Joel and the Temple Cult of Jerusalem* (VTSup 21; Leiden: E. J. Brill, 1971).

[6]O. Loretz, *Regenritual und Jahwetag im Joelbuch* (UBL 4; Altenberge: CIS Verlag, 1986).

[7]A. S. Kapelrud, *Joel Studies* (UUA 48:4; Uppsala: A. B. Lundequistska Bokhandeln, and Leipzig: Otto Harrassowitz, 1948).

[8]H. W. Wolff, *Joel and Amos* (Philadelphia: Fortress Press, 1977 [Original, *Dodekapropheton 2. Joel und Amos,* BKAT XIV, 2.2[e], 1975]).

[9]G. Wanke, "Prophecy and Psalms in the Persian Period," pp. 174–77 in *The Cambridge History of Judaism,* eds. W. D. Davies and L. Finkelstein, vol. I (Cambridge: Cambridge University Press, 1984).

[10]P. L. Redditt, "The Book of Joel and Peripheral Prophecy," CBQ 48 (1986) 225–40.

[11]L. C. Allen, *The Books of Joel, Obadiah, Jonah and Micah* (NICOT 13/2; Grand Rapids: William B. Eerdmans Publishing Company, 1976).

[12]R. Simkins, *Yahweh's Activity in History and Nature in the Book of Joel* (ANETS 10; Lewiston, Queenston, Lampeter: The Edwin Mellen Press, 1991).

[13]M. Greenberg, "Reflections on Apocalyptic," pp. 163–73 in *Studies in the Bible and Jewish Thought* (JPS Scholar of Distinction Series; Philadelphia & Jerusalem: The Jewish Publication Society, 5755/1995).

[14]When this paper was read in Cambridge at the IOSOT, J. Blenkinsopp observed that the designation of Judeans as *šikkôrîm* implied guilt, the natural meaning of the word being "drunkards." I rejected this translation on the basis of its immediate context. Moreover, I observed that everyone drank wine in the ancient world, with notable exceptions of Rechabites and Nazarites, and that the subsequent divine restoration of wine would constitute a strange gift if its misuse caused the calamity in the first place.

Chapter 19: Transmitting Prophecy across Generations

[1]John Barton, *Oracles of God: Perceptions of Ancient Prophecy in Israel after the Exile* (New York and Oxford: Oxford University Press), 1986 has highlighted the sharp disjunction between the modern critical interpretation of ancient Israelite prophecy and the way it was understood before the development of historical criticism. He explores four modes of reading ancient prophecy: (1) as halakah, or ethical instruction; (2) as eschatological promise, containing foreknowledge of the present moment of interpreters; (3) as prognostication but without a sense of an imminent inbreaking of the divine; and (4) as speculative theology about God's character and the heavenly realm. Interpreters after the exile, both Jewish and Christian, viewed prophets as recipients of divine secrets, and this understanding of prophecy spurred them on to develop hermeneutical principles capable of unlocking the mystery pertaining to the present situation. They did not employ distinctions of genre, however, and that failure allowed them to discover prophecy in Torah, Psalms, wisdom literature, indeed in any sacred book. The decisive issue was whether or not God spoke in the text; if so, it was prophecy. Merely warning people of their own day required no word from God; prediction in its true sense did depend on revelation, in the

view of ancients. Using the image of looking into a well of the past, Barton accuses pre-critical readers of seeing their own reflection rather than the great classical prophets Amos, Hosea, Isaiah, and Jeremiah. Has Barton exaggerated the differences between "lone laymen" and post-exilic prophecy? Perhaps the promised sequel to the present volume will address this important question in the light of extensive redaction of older prophetic literature during the post-exilic period.

[2]Those shifts in fortune include the termination of the northern kingdom, the exile of a large segment of Judah and the eventual return of a small group to a province lacking the power of self-rule. These momentous events, spanning more than two centuries, witnessed a growing chasm between rich and poor, subjects and kings. Older family structures gave way to executive privilege, which in turn collapsed before foreign rule. In the restored community priestly hierarchy emerged, and competition for inherited land ruled the day, along with struggles to determine rights of inclusion. Given the scope of these changes, the formidable task of describing social characteristics in any given historical situation is humbling. Determining motives for actions of an ancient group of people poses an even more daunting challenge.

[3]The distinction between mantics and visionaries became blurred over time, as did the various terms designating prophetic figures: *rō'eh*, *ḥōzeh*, *'îš 'elôhîm*, *'îš hārrûaḥ*, and *nābî'*. The superscription to the book of Amos deftly combines the visionary and the oracular types of intermediation ("The words of Amos which he saw..."). The decisive issue pertained to the source of the prophecy, regardless of its form. If the prophecy derived from the deity, it was thought to have permanent relevance for individuals who possessed sufficient insight to decode it.

[4]This shift is more than a retreat to familiar territory when in doubt. The move occurs because sages reflected openly about the potential of cited words to immortalize their dead source. To put the matter succinctly, "When the dead are quoted their lips move." Stated another way, the written tablet keeps the memory of its scribe/author alive long after death has silenced the teacher. Similarly, the quoted prophetic oracle amounted to a death-defying act, a refusal to concede that the spirit infusing that word or vision has abandoned the religious community.

[5]When Miriam Lichtheim wrote "Egyptians, Mesopotamians, and Israelites, all three had the same approach to retaliation, vengeance, and forgiveness," she did not superimpose modern concepts of forgiving one's enemies upon ancient texts (*Moral Values in Ancient Egypt* [OBO 155; Fribourg: University Press and Göttingen: Vandenhoeck & Ruprecht, 1997, p. 46]). Nor was she a victim of the evolutionary approach adopted in interpreting ancient literature. Instead, she simply called attention to one feature of ancient thought that transcends space and time. One can concur with her that contemporary research has fallen into a terminological muddle as a result of a too-free use of the category "wisdom literature" by specialists in Egypt and Mesopotamia without surrendering the insight that both these civilizations had a corpus of literature reflecting on the most efficient means of attaining success and shaping character, as well as serious pondering of life's deeper mysteries.

[6]This sentence presupposes a central core of proverbial teachings during the monarchy, as well as accurate historical memory lying behind the superscription in Prov 25:1 ("These, too, are proverbs of Solomon that the men of Hezekiah, king of Judah, transmitted" ([*he'tîqû*]). The latter view has recently come under attack (M. Carasic, "Who were the Men of Hezekiah (Proverbs XXV:I?" *VT* 44 [1994] 291–300), and the former has been reinforced (Claus Westermann, *Roots of Wisdom* [Louisville: Westminster John Knox, 1995]). On Ben Sira's reliance on earlier wisdom literature see James L. Crenshaw, "Sirach," pp. 601–867 in *NIB*, vol V (Nashville: Abingdon, 1997).

[7]Concomitant with societal interest in "family values" has come renewed attention to the formation of character in the ancient world. The first full-scale analysis, William P. Brown, *Character in Crisis: A Fresh Approach to the Wisdom Literature of the Old Testament* (Grand Rapids: William B. Eerdmans, 1996) juxtaposes the efforts at community maintenance in the book of Proverbs with more crisis-centered approaches within the books of Job and Ecclesiastes. For him, the move of the self charts a journey outward but does not end there. The final resting place entails a return to the communal ethos by one whose journey has brought fresh insights and growth in moral fiber.

[8]The familial locus of teachings in the initial collection of the book of Proverbs, chapters 1–9, is no mere literary fiction. The memory of parents' role in formulating earlier collections of sayings exercised remarkable power over later traditionists, for whom

professional *ḥakāmîm* may have been a reality (see James L. Crenshaw, *Old Testament Wisdom*, Revised and Enlarged [Louisville: Westminster John Knox, 1998], *Urgent Advice and Probing Questions: Collected Writings on Old Testament Wisdom* [Macon: Mercer University Press, 1995], and Westermann, *Roots of Wisdom*).

[9]A weakness of the argument from analogy with Mesopotamia and Egypt arises from distinct differences in urban complexity and cultural development. Nili Shupak's stimulating analysis of affinities between Israelite and Egyptian concepts of education does not give sufficient attention to this important detail (*Where Can Wisdom be Found? The Sage's Language in the Bible and in Ancient Egyptian Literature* [OBO 130; Fribourg & Göttingen: University Press and Vandenhoeck & Ruprecht, 1993]). Friedemann W. Golka, *The Leopard's Spots* (Edinburgh: T. & T. Clark, 1993) has seen this disjunction between Israel and her more advanced neighbors with sharp clarity.

[10]I have explored the primary reason for this decline, the people's inability to distinguish between authentic intermediaries and religious charlatans (*Prophetic Conflict: Its Effect upon Israelite Religion* [BZAW 124; Berlin and New York: Walter de Gruyter, 1971). The scope of disenchantment with prophecy in this astonishing snippet within Zechariah is unclear, with some interpreters viewing it as absolute and others thinking it pertains only to a certain type of prophecy.

[11]When this early second century teacher issues specific advice to his audience, he instructs them to enter into lively dialogue with thoughtful people, not to pick up a scroll and read it–notwithstanding the present reality of that counsel in written form. The long tradition of teaching by means of oral instruction has persisted to the twentieth century, despite frequent attacks on lecture as a pedagogical method. The importance of hearing did not immediately vanish from education with the rise of reading texts, for people usually read aloud. By this means the two senses, seeing and hearing, heightened understanding. I have discussed Ben Sira's manner of teaching in James L. Crenshaw, "The Primacy of Listening in Ben Sira's Pedagogy," in chapter 3 above, originally published in *Wisdom, You Are My Sister. Studies in Honor of Roland E. Murphy, O. Carm., on the Occasion of His Eightieth Birthday*, ed. Michael L. Barré (CBQMS 29; Washington, D.C.: The Catholic Biblical Association of America, 1997), 172–187.

[12]Recent assessments of literacy in ancient Greece (William V. Harris, *Ancient Literacy* [Cambridge and London: Harvard University Press, 1989]) and in Egypt (John Baines, "Literacy and Ancient Egyptian Society," *Man* 18 [1983], 572–99) occasion little surprise when estimating a low percentage of literate citizens, less than 10% in classical Greece, about a half of one per cent in Egypt. The complex writing systems in both countries only partially explain this phenomenon. The alphabetic system in ancient Hebrew was much simpler, but the Israelites possessed few incentives to master it, and a number of disincentives (James L. Crenshaw, *Education in Ancient Israel: Across the Deadening Silence* [ABRL; New York: Doubleday, 1998]).

[13]Postmodernism functions as a healthy reminder that assured results of a previous generation's scholarship reflect biases of the elite and powerful. The many substitutes being offered today–feminist, Marxist, Afro-Americanist, liberationist, fundamentalist–only replace the white male bias with others equally one-sided. Their value consists in bringing a whole range of issues to the table where, one hopes, rational assessment will eventually occur. Debate also rages over the most effective method by which to illuminate the prophetic literature: an evolutionary history of ideas or a sociological model. Each method has serious drawbacks.

[14]The ecstatic, the cultic diviner, and lone lay person at Mari correspond to the prophetic types referred to in biblical literature. Similarly, several literary expressions link the two prophetic phenomena despite their distance in time and place (e.g., fear not; the God X has sent me; thus you shall say).

[15]The most plausible reading of this poem chronicles the astonishing journey of these disciples from a position similar to that of Job's three friends to a directly opposing viewpoint. The author gives no hint as to the basis for the decisive shift from viewing the servant as suffering for his sins to understanding his affliction as vicarious, redemptive, and undeserved.

[16]The episodes involving these two prophets have more affinities with post-exilic understandings of earlier prophecy than do the oracles and visions attributed to classical prophets. In the case of Amos, Hosea, Isaiah, Jeremiah and Micah one observes a radical disjunction between the preserved traditions and the view of prophecy in post-exilic

Judaism. That element of discontinuity may suggest that authentic memories have survived later editing.

[17]A legal background seems to be implied, e.g. the sealing of official documents for subsequent validation, if necessary. Such a practice would naturally apply to prophetic predictions so long as one accepts Deuteronomy's criterion of fulfillment as a mark of genuine prophecy.

[18]Who does the reading? If the prophet, then the text describes a herald rapidly scurrying about in order to proclaim a word to the entire citizenry. The alternative interpretation is less plausible because it presupposes an ability to read on the part of the populace.

[19]Such thinking carries within itself a fundamental core of eschatology, the conviction that the divine word will inevitably attain closure. Israel's experience with partial fulfillments gradually gave rise to expectations of final resolution some day, a tieing up of all loose ends. Frank Kermode, *The Sense of an Ending* (Oxford: Oxford University Press, 1966/67) writes of the tic/toc movement in linear thought, an inevitable anticipation of something yet to arrive on the scene.

[20]This endeavor to rescue all predictions by any available means led to extensive hermeneutical development of interpretive strategies, which come to light in various communities (e.g., Qumran, the New Testament, intertestamental Judaism, rabbinic Judaism, the Church Fathers). Michael Fishbane, *Biblical Interpretation in Ancient Israel* (Oxford: Clarendon Press, 1985) treats the interpretative tradition in prophecy under the title, mantological exegesis (443–524).

[21]The problem with becoming specific is acute, for the generation affected by the prophecy experiences its disconfirmation and is forced to explain the failure. Religious people have remarkable resilience when confronted with cognitive dissonance (Robert P. Carroll, *When Prophecy Failed* [London: SCM Press, 1979]).

[22]In the ancient writer's view, Moses had direct access to the deity, whereas every other prophet received the divine word derivatively–that is through riddles that had to be interpreted. Similarly, later readers believed that classical prophets received divine oracles and post-exilic prophets worked with derivative traditions, interpreting them rather than transmitting oracles directly from the deity. Ellen F. Davis, *Swallowing the Scroll: Textuality and the Dynamics of Discourse in Ezekiel's Prophecy* (JSOT SS 78; Sheffield: Almond Press, 1989) may be correct that Ezekiel brought about a decisive shift to the *text* as opposed to a word spoken by the deity to a prophet. "Nostalgia, not theocracy, was the death of prophecy" (Barton, *Oracles of God*, 115).

[23]This description, largely conjectural, relies on information gleaned from visionary accounts in the books of Amos and Jeremiah.

[24]Crenshaw, *Prophetic Conflict*.

[25]Robert R. Wilson, *Prophecy and Society in Ancient Israel* (Philadelphia: Fortress Press, 1980) employed this concept of central and peripheral prophecy as a means of clarifying the power structures of competing groups.

[26]On Assyrian prophecy, see Martti Nissinen, *References to Prophecy in Neo-Assyrian Sources* and Simo Parpola, *Assyrian Prophecies*, vols. VII and IX in State Archives of Assyria (Helsinki: Helsinki University Press, 1998 and 1997 respectively). Nissinen concludes that prophecy functioned in imperial ideology to provide divine directions for the king and propaganda for royal policies (164), although he adduces an example of a private citizen, Urad Gula, consulting a prophet. Parpola explains the paucity of prophetic texts by the oral nature of the phenomenon, stresses its ecstatic character, notes that only Esarhaddon and Assurbanipal mention prophetic oracles in their inscriptions, lists several similarities with biblical prophecy, and offers a translation and extensive notes of twenty-eight oracles from thirteen different prophets (four male, nine female). Collection 2.4 has a striking reference to sealing the writing of the Urartian (cf. Isa 8:16). Parpola's account of the worship of Ishtar of Arbela as monotheistic, indeed his description of Assyrian religion in general, is highly speculative.

[27]The elitist attitude represented by the author of this text attributed to Jeremiah may strike readers as strange, given the prophet's ill treatment by certain elements in power. The issue is more complex than that, for the biblical record also suggests that Jeremiah enjoyed considerable support from highly placed persons in Jerusalem. The contemptuous view of the poor contrasts with the equation elsewhere of the poor and the devout, an attitude with a long history.

[28]Joseph Blenkinsopp, *Sage, Priest, Prophet: Religious and Intellectual Leadership in Ancient Israel* (LAI; Louisville: Westminster John Knox, 1995) offers a thorough evaluation of the dominant social roles in the biblical world. His analysis of prophecy pays scant attention to the problem posed by competing voices and the struggle to escape the dilemma arising from an inability to distinguish between an authentic and a bogus prophet.

[29]Interpreters have understood the harsh attacks on the cult as either absolute or conditional. The infusion of Roman Catholic scholars into the mix, as well as renewed appreciation among Protestants for liturgy, has brought about a shift in favor of the latter interpretation, criticism of certain features of the cult but coming short of rejecting it entirely.

[30]On this complicated issue, see my "The Deuteronomist and the Writings," chapter 13 in this volume, originally published in *Those Elusive Deuteronomists: The Phenomenon of Pan-Deuteronomism*, ed. Steven McKenzie and Linda Schearing (Sheffield, JSOTSup 268, 1999), 145-68.

[31]Scholars would do well to avoid the assumption that a single group held a monopoly on lofty ethics (cf. Moshe Weinfeld, *Deuteronomy and the Deuteronomic School* (Oxford: University Press, 1972; reprint Eisenbrauns, 1992). Israelite society was not so insular as to yield specialists in morality; instead, fundamental values found champions among priests, prophets, and sages. Not every piece of legislation in the book falls into the category of humane. The law about recalcitrant sons seems particularly harsh, even when one takes into account the concept of honor and shame, as well as the importance of protecting communal solidarity.

[32]Gerhard von Rad championed the view that levitical preaching lay behind the book of Deuteronomy. See *Deuteronomy* (Philadelphia: Westminster, 1966), *Das Gottesvolk im Deuteronomium* (BzWANT, 47; Stuttgart: W. Kohlhammer, 1929), and *Studies in Deuteronomy* (London: SCM, 1953).

[33]Priestly features of these prophetic books abound (e.g., the importance of the temple, the role of the priest, the centrality of ritual and mediation by the ministers of the altar, the significance of adjudicating matters of purity and impurity). For Blenkinsopp, prophecy was swallowed by the cult, a view that David L. Petersen challenges ("The Temple in Persian Period Prophetic Texts," pp. 125–44 in *Second Temple Studies. 1 Persian Period*, ed. Philip R. Davies (JSOTSup 117; Sheffield: JSOT Press, 1991).

[34]The juxtaposition of Psalms 50 and 51 makes this issue all the more interesting. The rejection of sacrificial worship in Psalm 50 gives rise to copious ritual language in Psalm 51, together with language pointing beyond the penitential ritual to a shattered spirit.

[35]The nature of the Israelite family is the subject of a recent monograph by Leo G. Perdue, Joseph Blenkinsopp, John J. Collins, and Carol Meyers, *Families in Ancient Israel* (Louisville: Westminster John Knox, 1997). The discussion does not encourage one to think that ordinary families devoted themselves to preserving religious traditions for posterity. Their chief aim was survival in a hostile environment.

[36]*Oral World and Written Word: Ancient Israelite Literature* (LAI; Louisville: Westminster John Knox, 1996) proposes four models for evaluating biblical material on the literacy/orality continuium: (1) oral performance; (2) slow crystallization of a pan-Hebraic literary tradition; (3) written imitation of oral-style literature; and (4) the production of a written text excerpted from another.

[37]*Biblical Interpretation in Ancient Israel.*

[38]See note 12.

[39]See the conclusions of Charles E. Carter, "The Province of Yehud in the Post-Exilic Period: Sounding in site Distribution and Demography," pp. 106–45 in *Second Temple Studies 2. Temple Community in the Persian Period*, eds. T. C. Eskenazi and K. H. Richards (Sheffield: JSOT Press, 1994) and Ehud Ben Zvi, "The Urban Center of Jerusalem and the Development of the Literature of the Hebrew Bible," pp. 194–209 in *Aspects of Urbanism in Antiquity*, eds. W. G. Aufrecht, N. A. Mirau, and S. W. Gauley (Sheffield: JSOT, 1997).

[40]The term "managed scarcity" aptly describes scribal practices in ancient Egypt. The secret was to train just enough scribes to handle the demand for their services. The existence of too many scribes at a given time would compromise their employment and reduce their income appreciably. Presumably, a similar practice characterized Mesopotamian scribes.

[41]Bengt Holbek, "What the Illiterate Think of Writing," *Literacy and Society*, eds. Karen Schousboe and Mogens Trolle Larsen (Copenhagen: Akademisk Forlag, 1989) 183–96

writes that written letters and words shimmered with the very power of the gods. For most people, then, words functioned as icons. Their magical character did not escape those in power, who benefitted most from royal stelae.

[42]Much nonsense has been written about the magical power of the spoken word to bring about what it proclaims. This claim overlooks the instances in which the biblical text acknowledges the failure of oaths and curses, supposedly the most power-laden of all speech.

[43]See the exhaustive treatment of this phenomenon by Shalom M. Paul, "Heavenly Tablets and the Book of Life," *JANESCU* 5 (1973) 345–53 (with a postscript by William W. Hallo) and the comments of Hans Wildberger, *Isaiah* 1–12 (Minneapolis: Fortress, 1991) 169–70. Besides listing a book in which was recorded the name of everyone destined for life, the Bible also refers to a book of memorable deeds (Ps 139:16), one in which the tears of the righteous are recorded (Ps 56:9), and a book of remembrance (Mal 3:16). The idea of a book of life (Exod 32:32–33) has a long history (cf. the Tablets of Destiny in Babylon).

[44]Ellen F. Davis, *Swallowing the Scroll*, underestimates the symbolic aspects of such language and overplays the written character of prophetic traditions.

[45]According to David L. Petersen, *Haggai and Zechariah 1–8* (Philadelphia: Westminster, 1984) 245–54 the unrolled scroll portends punishment for violations of two laws, theft and false swearing. Thus old values persist in a new community, the diarchy that has replaced monarchy. Punishment falls to YHWH, and it hovers over all. Carol L. Meyers and Eric M. Meyers, *Haggai, Zechariah 1–8* (New York: Doubleday, 1987) 277–93 emphasize the correspondence of size between the temple vestibule and the scroll. They also consider the oath administered by priests to be important.

[46]"Beware of saying: 'Everyone is according to his nature
(bi't)
ignorant and learned ones alike,
Fate and fortune are graven in the nature
in the god's own writing...'" (P. Chester Beatty IV).
The translation is taken from Lichtheim, *Moral Values in Ancient Egypt*, 32.

[47]Is their offense the abuse of wine or sacrilege involving sacred vessels obtained through victory over Jerusalem?

[48]Crenshaw, "The Primacy of Listening in Ben Sira's Pedagogy," chapter 3 above.

[49]One may compare a Yaruba proverb: "The white man who created writing also created the eraser."

[50]I have examined the use of this confessional expression in "Who Knows What YHWH Will Do? The Character of God in the Book of Joel," 185–96 in *Fortunate the Eyes that See. Essays in Honor of David Noel Freedman in Celebration of his Seventieth Birthday*, eds. Astrid Beck et. al. (Grand Rapids: Eerdmans, 1994). See chapter 16 in this volume.

[51]See James L. Crenshaw, *Joel* (New York et. al.: Doubleday, 1995) 47–50 and passim for analysis of this expression.

[52]On the importance of this theme, see Northrop Frye, *The Great Code: The Bible and Literature* (New York: Harcourt Brace Jovanovich, 1982). Note also the different treatments of YHWH's vineyard in Isaiah 5 and 27.

[53]I treat this phenomenon in "Freeing the Imagination: The Conclusion to the Book of Joel," chapter 17 in this volume, originally published in Yehoshua Gitay, ed. *Prophecy and Prophets: The Diversity of Contemporary Issues in Scholarship* (SBLSymS; Atlanta: Scholars Press, 1997), 129–47.

[54]The goal of objectivity has come under attack by those who wish to replace it with passionate involvement similar to that of religious communities. I continue to value objective reading insofar as possible, chiefly as a means of dealing with the tower of Babel resulting from contemporary voices.

Chapter 20: Theodicy in the Book of the Twelve

[1]Steven T. Katz, "Holocaust: Judaic Theology and the," in *The Encyclopedia of Judaism*, (ed. Jacob Neusner, Alan Avery-Peck, and William Scott Green; Leiden: E. J. Brill, 1999), 406–20. Perhaps one should distinguish between theodicies and responses to the sheer magnitude of evil encountered in the Holocaust such as mystery and silence (William Scott Green, "Facing the One God Together," *Perspectives in Religious Studies* 26 (1999):308. With few exceptions, Judaic responses have exonerated God or left the traditional conception of

God intact, according to Green, who adds that "Post-Holocaust Jewish prayer is like pre-Holocaust prayer: same blessings, same petitions, same questions, same answers" (*ibid.*, 309). One is reminded of a story by Eli Wiesel about a trial of God by three Talmudic scholars at Auschwitz. They listened to witnesses and weighed evidence for several evenings, finally issuing a unanimous judgment. "The Lord God Almighty, Creator of Heaven and Earth, was found *guilty* of crimes against creation and humankind. And then, after what Wiesel calls an infinity of silence, the Talmudic scholars looked at the sky and said, 'It's time for evening prayers,' and the members of the Tribunal recited Maariv, the evening service" (Robert McAfee Brown, introduction to E. Wiesel's play, *The Trial of God* [New York: Schocken, 1995]), 7.

[2]The single term, lawlessness, captures best the lack of rhyme or reason that has replaced an earlier view of an order governing the entire universe. The resurgence of religious intolerance represents the conservative response to a threatened collapse in theological orthodoxy. When individuals see cherished doctrine under attack, the natural inclination is to reaffirm it rather than explore the reasons others consider the belief no longer adequate. Aggressive reaffirmation thus undercuts any possible dialogue with persons who hold different religious views. For the term *anomie* and the social aspects of theodicy, see Peter L. Berger, *The Sacred Canopy: Elements of a Sociological Theory of Religion* (Garden City: Doubleday, 1969), 53–80. Walter Brueggemann, "Theodicy in a Social Dimension," *JSOT* 33 (1985):3–24 faults Old Testament scholars for ignoring the social aspect of theodicy, but James L. Crenshaw, "The Sojourner Has Come to Play the Judge: Theodicy on Trial," chapter 22 in this volume, originally published in *God in the Fray: A Tribute to Walter Brueggemann*, eds. Tod Linafelt and Timothy K. Beal (Minneapolis: Fortress, 1998), 83–92 demurs.

[3]Clark M. Williamson, *Way of Blessing Way of Life: A Christian Theology* (St. Louis; Chalice, 1999), 67–72 deals helpfully with the question, "Is there one true religion, or are there many?" and discusses the possibility of inter-religious dialogue. He examines five options to this question: (1) the exclusivist claim that Christianity is the only true religion and that salvation is granted only to Christians; (2) the inclusivist position that Christianity is the one true religion but one's ultimate salvation is a separate issue; (3) the pluralist option, in which all religions are equally true and salvation is granted to all; (4) a view that salvation does not adhere to a single religion, for other religions may be true; and (5) Christian claims are true but stand under the judgment of revelatory events that make Christians forgiven sinners.

[4]In the introduction to the journal referred to in note 1, David Nelson Duke conveniently specifies various types of theodicy at the turn of the twentieth century. He lists theodicies of: (1) fatalism, (2) accountability and calculation, (3) instrumental purpose, (4) expressivity, and (5) denial. Duke includes theodicies emphasizing God's impenetrable mystery in the first category, and he notes the magical dimensions of control underlying the second type, the human attempt to escape the consequence of evil through mental gymnastics such as prayer or positive thinking, akin to bootstrapism. In the third type he sees the danger of self-abuse encouraged by an abusive deity; in the fourth he recognizes a form of escapism from the real world; and in the fifth category he notices signs of trivializing evil through sloppy language and improper use of analogies. Other contributors to this volume of *Perspectives in Religious Studies* address the general problem of theodicy in the Hebrew Bible (Walter Brueggemann), the particular case of Job (Samuel E. Balentine), insights from Buddhism and the possibility of compassion as a practical theodicy (Wendy Farley), the problem of the white Christ from the perspective of Dietrich Bonhoeffer (Josiah Ulysses Young), and Dostoevsky on evil as a perversion of personhood (Ralph C. Wood). The editors, Duke and Balentine, conclude the issue with an impassioned plea that Jews and Christians rethink the concept of God. The ramifications of bold rethinking can be seen in my forthcoming article entitled "The Reification of Divine Evil" and in David Penchansky, *What rough Beast? Images of God in the Hebrew Bible* (Louisville: Westminster John Knox, 1999), as well as the various articles in *Shall Not the Judge of all the Earth Do What Is Right: Studies on the Nature of God in Tribute to James L. Crenshaw*, (ed. David Penchansky and Paul L. Redditt; Winona Lake: Eisenbrauns, 2000).

[5]Terrence W. Tilley, *The Evils of Theodicy* (Eugene, Oregon: Wipf and Stock, 2000) argues that theodicy creates evil by silencing powerful voices of insight and healing (p. 1). On the basis of a theory of speech act, he considers the silencing of Job and the distortion of subsequent texts; specifically Augustine's *Enchiridion*, Boethius' *The Consolation of*

Philosophy, Hume's *Dialogues Concerning Natural Religion*, and George Eliot's *Adam Bede*. Tilley dislikes the theoretical nature of Post-enlightenment theodicies and insists on the need for practical responses to evil, together with the use of spiritual texts such as Job, Boethius, Julian of Norwich, and Simone Weil. For Tilley, the most shocking feature of modern theodicies is the effacement of Job (p. 245), which may be true of theologians in general but does not apply to biblical scholars. *Theodicy in the Old Testament* (Philadelphia: Fortress, 1983) which I edited will soon give way to a comprehensive *Handbook of Theodicy* in the ancient Near East to be edited by Antti Laato and Johannes C. de Moor and published by E. J. Brill and by a volume that I have given the provisional title *Deities on Trial: Questioning Divine Justice in the Bible*, to be published by Oxford University Press. The present essay should be supplemented by my "Theodicy and Prophetic Literature," chapter 21 in this volume, originally published in *Theodicy in the World of the Bible*, ed. A. Laato and C. de Moor (Leiden: Brill, 2003), 236–55.

[6]In a forthcoming article entitled "Theodicy, Theology, and Philosophy: Early Israel and Judaism," I describe the cultural assumptions in the ancient Near East that underlie discussions of evil (*Religions of the Ancient World: A Guide* [Cambridge, Mass.: Harvard University]).

[7]Classifying the book of Job as wisdom literature requires that one put more emphasis on content than style, as various critics have underscored. The prominence of lament does not override the dominant intellectual query about the adequacy of interpreting suffering on the basis of a rigid theory of act and consequence. The cognitive dimension almost equals the affective one in the powerful exploration of the right response to suffering and the possibility of disinterested virtue. Still, it must be conceded that the book of Job includes features otherwise absent from wisdom literature, most notably theophanic addresses.

[8]The interplay of realism and imagination turns this majestic psalm into what is arguably the theological center of the Psalter, despite unresolved questions about the exact scope of the union with the deity in the closing verses, or even the nature of the transforming experience in El's sacred place (v. 17). Both the literary artistry and theological profundity of this assessment of the belief that God is good to the pure in heart occupy pride of place in my discussion of this psalm in *The Psalms: an Introduction* (Grand Rapids: Eerdmans, 2001), 109–27.

[9]Few investigators into the level of literacy in ancient Israel consider it high, given the agrarian economy and managed control by the elite scribes who profited from its scarcity. Analogies with the sophisticated cultures in Mesopotamia and Egypt cut both ways. The tiny percentage of literate people, perhaps approximating one percent, and the greater demand for scribes than in Israel point one way, even as the simplicity of Hebrew when compared with cuneiform and hieroglyphics points another way. On this complex issue, see James L. Crenshaw, *Education in Ancient Israel: Across the Deadening Silence* (New York: Doubleday, 1998).

[10]The investigation of popular belief, which captured my imagination over three decades ago (*Prophetic Conflict: Its effect Upon Israelite Religion* [BZAW, 124; Berlin and New York: Walter de Gruyter, 1971] and "Popular Questioning of the Justice of God in Ancient Israel," *ZAW* 82 [1970]: 380–95) has begun to intrigue others who bring different questions to the table from those preoccupying me then. Without assuming that citations attributed to the people accurately reflect fact on one level, we may credibly imply verisimilitude; otherwise the literary fiction would have floundered. There is no evidence that readers rejected the attributions as unreliable descriptions of popular belief. Moshe Greenberg, *Biblical Prose Prayer as a Window to the Popular Religion of Ancient Israel* (Berkeley: University of California, 1983) uses a similar argument to justify his treatment of fictional prayers as true to life.

[11]Recent interpreters of these prophetic texts have concentrated on their social context more than their theological content, with the exception of Simo Parpola, *Assyrian Prophecies* (SAA 9; Helsinki University, 1997), whose speculative description of a monotheistic religion involving Ishtar of Arbela argues for a continuity with later Graeco-Roman and Hellenistic philosophy. Martti Nissinen, *References to Prophecy in Neo-Assyrian Sources* (SAAS 7; Helsinki: The Neo-Assyrian Text Corpus Project, 1998) and "Spoken, Written, Quoted, and Invented: Orality and Writtenness in Ancient Near Eastern Prophecy," in *Writings and Speech in Israelite and Ancient Near Eastern Prophecy* (ed. Ehud Ben Zvi and Michael H. Floyd; Atlanta: Society of Biblical Literature, 2000), 235–71 and Karel van der Toorn, "From the Oral to the Written: The Case of Old Babylonian Prophecy," in *Writings and Speech in*

Israelite and Ancient Near Eastern Prophecy, 219–34 examine the phenomenon of prophecy--its institutional setting, official titles, mode of proclamation, and preservation in writing.

[12]These five occasions for theodicy are developed in my "Theodicy and Prophetic Literature," chapter 21 in this volume, originally published in *Theodicy in the World of the Bible*, ed. A. Laato and C. de Moor (Leiden: Brill, 2003), 236–55.

[13]John F. Kutsko, *Between Heaven and Earth: Divine Presence and Absence in the Book of Ezekiel* (Biblical and Judaic Studies 7; Winona Lake, Ind.: Eisenbrauns, 2000) clarifies the importance of theodicy to the prophet Ezekiel, particularly in regard to idolatry. Kutsko emphasizes the means by which Ezekiel comes to Yahweh's defense, above all the relegation of idols to non-entities and the departure of the divine presence but ultimately its return and the restoration of a chastened people. Kutsko's argument, thoroughly philological, makes good use of literary features to illuminate the theological context in which Ezekiel moved.

[14]Raymond C. Van Leeuwen, "Scribal Wisdom and Theodicy in the Book of the Twelve," in *In Search of Wisdom: Essays in Memory of John Gammie* (ed. Leo G. Perdue, Bernard Brandon Scott, and William Johnston Wiseman; Louisville: Westminster John Knox, 1993), 31–49. Van Leeuwen traces allusions to Exod 34:6–7 in the Book of the Twelve, arguing that forerunners of Ben Sira introduced theodicy as an explanation for the catastrophic events in 722 and 587 BCE. He discusses Hos 14: 10 (also 1:6, 9); Mic 2:7–8a; 7:18–20 via 4:5 and Ps 25:4–13; Joel 2:12–14; 4:21 [3:21]; Amos 4:13; 5:8–9; 9:5–6, Obad (the references to Yahweh's day); Jonah 3:5–10; 4:1–2, 3–11; Nah 1:2b-3a; and Habakkuk. Indeed, Van Leeuwen thinks Mic 6–7 comprises a miniature theodicy.

[15]By placing the controversy over Yahweh's justice in the circle of the wise, Van Leeuwen isolates biblical prophets from daily life in a way that flies in the face of their frequent readiness to wrestle with difficult theological questions. It is more probable that biblical prophets joined the fray and thus were not insulated from the challenges to traditional belief but experienced them both professionally and personally. Their concept of God and theology of election guaranteed the emergence of theodicy. Nevertheless, Van Leeuwen's initial insight, that some of these texts that rush to defend divine justice are editorial glosses, can not be faulted. The issue, then, becomes one of origin, whether scribal or prophetic.

[16]The modern references to a shift in paradigm from history to literature indicate an awareness that the manner of interpreting texts for nearly two centuries has given way to a rival one that never really disappeared. Similarly, the furor over Post-Enlightenment views and the desire to replace them with older ways of viewing the world reveal the emotional involvement in cultural assumptions.

[17]The translations in this article come from the NRSV.

[18]Ignoring the first half of verse 5, the assertion that the righteous Yahweh can do no wrong, Adele Berlin concentrates on the concluding half-verse and compares its single idea, in her view, to Psalm 19, which associates judgment and sunlight (*Zephaniah* [New York: Doubleday, 1994), 130. J. Schreiner, "'āwel, 'awlâ, 'wl, 'iwwāl," *TDOT* 10 (1999), 529 contrasts the biblical insistence on Yahweh's freedom from wrongdoing (e.g., in Ps 92:15 [16], Zeph 3:5; Deut 32:4) with the people's proclivity to engage in sinful acts.

[19]For Joel's anticipation of a day when Yahweh will sit in judgment over the nations, see James L. Crenshaw, *Joel* (New York: Doubleday, 1995), 186–96. Historical events made it increasingly necessary to explain the dominance of foreigners over a covenant people, and the resulting sense of helplessness fueled eschatological hope that Yahweh would eventually punish the nations for their harsh treatment of his devotees. (According to Zech 1:7–17 those nations who exceded the divine mandate to punish [Israel and] Judah were particularly vulnerable to Yahweh's wrath). The fundamental basis for this optimism was the conviction that Yahweh's justice could not be compromised.

[20]The claim that the gloss in Hos 14:10 derives from sages rests on the dubious assumption that they held a monopoly on cognitive vocabulary. Were the prophets interested in being understood and in addressing discerning hearers? The answer to this question can only be a resounding "yes." It follows that the open expression of this wish to have astute hearers (and readers) does not necessarily indicate the interests of a different sociological group. The language consists of nothing that belongs exclusively in wisdom literature, for everything in the verse fits nicely within prophecy.

[21]Like the book of Jonah with its single oracle of five words, Malachi rests uneasily in the prophetic corpus. The prevailing tone is that of discussion, or even argument, with a

wide range of issues from moral to ritual (Julia O'Brien, *Priest and Levite in Malachi* [Atlanta: Scholars, 1990]).

[22]Shalom M. Paul, "Heavenly Tablets and the Book of Life," *JANESCU* 5 (1973): 345–53 discusses the scope of ancient Near Eastern speculation about the deity's active role in determining an individual's ultimate destiny by means of a written record. This early version of "Santa Claus lore" ("He's making a list and checking it twice; gonna find out who's naughty or nice") blossomed in later apocalyptic, bringing comfort to an oppressed people. Underlying the idea is a calculating morality, according to which one's fate depends entirely on a final weighing of good deeds against evil ones reminiscent of the Egyptian belief that one's virtues would be weighed against the goddess of justice, Maat.

[23]The language of lament, by nature raw, includes subtle indictment, for the champion of the oppressed should hasten to the rescue on hearing about bloodshed and violence. In this instance, the prophet has cried out repeatedly, without receiving any answer. This rare cluster of words (*'ad 'ānāh, 'ez'aq*, and *ḥāmās*) pertaining to theodicy refutes any suggestion that the issue was merely an intellectual enterprise.

[24]Justice is always conflicted, as Ralph Waldo Emerson observed: "One man's justice is another man's injustice." A better articulation of the idea would substitute the word "tyranny" for "injustice." The struggle for justice often becomes a striving for power, which engenders rival theodicies, one for the group in control and another for the disenfranchised.

[25]On the antecedent of the suffix attached to *'emûnâ*, with a prefixed preposition, see J. J. M. Roberts, *Nahum, Habakkuk, and Zephaniah* (Louisville: Westminster/John Knox, 1991) and Robert D. Haak, *Habakkuk* (VTSup 44; Leiden: Brill, 1991). Donald E. Gowan, *The Triumph of Faith in Habakkuk* (Atlanta: John Knox, 1976), 20–50 raises the theological issue of divine justice.

[26]James L. Crenshaw, "Who Knows What Yahweh Will Do? The Character of God in the Book of Joel,"chapter 16 in this volume, originally published in *Fortunate the Eyes That See: Essays in Honor of David Noel Freedman*, (ed. Astrid Beck et. al. [Grand Rapids: Eerdmans, 1995]), 185–96 and Terence E. Fretheim, "Jonah and Theodicy," *ZAW* 90 (1978): 227–37.

[27]In trying to justify curses against enemies in the Psalter, C. S. Lewis reflects on the consequences of letting evildoers escape punishment. For him, anger over wickedness demonstrates a conscience, whereas tolerating cruelty indicates indifference. He also stresses the harm inflicted on the innocent by generating hatred within them (*Reflections on the Psalms* [New York: Harcourt, Brace and Company, 1958], 20–33).

[28]Jack M. Sasson, *Jonah* (New York: Doubleday, 1990), 234–37 recognizes the ambiguity of the word *nehpaket*, its potential for both a threatening and a hopeful sense. Nineveh faced a choice, whether to be overturned through external force or to be turned around in repentance.

[29]On this dynamic, see James L. Crenshaw, "The Concept of God in Old Testament Wisdom," in *In Search of Wisdom*, 1–18 (also in Crenshaw, *Urgent Advice and Probing Questions: Collected Writings on Old Testament Wisdom* [Macon: Mercer University, 1995], 191–221; pages 141–221 of this book deal with theodicy).

[30]James L. Crenshaw, "Joel's Silence and Interpreters' Readiness to Indict the Innocent," chapter 18 in this volume, originally published in "*Lasset uns Brücken bauen...*" *Collected Communications to the XVth Congress of the International Organization for the Study of the Old Testament, Cambridge 1995*, ed. Klaus-Dietrich Schunck and Matthias Augustin (BEATAJ 42; Frankfurt: Peter Lang, 1998), 255–59.

[31]From a human perspective, the discipline amounts to a squandered opportunity, whereas from a divine viewpoint it represents a pedagogical failure (James L. Crenshaw, "A Liturgy of Wasted Opportunity: Am. 4:6–12; Isa. 9:7–10:4," *Semitics* 1 [1971]: 27–37).

[32]James L. Crenshaw, *Hymnic Affirmation of Divine Justice* (SBLDS 24; Missoula, Montana: Scholars, 1975).

[33]On this extraordinary instance of rational deduction within prophetic literature, see Jörg Jeremias, *The Book of Amos* (Louisville: Westminster John Knox, 1998), 51–5; Hans Walther Wolff, *Joel and Amos* (Philadelphia: Fortress, 1977), 179–88; and Shalom Paul, *Amos* (Minneapolis: Fortress, 1991), 104–14.

Chapter 21: Theodicy and Prophetic Literature

[1]As used here, theodicy refers to the attempt to pronounce God innocent of the evil that befalls human beings. This understanding of the term differs from Post-Enlightenment

efforts to demonstrate the intellectual credibility of an infinite being or power and to show that belief in deity can coincide with belief in a mechanistic universe. Theodicy is therefore an *articulate* response to the *anomie* of existence, one that goes beyond silence, submission, and rebellion to thoughtful justification of the deity in the face of apparently contradictory evidence. The *concept* antedates by millennia the origin of the word theodicy, a neologism coined by G. W. Leibniz in 1710 (*Theodicy: Essays on the Goodness of God, the Freedom of Man and the Origin of Evil*, transl. E. M. Huggard, London 1952).

[2]The pervasive influence of a theological historiography shaped by the ideas of Deuteronomy has led modern critics to what has recently been dubbed pan-Deuteronomism, on which see L. S. Schearing and S. L. McKenzie (eds.), *Those Elusive Deuteronomists: The Phenomenon of Pan-Deuteronomism* (JSOTSup 268), Sheffield 1999.

[3]The slightest hint of weakness on YHWH's part continued to trouble Jewish writers during the period of Roman dominance. A fine example of sensitivity over this issue occurs in the Apocalypse of Baruch (early second century CE). Baruch has a vision in which angels come to a besieged Zion; take away for safe-keeping the veil, the holy ephod, the mercy seat, the two tables, the holy raiment of the priests, the altar of incense, the forty-eight precious stones adorning priestly garments, and all the holy vessels of the tabernacle; entrust them to earth's care until the future restoration of the temple; demolish the wall protecting the city; and tell the Babylonian soldiers that they can enter since the guard (YHWH) has left the house. The text goes on to proclaim that the conquerors have no reason to boast about their victory over Jerusalem (chs 6–7).

[4]'The Lamentation over the Destruction of Sumer and Ur' gives voice to the pathos evoked by deities' abandonment of their temple and its environs to destruction. The book of Lamentations expresses similar dismay over YHWH's seeming lack of interest in Zion's fate.

[5]The prophetic figures mentioned in the Deuteronomistic History effectively shape historical events through their messages, in sharp contrast with most prophets whose names are associated with biblical books, who were largely ignored by those they hoped to influence. The exceptions, Haggai and Zechariah, are credited with supplying primary motivation for rebuilding the temple in Jerusalem. The nature of ancient historiography and the utilitarian features of redactional effort, even during the initial composition of prophetic literature, make it difficult if not impossible to distinguish fact from fiction. The case of Jonah, however, is easy to decide, for his extraordinary success in evoking repentance belongs to the genre of fiction.

[6]Translations in this article are the author's. For the idea of testing, both human and divine, see J. L. Crenshaw, *A Whirlpool of Torment*, Philadelphia 1984. J. O'Brien, *Priest and Levite in Malachi*, Atlanta 1990, treats the combative character of this book, its excessive verbal exchanges, in the context of lawsuits. A. E. Hill, *Malachi*, New York 1998, 34–7 favors a didactic interpretation of the discussions, dubiously relating them to sapiential circles.

[7]According to T. W. Tilley, *The Evils of Theodicy*, Eugene, OR 2000, every theodicy not only fails but also damages both the intellectual endeavor among theists and victims of injustice. The contributors to *Perspectives in Religious Studies* 26 (1999), a volume on theodicy edited by D. N. Duke and S. E. Balentine, do not share this negative view of theodicy.

[8]James L. Crenshaw, "The Sojourner Has Come to Play the Judge: Theodicy on Trial," chapter 22 in this volume, originally published in *God in the Fray: A Tribute to Walter Brueggemann*, eds. Tod Linafelt and Timothy K. Beal (Minneapolis: Fortress, 1998), 83–92.

[9]I. Kant, 'Über das Misslingen aller philosophischen Versuche in der Theodizee', *Werke* (ed.), W. Weischedel, Darmstadt 1946 vol. 6, 103–24 (ET M. Despland [trans.], 'On the Failure of All Attempted Philosophical Theodicies', in: *Kant on History and Religion*, Montreal 1973, 283–97).

[10]J. L. Crenshaw, *Urgent Advice and Probing Questions: Collected Writings on Old Testament Wisdom*, Macon 1995, 141–221; J. Ebach, 'Theodizee: Fragen gegen die Antworten. Anmerkungen zur biblischen Erzählung von der Bindung Isaaks "(1 Mose 22)",' 1–25 in: *Gott im Wort: Drei Studien zur biblischen Exegese und Hermeneutik*, Neukirchen-Vluyn, 1997; D. Penchansky, and P. L. Redditt (eds.), *Shall Not the Judge of All the Earth Do What Is Right? Studies on the Nature of God in Tribute to James L. Crenshaw*, Winona Lake, IN 2000.

[11]T. Jacobsen, *The Treasures of Darkness*, New Haven and London 1976, detects this shift in Mesopotamian religions.

[12]L. Feuerbach, *The Essence of Christianity*, New York 1957, recognized an intimate connection between human desire and the imaging of deity. As Peter Berger and Thomas

Luckman, *The Social Construction of Reality: A Treatise in the Social Construction of Knowledge*, New York 1966, perceived with great clarity, humans construct a world view, which then exercises remarkable power over them. The detrimental effect of such absolutizing of concepts is discussed in J. L. Crenshaw, 'The Reification of Divine Evil', forthcoming.

[13]J. Day, *God's Conflict with the Dragon and the Sea*, University of Cambridge Oriental Publications 35), Cambridge 1985, emphasizes Canaanite influence on biblical imagery, whereas J. D. Levenson, *Creation and the Persistence of Evil*, San Francisco 1985, focuses on the connection of such mythic combat with ideas about origins.

[14]R. P. Carroll, *Jeremiah*, Philadelphia 1986, 168–70 may be correct in finding apocalyptic themes in this poem, which he considers non-Jeremianic. Carroll relates the imagery to the holocaust, quoting E. Wiesel, *Five Biblical Portraits*, Notre Dame 1981, 126. The connections with Genesis 1, although real, are less extensive than thought by M. Fishbane, 'Jeremiah IV 23–26 and Job III 3–13: A Recovered Use of the Creation Pattern', *VT* 21 (1971) 151–67.

[15]R. W. L. Moberly, *The Bible, Theology, and Faith: A Study of Abraham and Jesus*, Cambridge 2000, argues for the positive role of divine testing in the life of faith, but he does not give sufficient attention to the destructive aspects of this pedagogy, whether emotional (as seen in rabbinic reflections about Eve's response to the story about Isaac's ordeal), physical (as exemplified by Job's ten children), or mental (as experienced by countless individuals enduring trials too difficult to bear). Moberly perceives the potential for both glory and tragedy in the process of testing, although this knowledge does not compel him to question YHWH's actions when they are immoral from a human standpoint. ('The paradox, with the potential for both glory and tragedy, is that the very process which can develop and deepen human life [divine testing] is the one which can stunt, corrupt, and destroy human life [satanic temptation]', 240).

[16]Crenshaw, 'The Reification of Divine Evil', Penchansky, *What Rough Beast?*, and R. N. Whybray, 'Shall Not the Judge of All the Earth Do What Is Just?', 1–20 in: *Shall Not the Judge of All the Earth Do What Is Right?*

[17]A distinction between orthodox and heterodox, as well as syncretistic Yahwism, is required by onomastic and theophoric evidence, perhaps also family religion and official national religion (P. D. Miller, *The Religion of Ancient Israel*, Louisville 2000). The claim that Yahwism evolved from early polytheism through henotheism to the monotheism of Deutero-Isaiah, once taken for granted by scholars, did not take into account the fact that certain segments of the population probably never completely abandoned belief in other deities than YHWH. For arguments in favor of early aniconism and monotheistic leaning, see T. Mettinger, *No Graven Image? Israelite Aniconism in its Ancient Near Eastern Context* (ConBOT 42), Stockholm 1995 and J. C. de Moor, *The Rise of Yahwism: The Roots of Israelite Monotheism*, Leuven 1990.

[18]Much has been written on this psalm, but the following works cover a wide range of interpretation: H.-W. Jüngling, *Der Tod der Götter. Eine Untersuchung zu Psalm 82* (StB 38), Stuttgart 1969, J. S. Ackerman, *An Exegetical Study of Psalm 82*, Ph.D. Dissertation, Harvard University, 1966, and P. Höffken, 'Werden und Vergehen der Götter: Ein Beitrag zur Auslegung von Psalm 82', *TZ 39* (1983), 129–37.

[19]For notable exceptions, see O. Kaiser, 'Deus absconditus and Deus revelatus: Three Difficult Narratives in the Pentateuch', 73–88 in: *Shall Not the Judge of All the Earth Do What Is Right?;* L. H. Silberman, '"You Cannot See My Face": Seeking to Understand Divine Justice', 89–96 in: ibid., and S. E. Balentine, 'Who Will Be Job's Redeemer?' PRS 26 (1999), 269–89.

[20]'One man's justice is another man's injustice'--Ralph Waldow Emerson. J. L. Crenshaw, 'Popular Questioning of the Justice of God in Ancient Israel', *ZAW* 83 (1970), 380–95 (175–90 in *Urgent Advice and Probing Questions*) underscores the seething discontent among the populace over simple answers by leaders of state religion.

[21]M. Nissinen, *References to Prophecy in Neo-Assyrian Sources* (JAAS 7), Helsinki 1998, and 'Spoken, Written, Quoted, and Invented: Orality and Writtenness in Ancient Near Eastern Prophecy', 235–71 in: *Writing and Speech in Israelite and Ancient Near Eastern Prophecy*, (eds.), E. Ben Zvi and M. H. Floyd, Atlanta 2000; and K. van der Toorn, 'From the Oral to the Written: The Case of Old Babylonian Prophecy', 219–34 in: *ibid.* Whereas these works concentrate on the phenomenon of prophecy--its institutional setting, official titles, mode of proclamation, and preservation in writing--, S. Parpola, *Assyrian Prophecies* (SAA 9), Helsinki 1997, emphasizes theological features of prophecy.

[22]R. R. Wilson, *Prophecy and Society in Ancient Israel*, Philadelphia 1980, introduced this language into the analysis of biblical prophecy.

[23]On the relationship between theology, theodicy, and philosophy, see J. L. Crenshaw, 'Theodicy, Theology, and Philosophy: Early Israel and Judaism', forthcoming in: *Religions of the Ancient world: A Guide*, Cambridge.

[24]G. M. Landes, 'Jonah: A Māšāl?' 137–58 in: *Israelite Wisdom: Theological and Literary Essays in Honor of Samuel Terrien* (eds.), J. G. Gammie et. al., Missoula 1978; J. M. Sasson, *Jonah*, New York 1990; P. L. Trible, 'Studies in the Book of Jonah', Ph.D. Diss., Columbia University, 1963; K. M. Craig, Jr., *A Poetic of Jonah: Art in the Service of Ideology*, Columbia 1993; and T. E. Fretheim, 'Jonah and Theodicy', *ZAW* 90 (1978), 227–37.

[25]J. L. Crenshaw, *Prophetic Conflict: Its Effect upon Israelite Religion* (BZAW 124), Berlin 1971, drew attention to differences between official state religion and popular piety. Recent scholarship has reinforced that diversity, but critics differ on whether or not it was salutary.

[26]Crenshaw, *A Whirlpool of Torment*, 31–56 explores the depth of this rift between prophet and deity as expressed in the so-called confessions. The move from literary text to biography is far too complex to rely on these laments for personal information about Jeremiah, but they do give voice to the author's sentiments and reveal something about the audience's religious tolerances.

[27]The language is that of the judiciary, with *ṣaddîq* functioning as a declaration of innocence equivalent to the modern 'Not guilty'.

[28]G. Matties, 'Ezekiel 18 and the Rhetoric of Moral Discourse in the Book of Ezekiel', Ph.D. Diss., Vanderbilt University, 1989.

[29]This text has been widely discussed, most helpfully by M. Fishbane, *Biblical Interpretation in Ancient Israel*, Oxford 1985, 335–50. For more recent analysis, see J. L. Crenshaw, 'Who Knows What YHWH Will Do? The Character of God in the Book of Joel', 185–96 in: *Fortunate the Eyes That See: Essays in Honor of David Noel Freedman in Celebration of his Seventieth Birthday*, (eds.), A. B. Beck et. al., Grand Rapids 1995. Chapter 16 in this volume.

[30]J. Crenshaw, *Joel*, New York 1995. This prophet's ambiguous attitude toward guilt and punishment has not always been recognized, on which see my article, "Joel's Silence and Interpreters' Readiness to Indict the Innocent," chapter 18 in this volume, originally published in "*Lasset uns Brücken bauen...*" *Collected Communications to the XVth Congress of the International Organization for the Study of the Old Testament, Cambridge 1995*, ed. Klaus-Dietrich Schunck and Matthias Augustin (BEATAJ 42; Frankfurt: Peter Lang, 1998), 255–59.

[31]L. G. Perdue, *The Collapse of History: Deconstructing Old Testament Theology,* Minneapolis 1994, and R. Gnuse, *Heilsgeschichte as a Model for Biblical Theology,* Lanham, NY 1989.

[32]On narrativity in ancient inscriptions, see S. Parker, *Stories in Scripture and Inscriptions,* New York 1997. He views the Mesha stela as a memorial inscription that uses earlier ones to show that Chemosh has given the king victory over hostile forces (55).

[33]S. B. Frost, 'The Death of Josiah: A Conspiracy of Silence', JBL 87 (1968), 369–82 expresses surprise over the biblical authors' failure to address this shocking affront to the dominant understanding of divine solicitude.

[34]D. E. Gowan, *The Triumph of Faith in Habakkuk,* Atlanta 1976, 20–50 relates the prophet's complaint to the larger issue of theodicy.

[35]Reading (with Tiqqune Sopherim) *lō' tāmût*.

[36]This psalm must have been truly revolutionary, both in open acknowledgment of the reality of the gods and in declaring their mortal nature on the basis of ethical standards. The claim that they were subservient to YHWH was equally bold, if, as many think, the name Elohim actually replaces an original YHWH.

[37]The long history of ridiculing idols reaches a high point in the Apocalypse of Abraham (c. 100 CE), where a wooden image that Abraham instructed to watch over the fire on which Terah's food was cooking ignites and burns, convincing Terah that the god Barisat sacrificized itself for its devotee. This reference to a god's self-immolation for another's benefit shares the stage with other easily destroyed images as well as man-made replacements that, when thrown in the river, cannot save themselves, or when sold to foreigners, cannot control their own destiny.

[38]I owe these observations to the perceptive insights of J. F. Kutsko, *Between Heaven and Earth: Divine Presence and Absence in the Book of Ezekiel* (JBS 7), Winona Lake, IN 2000.

[39]J. L. Crenshaw, 'A Liturgy of Wasted Opportunity: Am 4:6–12; Isa 9:7–10:4,' *Semitics 1* (1971), 27–37.

[40]F. Crüsemann, *Studien zur Formgeschichte von Hymnus und Danklied in Israel* (WMANT), Neukirchen-Vluyn 1965, stresses the hymnic features of these fragments, whereas J. L. Crenshaw, *Hymnic Affirmation of Divine Justice: The Doxologies of Amos and Related Texts in the Old Testament* (SBLDS 24), Missoula 1975, emphasizes their present context, hence their function as doxologies of judgment, a term derived from Friedrich Horst.

[41]Saadia Gaon, *The Book of Theodicy,* (transl.) L. E. Goodman (Yale Judaica Series 25), New Haven and London 1988, understood the book of Job in this light, arguing that God did not "shortchange" anyone, for life itself is the greatest gift possible. The argument does not do justice to the differences in quality of life which cannot be explained on the basis of guilt or merit, or to length of life, Dostoevsky's primary concern, graphically depicted in the suffering of a child.

[42]This extraordinary claim that YHWH always conveys his intentions to intermediaries is usually taken to be a later addition. It assumes that like Amos they will intercede for the people, although his record at intercession was hardly encouraging. S. Paul, *Amos,* Philadelphia 1991, 113 defends its contextual integrity as well as its appropriateness to Amos' views, but as he admits a skilful editor could integrate the verse into its setting and adjust Deuteronomistic phraseology to the prophet's understanding of reality.

[43]J. L. Crenshaw, 'The Problem of Theodicy in Sirach: On Human Bondage', JBL 94 (1975), 49–64 (*Urgent Advice and Probing Questions,* 155–74) and *The Book of Sirach* (NIB vol. V) Nashville 1997.

[44]M. E. Stone, *Fourth Ezra,* Minneapolis 1990, writes: 'The answers given by the angel, however, are rather conventional. God's workings are a mystery and beyond human comprehension; God loves Israel and will vindicate Israel in the end; God rejoices over the few saved and is not concerned over the many damned; God's mercy works in this world, while his justice is fully active only in the world to come' (36).

[45]For further analysis, see J. L. Crenshaw, "Theodicy in the Book of the Twelve," chapter 20 above, originally published in *Thematic Threads in the Book of the Twelve,* ed. P. L. Redditt and A. Schart (BZAW 325; Berlin/New York: de Gruyter, 2003), 175–191.

Chapter 22: The Sojourner Has Come to Play the Judge

[1]Hermann Gunkel, *Genesis* (GKAT; Göttingen: Vandenhoeck & Ruprecht, 1922) 203 follows Wellhausen in understanding Abraham's intercession for Sodom as a late interpolation into the Yahwistic narrative, primarily because of the way it deals with the problem of divine justice in the abstract. Classical prophets, he points out, saw no difficulty with the total punishment of a given community. Gerhad von Rad accepts Gunkel's general understanding of the two episodes in terms of the history of religions but goes on to emphasize theological dimensions of the narrative (*Genesis* [London: SCM Press, 1961]). Terrence Fretheim's sensitivity to the religious dimensions of the text stands out among the several commentaries consulted (*Genesis* [Nashville: Abingdon, 1994]). The attitude expressed by the people of Sodom has been replicated hundreds of times when confronted by "sojourners": an African American professor who assails the culture that welcomed him, a new congress-woman who attacks those doing things the traditional way, a new clerk in a law firm who dares to raise objections to company policy, a novice minister who challenges ecclesiastical procedure, and so forth.

[2]The expression for brotherhood, *'aḥai,* and evil behavior *tārēʿû...kaṭṭôb beʿênêkem,* links this text with Jdg 19:23–24, where citizens of Gibeah demand a visitor for homosexual purposes and are offered a virgin daughter and a concubine instead.

[3]The term "sodomy" derives from this biblical story and should not be projected onto the narrative, hence the quotation marks.

[4]In ancient Egypt the notion of divine judgment led to the picture of scales on which were placed at death the human heart and a feather symbolizing justice. This powerful ethical motivation was familiar throughout the ancient Near East, as the frequent epithets for divine judge demonstrate.

[5]John Bunyan's classic, *Pilgrim's Progress,* gave expression to the idea that human beings merely pitch their tents on earth, that earthly existence offers opportunity to form character for life in eternity. Given the brevity of human life, whatever understanding that

accrues is limited from the temporal and the spatial viewpoints. Criticizing the Eternal One from a transitory perspective demands considerable nerve, as Immanuel Kant noted: "It is arrogant to attempt to defend God's justice; it is still more arrogant to assail the deity" ("Über das Misslingen aller philosophischen Versuche in der Theodizee," *Werke,* ed. W. Weischedel [Darmstadt, 1964] 6:103–24).

[6]We shape our own culture and then become subject to its claims. Ethos thus owes its origin to human beings even when it sits in judgment on its originators.

[7]The ancient *gēr* came under royal protection, at least in ideology (Norbert Lohfink, "Poverty in the Laws of the Ancient Near East and the Bible," ThSt 52 [1991] 34–50 and Leonidas Kalugila, *The Wise King* [ConBOT 15; Lund: CWK Gleerup, 1980]). According to the sapiential tradition, one type of sojourner, the foreign woman (*nokrîyyâ; 'iššâ zārâ*) flaunted her outsider status for seductive advantages.

[8]Considerable debate has raged over the extent, if any, of Yahweh's subjection to an external order, whether in Klaus Koch's words Yahweh did midwife service for the principle of deed/consequence or was thought to rule in majestic indifference to the concept. Walter Brueggemann, *Genesis* (Atlanta: John Knox, 1982) 171 recognizes the centrality of divine character in this argument. The character of Yahweh, not equity in history, is the issue here.

[9]The biblical deity often engages in dubious practices, from the modern perspective, a point that provokes provocative comments from Jack Miles, *God: A Biography* (New York: Vintage Books, 1995), especially 308–28 dealing with God as fiend.

[10]Contrast this accusing mood with the prophetic intercession in Amos 7 ("Lord, Yahweh, please forgive! How can Jacob stand, for he is small?"). Here, too, the intercession stops short, for after two successful attempts to stay divine judgment Amos abandons the effort.

[11]Claus Westermann, *Genesis* 12–36 (Minneapolis: Augsburg, 1984–6) 292. Other possibilities, however, come to mind–reluctance to become too precise; the recognition that the smallest military units consisted of ten; a smaller number will be treated as individuals; Abraham has made his point and to press it further would be useless.

[12]That, not homosexuality, is the specific offense that comes in for censure, although the text also denounces the people for the way in which they broke the code.

[13]For that matter, Abraham never appeals to his kinship with Lot as a bargaining chip. The story offers no hint that Lot would be a salvific influence over the people of Zoar.

[14]Anger over Yahweh's sparing of a wicked but repentant Nineveh moves Jonah to morbid thoughts that death would be better under the circumstances. The natural question, "Why did Yahweh relent in this instance but not in the case of Israel and Judah?" lies under the surface (Terrence E. Fretheim, "Jonah and Theodicy," ZAW 90 {1978] 227–37).

[15]The initial story, a mirror image of an earlier episode involving Abraham, involves a pun on the name Isaac.

[16]James L. Crenshaw, "Who Knows What YHWH Will Do? The Character of God in the Book of Joel," 197–209 in *Fortunate the Eyes That See: Essays in Honor of David Noel Freedman in Celebration of his Seventieth Birthday,* eds. A. B. Beck, et. al. (Grand Rapids: Eerdmans, 1995). See chapter 16 in this volume.

[17]Ronald J. Williams, "Theodicy in the Ancient Near East," CJT 2 (1956) 14–26, Wolfgang von Soden, "Das Fragen nach der Gerechtigkeit Gottes im Alten Orient," *Bibel und Alter Orient* BZAW 162 (Berlin & New York: W. de Gruyter, 1985) 57–76; J. J. Stamm, Das Leiden des Unschuldigung in Babylon und Israel (AThANT, 10; Zurich: 1946); Rainer Albertz, "Der sozial geschichtliche Hintergrund des Hiobsbuches und der 'Babylonischen Theodizee'," 349–72 in *Die Botschaft und die Boten,* F.S. H. W. Wolff, ed. J. Jeremias & L. Perlitt (Neukirchen/Vluyn: Neukirchener Verlag, 1981); Moshe Weinfeld, "Job and its Mesopotamian Parallels: A Typological Analysis," 217–26 in *Text and Context: Old Testament and Semitic Studies for F. C. Fensham,* ed. W. Claassen (JSOTSup 48; Sheffield: JSOT Press, 1988).

[18]The Admonitions of Ipuwer. Often believed to be intrusive, this brief section gives the impression of a society in considerable disarray.

[19]This text, Ludlul ("I Will Praise the God of Wisdom") has recently been translated by Benjamin R. Foster under the title, "Poem of Righteous Sufferer" (*From Distant Days: Myths, Tales, and Poetry of Ancient Mesopotamia* (Bethesda: CDL Press, 1995) 300–313.

[20]"The Babylonian Theodicy," 316–23 in *From Distant Days.*

[21]Magic was not the only instrument for controlling the gods; subjecting them to a human concept of order arose from a similar desire. At least the author of Ludlul recognized the impossibility of knowing what the gods liked or hated. Some biblical authors also emphasized the incomprehensibility of Yahweh.

[22]James L. Crenshaw, *A Whirlpool of Torment: Israelite Traditions of God as an Oppressive Presence* (Philadelphia: Fortress, 1984) 31–56.

[23]Donald E. Gowan, *The Triumph of Faith in Habakkuk* (Atlanta: John Knox, 1976) 20–50.

[24]W. A. M. Beuken, ed. *The Book of Job* (BETL 114; Leuven: University Press, 1994) indicates the rich diversity of opinion regarding this provocative text.

[25]Job's silence has not generated comparable reticence among interpreters, who view the text from vastly different perspectives. Does he find reconciliation as a result of the divine speeches, or does he express hidden contempt for such a deity? Are his words sincere, or does he resort to irony? What does he actually say?

[26]James L. Crenshaw, "Popular Questioning of the Justice of God in Ancient Israel," ZAW 84 (1970) 380–95, reprinted in Crenshaw, *Urgent Advice and Probing Questions: Collected Writings on Old Testament Wisdom* (Macon: Mercer University Press, 1995) 175–90.

[27]Martin Buber, "The Heart Determines (Psalms 73)," 199–210 in *On the Bible* (New York: Schocken Books, 1968); Crenshaw, *A Whirlpool of Torment,* 93–109.

[28]Michael Edward Stone, *Fourth Ezra* (Minneapolis: Fortress Press, 1990) and A. L. Thompson, *Responsibility for Evil in the Theodicy of IV Ezra* (SBLDS 29; Missoula: Scholars Press, 1977).

[29]This chapter (18) has long been seen as the watershed of individualism, but it more correctly may be viewed as the prophetic insistence that Yahweh deal with Israel on the basis of its actions, whether good or evil.

[30]Walter Brueggemann, "Theodicy in a Social Dimension," JSOT 33 (1985) 13.

[31]Crenshaw, "The Shift from Theodicy to Anthropodicy," *Theodicy in the Old Testament* (Philadelphia: Fortress, 1983) 1–16 = *Urgent Advice and Probing Questions,* 141–54 (especially 144).

[32]Brueggemann, "Theodicy in a Social Dimension," 8.

[33]The incessant denunciation of Israel and Judah in the Deuteronomistic history and in prophetic literature, together with confessions in liturgical prayers, have had unfortunate consequences, for they give the impression that God's people were intractable from the very beginning. The problem arises when outsiders fail to acknowledge the context of such denunciation and take a further step toward antisemitism.

[34]Brueggemann, "Theodicy in a Social Dimension," 13, 19.

[35]The incongruity of the epilogue has commanded the attention of many interpreters, who see the ending as undercutting the essential insight in the poem. Having pressed forward to the conclusion that one's external circumstances do not signify one's inner being, the book now has Yahweh deal with Job in a manner predicated on the assumption that goodness must be rewarded in tangible ways.

[36]Brueggemann, "Theodicy in a Social Dimension," 13, 21.

[37]On this text, see James L. Crenshaw, "Clanging Symbols," 51–64 in *Justice and the Holy,* ed. D. A. Knight & P. J. Paris (Philadelphia: Fortress, 1989), reprinted in *Urgent Advice and Probing Questions,* 371–82.

[38]Brueggemann, "Theodicy in a Social Dimension," 18–21.

[39]Ibid., 21.

[40]David Noel Freedman, "Son of Man, Can these Bones Live?" *Inter* 29 (1975) 185–6.

[41]Gerhard von Rad, "The Joseph Narrative and Ancient Wisdom," *The Problem of the Hexateuch and Other Essays* (Edinburgh & London: Oliver & Boyd, 1966) 297 uses the image of God as puppeteer ("God has all the threads firmly in his hands even when men are least aware of it").

[42]Ludwig Schmidt, *"De Deo": Studien zur Literaturkritik und Theologie des Buches Jona, des Gesprächs zwischen Abraham und Jahwe in Gen 18:22ff. und von Hi 1* (BZAW 143; Berlin & New York: W. de Gruyter, 1976) attributes Gen 18:17–18, 22b-33 to a single hand and understands the late text as an expression of new collective thinking. He considers such an attitude impossible in pre-exilic Israel, for its main concern is not "that God is just" but "why God is just"–an abstract problem. Schmidt thinks the author of this story came from the same circle as the person responsible for the book of Jonah.

[43]For discussion of limits to knowledge, see James L. Crenshaw, "Wisdom and the Sage: On Knowing and Not Knowing," chapter 2 above, originally published in *Proceedings of the Eleventh World Congress of Jewish Studies*, Division A (Jerusalem: World Union of Jewish Studies, 1994), pp. 137–44 and chapter 10, "Probing the Unknown: Knowledge and the Sacred," *Education in Ancient Israel: Across the Deadening Silence*, Anchor Bible Reference Library (New York: Doubleday, 1998).

[44]Both Ben Sira and Wisdom of Solomon added psychological and philosophical arguments to the conventional ones in discussions of theodicy (James L. Crenshaw, "The Problem of Theodicy in Sirach: On Human Bondage," JBL 94 [1975] 49–64 = *Urgent Advice and Probing Questions*, 155–74).

[45]Seyyed Hossein Nasr, *Knowledge and the Sacred* (Albany: State University of New York Press, 1989). These Gifford Lectures argue powerfully against the hegemony of secularism.

[46]As I argue in "The Shift from Theodicy to Anthropodicy," the usual defenses of divine justice come at considerable expense to human dignity. In such a context, defense of humankind may be appropriate–but it is not theodicy.

Hebrew/Greek Index

Hebrew

'āb 36, 66, 128
'ādām 7, 9-10, 62, 67, 226n17
'ādāmâ 9
'ašre 77, 116
'eḥād 89-90
'elep 91
'elōhîm 191, 193
'ēn 88-89, 94, 220n40
'enōš 7, 67
'îš 7, 67-68, 128
'îš ha'elōhîm 175, 249n3
'iššâ 7
'iššâ zārâ 16, 262n7
'lp 35-36
bārak 116
bāṭaḥ 76, 223n10, 224n30
bēt hammidraš 26
beqaš 27
bḥn 80, 224n29
dābār 38, 226n15, 233n45
deraš 27, 106, 108
geber 7, 11
hakkōl 83-87, 94, 225n5, 226n13, 226n18
hebel 10, 34, 63, 83, 86-87, 93-94, 217n5, 218n10, 221n48, 225n6
hinnēh 148, 242n9
hwh 1
hyh 1
ḥākām 24, 26, 32, 38, 47, 67, 204n2, 212n18, 215n16, 250n8
ḥāqar 27, 39-40, 80, 224n29
ḥatum 7
ḥāzâ 37
ḥdl 11
ḥešbôn 38, 90, 92, 94, 209n17, 221n44, 226n14
ḥesed 96, 245n39
ḥokmâ 2, 19, 27, 37, 40, 46, 57, 220n34, 223n20
ḥōzeh 158, 175, 186, 249n3
ḥlš 11
ḥoq 7
yēš 87-89, 220n40, 228n43, 228n45
yešivâ 26
ysr 35-36
yrh 36
kābôd 176, 191
kāsap 201n6
kātab 23, 37
kelāyôt 80, 231n22
kî 62, 64, 87-88, 98, 218n14, 226n13
lēb/lēbāb 23, 36-37, 76, 79-80, 98, 221n43, 223n9, 224n27
leḥem 63-65
lmd 35-36
ma'aśeh 209n17, 221n44, 226n14
māšāl 34, 180, 186, 215n21
mî yôdēa' 79, 150-51, 164, 211n44, 223n24
miqreh 67, 84, 209n17, 221n44, 226n14
mispar 92, 94
mišpāṭ 178, 193
mût 11
mûsār 18, 27, 36
nābî' 158, 175, 186, 249n3
natan 228n41

ne'um-YHWH 148, 243n13, 247n12
niḥām 164
nokrîyyâ 16
sôpîyya 24
sûr 27
'ābar 208n3
'am 59, 219n22,
'ēṣ 65, 76, 223n11
'ôlām 209n17, 221n44, 226n14
pešat 106, 108
pešer 38, 107, 131, 211n43, 238n47
ṣaddîq 151, 176-78, 260n27
qāra' 23, 244n29
rā'â 37, 40, 63, 81, 90
rē'šît 103
rō'eh 158, 175, 186, 249n3
śākal 37
śiḥâ 28
šalîṭ 32
šālôm 113
šûb 148, 151, 164-65, 243n17
talmîd 37

Greek

dike 199
eros 18
eukairia 32
theos 199–200
sorites 18
sophia 19, 24
tò pân / tà pánta 84–85
psyche 36

Scripture Index

OLD TESTAMENT
(English versification in parentheses)

Genesis
1 116, 185, 259n14
1–11 125
2–3 9, 44
3:9 12
3:19 55
6:5 78
6:5–6 222n1
8:1 7
8:21 78
8:21–22 219n21
15 98
18 237n24
18–19 197
18:17–18 263n42
18:22–33 263n42
18:26 196
19 184
19:9 184, 195
22:2 108
22:6 108
35:29 10
37–50 125
39:9 64
49:10–12 160
49:11 233n38

Exodus
3:8 233n38
3:14 1
13:5 233n28
22:29–30 189
29:24 226n21
31:18 171
32–34 150
32:12 150–51, 244n34
32:14 150
32:29 150
32:32–33 202n12, 253n43
33:3 233n38
33:19 150, 244n32
34:6 147, 150, 164, 181, 244n29, 244n33, 244n34
34:6–7 3, 56, 116, 150–51, 156, 172, 180–81, 189, 241n1, 248n2, 256n14
34:7 150
34:10 150

Leviticus
1:9 226n21
20:24 233n38

Numbers
11:29 158
12:6–8 158, 169
14:9 64
14:17–18 244n29
14:18 151

Deuteronomy
1:17 127
4:2 126
4:6 128, 237n27
4:30–31 149
6:7–9 127
7:3 129
8:5 128
10:16 149
11:18–20 127
13:1 (12:32) 126
16:19 127
16:20 127
18:15–22 168
19:14 127
23:15–16 127
23:22 129
23:22–24 (21–23) 128
25:18 128
28:15–45 129
29:28 (29) 41
29:29 129
30:2 149
30:3 149
32 139
32:4 256n18
32:6 98
32:13–14 102, 232n35
32:39 182

Joshua
24 110

Judges
7:1 35
14:14 219n25
14:18 219n25
16:13 231n7
19–21 53
19:1 53
19:23–24 261n2
21:25 53

1 Samuel
9:5–10 247n17
9:9 158, 186
17:43–47 215n18
24:14 (13) 215n21
25:29 7

2 Samuel
1:9 226n21
9–20 125
12:6 214n5
12:15–23 149
12:22 151
12:23 55
13:3 215n16
14:3b 55
14:14 55
17:7–13 215n18
22:15 220n32

1 Kings
1–2 125
13 143
20:11 56
22 158

2 Kings
18:19–25 215n18

18:28–35 215n18
20:1–11 244n28

1 Chronicles
5:13 35
25:8 37
29:14 85
29:17 80
29:28 10

2 Chronicles
26:15 92
30:9 149
32:10–15 215n18

Ezra
2:64 90
3:9 90
6:20 90
9 129

Nehemiah
7:66 90
9 129
9:17 151
9:31 151
10:39 233n38
13:22 156

Esther
4:3 149
4:14 151

Job
1:22 242n8
2:10 242n8
3:13–17 201n8
3:17–19 201n8
5:1 88
5:9 39
6:6 88
6:15–20 223n16
6:30 88
7:1 202n11
7:18 80
8:8, 10 36, 40
9:2–3 92
9:5–10 95
9:10 39
9:22–24 95
9:27 216n36
9:32–34 201n5
9:33 88, 95
10:3 201n6
10:3–22 96
10:6 39
10:8–12 95–96, 218n7
10:11 231n7
10:11–12 220n38
11:7 40
13:20–22 201n1, 201n5
13:26 37
14:1–6 9–11
14:2 99
14:7 87, 99
14:7–12 9, 11–12
14:10 87
14:12 99
14:13–17 2, 6–13
14:14 202n10
14:18–19 99
14:18–22 6, 9, 12–13
14:22 203n28, 203n29
15:4 28
15:5 36
15:19 127
16:4 88
16:19 148
19:23 37
19:25–27 201n5
22:8 127
23:10 80
25:3 88
28 40, 50
28:23 40
28:27 40
29:18 216n36
31 3, 42–45
31:15 228n49
33:23 88
33:32 88
33:33b 36
34:6 79
34:24 39
35:10 157
35:11 35
36:26 39
37:14 36
38–41 190
38:1–41:6 16
38:5 30
38:16 40
38:28 88
42:2 85
42:5 25
42:17 10

Psalms
1–41 107
1 76–77, 113, 116, 203n24
1:4 77
2 115–16
4:2 107
6 116
7:7–21 201n2
7:10 80
8 10, 58–59, 98, 110
8:7–8 85
9–10 108
10 231n16
10:2–22 201n2
13:20–14:22 201n2
14 222n1, 231n16
14:1 82, 222n1
14:3 222n1
14:5 222n1
15 110, 112
16:7–8 201n2
17:3 80
17:3–4 201n2
19 113, 116, 256n18
19:2–7 110
20 110
21 110
22:4 234n13
23 116, 120
24 112, 119
24:1–6 110
24:7–10 110
25 59
25:4–13 256n14
29 110, 114
30:5 182
30:20–23 201n2
32–33 108
34 113, 130
37 48, 107, 113, 116

37:11 107
37:25 208n3
37:38 128
39 59
39:5–7 218n7
39:6–7 87
39:12 87, 218n7
39:14 (13) 12
40:3–5 201n2
41:13 107
42–43 108
42:1–6 201n2
42:4 (3) 65, 157
42:11 (10) 157
45 110
48 110
49 48, 113
49:16 98
50 110, 252n34
51 110, 170, 252n34
52 59
52:10 78
53 222n1
53:2 82
54 231n16
56:9 253n43
57:8–11 110
60 110
62 59
62:10 87
63:9 (8) 130
65:10 110
68 110–11, 114
69:21 79
70–71 108
71 116, 119
72 115
72:19 107
73 48, 58–59, 116, 119–20, 134, 174, 180, 198, 212n24, 221n43, 222n3
73–89 107
73:17 128
73:23 97
73:24 98, 201n3
76 110
78 58, 110, 113, 116
79 157
80:6 65
81:6–17 110
82 185
82:7 191
83:19 (18) 130
84 111
86:10 130
86:15 151
88 59
89 110, 115–16
89:52 107
90 58–59
90–100 108
90–106 107
90:11 151
92 177
92:5–6 177
92:13–15 78
92:15 (16) 256n18
93 116
94:7–9 59
94:11 87
94:12 35
94:14 59
94:53 59
95 110
95–99 116
100 110
102 118
102:18 223n11
103–104 108
103:8 151
103:19 85
104 110, 114, 117
105 110, 113
106 113
106:48 107
107–150 107
111 113
111:4 151
112 113
112:4 151
113–118 116
114 110
115 119, 157
115:1–2 157
118:26 107
119 48, 59, 116, 123, 216n36, 233n45
119:10 130
119:31 130
119:34 130
119:69 130
119:91 85
119:97, 99 28
119:108 35
120–134 108, 116, 120
127 108, 113
131 93, 108
132 108, 112
134:6 116
135:17 228n45
136 110
137 166
137:2 107
139 39, 48, 60, 118
139:1–3 38
139:4 39
139:7–12 8
139:13–18 96–97, 216n7, 220n38
139:16 202n12, 216n7, 253n43
139:19–22 60, 97
139:23–24 39, 80
141:3 43
144:3 10
144:4 10, 87
145 108, 111
145:3 39
145:8 151
146–150 108
150 107

Proverbs

1 18
1–9 63, 249n8
1:1–9:18 26
1:2–7 50
1:7 103
1:8–19 15, 235n1
1:10 218n15
1:20–33 235n1
1:28 236n11

2:21–22 127
3:3 23, 37
3:11–12 36
3:12 128
3:18 78
3:32 127
3:70 201n1
4:1–9 15
4:13 38
4:24 78
5:7–14 15
5:13 36
5:13–14 23
5:15–20 57, 219n25
6:1–19 235n1
6:20–22 127
6:20–35 214n5
6:30 53, 214n5
7:3 23, 37, 127
7:6–27 30, 208n2, 208n3
8 18
8:22–31 85, 93, 233n46
8:22–36 33
8:32 218n15
9 18
9:5 103
9:17 57, 64, 103
9:18 57
10:1–22:16 34, 219n22
10:30 127
11:1 127
11:20 127
12:9–10 23
12:22 127
15:8–9 127
15:26 127
16:5 127
17:15 127
18:5 23
18:15 39
18:24 87
19:23–24 23
19:27 24
20:5 80
20:10 127
20:23 127
21:21 127
22:17 24
22:17–24:22 23
22:20 24
23:5 78
23:10 127
23:12 24
23:18 128
23:26 24
24:14 128
24:23 127
24:30–34 24, 30, 208n3
25–29 34, 219n22
25:1 249n6
25:3 39, 40
25:27 40
26:7 57
26:9 56–57
27:26–27 103
28:21 127
28:26 36
30:1 231n15
30:1–4 223n24
30:1–14 24, 30, 126, 231n21, 236n7
30:4 98
30:7–9 201n1
30:8–9 53, 102
30:10 127
30:18–23 91
30:20 219n25
30:29–31 91
31:1–9 24, 208n2
31:10–31 24
31:14 220n28
31:26 24
31:27 24

Ecclesiastes
1:1 34, 62
1:2 62, 84, 86, 217n4, 218n9, 226n13, 228n38
1:2–3 34
1:3–12:7 62
1:4 226n13
1:4–11 32, 34, 64, 84, 220n31
1:7 89
1:8 67, 226n15
1:9 89
1:9–11 221n51
1:10 87, 228n43
1:11 88
1:12–2:26 31, 34, 221n52
1:14 84, 87
1:15 93
1:16 92
1:18 92
2:1 216n36
2:3 92
2:4–9 221n52
2:7 92
2:10 92
2:11 84, 87, 89, 226n13
2:13 88
2:13–14 217n2
2:16 88
2:17 84, 226n13
2:19 66, 151
2:21 88, 92, 228n43
2:24 88, 217n4
2:26 217n4
3:1–8 32
3:1–22 34
3:2–8 24, 32
3:6 39
3:9 88
3:9–22 32
3:11 39, 86–87, 101, 220n36
3:12 89, 217n4
3:14 89, 92
3:14–15 33
3:15 86
3:18 226n13
3:19 84, 87, 226n13
3:20 12, 84, 226n13
3:21 151
3:22 89, 92, 217n4
4:1 89
4:4 67
4:7 90
4:8–12 90, 221n52
4:8 87, 89

4:9 88
4:10 89
4:16 88
4:17 89
5:1 92
5:1–5 128–29
5:2 92
5:3 89
5:6 92
5:7 91
5:8 91
5:11 67, 89, 92
5:12 87
5:12–16 65
5:13 89
5:15 129
5:16 92
5:17 92, 217n4
5:17–18 92
5:19 92, 233n44
6:1 87
6:2 89, 92
6:3 67, 91
6:6 84, 91
6:11 88, 92
6:12 10, 92
7:15 83, 88
7:17 92
7:19 91
7:20 89
7:22 92
7:23b 38
7:24 38, 79
7:25 38, 92
7:27 38, 90, 92
7:28 38, 91, 222n53
7:29 91–92
8:1 38, 91, 151, 217n1
8:6 88
8:7 89
8:8 88
8:10–17 32
8:11 89
8:12 91
8:12–13 33
8:13 89
8:14 87
8:15 89, 217n4
8:16 89
8:17 39
9:1 84, 87, 89
9:2 89
9:4–5 12
9:4 88
9:5 89
9:6 89, 92, 226n16
9:7–9 102, 217n4
9:7–10 217n1
9:9 92, 217n4
9:10 89
9:11 85
9:14 67, 92
9:15 67, 92
9:16 89
10:5 87
10:11 89
10:14b 63
10:18 63
10:19 63–64, 103
10:20 218n9
11:1 92, 214n2, 218n9, 218n14, 220n28
11:1–8 3, 61–68
11:2 92, 218n14
11:3 218n14, 220n32, 220n37
11:4 214n2
11:5 60, 87, 89, 98, 216n44, 218n14, 220n37
11:6 89–90, 220n26
11:7–12:1 217n4
11:7–12:7 34, 220n26
11:8 63, 86, 92, 218n8, 218n14, 221n49, 226n13
11:9 63
11:9–12:7 63, 67
12:1 63, 89
12:1–7 217n4, 221n51
12:2–3 63
12:3 67, 92
12:6 99
12:7 98
12:8 34, 62–63, 84, 86, 99, 217n4, 225n10, 226n13, 228n38
12:8–14 34
12:9 24, 92, 219n15, 219n22
12:9–14 62
12:9–10 38
12:10 37
12:11 90
12:12 84–85, 103
12:13–14 128, 216n37, 237n27

Isaiah
2:2–4 160–61
5 253n52
6:9–13 189
8:16 169, 251n26
9:1–7 161
10:5–19 163
11:1 11
11:6–9 160–61
17:11 79
18:12 220n28
26:19 201n3, 203n27
27 253n52
28:23–29 35, 192, 219n21
28:26 35, 193
29:11–12 23
29:15–16 193
30:20 35
36:4–10 215n18
36:13–20 215n18
40–55 192
40:2 148, 202n10
40:6–8 9
40:28 39
44:22 148
44:24 85, 226n19
45:7 85, 182
51:6 86

51:9–11 185
52:13–53:12 168
54:7–8 182
55:10–11 169
58:3–9 149
65:17 86
65:25 90
66:24 203n29, 221n47

Jeremiah

1 139
1–20 138
1–25 137
1–45 137, 140
1:4–11:6 142
1:4–6:30 239n7
1:4–14 138
1:5 138, 142
2:2–3 138
2:5–37 138
3 96
3:1–5 138
3:12–14 138
3:19–25 138
4:1 244n30
4:1–6:30 138
4:4 149
4:23–25 185
4:23–26 96
5:4–5 170
5:30–31 144
5:40 216n36
6:9–15 144
6:27 79
8:4–10 138
8:13 138
8:14–10:25 138
10:16 85–86
11:19 65
11:20 80
12:1 245n40
12:1–2 188
12:4 188
13:23–28 202n20
14:1 203n22
14:1–6 202n20, 240n39
14:1–15:9 142, 247n13
14:7–22 202n20
15:3 202n16
15:5–9 240n39
15:10–21 240n33
15:14 203n22
15:18 79, 188
17:5–11 2, 73–82, 224n32
17:6 222n5
17:8 222n5
17:9 87
17:16 79
18:8–11 196
18:20 188
19:1–20:6 140
20:7 188, 231n15, 241n56
20:12 80
20:14 188
20:18 138
24 139
24:9 246n54
25:4 202n22
25:11–12 169
26–29 140
26–45 137
26:20–23 187
29:10 169
30–31 137, 140–41
30:12 79
30:15 79
31:2–6 140
31:12 233n38
31:15–20 140
31:29 56
31:33 37, 171
32:19 74
32:33 35
32:39 228n49
36 140
37–44 140
44:15–19 193
45 140
46–52 137
51:19 85–86
51:59–64 140

Ezekiel

12:1 176
14:12–20:18 196
18 189
18:2 56
18:3 246n54
20:7 176
20:25–26 189
22:23–31 177
34:22 228n49
37:22 228n49
37:24 90
47:1–12 160–61
47:12 77
48:8–14 247n16

Daniel

4 203n24
5:5 171
9 129
9:1–27 169
9:15 129
12:1 202n12
12:2 201n3, 203n27

Hosea

1:6 256n14
1:9 256n14
2:2 228n49
2:10 233n38
2:14–15 (16–17) 182
2:16 243n13
2:21 243n13
4:12 65
11:11 243n13
13:14 182
14:5–7 (4–7) 160–61
14:10 178, 256n14, 256n20

Joel

1:1–2:1 155
1:1–2:11 154–56
1:1–4:16 153
1:9–2:17 155
1:12 155
1:13 155
1:16 155
2:1 155
2:3 151, 154, 156
2:11 156
2:12 156, 165
2:12–14 147–52, 189, 256n14
2:12–27 156–57, 181
2:13 156, 244n33, 245n43

2:14 156
2:16 156
2:17 150, 245n44, 246n54
2:18 157
2:18–27 245n43
2:19 246n54
2:23 246n55
2:26–27 157, 245n44
2:27 154
3:1–5 247n19
3:1–4:16 157–60
4:8 148
4:9–16 154
4:10 (3:10) 150
4:14 160
4:16 160
4:17–21 (3:17–21) 153–61
4:21 (3:21) 256n14

Amos

1:2 160
1:3 91
1:6 91
1:9 91
1:11 91
1:13 91
2:1 91
2:4 91
2:6 91
3:3–8 182, 193
3:6 193
3:7 41
3:8 182
4:6–11 164
4:6–12 181, 191
4:13 182, 192, 256n14
5:8–9 182, 192, 256n14
5:18–20 156
7 262n10
7:10–15 187
9:2–4 8, 98, 231n17
9:5–6 182, 192, 256n14
9:11–15 160
9:13 77

Obadiah

15 181

Jonah

3:5–10 256n14
3:9 150–51
4:1–2 150, 180, 256n14
4:3–11 256n14

Micah

1:9 79
2:7–8 256n14
3:8 158
4:1–4 160–61
4:5 256n14
5:4 64, 91
6–7 256n14
7:10 157
7:18–20 181, 245n39, 256n14

Nahum

1:2–3 181
1:3 151

Habakkuk

1:2–4 179, 190
1:5 190
1:5–11 179
1:7 179
1:11 179
1:12 190
1:13 179, 190
2:1–4 179
3 180

Zephaniah

3:1–5 177
3:5 256n18
3:6–13 178
3:9 228n49

Zechariah

1:7–17 256n19
7:3 149, 243n26
7:5 149, 243n26
13:1–6 186
13:2–6 168
13:9 80
14:1–21 160–61

Malachi

1:2–5 178
2:10 228n49
2:13–15 178
2:17 157, 178, 183
3:6 149
3:13–15 184
3:16 253n43
3:19–21 (4:1–3) 160–61

APOCRYPHA

1 Esdras

3:1–4:41 44
4:37–38 75

Judith

16:17 203n29

2 Maccabees

7:9 201n3
7:22 220n38

Sirach

1:1–23:27 205n20
3:12 219n15
3:17–24 40–41
3:21–24 94, 224n37
5:3 39
6:6 92
6:17–20 18
6:18–37 18, 27–28
6:27 38
10:18 203n22
11:10–14 85
11:28 81
15:2 18
16:3 92
21:15 18
22:16–17 18
22:27–23:6 201n1
23:17 64
24 93
24:30–34 208n5
26:12 219n25
27:6 18
29:21 54, 100, 217n1, 232n35
33:16–18 208n5
34:7 100
34:9–12 208n5
36:1–22 201n1
36:1 86
38:9 219n15
38:23–24 247n10

38:24–39:11 238n43
38:24–30 229n63
39:11 92
39:12 208n5
39:12–35 86
39:25–27 100
39:26 54, 217n1
39:32 23, 37
39:32–35 208n5
39:33 101
40–50 58
41:1–4 100
41:12 92
42:2 92
42:3 92
42:7 37
43:26b–28 85
44–50 48
44:5 23, 37
45:11 23, 37
48:5 100
48:10 23, 37
50:15 86
50:25–26 60, 91
50:25–29 208n5
51:1–30 205n20
51:12 86
51:13–30 18, 208n5, 208n6
51:17 35
51:23 219n22

Wisdom of Solomon
3:3–4 100
3:13–14 229n56
4:1 229n56
7:2 96
8:19–20 100
10–19 58
14:18–20 96

NEW TESTAMENT

Matthew
11:29 27

John
3:2–15 221n41
3:8 66
14:3–4 247n16

Acts
2:1–21 247n19

Romans
3:10–12 222n1

Author Index

A

Ackerman, J.S., 259n18
Ahlström, G., 154, 164, 243n18, 246n55, 248n5
Albertz, Rainer, 216n41, 245n52, 262n17
Albrektson, B., 242n5
Albright, W.F., 115, 132
Allen, Leslie C., 154, 165, 243n22, 248n11
Alonso-Schökel, Luis, 115, 206n35, 234n15
Alter, Robert, 115, 133, 158, 234n17
Amir, Y., 84, 225n9
Anderson, Bernhard, 117
Anderson, G., 243n27
Anderson, Hugh, 232n26
Atkinson, Kenneth, 234n4
Auffret, P., 115

B

Backhaus, Franz Josef, 63, 211n42
Bains, John, 206n41
Baker, Joshua, 234n6
Bakhtin, Mikhail, 167
Bal, M., 158
Balentine, Samuel E., 201n1, 254n4, 258n7, 259n19
Baltzer, K., 229n55
Bar-Efrat, S., 158
Barthélemy, Dominique, 204n10
Bartholomew, C.G., 230n72
Barton, John, 218n12, 223n19, 248n1, 251n22
Bauks, Michaela, 233n46
Baumann, Gerlinda, 211n1, 215n25, 230n68, 233n46
Baumgartel, F., 242n10
Becker, Ernest, 202n18
Beckman, Gary, 214n14
Beentjes, P.C., 206n31, 227n27, 232n34, 232n36
Begg, Christopher, 204n3
Begrich, Joachim, 234n11
Ben Zvi, Ehud, 252n39
Berger, Peter L., 254n2, 258n12
Bergler, S., 244n36
Berlin, Adele, 115, 158, 234n17, 256n18
Berquist, J.L., 229n54
Berridge, John, 142, 240n34
Beuken, W.A.M., 240n39, 263n24
Bewer, J.A., 154
Bickerman, Elias, 209n22, 220n28, 224n2
Birkeland, H., 112
Blank, Sheldon, 142, 240n34
Blenkinsopp, Joseph, 32, 204n5, 209n25, 210n35, 237n21, 248n14, 252n28, 252n33, 252n35
Bogaert, P.M., 238n1
Bohlen, Reinhold, 206n30, 218n13, 232n31
Boström, L., 242n5
Bourke, J., 241n3, 246n8
Bracke, J.M., 243n17
Braun, Rainer, 218n13
Brenner, Athalya, 209n25, 211n1
Brettler, Marc, 114
Brichto, Hebert Chanan, 234n17
Bright, John, 139, 142, 237n28, 240n34
Brongers, H.A., 242n6
Brown, Robert McAfee, 254n1
Brown, William P., 114, 212n19, 214n12, 221n45, 230n2, 249n7
Brueggemann, Walter, 114, 117, 135, 254n2, 254n4, 262n8, 263n30, 263n32, 263n34, 263n36, 263n38
Bruner, J.S., 203n2
Brünner, Hellmut, 220n27, 228n40
Bryce, Glendon E., 223n18
Buber, Martin, 156, 221n43, 263n27

Buccellatti, Giorgio, 142, 212n23, 246n6
Burkes, Shannon, 221n50
Buttenweiser, Moses, 110–11, 234n9, 234n10

C

Calduch-Benages, N., 227n23, 227n28
Camp, Claudia V., 204n5, 211n1, 215n25
Carasic, M., 249n6
Carney, T.F., 235n5
Carr, David M., 219n25, 233n39
Carroll, Robert, 138, 140–45, 239n4, 239n9, 241n54, 251n21, 259n14
Carter, Charles E., 252n39
Cathcart, K.J., 219n23, 219n24
Ceresko, Anthony, 115
Cerny, L., 245n49
Childs, B.S., 244n29, 245n50
Christianson, E.S., 225n10, 226n13, 230n72
Clements, R., 235n4
Clifford, Richard J., 215n23, 245n51
Clines, D.J.A., 233n1
Coggins, Richard, 235n2, 235n4
Collins, John J., 210n35, 212n29, 222n7, 231n20, 232n36, 237n21, 247n20, 252n35
Collins, T., 243n25
Cotter, D.W., 242n4
Craig, K.M. Jr., 260n24
Creach, Jerome F.D., 114, 214n12
Crenshaw, James L., 63, 113, 156, 158, 201n1, 202n21, 203n28, 203n30, 204n7, 205n25, 206n29, 206n31, 206n36, 206n38, 207n50, 208n7, 208n10, 208n12, 210n30, 210n34, 210n39, 211n44, 211n45, 211n48, 212n15, 212n18, 212n22, 212n24, 212n25, 213n43, 213n51, 213n53, 215n19, 215n28, 215n29, 216n32, 216n38, 216n42, 216n43, 217n3, 217n4, 219n22, 219n25, 220n40, 221n50, 222n1, 222n7, 224n28, 224n29, 224n35, 224n38, 227n29, 227n30, 227n32, 227n33, 227n34, 228n37, 228n42, 228n44, 228n47, 229n51, 230n1, 231n14, 231n21, 232n24, 232n25, 232n27, 232n28, 232n29, 232n30, 232n36, 233n40, 233n1, 236n12, 237n24, 237n26, 237n30, 238n39, 238n44, 240n46, 242n5, 243n17, 245n38, 245n42, 247n10, 247n13, 247n26, 248n1, 248n2, 248n3, 248n4, 249n6, 250n8, 250n11, 250n12, 251n24, 252n30, 253n48, 253n50, 253n51, 253n53, 254n2, 255n6, 255n9, 256n12, 256n19, 257n26, 257n29, 257n30, 257n31, 257n32, 258n6, 258n8, 258n10, 259n12, 259n16, 259n20, 260n23, 260n25, 260n26, 260n29, 260n30, 261n39, 261n40, 261n43, 261n45, 262n16, 263n22, 263n26, 263n27, 263n31, 263n37, 263n43, 263n44
Cross, Frank Moore, Jr., 115, 234n14
Crüsemann, Franz, 113, 220n28, 224n2, 261n40

D

Dahood, Mitchell, 115, 224n2
Daley, B.E., 230n71
Davies, Graham I., 206n38
Davis, Ellen F., 251n22, 253n44
Day, J., 259n13
de Jong, Stefan, 209n24, 210n38, 217n3, 230n66
de Moor, Johannes C., 215n20, 232n25, 255n5, 259n17
de Wette, W.M.L., 109

de Wilde, A., 203n22
Deist, F.E., 241n3
Delitzsch, Franz, 63
Dell, Katherine J., 211n1, 211n6, 213n46, 242n4
Demsky, Aaron, 206n42
Dentan, R.C., 241n1
Dhorme, Edouard, 203n26, 231n6
DiLella, A.A., 204n8, 205n21, 206n35, 227n32, 232n37, 232n38
Dor-Shaw, Ethan, 217n5
Dozeman, T.B., 241n1, 244n31, 244n35, 244n36, 246n58
Duhm, Bernhard, 138, 168
Duke, David Nelson, 254n4, 258n7
Dutcher-Walls, Patricia, 235n5

E

Ebach, J., 258n10
Ehlich, Konrad, 217n5, 225n6
Eissfeldt, Otto, 215n15
Everson, A.J., 242n3

F

Farley, Wendy, 254n4
Feininger, B., 233n1
Feuerbach, L., 258n12
Fichtner, J., 227n31
Fischer, A., 210n38, 219n19, 230n72
Fischer, Balthasar, 116
Fishbane, Michael, 93, 171, 234n2, 236n14, 236n16, 241n1, 244n37, 245n39, 251n20, 259n14, 260n29
Flint, P.W., 234n3
Fohrer, Georg, 238n2
Fokkelman, J., 242n9
Fontaine, Carol R., 211n1, 215n15, 229n55
Foster, Benjamin, 54, 78–79, 214n8, 214n10, 214n14, 262n19
Fox, Michael, 33, 202n21, 207n49, 207n1, 208n9, 209n15, 210n31, 210n36, 211n7, 211n9, 213n37, 213n43, 214n5, 215n27, 217n45, 217n3, 217n5, 218n8, 219n17, 220n30, 221n48, 221n51, 222n53, 225n6, 225n10, 226n16, 226n17, 227n34, 229n55, 230n1
Fredericks, Daniel, 32, 209n15, 209n19, 213n50
Freedman, David Noel, 115, 234n14, 241n53, 241n1, 263n40
Fretheim, Terence E., 257n26, 260n24, 261n1262n14
Frost, S.B., 260n33
Frye, Northrop, 253n52
Fuchs, Gisela, 203n23

G

Galling, Kurt, 62
Gammie, John G., 218n13
Geertz, C., 244n27
Geller, Stephen A., 213n41
Gericke, Jacobus Wilhelm, 217n2
Gersternberger, Erhard S., 113–14, 213n31, 223n10, 224n30, 240n33
Gese, Hartmut, 209n26, 225n7
Gilbert, M., 227n28, 228n40, 230n4
Gilkey, Langdon, 132
Gillingham, S.E., 235n19
Gillman, Neil, 202n18
Glatzer, N.N., 242n4
Gnuse, R., 242n5, 260n31
Golka, Friedemann, 206n38, 212n11, 216n39, 250n9
Good, Edwin M., 202n20, 242n7
Gordis, Robert, 208n14, 222n53
Gorssen, L., 217n3, 230n66
Gottwald, Norman, 114
Goulder, Michael, 114
Gowan, Donald E., 257n25, 260n34, 263n23
Green, William Scott, 253n1
Greenberg, Moshe, 166, 201n1, 248n13, 255n10
Gressmann, Hugo, 138
Grønbech, V., 112
Gunkel, Hermann, 111–14, 133, 138, 234n11, 234n13, 261n1

Gunn, David, 133
Gutiérrez, Gustavo, 114, 211n2

H

Haak, Robert D., 257n25
Habel, Norman C., 201n8, 202n11, 202n20, 242n7
Hadot, Jean, 205n28
Hakham, Amos, 223n16, 232n23
Halivni, David Weiss, 234n2
Hallo, William W., 214n14, 215n21, 253n43
Hamp, V., 243n25
Haran, M., 204n6
Harrelson, Walter, 135
Harrington, Daniel J., 204n1, 224n37
Harris, Scott L., 235n1
Harris, William V., 238n42
Harrison, C. Robert, 209n24, 218n13, 224n1
Hartley, John E., 203n27
Haspecker, Josef, 205n27
Hausmann, Jutta, 211n1
Hayman, A.P., 203n13
Heijerman, Meike, 208n2
Hengel, Martin, 205n17, 209n16, 218n13, 227n32, 232n31
Herder, J.G., 109
Herrmann, Siegfried, 143, 238n2, 239n4
Hertzberg, Hans Wilhelm, 63
Hiebert, T., 245n48
Hill, A.E., 258n6
Hobbs, T.R., 238n2
Höffken, Peter, 90, 204n3, 208n5, 221n52, 233n43, 259n18
Hoffmann, Yair, 201n9, 211n5, 213n36, 242n3, 246n8
Hoffner, Harry A. Jr., 214n11
Holbek, Bengt, 252n41
Holladay, William, 116, 138–39, 142, 224n31, 234n5, 239n6, 239n7, 239n9, 239n11, 240n39, 243n17
Horst, F., 154, 261n40
Hubbard, D.A., 154
Hubmann, Franz D., 141
Hugger, P., 214n12
Humphreys, W. Lee, 211n10
Hunter, A. Vanlier, 239n14
Hurvitz, Avi, 216n42, 227n26, 233n45
Hyatt, J. Philip, 135, 139, 142

I

Isakson, Bo, 228n43, 228n46

J

Jacobsen, Thorkild, 78–79, 214n13, 258n11
Jaki, Stanley J., 117
Janowski, B., 226n16
Janssen, E., 239n18
Janzen, J. Gerald, 240n26
Jenni, Ernst, 224n29
Jeremias, Jörg, 245n48, 257n33
Johnson, A. R., 233n1
Johnston, Sarah Iles, 222n1
Junge, Friedrich, 223n19
Jüngling, H.W., 259n18

K

Kaiser, Otto, 85, 210n32, 210n38, 218n13, 227n24, 232n31, 259n19
Kalugila, Leonidas, 262n7
Kant, I., 258n9, 262n5
Kapelrud, A.S., 154, 165, 233n1, 245n45, 246n2, 247n22, 248n7
Katz, Steven T., 253n1
Keel, Othmar, 114, 221n45
Kermode, Frank, 251n19
Kerrigan, A., 245n52
Kieweler, Volker, 205n15
Klein, Christian, 34, 210n37, 230n65
Klopfenstein, Martin A., 210n32, 245n44
Knight, Douglas A., 145, 241n52
Knuth, Hans C., 116
Koch, Klaus, 262n8
Kolarcik, Michael, 202n19, 213n45, 232n33

Koole, J.L., 204n4
Kraeling, Emil G., 202n14
Kraemer, David, 203n28
Kramer, S.N., 203n3
Kraus, Hans Joachim, 114
Kremers, Heinrik, 140
Krüger, Thomas, 62, 211n42, 218n8, 219n19, 221n48, 221n51, 222n53, 226n11, 226n16, 229n55
Kugel, James, 220n28, 224n2
Kuntz, J. Kenneth, 216n43
Kutsko, John F., 231n4, 256n13, 260n38

L

Laato, Antti, 215n20, 232n25, 255n5
Labuschagne, C.J., 246n56
Lamb, Jonathan, 203n28
Landes, G.M., 260n24
Lang, Bernard, 212n20, 230n68
Lauha, Aarre, 217n5, 225n6
Lee, Thomas, 205n23
Leibniz, G.W., 258n1
Lemaire, Andre, 206n37
Lemke, Werner E., 240n45
Lenski, Gerhard, 235n5
Levenson, Jon D., 203n23, 245n51, 259n13
Lewis, C.S., 117, 257n27
Lichtheim, Miriam, 76, 203n3, 204n8, 211n1, 211n8, 214n1, 214n2, 214n3, 214n7, 214n9, 217n44, 218n7, 220n26, 223n19, 249n5, 253n46
Limburg, James, 115, 233n1
Lindenberger, James M., 206n44
Loader, J.A., 246n7
Lohfink, Norbert, 62, 84, 86, 142, 206n40, 207n56, 209n15, 209n18, 210n32, 210n42, 217n4, 217n5, 222n53, 225n4, 225n6, 225n9, 226n11, 226n12, 226n16, 229n55, 233n44, 233n46, 235n2, 235n3, 238n40, 238n45, 262n7
Longman, T. III, 226n10
Lopreno, Antonio, 214n7
Loretz, Oswald, 31, 67, 165, 208n13, 214n53, 218n10, 246n55, 248n6
Luckman, Thomas, 258n12
Lundbom, Jack, 138–39, 224n31, 239n9
Lust, J., 141
Lux, Rüdiger, 209n27

M

Machinist, Peter, 90, 209n16, 210n41, 218n6, 221n44, 226n14, 230n1
Mack, Burton, 205n22, 207n55, 213n44
Magonet, J., 244n34
Maier, Christl, 212n20, 215n26
Marböck, Johannes, 204n1, 205n26, 206n31, 227n28
Martin, James D., 206n33, 207n55
Matties, Gordon H., 241n54, 260n28
Mattila, S.L., 227n24, 232n31
Mays, James L., 116
McCann, J. Clinton, Jr., 116
McGlynn, M., 227n29
McKane, William, 215n23, 224n31, 224n35, 239n4, 239n19
McKenna, John E., 217n5
McKenzie, S.L., 258n2
McKinlay, Judith E., 215n25, 230n68
Melchert, C.F., 208n11
Mettinger, T.N.D., 242n5, 259n17
Meyer, Ivo, 143–44
Meyers, Carol, 160, 210n35, 237n21, 242n12, 243n26, 252n35, 253n45
Meyers, E., 160, 242n12, 243n26, 253n45
Michel, Diethelm, 63, 217n3, 230n66
Middendorp, Theophil, 205n14
Miles, Jack, 262n9
Millard, Alan, 207n52

Miller, Patrick D., 114, 224n33, 259n17
Moberly, R.W.L., 259n15
Moran, William L., 214n10
Morgenstern, Julien, 110
Mowinckel, Sigmund, 3, 112–14, 117, 139, 234n13, 247n18
Muilenburg, James, 115, 234n16, 239n21, 240n34, 241n56
Müller, Hans Peter, 217n3, 225n4, 230n66
Murphy, Roland E., 205n25, 207n58, 209n26, 212n27, 213n43, 232n27
Myers, J.M., 248n27

N

Nash, K.S., 246n55
Nasr, Seyyed Hossein, 264n45
Nelson, Milward D., 205n12
Newsom, Carol A., 6, 203n29, 204n4, 210n29, 211n1, 211n5, 231n6
Nicholson, Ernest W., 139–40, 143, 234n6, 235n4
Niditch, Susan, 34, 171, 206n39, 207n48, 210n33, 212n15, 236n9
Nissinen, Marti, 213n34, 251n26, 255n11, 259n21
Nogalski, James D., 234n11
Novick, Tsvi, 224n25

O

O'Brien, Julia, 257n21, 258n6
O'Connor, M., 226n20
Oeming, Manfred, 216n29, 233n1
Oesterley, W.E., 215n23, 215n24
Ogden, Graham S., 217n5
Olyan, Saul M., 204n2
Oppenheim, A.L., 202n13
Overholt, Thomas W., 145

P

Pahk, J.Y.S., 229n55
Parker, S., 260n32
Parpola, Simo, 213n34, 251n26, 255n11, 259n21
Paul, Shalom M., 202n12, 223n15, 231n12, 231n17, 253n43, 257n22, 257n33, 261n42
Pautrel, Raymond, 205n19
Penchansky, David, 254n4, 258n10, 259n16
Perdue, Leo G., 202n10, 203n32, 210n35, 213n48, 216n31, 237n21, 238n3, 252n35, 260n31
Person, Raymond F., 237n34, 238n38
Pestmann, P.W., 229n62
Petersen, David L., 213n33, 242n12, 252n33, 253n45
Pfeiffer, E., 229n60
Pfeiffer, Robert H., 110
Pleins, J. David, 114
Pohlmann, Karl-Friedrich, 239n20
Polk, Timothy, 217n5
Potok, Chaim, 31
Prato, Gian Luigi, 206n29, 227n29
Preuss, Horst-Dietrich, 212n28, 222n7
Prinsloo, W.S., 154, 243n16, 247n22
Puech, Emile, 206n34

R

Raitt, T.M., 243n17
Redditt, P.L., 165, 243n21, 248n10, 258n10
Reindl, J., 116
Reines, C.W., 224n2
Reiterer, Friedrich Vincent, 204n11
Reuchlin, Johannes, 109
Reventlow, Henning Graf, 142
Rickenbacher, Otto, 204n10
Riede, Peter, 114
Rietzschel, Claus, 239n7
Robert, A., 244n36
Roberts, J.J.M., 257n25
Robinson, T., 154
Rollston, Chris A., 205n24
Rosenmüller, E.J.K., 109
Rostovtzeff, M., 229n62
Roth, Wolfgang, 205n20, 229n53
Rudman, D., 229n55

Rudolph, Wilhelm, 139, 154, 223n23, 243n15, 246n54, 248n27
Rüger, Hans Peter, 204n11

S

Salyer, G.D., 230n72
Sanders, Jack T., 205n18
Sanders, James A., 240n46
Sarna, Nahum, 117
Sarot, Marcel, 216n33
Sasson, J., 244n34, 245n38, 257n28, 260n24
Sauer, G., 226n18, 228n49, 229n53, 232n35
Sawyer, John D., 204n2
Scharbert, J., 241n1
Schearing, L.S., 258n2
Schellenberg, Annette, 217n3, 227n34, 230n1
Schmandt-Besserat, Denise, 202n13
Schmid, Hans-Heinrich, 213n49, 232n27
Schmidt, L., 241n1, 245n46, 263n42
Schmitt, Armin, 213n38
Schoors, Antoon, 62, 83, 87–88, 209n19, 211n42, 213n50, 217n3, 219n24, 222n53, 225n8, 229n55
Schrader, Lutz, 206n32, 230n66, 238n48
Schreiner, J., 256n18
Schroer, Sylvia, 215n25, 223n20, 230n68
Schunk, K.D., 242n3
Schwienhorst-Schönberger, Ludger, 63, 225n4, 232n31, 233n44
Sellin, E., 242n6, 246n2
Seow, Choon-Leong , 32, 63, 65, 203n21, 209n20, 209n21, 209n23, 213n43, 213n50, 218n8, 221n48, 221n51, 226n16, 227n26, 237n27
Seybold, Klaus, 116, 234n3
Sharp, Carolyn J., 217n6
Sheppard, G., 116, 213n40, 237n27
Shupak, Nili, 207n51, 210n39, 211n1, 223n14, 250n9
Silberman, Lou H., 135, 259n19
Simkins, R., 165, 241n2, 243n23, 245n44, 246n54, 248n12
Simon, Uriel, 234n6
Sitzler, Dorothea, 211n1
Skehan, P.W., 204n8, 205n21, 206n35, 227n32, 232n37, 232n38
Smend, Rudolf, 205n16
Smith, Jonathan Z., 74, 247n20
Snaith, J.G., 204n2
Snaith, Norman, 110
Stadelmann, Helga, 204n2, 211n1
Stähli, H.P., 157
Stamm, J.J., 233n1, 262n17
Steiert, Franz-Josef, 212n28
Sternberg, Meier, 115, 158, 234n17
Stoebe, H. J., 243n24
Stolz, F., 223n9, 231n22, 247n15
Stone, M.E., 230n70, 261n44, 263n28
Stuhlmueller, Carroll, 116
Stulman, Louis, 236n11
Sweeney, Marvin A., 224n32

T

Taylor, A., 241n2
Terrien, Samuel, 58–60, 114, 116, 215n28, 216n30, 216n33, 216n36, 216n38, 223n16, 227n22, 231n13, 231n18
Thiel, Winfried, 140, 239n19
Thompson, A.L., 263n28
Thompson, John, 239n4, 241n2
Tilley, Terrence W., 216n33, 254n5, 258n7
Trenchard, W.C., 204n5
Trible, Phyllis, 133, 218n12, 234n16, 241n48, 241n1, 260n24
Tsevat, Matitiahu, 39, 242n8
Tur-Sinai, N.H., 202n14

U

Uehlinger, Christoph, 218n13, 229n52

V

van der Lugt, Pieter, 202n20
van der Toorn, Karel, 231n21, 255n11, 259n21
van Grol, H.M.W., 240n39
Van Leeuwen, Raymond C., 231n21, 236n7, 256n14, 256n15
Vanderkam, James C., 231n19
Vanoni, G., 241n1, 244n34
Vattioni, Francesco, 205n13
Vermeylen, J., 141
Vetter, D., 156, 242n10
Vollmer, J., 231n5
Volz, Paul, 224n26, 224n27
von Rad, Gerhard, 132–33, 140, 142, 203n1, 212n26, 219n20, 222n7, 230n2, 235n4, 242n3, 252n32, 261n1, 263n41
von Soden, Wolfgang, 262n17

W

Waltke, B.K., 226n20
Wanke, Gunther, 140, 165, 243n20, 248n9
Washington, Harold C., 223n17
Weeks, Stuart, 206n38, 211n3, 212n21
Weil, Eric, 209n28
Weinfeld, Moshe, 126, 130, 212n26, 235n4, 236n7, 236n11, 236n13, 236n20, 237n22, 237n23, 237n29, 237n32, 252n31, 262n17
Weippert, Helga, 139, 239n19
Weiser, Artur, 114, 139, 237n28
Weiss, Meir, 115, 234n15, 242n3
Wellhausen, Julius, 110–12, 261n1
Westermann, Claus, 113, 116, 134, 207n49, 210n35, 211n4, 212n13, 215n26, 219n22, 245n52, 249n6, 250n8, 262n11
Whitley, Charles F., 207n47
Whybray, R. Norman, 116, 125, 208n3, 211n3, 213n39, 216n40, 217n4, 222n53, 225n4, 236n7, 259n16
Wicke-Reuter, U., 227n24, 232n31
Wiesel, E., 259n14
Wilcox, J.T., 242n8
Wildberger, Hans, 253n43
Williams, Ronald J., 262n17
Williamson, Clark M., 254n3
Willmes, Bernd, 217n6
Wilson, Gerald H., 115–16
Wilson, Robert R., 145, 158, 241n50, 243n21, 251n25, 260n22
Winston, David, 205n19, 213n38, 227n29, 232n32
Wischmeyer, Oda, 204n6, 207n53, 211n1, 213n52, 216n42, 219n22, 224n3, 233n41
Wolff, H.W., 134, 154, 165, 242n6, 243n15, 243n17, 243n19, 246n54, 247n22, 247n24, 248n8, 257n33
Wolters, A., 207n46
Wood, Ralph C., 254n4
Wright, Addison D.G., 62
Wright, J. Edward, 215n17, 221n47

Y

Young, Josiah Ulysses, 254n4

Z

Zenger, Erich,117, 202n17, 216n29, 233n1234n13
Ziegler, J., 204n9
Zimmerli, Walther, 63, 213n47, 216n31, 218n9, 229n64, 245n53, 246n9
Zuckerman, B., 242n4

Subject Index

A

Aging, 11, 92, 217n4
Allegory, 31, 107
Anomie, 174, 254n2, 258n1
Anthropodicy, 200
Apocalypticism, 82, 86, 98, 107, 131, 159, 166, 203n24, 221n51, 222n3, 247n20, 242n22, 248n27, 257n22, 259n14

B

Ben Sira, Hellenistic influence on, 20, 86, 227n23
Birth, *see* Embryology

C

Chaos/Chaos monster, 11, 59, 96, 112, 184, 185, 202n15, 203n23
"Confessions" of Jeremiah, 137–38, 141–45, 176, 260n26
Cosmic order, 11, 86–87, 96, 101, 175, 184–85, 187, 232n26, 262n8
Creation, *see* Nature/Creation
Critical theory, *see* Literary theory

D

Day of YHWH, 147, 152, 155–56, 159–60, 172, 241n3, 256n14, 256n18
Death, 3, 9–12, 21, 51, 56, 67, 96, 99, 100, 197, 201n3, 202n19, 221n48, 221n50, 225n4, 262n14
Divine anger, 7, 154, 178, 180
Divine council, 187
Divine freedom, 156, 164
Divine justice, *see* Theodicy
Divine recompense, 58, 80, 82, 93, 127–28, 163–64, 175, 178–79, 181, 184, 188–89, 193, 200, 215n18, 236n8
Divine sovereignty, 85
Divine word, 9, 85, 112, 141, 143, 145, 158, 169, 179, 197, 238n47, 251n19
Divination, 2, 35, 49, 65–66, 158, 175
Doubt, 59, 174–75, 182

E

Education: oral pedagogy, 16, 20–28, 47, 130, 150, 171–72, 236n9, 250n11; parental instruction, 22, 47, 125, 127, 134, 168, 207n2, 210n35, 249n8; religion, 17, 19, 50, 103; use of force in, 15, 17, 36, 237n25
Embryology, 60, 67, 95, 99, 216n44, 218n7, 228n47, 232n24
Ethical monotheism, 109, 144
Evil, 198, 228n36, 253n1, 254n5, 255n5

F

False prophecy, 134, 252n28
Fate, 54, 209n17, 221n44, 226n14
Fear of YHWH, 21, 26, 50, 103, 128–29, 216n37, 229n60, 236n13, 237n22, 237n23
Foreign woman, *see* Strange woman
Forensic language, 7, 96–97, 245n40, 247n25, 251n17, 258n6
Form criticism, 112, 132–33, 199, 234n13
Free will (human), 21, 97, 228n40

G

Gilgamesh, 8, 9, 90, 102, 203n32, 233n42

H

Heavenly book, 171, 179, 202n12, 253n43, 257n22
Historical positivism, 109

Holocaust, *see* Shoah
Honor, 175, 177, 245n44, 252n31
Hope, 6, 9, 12, 56, 140, 164, 203n31, 241n52, 256n19
Hospitality, 196
Human nature, 16, 78, 101, 164, 174
Humility, 19
Hymns/Hymnic texts, 51, 53, 55, 86, 93, 95, 111, 113, 133, 150–51, 180–82, 192, 227n28, 243n14, 261n40
Idolatry, 76, 81, 96, 102, 176, 191, 230n4, 231n4, 234n2, 256n13, 260n37

I

Immortality of soul, 9, 51, 99, 202n18
Intellect: limits of, 2, 31, 62, 67, 93–94; perversity of, 73, 76, 78–79, 222n1

J

Jerusalem, inviolability of, 176
Judicial proceedings, 8, 201n5

K

King, 40, 54–55, 112, 115–16, 169, 186–87
Knowledge and eroticism, 18, 64, 208n6, 219n25

L

Lament, 47–48, 58, 111, 187, 203n25, 255n7, 257n23
Libraries, 130
Life after death, 8, 13, 26, 56, 215n17
Literacy in ancient Israel, 20, 22, 34, 47, 126, 130, 168, 171, 235n3, 238n39, 251n18, 255n9
Literal sense, 1, 107, 131
Literary theory, 94, 208n8, 211n5, 218n12

M

Magic, 64–65, 67, 220n33, 263n21
Messiah/Messianism, 21, 108, 160
Mortality, 9–10, 36, 55, 84, 195

N

Nature/Creation, 1, 9–11, 33, 42, 44, 57, 64–66, 75, 101, 160, 173, 184, 192–93, 219n25, 220n31, 220n37, 242n8
Neo-Orthodoxy, 132, 174
Numerical gradation, 64, 91

O

Omen texts, 47, 238n46
Omniscient narration, 30, 242n11
Oral/Literacy continuum, 24, 25, 34, 51, 168, 171–72, 206n39, 252n36

P

Pan-Deuteronomism, 125, 130, 258n2
Pan-sapientialism, 125, 134
Philo, 31, 107
Postmodernity, 230n71, 260n13
Practical atheism, 82, 97, 216n32, 222n1
Prayer, 3, 6, 21, 55, 107, 112, 201n1, 222n4, 233n40, 237n30, 254n1, 254n4
Prophecy: central and peripheral, 186, 243n21, 251n25; cultic, 142, 157, 186; ecstatic, 175, 186, 251n26
Prophetic bands, 170
Prophetic conflict, 138, 143
Prophetic disciples, 168–70
Psalter, sapiential redaction, 2, 108, 116, 216n30

Q

Qoheleth: epistemology of, 29–41, 207n1, 225n4, 227n34, 230n1; Hellenistic influence on, 3, 31, 50–51, 63, 84, 100, 218n6, 220n40
Qumran, 106–7, 131, 224n37, 230n69, 238n45

R

Reception history, 117
Resurrection, 21, 100, 201n3, 202n18
Revelation, 41, 49, 221n45, 231n21, 248n1
Rhetorical criticism, 115, 144, 239n9
Romanticism, 109
Royal enthronement festival, 111–13

S

Salvation history, 125
Sapiential ethics, 59
Schools, 22, 52, 59, 168, 206n37, 235n4
Scribes, royal court and, 22–23, 47, 125, 134, 171, 212n10
Serpent, 9
Shame, 17, 157, 177, 245n44, 252n31
Sheol, 8, 12, 40, 57, 67, 86, 98, 201n8, 203n25, 218n8, 221n47, 226n17
Shoah, 173, 253n1, 259n14
Sickness, 12, 203n25
Slavery/Slave trade, 7, 26, 159, 163, 181, 202n10, 247n24
Solomonic Enlightenment, 133
Stoicism, 21, 32–33, 85, 227n23, 232n26
Strange woman, 48, 57, 208n6, 262n7
Subjectivity and objectivity, 29, 41, 106, 172, 253n54
Suffering, vicarious, 173, 192, 198, 250n15
Superscriptions, 106, 249n3, 249n6
Symbolic actions, 169
Syncretistic worship, 164

T

Temple, 21, 75, 111, 165
Testing, 258n6, 259n15
Theodicy: definition, 257n1; in the Book of the Twelve, 173–82; in Genesis, 195–200; in prophetic literature, 183–94
Time, 12, 24, 228n39
Torah Psalms, 116, 130
Tradition-history, 132
Tree, 11–12, 77–78, 99, 100, 203n24; of life, 9, 11, 203n24

U

Universalism, 26, 135, 158, 192
Utopia, 73–75, 82, 86, 90, 153, 160, 172, 222n3

V

Vows, 128

W

Water, 11–12, 77, 81, 101, 155, 192, 203n31
Wisdom: apocalyptic and, 49, 51, 174; creation theology and, 58, 216n31; female personification of, 46, 51, 85, 93, 211n42, 215n25, 219n15, 223n20; personal experience and, 30–32, 57, 75, 225n5, 227n34; Psalms, 48, 113, 116, 215n28; role of observation in, 24, 37, 152
Women, 20, 26, 43, 133, 203n22, 229n55
Words, magical character of, 253n41, 253n42
Writing, 22–23, 37, 101, 150, 233n39
Written documents, 8, 131, 150, 171, 249n4

Printed in the United States
69291LVS00002B/1-84

9 780827 229884